Advanced SNA Networking
A Professional's Guide to VTAM/NCP

Ranade IBM Series

ISBN	AUTHOR	TITLE
0-07-006551-9	K. Booler	*CLIST Programming*
0-07-044129-4	H. Murphy	*ASSEMBLER For COBOL Programmers: MVS, VM*
0-07-006533-0	H. Bookman	*COBOL II*
0-07-010071-0	P. McGrew, W. McDaniel	*In-House Publishing In a Mainframe Environment, Second Edition*
0-07-051265-5	J. Ranade	*DB2 Concepts, Programming and Design*
0-07-054594-4	J. Sanchez	*IBM Microcomputers Handbook*
0-07-002467-7	M. Aronson	*SAS: A Programmer's Guide*
0-07-002673-4	J. Azevedo	*ISPF: The Strategic Dialog Manager*
0-07-007250-7	K. Brathwaite	*System Design In a Database Environment*
0-07-009816-6	M. Carathanassis	*Expert MVS/XA JCL: A Complete Guide To Advanced Techniques*
0-07-015231-4	M. D'Alleyrand	*Image Storage and Retrieval Systems*
0-07-016188-7	R. Dayton	*Integrating Digital Services*
0-07-017606-X	P. Donofrio	*CICS: Debugging, Dump Reading and Problem Determination*
0-07-018966-8	T. Eddolls	*VM Performance Management*
0-07-033571-0	P. Kavanagh	*VS COBOL II For COBOL Programmers*
0-07-040666-9	T. Martyn	*DB2/SQL, A Professional Programmer's Guide*
0-07-050054-1	S. Piggot	*CICS: A Practical Guide To System Fine Tuning*
0-07-050686-8	N. Prasad	*IBM Mainframes: Architecture and Design*
0-07-051144-6	J. Ranade, G. Sackett	*Introduction To SNA Networking: A Guide To VTAM/NCP*
0-07-051143-8	J. Ranade, G. Sackett	*Advanced SNA Networking: A Professional's Guide For Using VTAM/NCP*
0-07-065086-1	J. Towner	*CASE*
0-07-054528-6	S. Samson	*MVS Performance Management*
0-07-032673-8	B. Johnson	*MVS: Concepts and Facilities*
0-07-046263-1	P. McGrew	*On-Line Text Management*
0-07-065087-X	L. Towner	*IDMS/R Cookbook*
0-07-071136-4	A. Wipfler	*Distributed Processing In The CICS Environment*
0-07-071139-9	A. Wipfler	*CICS Application Development Programming*
0-07-05-1244-2	J. Ranade	*VSAM: Concepts, Programming and Design*
0-07-051245-0	J. Ranade	*VSAM: Performance, Design and Fine Tuning, Second Edition*

Advanced SNA Networking
A Professional's Guide to VTAM/NCP

Jay Ranade
George C. Sackett

McGraw-Hill, Inc.

New York St. Louis San Francisco Auckland Bogotá
Caracas Hamburg Lisbon London Madrid Mexico
Milan Montreal New Delhi Paris
San Juan São Paolo Singapore
Sydney Tokyo Toronto

Library of Congress Cataloging-in-Publication Data

Ranade, Jay.
    Advanced SNA networking : a professional's guide to VTAM/NCP / Jay Ranade and George C. Sackett.
        p.   cm.—(J. Ranade IBM series)
    Includes index.
    ISBN 0-07-051143-8
    1. SNA (Computer network architecture)   2. Virtual computer systems.   I. Sackett, George C.   II. Title.   III. Series.
TK5105.5.R358   1991
004.6'5—dc20   90-53694
                                                                                               CIP

Copyright © 1991 by Jay Ranade and George C. Sackett. All rights reserved. Printed in the United States of America. Except as permitted under the United States Copyright Act of 1976, no part of this book may be reproduced or distributed in any form or by any means, or stored in a database or retrieval system without the prior written permission of the publisher.

2 3 4 5 6 7 8 9 0 DOC/DOC 9 6 5 4 3 2 1

ISBN 0-07-051143-8

IBM is a trademark of International Business Machines, Inc. Multiple Virtual Storage (MVS), MVS/SP, MVS/XA, MVS/ESA, ESA/370, NetView, NetView/PC, PS/2, VM/SP and VM/XA are trademarks of the IBM Corporation, Poughkeepsie, NY 12602.

Line art composed in Micrografx Designer by VisionQuest USA, Inc., Rutherford, NJ 07070.
Typesetting and indexing composed in Xerox Ventura Publisher by VisionQuest USA, Inc., Rutherford, NJ 07070.

LIMITS OF LIABILITY AND DISCLAIMER OF WARRANTY

The author and publisher have exercised care in preparing this book and the programs contained in it. They make no representation, however, that the programs are error-free or suitable for every application to which a reader may attempt to apply them. The author and publisher make no warranty of any kind, expressed or implied, including the warranties of merchantability or fitness for a particular purpose, with regard to these programs or the documentation or theory contained in this book, all of which are provided "as is." The author and publisher shall not be liable for damages in an amount greater than the purchase price of this book, or in any event for incidental or consequential damages in connection with, or arising out of the furnishing, performance, or use of these programs or the associated descriptions or discussions.

Readers should test any program on their own systems and compare results with those presented in this book. They should then construct their own test programs to verify that they fully understand the requisite calling conventions and data formats for each of the programs. Then they should test the specific application thoroughly.

Subscription information to BYTE magazine:
Call 1-800-257-9402 or write Circulation Dept.,
One Phoenix Mill Lane, Peterborough, NH 03458

*This book is dedicated to my brothers,
Jan Ranade and Hirday Ranade,
and my sister,
Chander M. Ranade,
who have always stood beside me when I needed them.*

Jay

*This book is dedicated to my parents,
Ray and June Sackett,
and my brother,
Raymond.
Thanks for your support throughout my life.*

George

Contents

Acknowledgments		**xix**
Preface		**xxi**
Part 1	**Advanced Communications Hardware**	**1**
Chapter 1	**IBM 3174 Establishment Controller**	**3**
	1.1 Functions and Features	3
	1.1.1 Functions of ECs	4
	1.1.2 Features	5
	1.2 Advantages over 3274s	9
	1.3 Host Connectivity	9
	1.3.1 Channel-Attached	9
	1.3.2 Link-Attached	10
	1.3.3 Token-Ring Attached	11
	1.3.4 ASCII Host Connectivity	12
	1.4 Large IBM 3174 Models	14
	1.4.1 Models 1L and 11L	14
	1.4.2 Models 1R and 11R	15
	1.4.3 Models 2R and 12R	15
	1.4.4 Models 3R and 13R	15
	1.5 Medium-Size IBM 3174 Models	16
	1.5.1 Model 51R and 61R	17
	1.5.2 Models 52R and 62R	18
	1.5.3 Models 53R and 63R	18
	1.6 Small IBM 3174 Models	18
	1.6.1 Models 81R and 91R	18
	1.6.2 Models 82R and 92R	19
	1.7 Summary	20
Chapter 2	**IBM 3745 Communications Controller - Function and Architecture**	**21**
	2.1 Introduction	21
	2.2 Functions and Characteristics	22

	2.2.1 Major Functions	22
	2.2.2 Functional Categories	23
	2.2.3 Channel-Attached, Link-Attached and Token-Ring-Attached	25
2.3	Architecture	25
2.4	Control Subsystem	28
	2.4.1 Central Control Unit (CCU)	28
	2.4.2 Cache Buffers	29
	2.4.3 Main Storage	29
	2.4.4 Storage Control	30
	2.4.5 Direct Memory Access (DMA)	30
	2.4.6 Input/Output Control (IOC) Buses	30
	2.4.7 Channel Adapters (CAs)	30
	2.4.8 Data Streaming Feature	31
	2.4.9 Two-Processor Switch (TPS)	31
2.5	Communications Subsystem	33
	2.5.1 High Performance Transmission Subsystem (HPTSS)	34
	2.5.2 Transmission Subsystem (TSS)	35
	2.5.3 Token-Ring Subsystem (TRSS)	36
2.6	Maintenance and Operator Subsystem (MOSS)	37
	2.6.1 MOSS Components	38
	2.6.2 MOSS Consoles	40
	2.6.3 Remote Support Facility (RSF)	42
	2.6.4 MOSS Functions	43
2.7	Summary	43

Chapter 3 IBM 3745 Communications Controller - Types and Models 45

3.1	Types and Models	45
	3.1.1 Model 130	47
	3.1.2 Model 150	49
	3.1.3 Model 170	50
	3.1.4 Model 210 (base)	51
	3.1.5 Model 410	53
3.2	Expansion Units	53
	3.2.1 3746 Model A11	54
	3.2.2 3746 Model A12	55
	3.2.3 3746 Model L13	55
	3.2.4 3746 Model L14	56
	3.2.5 Model L15	56
3.3	3745 Model 410 Modes of Operation	56
	3.3.1 Twin-Dual Mode	56
	3.3.2 Twin-Standby Mode	57
	3.3.3 Twin-Backup Mode	59
3.4	Summary	60

Chapter 4 IBM 3745 Communications Controller - Configuration 61

- 4.1 Communications Components — 61
  - 4.1.1 Scanners — 62
  - 4.1.2 Line Attachment Base (LAB) / Double Multiplexers (DMUX) — 63
  - 4.1.3 Hierarchy of Components — 63
  - 4.1.4 Line Interface Coupler (LIC) — 64
  - 4.1.5 LIC Unit (LIU) — 66
  - 4.1.6 Line Interface Base (LIB) — 67
- 4.2 Line Weight Considerations — 67
  - 4.2.1 Selective Scanning — 68
  - 4.2.2 Maximum Line Configurations — 68
- 4.3 Configuration Rules — 70
- 4.4 Overloading Scanners — 71
- 4.5 Summary — 72

Part 2 Beyond Single Domain 73

Chapter 5 Multi-Domain VTAM Definitions 75

- 5.1 Cross-Domain Resource Manager (CDRM) — 77
  - 5.1.1 VBUILD Statement for CDRM — 77
  - 5.1.2 CDRM Definition Statement — 78
- 5.2 Cross-Domain Resources (CDRSC) — 81
  - 5.2.1 VBUILD Statement for CDRSC — 81
  - 5.2.2 CDRSC Definition Statement — 81
- 5.3 Adjacent SSCP Table (ADJSSCP) — 83
  - 5.3.1 ADJSSCP Start List Options — 85
  - 5.3.2 ADJCDRM Definition Statement — 86
- 5.4 Channel-to-Channel Attachment — 87
  - 5.4.1 CTCA GROUP Definition Statement — 88
  - 5.4.2 CTCA LINE Definition Statement — 88
  - 5.4.3 CTCA PU Definition Statement — 89
- 5.5 VTAM Path Table Considerations — 90
  - 5.5.1 Defining the Multi-Domain Path Table — 91
- 5.6 Parallel Transmission Groups — 94
  - 5.6.1 Defining Parallel Transmission Groups — 95
- 5.7 Summary — 98

Chapter 6 Multiple Domain Definitions for an NCP 99

- 6.1 PCCU Definition Statement for Additional Hosts — 100

	6.2 BUILD Definition Statement Considerations for Multiple Domains	102
	6.3 HOST Definition Statement for a Multi-Domain NCP	103
	6.4 SDLCST Definition Statement for a Multi-Domain NCP	104
	6.5 GROUP Definition Statements for a Multi-Domain NCP	108
	6.6 GROUP, LINE and PU Definition Statements for SDLC Subarea Links	110
	6.7 GROUP, LINE and PU Definitions for Multi-Point Subarea Links	113
	6.8 Switched Subarea Links	117
	6.9 Path Statement Updates for a Multi-Domain NCP	121
	6.10 Summary	123
Chapter 7	**SNI - Single Gateway for VTAM**	**125**
	7.1 Interconnection Considerations	126
	7.1.1 Determine Gateway Location	127
	7.1.2 Establish Physical Connectivity	128
	7.1.3 Assign Gateway NCP Subarea	129
	7.1.4 Define Gateway to VTAM	130
	7.1.5 Define Gateway to NCP	130
	7.1.6 Network Autonomy	132
	7.2 Single Gateway Definition for VTAM	134
	7.2.1 Non-Gateway VTAM Definition	135
	7.2.2 Gateway VTAM Definition	137
	7.2.3 Alias Name Translation	141
	7.3 Summary	144
Chapter 8	**SNI - Single Gateway for NCP**	**145**
	8.1 Non-Gateway NCP Definition	145
	8.2 Gateway NCP Definition	148
	8.3 Summary	154
Chapter 9	**SNI - Multiple Gateways and Back-to-Back Gateways**	**155**
	9.1 Gateway-Capable VTAM Definition	156
	9.2 Gateway VTAM Definition Updates	159
	9.3 Multiple Gateway Definition for NCP	160
	9.3.1 Gateway NCP Definition Updates	160
	9.3.2 Non-Gateway NCP Definition Updates	161
	9.4 Back-to-Back Gateway Definition for VTAM	162

	9.4.1 Non-gateway VTAM Definition Updates	163
	9.4.2 Gateway-Capable VTAM Definition Updates	163
	9.4.3 Gateway VTAM Definition Updates	165
9.5	Back-to-Back Gateway Definition for an NCP	166
	9.5.1 Gateway NCP Definition Updates	166
9.6	Summary	169

Chapter 10 VTAM Initialization 171

10.1	ATCSTR00 START Options	171
10.2	VTAM Major Node Configuration Table (ATCCON00)	172
10.3	Resource Definition Table (RDT)	172
10.4	Symbol Resolution Table (SRT)	174
10.5	Activation of the Host Node	174
	10.5.1 Activating the Channel between the Host and the NCP	175
10.6	Activating an NCP Subarea	177
	10.6.1 Activating a Channel-Attached NCP	177
	10.6.2 Activating Routes to a Channel-Attached NCP	178
	10.6.3 Loading a Remote NCP	179
	10.6.4 Activating Routes to a Remote NCP	181
10.7	Activating Nonswitched SDLC Nodes	182
	10.7.1 Establishing a Nonswitched SDLC Node SSCP-PU Session	183
	10.7.2 Establishing a Nonswitched SDLC Node SSCP-LU Session	184
10.8	Activating Switched SDLC Nodes	184
	10.8.1 Activating Switched SSCP-PU Sessions	186
	10.8.2 Activating Switched SSCP-LU Sessions	186
10.9	Activating an SSCP-SSCP Session	187
10.10	Establishing a Single-Domain LU-LU Session	188
10.11	Establishing a Cross-Domain LU-LU Session	189
10.12	Establishing a Cross-Network LU-LU Session	191
10.13	Deactivating a Host Node	193
10.14	Deactivating a Cross-Domain Session	193
10.15	Deactivating a Same Domain Session	193
10.16	Deactivating an SSCP-SSCP Session	195
10.17	Deactivating Switched SDLC Nodes	196

xii Contents

	10.17.1 Deactivating a Switched SSCP-LU Session	197
	10.17.2 Deactivating a Switched SSCP-PU Session	198
	10.18 Deactivating Nonswitched SDLC Nodes	198
	10.18.1 Deactivating a Nonswitched SSCP-LU Session	198
	10.18.2 Deactivating a Nonswitched SSCP-PU Session	198
	10.19 Deactivating Routes to a Remote NCP	199
	10.20 Deactivating a Channel-Attached NCP Subarea	200
	10.21 SNA Node T2.1 Activation	202
	10.22 Cross-Domain T2.1 ILU Sessions	203
	10.23 Summary	205
Part 3	**Network and Performance Management**	**207**
Chapter 11	**Network Management and Problem Analysis**	**209**
	11.1 Managing the Network with VTAM	210
	11.1.1 VTAM Operator USSTAB	210
	11.2 Managing Resource Ownership and Recovery	214
	11.2.1 LOGAPPL Operand	214
	11.2.2 ISTATUS Operand	216
	11.2.3 OWNER and BACKUP Operands	216
	11.3 Advanced Configuration Facilities	218
	11.3.1 Using Dynamic Reconfiguration	218
	11.3.2 Communication Management Configuration (CMC)	224
	11.3.3 Extended Recovery Facility (XRF)	226
	11.3.4 Dynamic Path Update	228
	11.3.5 Dynamic Table Replacement	230
	11.4 Using VTAM Commands to Manage the SNA Network	232
	11.4.1 The DISPLAY Command	232
	11.4.2 The VARY Command	236
	11.4.3 The MODIFY Command	237
	11.5 VTAM TRACE Facilities	238
	11.5.1 VTAM Trace Procedure for MVS	240
	11.5.2 VTAM Trace Procedure for VSE	241
	11.5.3 VTAM Trace Procedure under VM	241
	11.6 Summary	242

Chapter 12   NetView and NetView/PC   245

12.1 Open Network Management Architecture   246
   12.1.1 Focal Point   246
   12.1.2 Entry Point   247
   12.1.3 Service Point   248
12.2 SNA Network Services Flow   248
12.3 NetView Release 1 Overview   250
   12.3.1 Network Command Control Facility (NCCF)   251
   12.3.2 NetView Hardware Monitor   252
   12.3.3 NetView Session Monitor   253
   12.3.4 NetView Status Monitor   254
   12.3.5 Network Management Productivity Facility (NMPF)   255
12.4 NetView/PC Version 1   256
12.5 NetView Release 2   257
   12.5.1 Automation and Central Management   257
   12.5.2 Automation Enhancements   258
   12.5.3 Central Management Enhancements   258
   12.5.4 Message and Alert Notification Routing Facility   258
   12.5.6 Message-Driven Alert Facility   259
   12.5.7 LAN Support   259
   12.5.8 Communications Network Management Router Function   259
   12.5.9 Session Monitor SNA Node Type 2.1 Support   260
   12.5.10 Generic Alerts   260
12.6 Service Point Command Service   261
   12.6.1 SPCS RUNCMD Command   261
   12.6.2 SPCS LINKDATA Command   261
   12.6.3 SPCS LINKTEST Command   262
   12.6.4 SPCS LINKPD Command   262
12.7 NetView/PC Version 1.1   262
   12.7.1 NetView/PC Generic Alert Support   262
12.8 Service Point Command Service Support NetView/PC V1.1   263
12.9 Token-Ring Network Manager for NetView/PC   263
12.10 NetView R3 Enhancements   263
12.11 NetView/PC V1.2   264
12.12 Summary   265

Contents

Chapter 13 Network Performance and Tuning   267

    13.1 Performance and Tuning Methodology   267
        13.1.1 Performance Monitoring   268
        13.1.2 Analyze and Report Performance   269
        13.1.3 Performance Objectives   270
    13.2 VTAM Performance and Tuning Considerations   270
        13.2.1 VTAM Buffer Pool Usage   270
        13.2.2 Buffer Pool Specification   272
        13.2.3 Coat-Tailing   274
    13.3 NCP Performance and Tuning Considerations   277
        13.3.1 Facility and Link Configurations   278
        13.3.2 NCP Inbound Data Flow   280
        13.3.3 NCP Outbound Data Flow   283
        13.3.4 Link Scheduler Service   285
        13.3.5 Transmission Group Queuing/Resequencing   288
    13.4 Logical Data Flow Performance   289
        13.4.1 Chaining and Segmentation   290
        13.4.2 Session-Level Pacing   293
        13.4.3 Compression and Compaction   297
    13.5 Virtual Route Pacing   297
        13.5.1 VR Window Size   298
        13.5.2 VR States   299
        13.5.3 Network Congestion   301
    13.6 Summary   303

Part 4 New Connectivity Issues   305

Chapter 14 Low Entry Networking   307

    14.1 LEN Architecture   308
        14.1.2 SNA Node Type 2.1   310
        14.1.2 Logical Unit Type 6.2   313
    14.2 LEN Enhanced Connectivity Support   314
        14.2.1 LEN/VTAM/NCP Support   315
        14.2.2 Advanced Peer-to-Peer Networking (APPN)   316
    14.3 Defining a T2.1 Node to LEN/NCP   319
    14.4 Defining T2.1 / LU6.2 to LEN/NCP   320
    14.5 LEN/NCP BUILD Definition Parameters   323
    14.6 DR and Switched LEN Support   324
    14.7 Summary   325

Chapter 15	Token-Ring LAN Networking	327
	15.1 What is a Token-Ring LAN?	327
	15.2 Token-Ring Support Hardware	329
	15.2.1 Cables and Physical Transmission Media	330
	15.2.2 Multi-station Access Unit - IBM 8228	330
	15.2.3 Token-Ring Cards	331
	15.2.4 Repeaters and Converters	331
	15.3 Token-Ring LAN Devices	332
	15.3.1 IBM 3174 EC	333
	15.3.2 IBM Communications Controllers	333
	15.3.3 IBM 9370 Token-Ring Subsystem	336
	15.3.4 IBM AS/400	338
	15.4 Defining a Token-Ring to VTAM/NCP	340
	15.4.1 The OPTIONS and BUILD Defintion Statements for NTRI	340
	15.4.2 Defining the Physical GROUP Definition Statement for NTRI	341
	15.4.3 Defining the Physical LINE Definition Statement for NTRI	343
	15.4.4 Defining the Physical NTRI PU	345
	15.4.5 Defining a DSPU to NTRI	345
	15.4.6 Defining Subarea Connections over Token-Ring	346
	15.4.7 Defining the DSPU to VTAM	348
	15.4.8 Defining a Remote 3174 Establishment Controller Gateway	348
	15.5 Summary	350
Appendix A		351
Appendix B	**IBM Default USS Table**	353
Appendix C	**Product Support of SNA Network Addressable Unit Types**	355
Appendix D	**IBM 3720 and 3745 Line and Channel Adapter Considerations**	357
Appendix E	**VTAM and NCP Performance Tuning Tables**	359
Appendix F	**Subsystem and Device Performance Considerations**	363

Appendix G Bibliography of Suggested IBM Manuals 371

Appendix H List of Abbreviations 373

Glossary 377

Index 387

The following table of contents highlights the chapters from the preceding volume, *Introduction to SNA Networking: A Guide to VTAM/NCP*.

Part 1	**Introduction and Concepts**
Chapter 1	Data Communications and Telecommunications
Chapter 2	Communications Hardware-Cluster Controllers and Communications Controllers
Chapter 3	Communications Hardware-Miscellaneous
Chapter 4	SNA Telecommunications Access Methods
Chapter 5	Communications Protocols
Chapter 6	Communications Software
Part 2	**SNA Networks**
Chapter 7	SNA Domains and Networks
Chapter 8	Defining Network Topography
Part 3	**VTAM**
Chapter 9	Defining a Single-Domain Network
Chapter 10	VTAM Major Nodes-Application, Non-SNA, and SNA
Chapter 11	Switched Major Nodes and Path Tables
Chapter 12	VM and VSE Channel-Attached Configurations
Chapter 13	VTAM User Tables-USSTAB, MODETAB and COSTAB
Part 4	**NCP**
Chapter 14	NCP Macros-PCCU, BUILD and SYSCNTRL
Chapter 15	NCP Macros-HOST, LUDRPOOL, PATH and GROUP
Chapter 16	NCP Macros-LINE, SERVICE, CLUSTER and TERMINAL
Chapter 17	NCP Macros-PU, LU and SDLCST

Acknowledgments

Introduction to SNA Networking was published more than a year ago. It was mentioned in that book that the authors were working on a second volume, *Advanced SNA Networking*. Since then, George and I have received numerous phone calls and letters inquiring about the publication date for this book. We would like to thank all our readers for making the first book a best-seller. We have tried our best to keep this volume rich in content and simple in style. We hope you like this book as much as the first one. So first and foremost, we would like to acknowledge the readers of the first volume for expressing their faith in the authors' first joint work.

Our very special thanks are due to Carol Lehn for reviewing and copy editing the manuscript. Our thanks are also due to Kenya Sanders for typing some of the chapters. Our very special thanks are due to Peg Sackett, President of VisionQuest USA, Inc., Rutherford, New Jersey, for doing a magnificent job with art work, typesetting and indexing on such short notice.

Our special thanks to Theron Shreve, our senior editor, and Jim Fegen, editor-in-chief, McGraw-Hill, for showing extreme patience with delays in finishing the final draft (primarily due to Jay's involvement in a couple of dozen other writing projects).

George would like to thank little Chelsea for letting Daddy write when it was time for the weekly excursion to the park, and Helene LaChapelle and Frank LaChapelle for their constant support. A special thanks to Ruoh-Yann Huang for her encouragement and expert review of several chapters. Finally, special thanks to our spouses for not letting us write when they determined that it was time to quit.

Jay Ranade
George C. Sackett

Preface

It's been a long time since this project was conceived. It took more than 18 months to finish *Introduction to SNA Networking*, popularly known as SNA, Volume I, among our readers. It took a little longer to finish the current volume, which we think readers will call Volume II. A lot of research went into the writing and rewriting of the table of contents of this book. Due to the quantity of SNA information available, it became an arduous task to determine what should be included and what should be left out in a 350-400 page book. More effort went into the writing and rewriting of the material to make it easy to understand. It has been an enormous effort to determine how such an advanced and complete subject can be presented in a manner which will make it painless to comprehend. We sincerely hope that we have succeeded in our efforts.

THE 80/20 RULE

This book is not a summary of the IBM manuals, nor is its purpose to replace these manuals. As a matter of fact, it is difficult to replace the 20,000 pages of reference material contained in the IBM manuals. We have applied the 80/20 rule for material to be included in this text. The material on advanced SNA, used 80 percent of the time, constitutes 20 percent of the information supplied by IBM. This is what is covered in this text; the rest has been discarded. Although it will make you feel comfortable with the software, it does not qualify this book to be your only VTAM/NCP reference manual.

WHO THIS BOOK IS FOR

First let's talk about who this book is not for. If you do not have a basic knowledge of SNA or have some experience or knowledge about single domain networks, this book is not for you. It is not a theoretical book on SNA; it is meant to be an implementor's guide. Network engineers who already have some knowledge of linking physical networks and hardware will learn about how software makes the bits move in a large SNA network. CICS systems programmers and senior network operators who would like to assume additional responsibilities for VTAM/NCP will find this book very useful.

The first four chapters (Part I) will impart knowledge about IBM 3174s and 3745s. Part II will give you information about multi-domain VTAM/NCP definitions, SNI, and VTAM initialization. Part III discusses some advanced topics like problem determination, network management, NetView, and performance aspects of networking. Finally, Part IV goes into the details of new issues like LEN and LAN connectivity.

WHAT IS THE PREREQUISITE?

The book in your hands is an advanced book on SNA. It is not supposed to teach you SNA from scratch. It presupposes a basic understanding of VTAM/NCP on your part. In most cases, we assume that you already have read the authors' *Introduction to SNA Networking*. If not, you must have had at least some experience as a VTAM/NCP Systems Programmer. If you have no concept of how to define a single domain SNA network, we strongly recommend that you read Volume I before getting entangled in the complexities of a multi-domain network definition.

In many relatively small installations (specially DOS/VSE), responsibility for VTAM/NCP and CICS/VS lies with the same individual or group of individuals. This book will be especially useful for them when they move from a single domain to multiple domain network as a result of their business expansion.

The book has been structured so that it may be used as a self-teaching guide. It may also be used as a textbook for a 2-to-3-day in-house seminar on advanced SNA and VTAM/NCP.

WHAT ENVIRONMENT THIS BOOK IS FOR

This book covers the MVS/SP, MVS/XA, MVS/ESA, VSE, and VM operating systems environments. It is applicable to large mainframes (e.g., IBM 3084, 3090, ES/9000) as well as not-so-large mainframes (e.g., IBM 9370 and low-end ES/9000 models).

WORD ON THE STYLE USED

We have kept the style used in our previous book on SNA, which involves extensive use of figures, examples, diagrams, and illustrations. We would like our readers to understand the complexity of SNA networks, the underlying structure and the simplicity of multi-domain networks without presenting it in a complex manner.

Again, we could have gone into theory, but we did not. This is a practical book. This is meant for practitioners and implementors only.

WHY THIS BOOK IS COMPLETE

You will learn about IBM 3174s as well as IBM 3745s. The coverage is much more extensive (three chapters on 3745) than what was given in the previous volume. We have covered multi-domain definitions for VTAM and the NCP. There are three chapters on SNI to satisfy the requirements of very large networks. Network management aspects using NetView have been covered in sufficient detail. Practical aspects of network problem determination, performance management, and fine tuning are also given. Further, some new networking issues like low entry networking (LEN) and LAN connectivity introduce you to interesting SNA topics.

WHAT NEXT?

This book covers advanced topics on VTAM/NCP, networking hardware, and advanced architectures. The authors expect that after finishing this book, you will be able to design and code multi-domain networks with a high degree of confidence and competence. We intend to keep both volumes current if significant IBM announcements make portions of either book obsolete. Maybe a third volume is in the offing! Good Luck.

Jay and George

Advanced SNA Networking
A Professional's Guide to VTAM/NCP

Part

1

Advanced Communications Hardware

Chapter

1

IBM 3174 Establishment Controller

The IBM 3174's predecessor, the IBM 3274 Cluster Controller, was discussed in some detail in Chapter 2 of *Introduction to SNA Networking*. A vast majority of users still use IBM 3274s and may continue to do so for a long time. Display devices attached to these cluster controllers may be either non-programmable Control Unit Terminals (CUT), like the IBM 3278 and 3178, or intelligent PCs emulating CUTs by using IBM 3270 emulation boards like IRMA and AST. If you need more familiarity with the IBM 3274 Cluster Controllers, you are advised to read the relevant sections in Chapter 2 of the authors' previous SNA book entitled *Introduction to SNA Networking*.

1.1 FUNCTIONS AND FEATURES

When IBM 3174s were introduced a few years ago, they were called Subsystem Control Units or SCUs. Since then, IBM has enhanced the capabilities of the IBM 3174 Subsystem Controller. These capabilities allow SNA LU6.2 communications to the host as a dependent logical unit (DLU) and the ability to act as a Token-Ring gateway. These new connectivity establishment capabilities are found in the IBM 3174 Establishment Controllers (EC).

1.1.1 Functions of ECs

Establishment Controllers are used to control a cluster of terminals. Depending upon the model, you can attach anywhere from 8 to 32 terminals and printers to it. An IBM 3174 can be directly attached to a host computer channel, link-attached to a communications controller or may be attached to a Token-Ring Network. A 3174 also provides connectivity for ASCII terminals to talk to an ASCII host (e.g., DEC VAX equipment) as well as to an SNA host (e.g., IBM ES/9000 and 3090). It also enables IBM 3270 devices (e.g., IBM 3278) to talk to an SNA host as well as an ASCII host. An IBM 3174 Token-Ring SNA Gateway feature allows a single 3174 to act as a gateway to many other 3174s on a Token-Ring Network. Figure 1.1 shows various ways of providing connectivity for a 3174.

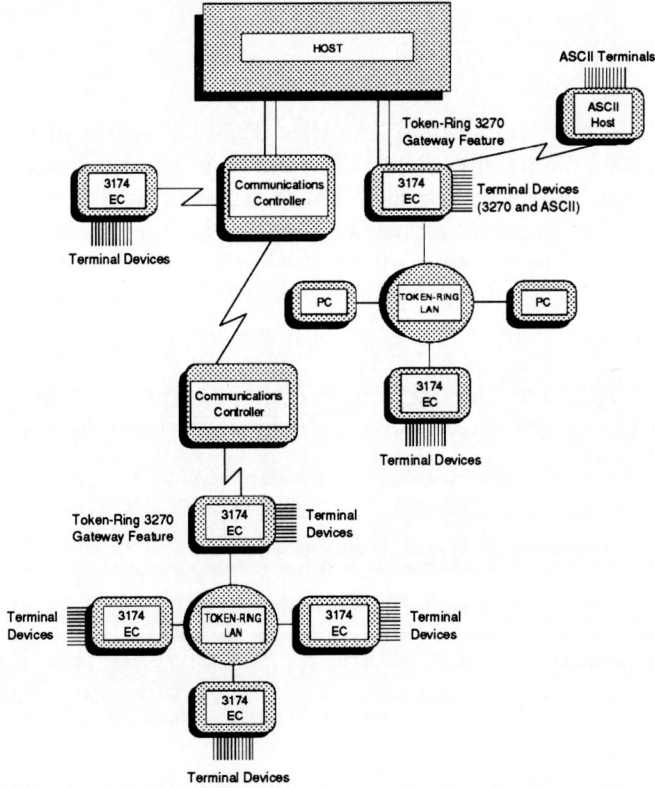

Figure 1.1 An example of different types of connectivity features provided by the IBM 3174 Establishment Controller.

We will discuss connectivity in more detail in subsequent sections of this chapter, so don't be alarmed if this figure looks too complex to understand.

A channel-attached EC is linked to the byte or block multiplexer channel of a mainframe host. It uses a bus and tag interface to the host channel. A link-attached cluster controller is linked to the communications controller (e.g., IBM 3745) through a communications link. The hardware that links an EC to it is called Data Communications Equipment (DCE). A DCE can be a modem for analog (voice) lines or a DSU/CSU for digital circuits. A token-ring-attached EC is linked to a Token-Ring Network via a multistation access unit (MAU). A number of ECs can be connected to a Token-Ring Network. A single EC with the Token-Ring SNA Gateway feature provides connectivity for itself and other ECs in the ring network to the host. An EC also provides connectivity to ASCII terminals (e.g., IBM's 3101 or DEC's VT 100) so that they may either have a session with their ASCII hosts (e.g., DEC VAX) or an SNA host. Similarly, it also allows SNA terminals to have connectivity not only to their SNA hosts but also to the ASCII hosts. More details on this are given later in this chapter.

1.1.2 Features

The IBM 3274 cluster controller is quite primitive when compared to the IBM 3174 EC. It has a limited amount of memory and only one or two floppy diskette drives for customization and microcode loading. Each IBM 3274 has to be customized at its physical site location. For a large installation with thousands of terminals scattered around the country, it becomes difficult to apply new fixes as well as perform new customizations. There are a number of new features that have enhanced the usability of an IBM 3174 EC over its predecessor the IBM 3274 CC. Some of those features are not available in all of the models of an IBM 3174 EC. These models will be mentioned in the following discussion, although details about the various models will be provided in a later section of this chapter.

20MB Fixed Disk Drive. A hard disk drive provides the same functions as a diskette drive except that it provides increased storage, further reducing the need for diskette swapping. Two fixed disk drives are supported for IBM 3174 ECs, with models between 1 and 13 (e.g., 1L, 11L, 1R, 11R, 2R, 12R, 3R, 13R). One disk drive is supported for model numbers between 51 and 63 (e.g., 51R, 61R, 52R, 62R, 53R, and 63R). Fixed disk is not supported for models between numbers 81 and 92 (e.g., 81R, 82R, 91R, 92R).

2.4MB Diskette Drive. Either a 1.2 megabytes (MB) or a 2.4MB diskette drive is supported on every model of the IBM 3174 family of ECs. A 2.4MB drive supports 2.4MB as well as 1.2MB diskettes. However, a 1.2MB drive cannot read from or write to a 2.4MB diskette.

Memory. Small models of the IBM 3174 EC like the 81R and 82R have 1MB of base memory. Models 91R and 92R have 2MB. Model 52R supports only 512 kilobytes (KB). Among the medium-size models, 51R and 53R have 1MB, while Models 61R, 62R and 63R have 2MB of base memory. Large models like 11L, 11R, 12R and 13R come with 2MB of main storage, while 1L, 1R, 2R and 3R support 1MB of base memory.

Memory in most of the the 3174 ECs can be expanded to support features like the Token-Ring SNA Gateway and the Asynchronous Emulation Adapter. 1MB and 2MB expansion cards can be inserted into the card slots to increase memory. We will talk about individual EC models in a later section.

Concurrent Communications Adapter (CCA). This is an optional feature which allows certain large and medium-size ECs to communicate simultaneously with many host processors. Keep in mind that this feature provides for *additional* physical links to the hosts. As far as logical links are concerned, distributed function terminals (DFT) already support it without the necessity of additional physical links.

Small controllers and Models 52R and 53R of medium-size controllers do not support this feature. Also this feature is different from the Asynchronous Emulation Adapter (AEA), which supports connectivity to ASCII hosts like DEC/VAX.

Single Link Multi-Host Support. Unlike the CCA discussed above, this is not an installable feature. Its support is provided in the microcode itself. This feature provides the *capability* to access up to eight IBM hosts attached to a particular Token-Ring Network. Terminals attached to Models 3R, 13R, 53R or 63R can communicate with up to five of these eight hosts. Installation of this option does not affect existing host software. Notice that only those controllers that *do not support* gateway features (discussed later) support this feature. These models are 3R, 13R, 53R and 63R. Other models that can be configured to act on those models will also support this feature.

Encrypt/Decrypt Adapter. This is an optional feature and is supported for large Models 1R, 2R and 3R.

Token-Ring Network Gateway Feature. This feature provides a gateway for multiple devices on a token-ring to communicate with an IBM host. Although there may be up to 140 such devices, their link to a host is a single IBM 3174 EC (Figure 1.2). Devices on a

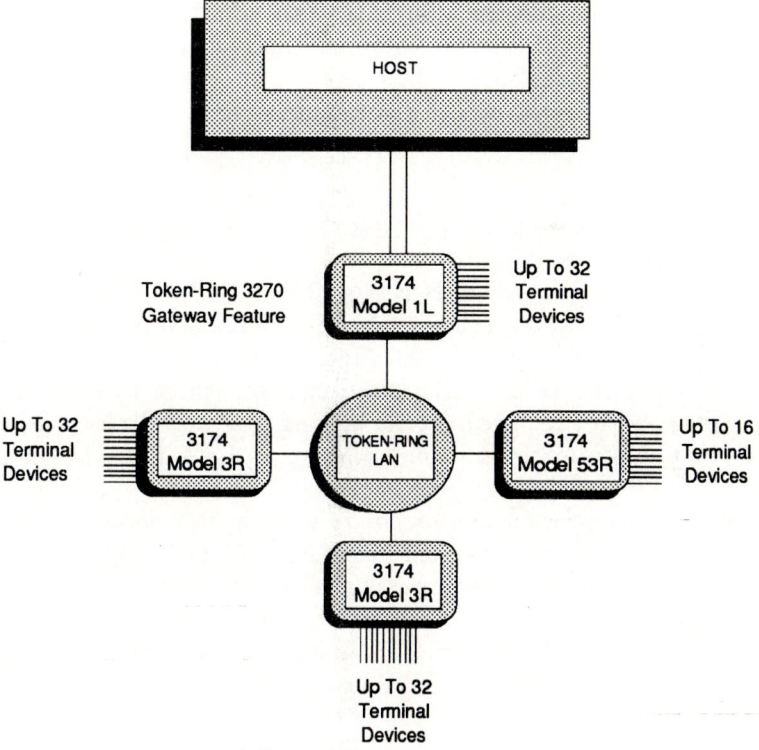

Figure 1.2 An example of the usage of Token-Ring Network Gateway feature. In this case, the IBM 3174 Model 1L has the gateway feature installed. This not only provides connectivity to the IBM host for the devices attached to itself, but also provides connectivity to the other IBM 3174s in the token-ring.

ring can be PCs running the DOS or OS/2 operating systems, other IBM 3174s without the gateway feature, and 3270 terminals attached to the 3174s. The 3174 with the gateway feature may also have terminals attached directly to itself. Also, the devices attached to the ring may also communicate with each other and are thus unaffected by the presence of the gateway feature. This feature is supported in Models 1L, 11L, 1R, 11R, 2R, 12R, 51R, 61R, 52R and 62R.

Asynchronous Emulation Adapter (AEA). This feature consists of both additional hardware and microcode. We will discuss this in greater detail in a later section of this chapter. The AEA provides connectivity as follows:

- An SNA terminal (e.g., 3270) can communicate with an ASCII host (e.g., DEC/VAX) by emulating an ASCII terminal.
- An ASCII terminal can communicate with an SNA host by emulating as an IBM 3270 device.
- An ASCII terminal can communicate with an ASCII host in the passthrough mode.

Communications Adapters. An IBM 3174 EC supports four types of communications adapters.

A Type 1 adapter provides EIA 232D or CCITT V.24 or CCITT V.35 interfaces to support SDLC, BSC or X.25 links to the host. When this adapter is used with Models 1L or 11L (channel interface models) and 3R or 13R (token-ring interface models) it provides them with the capability of having a remote link to the IBM host via a communications controller (e.g., IBM 3745) to the IBM host.

A Type 2 adapter is similar in functions and capabilities to a Type 1 except that its physical interface is X.21 (CCITT V.11) and the link-level protocols it supports are SDLC and X.25.

A Type 3 adapter provides a token-ring attachment capability at 4Mbps for Models 1L, 1R, 2R, 51R, and 52R. This capability is part of the base feature for Models 3R and 53R. However, if the Token-Ring Gateway feature is installed (discussed previously), the Type 3 adapter comes with it as part of that feature.

A Type 3A adapter is the same as a Type 3 adapter except that it supports dual speeds, i.e., 4 megabits per second (Mbps) as well as 16Mbps. It can be installed for Models 1L, 11L, 1R, 11R, 2R, 12R, 3R, 51R, 61R, 52R, 62R and 53R. It is part of the basic features for Models 13R and 63R.

IBM 3174 Establishment Controller   9

1.2 ADVANTAGES OVER 3274s

The capabilities of an IBM 3174 EC are far beyond what is possible with the IBM 3274s. Most of their prominent features have been discussed in the previous section. There are other features which enhance its capability considerably. They are:

- It provides for the customization of disks at remote sites from a central site and maintenance of them in a library.
- It provides for electronic distribution of microcode or customization parameters for remote IBM 3174s.
- It supports an Intelligent Printer Data Stream(IPDS), which supports All Points Addressability (APA) to position text, bar codes, images and vector graphics on a page.
- It provides for network asset management by supporting retrieval of a 3174's hardware product information from a central host. Such product information includes machine serial number, model, machine type, etc.
- It supports Multiple Logical Terminals (MLT) which enable an IBM 3270 CUT terminal to interact with up to five host sessions. However, a session can be connected to only one host at a time. The sessions can be for one IBM host and one or more ASCII hosts.
- It supports a Terminal Multiplexer Adapter (TMA), which can multiplex up to eight IBM 3270 devices into a single coaxial cable. A 3174 can support up to four TMAs, each TMA providing attachment for eight terminals. Thus, four TMAs provide connectivity to 32 terminals over four cable paths.

1.3 HOST CONNECTIVITY

IBM 3274s supported only two types of host connectivity, channel-attached and link-attached. IBM 3174 ECs additionally support token-ring attachment and ASCII host connectivity. Let's look into the various features for each type of connectivity.

1.3.1 Channel-Attached

This connectivity is only supported for those models which are suffixed with an L (Local), i.e., 3174 Models 1L and 11L. These models attach directly to the host byte or block multiplexer chan-

10 Advanced SNA Networking

nel. Since channel-attached devices have distance limitations, such 3174s should be in the same building as the host itself. The interface is bus and tag to the host channel. Figure 1.3 shows a 3174 attached to the host channel. Note that up to 32 terminal devices can be attached to the 3174. They can either have 32 individual cable connections or may use up to four IBM 3299 terminal multiplexers using four coaxial cable connections, or some combination of both.

1.3.2 Link-Attached

If all of the IBM 3174 ECs and their attached terminals were in the same building as the host processor, they would not need to be link-attached. However, in real life, the end-users executing their business transactions are usually at locations other than the data center. In order to establish host connectivity, you need remote IBM 3174s. Most of the models are remote (identified by suffix R) e.g., Models 1R, 11R, 62R, etc. Physical connectivity between a 3174 and a remote host is provided by analog (voice) or digital communications lines. Link-attached 3174s are connected to the host via one or more communications controllers. Figure 1.4 gives a pictorial view of such a connection.

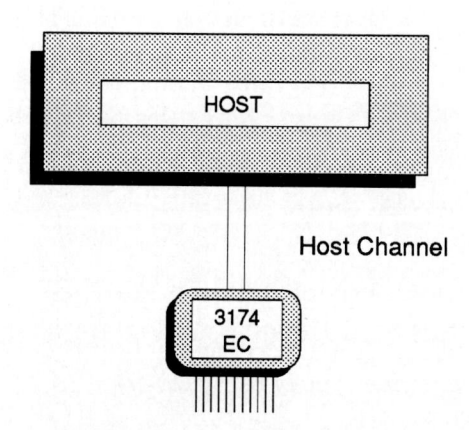

Figure 1.3 A channel-attached IBM 3174.

IBM 3174 Establishment Controller   11

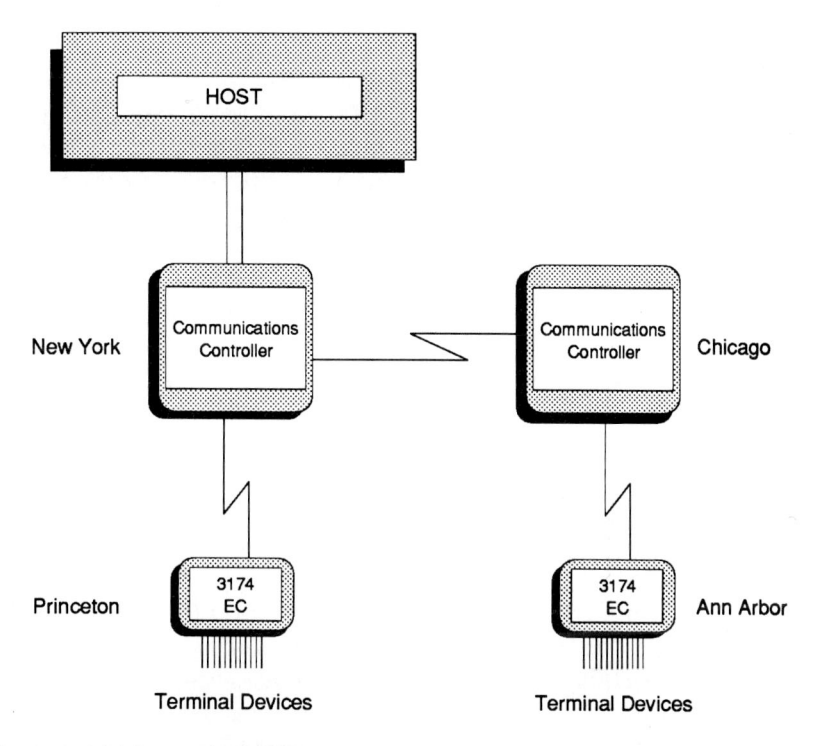

Figure 1.4 Link-attached IBM 3174s.

1.3.3 Token-Ring Attached

A Token-Ring is an implementation of a local area network (LAN) for the IBM environment. A LAN enhances connectivity between multiple scattered devices (e.g., between the floors of a single building) and helps them share resources such as files, printers, programs, etc., LANs are normally used to connect personal computers (e.g., IBM PCs and PS/2s) to share resources and communicate with each other. IBM has gone one step further by providing connectivity between 3174 ECs over a Token-Ring-based LAN.

How 3174s Fit in a LAN. Under normal circumstances, a cluster controller is either directly attached to a host channel or to a communications controller's port over a communications link. You can also multidrop a number of cluster controllers over a single link. A Token-Ring LAN provides an alternative to the multidrop approach for cluster controllers housed in a single building location.

Devices such as IBM PCs, PS/2s and 3174s can be attached to a Token-Ring LAN through a Multisystem Access Unit (MAU). When we talk about upgrading an IBM 3174 to support token-ring features, we are referring to the hardware, microcode, software, and physical interface needed to support token-ring protocols and physical connectivity to a MAU. A MAU looks like a wall-mounted plate with 10 physical interfaces. Two of the interfaces connect to other MAUs (i.e., MAU-in and MAU-out) and the other eight interfaces are used by the devices needing connectivity to the LAN.

Token-Ring Connectivity versus Token-Ring 3270 Gateway. The token-ring connectivity feature enables an 3174 to be connected to a token-ring through a MAU port. The Token-Ring 3270 Gateway feature enables a single 3174 to act as a gateway to the SNA network for *all* the 3174s attached to the Token-Ring Network through the Token-Ring connectivity feature.

While the connectivity feature provides for physical connectivity to the token-ring, the 3270 gateway feature provides the means to be connected to the outside world. A single 3270 gateway 3174 can provide connectivity to a number of LAN-attached 3174s. (Refer back to Figure 1.2). We have a channel-attached 3174 with the Token-Ring 3270 Gateway feature. It provides connectivity for itself and the other three 3174s through the token-ring connectivity feature. The gateway 3174 does not have to be channel-attached, it can be remote (link-attached).

Only 3174 Models 1L, 11L, 1R, 11R, 2R, 12R, 51R, 52R, 61R and 62R support the 3270 gateway feature. Models 3R and 53R can only support connectivity to a Token-Ring LAN, but cannot act as gateways. Models 81R and 82R neither support LAN connectivity nor the 3270 gateway feature.

We can define a maximum of 140 token-ring-attached devices to VTAM using an IBM 3174 EC. The channel-attached 3174 Model 1L acting as a 3270 gateway needs a single subchannel address to the host. A link-attached 3174 acting as a 3270 gateway requires a single SDLC station address.

1.3.4 ASCII Host Connectivity

The IBM terminal world consists primarily of 3270-like devices. For non-IBM hosts, the equivalent device is an ASCII terminal. Previously, if you worked in an environment in which you needed connectivity to IBM as well as non-IBM hosts, you had no choice

IBM 3174 Establishment Controller   13

but to have two separate display terminals. Now, it is possible to have connectivity to an IBM as well as an ASCII host from a single terminal device. Figure 1.5 gives an architecture for such a configuration. What you need is an IBM 3174 with an asynchronous emulation adapter (AEA) feature. This feature consists of a hardware card, microcode, and an additional 1.2MB disk drive. It can be installed on a local (channel-attached) as well as a remote (link-attached) 3174.

Each AEA supports up to eight ASCII devices. You can install up to three AEAs for Model 1L, 11L, 1R, 11R, 2R, 12R, 3R and 13R to support a maximum of 24 ASCII ports. These 24 ports are in

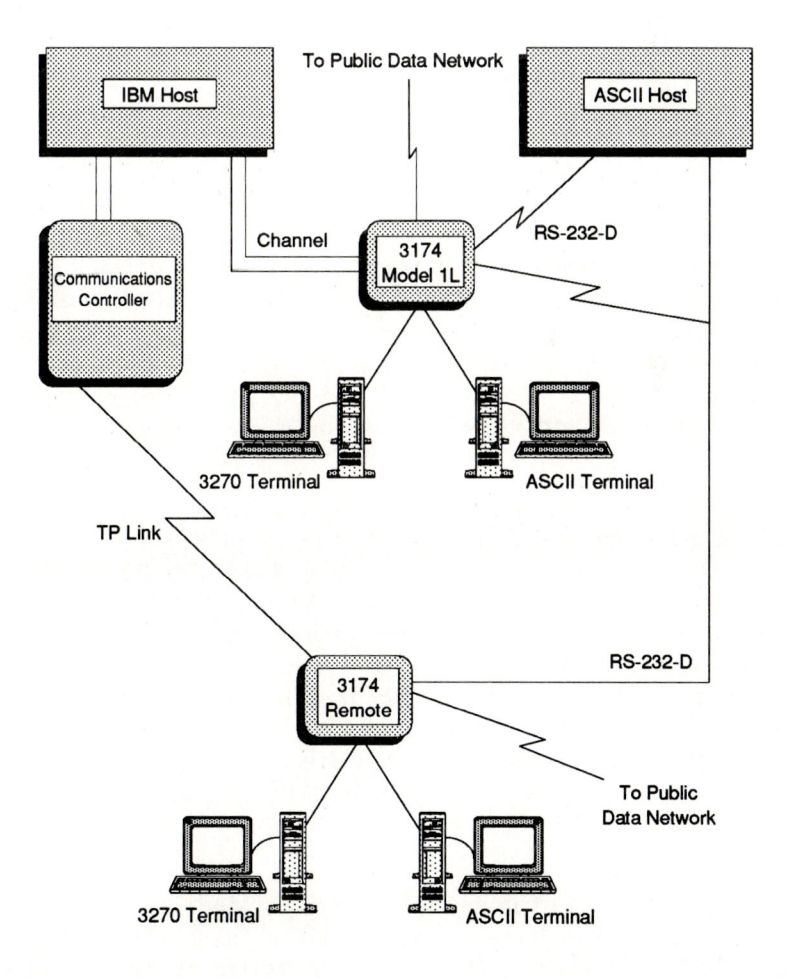

Figure 1.5 Interconnectivity between IBM 3270 and ASCII terminals, and IBM and ASCII hosts.

addition to the 32 terminal ports for 3270 devices. However, for Models 51R, 52R, 61R, 62R and 63R, you may not install more than one AEA which will support 8 ASCII ports in addition to 16 IBM 3270 ports. The three functions of AEAs are:

- IBM terminals can emulate ASCII terminals such as the VT-100 for connectivity to a DEC/VAX host. They can also emulate an IBM 3101 ASCII terminal.
- ASCII terminals can emulate 3270 terminals such as an IBM 3178 Model C2, a 3279 Model 2A, or a 3287 Model 2 printer.
- ASCII terminals, rather than emulating 3270 devices, can have a straight pass through to an ASCII host or a Public Data Network (PDN).

1.4 LARGE IBM 3174 MODELS

In this section we will discuss the various characteristics and features of the different models of IBM 3174 ECs. For sizing purposes, large controllers support 32 terminal ports, medium-size controllers support 16 terminal ports, and small controllers support eight ports.

1.4.1 Models 1L and 11L

Model 1L. Model 1L is a channel-attachment (local) support controller and provides connectivity to up to 32 terminals through four-port terminal adapters supporting four IBM 3299 terminal multiplexers. It has 1MB of base storage. The diskette drive supports 1.2MB of storage. Configuration and off-line tests are performed by attaching a CUT to Port 0 of the IBM 3174. Some of the optional features that may be installed are a 20MB fixed disk drive, a Token-Ring Network Gateway feature, an asynchronous emulation adapter, a second diskette drive, and additional memory. All types of communication adapters (Types 1,2,3, & 3A) are optionally supported.

Model 11L. This has the same features as Model 1L except that it supports 2MB of base memory. All of the optional features supported for model 1L can also be installed on an 11L except for a Type 3 communications adapter, which is *not* supported. Recall that a Type 3 adapter supports a 4Mbps token-ring.

However, a Type 3A adapter *is* supported, which provides LAN connectivity at 4Mbps as well as 16Mbps.

1.4.2 Models 1R and 11R

Model 1R. While Model 1L is meant for channel-attachment, Model 1R provides connectivity over communications lines. The physical interfaces supported are EIA 232D/CCITT V.24 and CCITT V.35. Remote link-attachment is done for SDLC, BSC and X.25. All other features are the same as in the Model 1L discussed above.

Model 11R. This controller has the same features as Model 1R except that it has 2MB of base storage and it does not support a Type 3 communications adapter.

1.4.3 Models 2R and 12R

Model 2R. While Model 1R supports physical interfaces EIA 232D/CCITT V.24 and CCITT V.35, Model 2R supports physical interfaces X.21 (CCITT V.11) for SDLC and X.25. Because of the popularity of RS-232-C and EIA232D interfaces in the United States, X.21 has not really gained wide acceptance.
Except for the differences in the physical interface, Model 2R has the same features as Model 1R.

Model 12R. This model is the same as Model 2R except that it comes with 2MB of base storage.

1.4.4 Models 3R and 13R

Model 3R. This model is, in fact, a Model 1R or 2R with a token-ring attachment. All other features and the capabilities are the same. Model 3R can also be converted back to Model 1R or 2R by installing a Type 1 communications adapter for Model 1R conversion and a Type 2 communications adapter for model 2R conversion. *Remember, although Model 3R has token-ring connectivity, it cannot be a Token-Ring 3270 Gateway.*

16   Advanced SNA Networking

FEATURES	MODELS							
	1L	11L	1R	11R	2R	12R	3R	13R
1 MB Base Storage	S	--	S	--	S	--	S	--
2 MB Base Storage	--	S	--	S	--	S	--	S
Type 1 Communications Adapter	O	O	S	S	N	N	O	O
Type 2 Communications Adapter	N	O	O	N	S	S	O	O
Type 3 (4Mbps) Communications Adapter	O	N	O	N	O	N	S	N
Type 3A (16/4 Mbps) Communications Adapter	O	O	O	O	O	O	O	S
Token-Ring Network Gateway feature	O	O	O	O	O	O	N	N
Asynchronous Emulation Adapter	O	O	O	O	O	O	O	O
20 MB Fixed Disk Drive	O	O	O	O	O	O	O	O
2.4 MB Diskette Drive	O	S	O	S	O	S	O	S
Encrypt/Decrypt Adapter	N	N	O	N	O	N	O	N
Concurrent Communications Adapter	O	O	O	O	O	O	O	O
Single Link Multi-Host Support	N	N	N	N	N	N	O	O

Note: S=Standard Feature   Number of terminals
        O=Optional Feature   supported for all
        N=Not Supported   large models = 32

Figure 1.6 Standard and optional features for *large* IBM 3174 Establishment Controllers.

Model 13R. This model is the same as Model 3R except that it comes with 2MB of base storage.

Figure 1.6 tabulates the standard and optional features of the large IBM 3174 models discussed in this section.

1.5 MEDIUM-SIZE IBM 3174 MODELS

Any 3174 controller that supports up to 16 terminals is classified as a medium-size controller. There are six models which fall into this category. The various features of these models are summarized in Figure 1.7 for quick reference.

IBM 3174 Establishment Controller 17

1.5.1 Models 51R and 61R

Model 51R. This model supports 16 terminals and has physical interfaces for communications links of EIA 232D/CCITT V.24 and V.35. It has 1MB of base storage and a 1.2MB floppy drive. Optional installable features include a Type 3 or Type 3A communications adapter (for token-ring connectivity), Token-Ring Network Gateway, Asynchronous Emulation Adapter, 20MB fixed disk drive and a concurrent communications adapter. However, the encrypt/decrypt adapter and Single Link Multi-Host support is not available for this model.

Model 61R. This model is similar to Model 51R with a few differences. It has a base memory of 2MB instead of the 1MB in Model 51R. It does not support a Type 3 communications adapter, and a 2.4MB floppy diskette drive is a standard feature.

FEATURES	MODELS					
	51R	61R	52R	62R	53R	63R
1 MB Base Storage	S	--	N (0.5 MB)	--	S	--
2 MB Base Storage	N	S	N	S	N	S
Type 1 Communications Adapter	S	S	N	N	N	N
Type 2 Communications Adapter	N	N	S	S	N	N
Type 3 (4Mbps) Communications Adapter	O	N	O	N	S	N
Type 3A (16/4 Mbps) Communications Adapter	O	O	O	O	O	S
Token-Ring Network Gateway feature	O	O	O	O	N	N
Asynchronous Emulation Adapter	O	O	O	O	N	O
20 MB Fixed Disk Drive	O	O	O	O	O	O
2.4 MB Diskette Drive	O	S	O	S	O	S
Encrypt/Decrypt Adapter	N	N	N	N	N	N
Concurrent Communications Adapter	N	O	N	O	N	O
Single Link Multi-Host Support	N	N	N	N	O	O

Note: S=Standard Feature   Number of terminals
       O=Optional Feature   supported for all
       N=Not Supported   medium models = 32

Figure 1.7 Standard and optional features for *medium-size* IBM 3174 Establishment Controllers.

18 Advanced SNA Networking

1.5.2 Models 52R and 62R

Model 52R. This model has the same capabilities and features as Model 51R except that it provides a Type 2 communications adapter instead of a Type 1. Thus, it supports an X.21 (V.11) interface and *not* an EIA 232D/V.24 interface. In addition, it has 512KB (0.5MB) of base storage instead of the standard 1MB in Model 51R. It also does not support a concurrent communications adapter.

Model 62R. This model is similar to Model 52R except that it supports 2MB of base memory. In addition, it does not support the old Type 3 communications adapter, a 2.4MB floppy diskette drive is standard, and the concurrent communications adapter is an optional feature.

1.5.3 Models 53R and 63R

Model 53R. This model does not support a telecommunications link to a communications controller via Type 1 or Type 2 communications adapters, but connects *only* to a Token-Ring Network. It has 1MB of base memory. It can optionally be configured for a 20MB hard disk and Single Link Multi-Host support.

Model 63R. This has the same capabilities as Model 53R except that it has a standard 2MB of base memory. It optionally supports an Asynchronous Emulation Adapter, while a Model 53R does not.

1.6 SMALL IBM 3174 MODELS

Any 3174 controller that supports a maximum of eight terminals is termed a small-size model. There are four models that fall into this category. The various features of these models are summarized in Figure 1.8 for quick reference.

1.6.1 Models 81R and 91R

Model 81R. This is a small controller with 1MB of base memory. It supports Type 1 CA, which provides EIA 232D/V.24 and V.35 physi-

IBM 3174 Establishment Controller 19

FEATURES	MODELS			
	81R	91R	82R	92R
1 MB Base Storage	S	--	S	--
2 MB Base Storage	N	S	N	S
Type 1 Communications Adapter	S	S	N	N
Type 2 Communications Adapter	N	N	S	S
Type 3 (4Mbps) Communications Adapter	N	N	N	N
Type 3A (16/4 Mbps) Communications Adapter	N	N	N	N
Token-Ring Network Gateway feature	N	N	N	N
Asynchronous Emulation Adapter	N	N	N	N
20 MB Fixed Disk Drive	N	N	N	N
2.4 MB Diskette Drive	N	S	N	S
Encrypt/Decrypt Adapter	N	N	N	N
Concurrent Communications Adapter	N	N	N	N
Single Link Multi-Host Support	N	N	N	N

Note: S=Standard Feature   Number of terminals
       O=Optional Feature   supported for all
       N=Not Supported   small models = 32

Figure 1.8 Standard and optional features for *small* IBM 3174 Establishment Controllers.

cal interfaces. There are *no* optional features that can be installed in this model.

Model 91R. This model has the same capabilities as Model 81R except that it provides 2MB of base memory and has a 2.4MB floppy diskette drive.

1.6.2 Models 82R and 92R

Model 82R. This is similar to Model 81R except that it supports a Type 2 CA instead of a Type 1 CA. Thus it provides an X.21 physical interface.

Model 92R. This is similar to Model 91R except that it supports a Type 2 CA instead of a Type 1 CA. It provides a physical interface of CCITT's X.21.

1.7 SUMMARY

In this chapter we learned about the IBM 3174 Establishment Controller. It has many additional features over its predecessor, the IBM 3274. A 3174 can be channel-attached, link-attached or token-ring-attached to the host. Different models support anywhere from 8 to 32 terminals. One of the important optional features is the support for ASCII host connectivity through the use of AEA cards. The AEA feature allows a 3270 terminal to emulate an ASCII terminal and vice versa. It also allows an ASCII terminal to have a session with an ASCII host in passthrough mode. Various models support EIA 232D/V.24, V.35 and X.21 interfaces for link-attached models. Token-Ring Network-attached models support 4Mbps as well as 16Mbps network spreads.

Chapter

2

IBM 3745 Communications Controller - Function and Architecture

SNA provides the underlying architecture for connecting various communications hardware and software. One of the most important components is the communications controller. We discussed various communications controllers in Chapter 2 of *Introduction to SNA Networking*. Before reading this chapter, you should read section 2.3 in that book. If you are already familiar with communications controllers, you may choose to skip it. Although we talked about all of IBM's communications controllers in the previous book, we will concentrate only on the IBM 3745 in this volume because it is the latest state-of-the-art.

2.1 INTRODUCTION

Communications controllers are intelligent systems that are dedicated to the control of communication lines and devices. Any communications device which cannot be channel-attached because of the distances involved has to be connected through a communications controller. Before we get into the details of the IBM 3745, let's talk about some of its predecessors that are still widely in use.

22 Advanced SNA Networking

IBM 3705. With a user base of over 48,000 units, this is the oldest and largest selling communications controller ever. After IBM started shipping it in the middle of 1976, it dominated the communications scene for over a decade. It is no longer marketed. It depended primarily upon the host for control and diagnostics because it did not support an attached terminal called a MOSS console (discussed later). Link-level protocols like BISYNC, SDLC and ASCII were supported and it could work with line speeds from 1200 bps to 230.4 kilobits per second. Depending upon the model, anywhere from 128 to 352 communication lines were supported.

IBM 3725. Announced in early March 1983, this communications controller supports anywhere from 80 to 256 communication lines. While the 3705 supported only 512 kilobytes of memory, a 3725 could support up to 3 megabytes of main storage. In 1986, support for attachment to a Token-Ring Network was also provided by IBM.

IBM 3720. Announced in May 1986, this controller is primarily intended for small and medium-size enterprises. Depending upon the various models and configurations, it can support anywhere from 28 to 60 communication lines. Some of its models support attachment to IBM Token-Ring Networks also. It is helpful as a low-cost concentrator for remote regional and branch offices of a company and was cost effective as a front-end to the 9370 family of processors. It appears that the newly introduced low-end models of the IBM 3745 could provide an effective replacement for the IBM 3720.

2.2 FUNCTIONS AND CHARACTERISTICS

The functions and characteristics of communications controllers were discussed in Chapter 2 of *Introduction to SNA Networking*. They are being repeated here for completeness and to minimize referring back to the previous volume.

2.2.1 Major Functions

A communications controller offloads communications-related functions from the host, leaving it to perform the function it was meant

IBM 3745 Communications Controller - Function and Architecture

for — running application systems. Without communications controllers, a host would be interrupted every time data is transmitted to or received from another source. The major functions of a communications controller are as follows:

1. It provides data buffers for temporary storage of data coming from the communication lines or host channels for subsequent transmission to the target location.
2. It controls the physical transmission and receiving of data on various communication lines.
3. Based on various communications protocols, it verifies the accuracy of transmission messages. It ensures data retransmission in case of errors. Thus, it isolates the host applications from the burden of checking transmission accuracy and performs such functions itself.
4. It maintains awareness of the capacity of other communications devices, thus controlling message pacing and ensuring a controlled flow of data to such devices.
5. It maintains awareness of the various paths to a destination and selects the appropriate route for sending data.
6. It logs and transmits transmission error data to the host computer.
7. It provides concentrator and intelligent switching functions.
8. It sequences the messages so that the receiving devices can reconstruct them from the sequence numbers assigned to the message segments.
9. It frees the host applications from the burden of polling the devices linked to that application.
10. It establishes and monitors its sessions with hosts and other communications controllers to provide logical connectivity between various nodes of the network.

2.2.2 Functional Categories

A communications controller can be split into the following three functional categories:

24 Advanced SNA Networking

1. *Front-End Processor (FEP).* As the name suggests, this acts as a front-end to a host processor. It is attached to the channels of one or more host systems and accepts data from the host communications access method (e.g., VTAM) for subsequent transmission to other nodes or devices. It also accepts data from terminal devices or other communications controllers for routing to the proper host system. In Figure 2.1, CC-1 and CC-2 are the FEPs. In this case, CC-2 is attached to two different hosts.

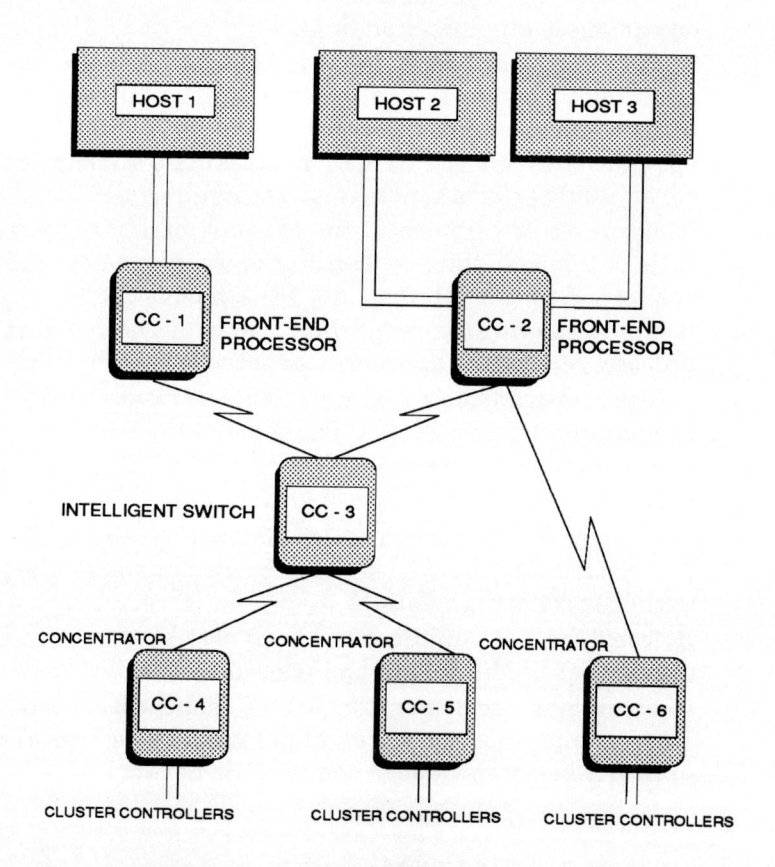

Figure 2.1 A sample network in which different communications controllers perform the functions of a front-end processor, a concentrator, and an intelligent switch.

2. *Concentrator.* A communications controller acting as a concentrator controls a number of cluster controllers, terminals, RJE/RJP devices, and other communications devices. In Figure 2.1, CC-4, CC-5 and CC-6 provide the concentrator function in a communications controller.
3. *Intelligent Switch.* An intelligent switch is an intermediary node which provides the switching and routing functions between other communications controllers. CC-3 in Figure 2.1 is an intelligent switch.

2.2.3 Channel-Attached, Link-Attached and Token-Ring-Attached

A communications controller can be either attached to the host channel or link-attached to another communications controller. In Figure 2.1, CC-1 and CC-2 are channel-attached while CC-3, CC-4, CC-5 and CC-6 are link-attached. In the IBM 3745 family, Models 130, 170, 210 and 410 have channel-attachment capabilities while Model 150 can only be link-attached. A channel-attached controller may have the capability to support a multiple attachments to more than one host. For example, an IBM 3745 Model 410 can have up to 16 channel attachments.

All communications controllers in the IBM 3745 family can be attached to IBM Token-Ring Networks. This capability provides an alternative to connectivity through traditional communications line ports. Other processors/devices that can be attached to an IBM Token-Ring Network are the IBM 9370, an IBM 3174 Subsystem Control Unit, and an IBM PC or PS/2. A Token-Ring Network provides a high-speed physical data path (4 or 16 megabits per second) between the various devices attached to a ring.

2.3 ARCHITECTURE

An IBM 3745 consists of three functional components as follows:

1. The Control Subsystem.
2. The Communications Subsystem.
3. The Maintenance and Operator Subsystem (MOSS).

Figure 2.2 gives a simple architectural view of such a controller.

26 Advanced SNA Networking

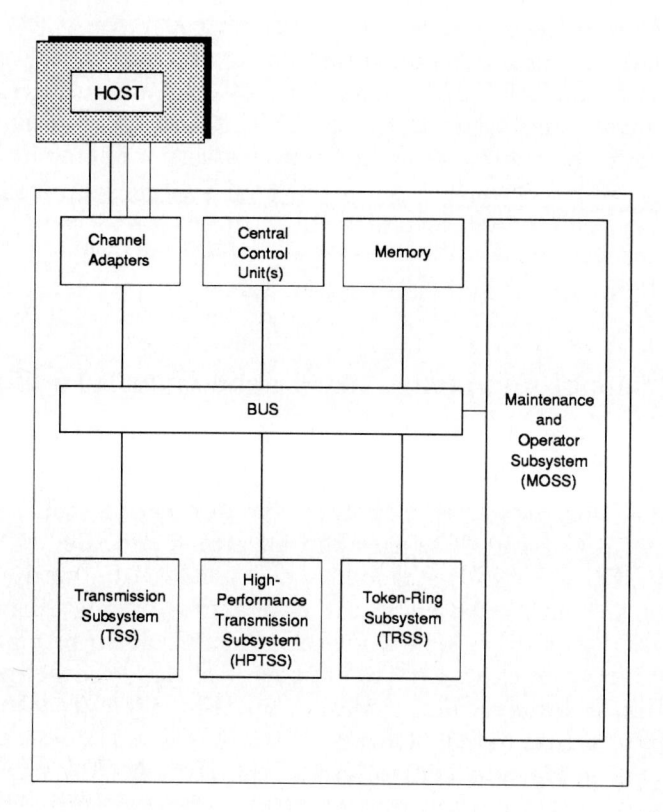

Figure 2.2 Architecture of an IBM 3745.

Control Subsystem. This is the brain of the communications controller. It is driven by the Network Control Program (NCP) or Partition Emulation Program (PEP). Its channel adapter interface receives and drives channel signals in a channel-attached FEP. Its memory component provides temporary buffers for data coming from or going to the channels or the communications subsystem. Central Control Units (CCUs) provide the necessary cycles to perform these functions. Some models, like the IBM 3745 Model 410, come with two CCUs and may be configured for enhanced availability or greater performance.

Communications Subsystem. This subsystem is the primary interface with low-speed, high-speed and token-ring communications media. It is a three-tiered architecture. Scanners, which are powerful microprocessors, provide for the control of a number of line interface couplers (LICs). A LIC, depending upon transmission line speed, controls one or more transmission lines. The speed of a scanner determines the ultimate transmission load a scanner can handle. The underlying principle is that every time a bit of data comes on the line, the scanner should be ready to grab the bit and pass it over the bus to the memory buffers of the control subsystem. Load balancing of communication lines over multiple scanners and LICs is a design issue and will be in Chapter 4.

A number of LICs constitute a Line Adapter Board (LAB). A LAB may further interface with one or two scanners. Thus there can be a single or a double scanner LAB. We can summarize as follows:

- One or two scanners control a LAB.
- A LAB interfaces with many LICs (e.g., 8).
- Each LIC provides one or more communications ports depending upon the line speed and other transmission characteristics.

In recent publications, IBM has been using different acronyms for a LAB. For 3745 Models 210 and 410, it sometimes calls it a LIC Interface Unit (LIU) and for 3745 Models 130, 150 and 170, it calls it a Line Interface Base (LIB). So be aware if you find confusing terminologies in the IBM Manuals. For all practical purposes, LIBs, LABs and LIUs refer to the component that controls multiple LICs.

The communications subsystem also provides an interface to high-speed transmission lines like T1 lines at 1.544 megabits/second in U.S.A., Canada and Japan, and CEPT lines at 2.048 megabits/second in Europe. In addition, it provides an interface for IBM Token-Ring Networks that support high-speed data transmission (4 or 16 megabits/second) within a particular location like a building or a campus environment.

Maintenance and Operator Subsystem (MOSS). Through a MOSS console, the communications subsystem provides utilities to support problem determination, maintenance, initialization and supervision. You can Initial Program Load (IPL) the controller or Initial Microcode Load (IML) a scanner from this console. You may perform online diagnostics, generate alarms and alerts, and isolate failures to a specific component. In a nutshell, MOSS provides a window into the IBM 3745 communications controller to determine the status of a component or event and to fix or switch a failed component.

28 Advanced SNA Networking

Now, since we have a bird's eye view of the entire architecture of an IBM 3745, let's get into more detail about each subsystem and their various components.

2.4 CONTROL SUBSYSTEM

Figure 2.3 gives a detailed view of the different components of the control subsystem in an IBM 3745. The following sections explain each of these components.

2.4.1 Central Control Unit (CCU)

The CCU constitutes the brain of the IBM 3745 communications controller. It runs under either the NCP or PEP. The NCP can be loaded into the controller using one of the following:

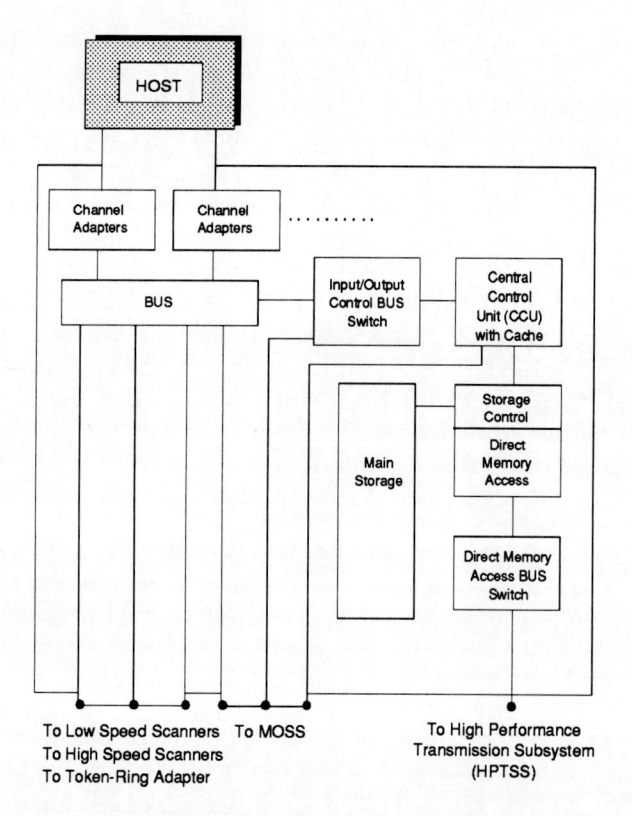

Figure 2.3 Architecture of the Control Subsystem of an IBM 3745.

IBM 3745 Communications Controller - Function and Architecture

1. Through a host channel for channel-attached controllers.
2. Through a communication line link for link-attached remote controllers.
3. Through the controller hard disk if such software resides on the controller hard disk.

The instruction set of an IBM 3745 is similar to that of a 3725. In addition, it has a few extensions to support additional capabilities. A CCU is a powerful processor with a machine cycle time of 75 nanoseconds in Models 210/410 and 131 nanoseconds in Models 130/150/170.

In Model 410, you have two CCUs instead of one. Depending on the different modes of operation, a twin-CCU environment provides for enhanced performance or increased availability. It will be discussed in more detail in a later section of this chapter.

2.4.2 Cache Buffers

A cache can be roughly defined as a high-speed buffer between a fast device and a slow device. In the context of a 3745, a CCU is a fast device (with a machine cycle of 75 nanoseconds) while the main storage (memory) has a relatively slower memory cycle. If the CPU has to fetch the next sequential instruction from main memory, it will be a slower process than if it could fetch the same instruction from its high speed cache buffers. So an intelligent algorithm is implemented to anticipate the CCUs action and transfer the appropriate set of instructions to its cache. Cache buffers provide instructions to the CCU at the CCU cycle rate.

IBM 3745 Models 210 and 410 have a capacity of 16 kilobytes of cache buffers, while the newer Models 130, 150 and 170 come with 32 kilobytes of cache buffers. The concept of high-speed cache buffers has been implemented in host processors for a long time.

2.4.3 Main Storage

In Models 210 and 410, you may have main storage of either 4 megabytes or 8 megabytes for each CCU. Since Model 410 has two CCUs, it can have a maximum of 16 megabytes of memory. Models 130, 150 and 170 can have a maximum of 4 megabytes of main storage only.

2.4.4 Storage Control

Storage control controls the movement of data between the CCU and main storage. It comes with the capability of enhanced error checking and correction (ECC), which can detect and correct all double-bit hard errors. It may also detect and correct some triple-bit errors.

2.4.5 Direct Memory Access (DMA)

Data can come from the High Performance Transmission Subsystem (HPTSS) at a very high speed. It supports T1 lines, on which bits could be coming at a speed of up to 1.544 megabits/second (2.048 megabits/second through CEPT lines in Europe). Since up to 8 T1 lines could be active concurrently, there could be a tremendous amount of data flowing to and from main storage. Allowing this much data to pass through the CCU could slow overall system performance. In order to improve performance, the IBM 3745 box provides DMA buses which can transfer data directly to main storage, bypassing the CCU. Two DMA buses are provided in an IBM 3745. Each bus can support up to four high-speed scanners (HSS).

2.4.6 Input/Output Control (IOC) Buses

Two pairs of IOC buses are supported in the IBM 3745. In Model 410, such buses are attached to each CCU. In Model 210, bus pairs are connected together. The first IOC bus in a pair is meant for channel adapters (CAs) and can support up to eight CAs. The second IOC bus is meant for communication line adapters and can support up to 16 such adapters. A line adapter may be attached to a high speed scanner (HSS), low speed scanner (LSS) or a token-ring adapter (TRA).

2.4.7 Channel Adapters (CAs)

A CA provides the interface between a host channel and the IOC bus of a communications controller. Internally, each CA is controlled by its own microprocessor. Thus, a maximum of 16 CAs in an IBM 3745 are controlled by 16 different microprocessors. The host channels may be byte-multiplexer, block-multiplexer or selector. Although a 3745 supports a maximum data transfer rate of only 3 megabytes per second, it may be connected to the 4.5 megabytes/second channels supported by the IBM 3090 hosts.

As we mentioned in the beginning of Section 2.3, a 3745 can be driven by the NCP or PEP. Further, an NCP and an emulation program (EP) can be run under PEP. When the controller is running under NCP, it is said to be running in native mode. In this mode, only one sub-channel address (one MVS UCB) is needed to transmit data to and from the host. When the controller is running under PEP, it is said to be running in partitioned mode. In this mode, it can only be attached to a byte-multiplexer channel. In addition, one sub-channel address will be required for each line in emulation mode.

2.4.8 Data Streaming Feature

Generally, a channel interface cable will allow a maximum of 200 feet of distance between a host and the communications controller. However, with the installation of a data streaming feature, this distance can be increased to a maximum of 400 feet. Be aware that data streaming is only supported in the IBM 3090 and 9370 processors. In addition, the host channel must be a block multiplexer channel for this purpose.

2.4.9 Two-Processor Switch (TPS)

The TPS feature provides the capability of attaching a 3745 channel adapter to two channel interfaces (CIs). Such CIs can be connected to the same host or to a different host. However, only one CI may be active at one time. Figure 2.4A illustrates a CA attached to two CIs through a TPS for a dual host environment.

A command can be executed at the MOSS console to select either host A or host B. A command can also be executed to enable interfaces both to host A as well as to host B. However, if both interfaces are enabled, the host is responsible for activating one of the two interfaces. Figure 2.4B illustrates a CA attached to two CIs through a TPS for a single host environment.

With proper configuration, a TPS can be used to enhance host availability. Remember that while the MOSS console is responsible for enabling one or both interfaces, the host is responsible for activating only one of them. Both interfaces cannot be enabled simultaneously.

32 Advanced SNA Networking

(A) Two-Processor Switch for Two Hosts

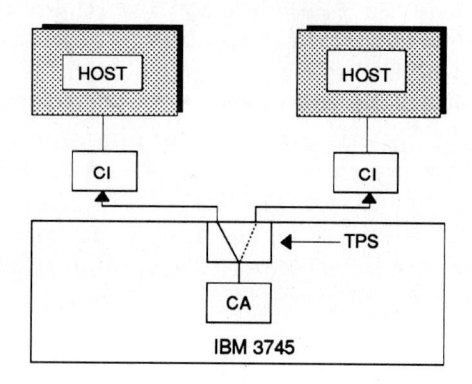

(B) Two-Processor Switch for Single Host

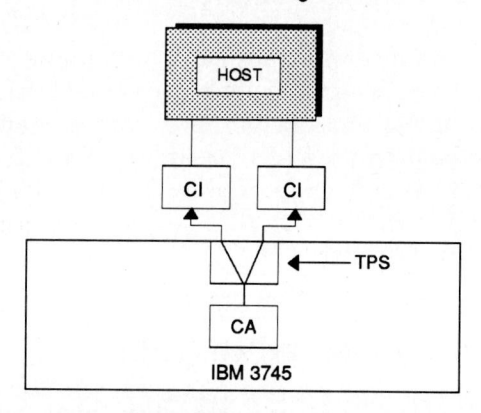

CI = Channel Interface
CA = Channel Adapter
TPS = Two-Processor Switch

Figure 2.4 Configurations with a two-processor switch (TPS).

While the IBM 3745 base unit for Models 210 and 410 supports eight CAs, the IBM 3746 expansion unit Model 11 (explained in the next chapter) supports eight additional CAs. Thus, we can install a maximum of 16 CAs. But a CA with a two-processor switch is considered to be the equivalent of two CAs. Therefore, the maximum number of CAs supported with TPS is eight and without TPS is 16. Models 130, 150 and 170 support a maximum of four CAs without TPS and two CAs with the TPS feature.

IBM 3745 Communications Controller - Function and Architecture   33

2.5 COMMUNICATIONS SUBSYSTEM

Figure 2.5 illustrates the general architecture of the communications subsystem of an IBM 3745. It consists of three sub-components as follows:

1. High Performance Transmission Subsystem (HPTSS).
2. Transmission Subsystem (TSS).
3. Token-Ring Subsystem (TRSS).

Scanners form the heart of the various subsystems mentioned above. In fact, each scanner has a microprocessor as its main component. There are various types of scanners used in a 3745.

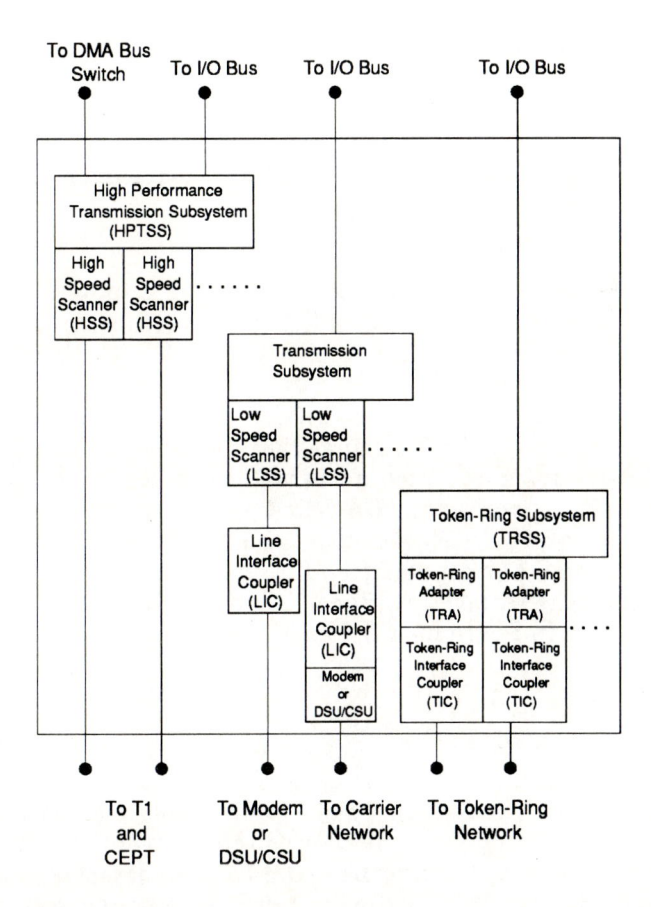

Figure 2.5 Architecture of the Communications Subsystem of an IBM 3745.

HPTSS, which supports high-speed lines like T1 and CEPT, uses high speed scanners (HSS). Low-speed scanners (LSS) are used for TSS where the maximum line speed may not exceed 256 kilobits/second.

2.5.1 High Performance Transmission Subsystem(HPTSS)

T1 and CEPT. HPTSS supports attachment to very high-speed digital lines like T1 and CEPT. T1 lines may carry data at the rate of 1.544 megabits/second and are popular in the U.S.A., Canada and Japan. CEPT lines are the equivalent of T1 lines in Europe and support a line speed of 2.048 megabits/second.

Limitation. Each high-speed scanner (HSS) can be connected to up to two high-speed lines. However, only one line can be active at a time for a particular HSS. A fully configured high-end model contains a maximum of eight HSSs, thus having the capability of being connected to 16 lines. However, only eight lines out of 16 can be active at a time.

Physical Interfaces. The physical interfaces supported by this subsystem are CCITTs V.35 and X.21. V interfaces and the X.21 interface were discussed in Sections 3.2.3 and 3.2.4 of *Introduction to SNA Networking*. As we discussed earlier, Data Circuit-Terminating Equipment (DCE) is needed to interface a physical line to the Data Terminal Equipment (DTE), which is an IBM 3745 in our case. Such an interface may be a data service unit/channel service unit (DSU/CSU) for digital data service (DDS) networks. In some countries, the interface may be network channel-terminating equipment (NCTE). An example of NCTE is an EIA-547 interface. DTEs, DCEs and DSU/CSUs were discussed in Sections 1.2.5 and 1.2.6 of *Introduction to SNA Networking*.

Direct Attachment. IBM 3745s may also be connected to each other using HPTSS. Using a V.35 or EIA-547 interface, the maximum distance allowable between 3745s is 325 feet. However, using X.21, the distance may not be more than 33 feet. An IBM 3745 may also be connected to another IBM 3725 in direct-attachment mode. In that case, V.35 is the only interface supported and the distance may not exceed 325 feet. While two 3745s may communicate with each other at a maximum speed of up to 1.8432 million bits/second, they can operate at up to 245.76 kilobits/second with an IBM 3725.

2.5.2 Transmission Subsystem (TSS)

While HPTSS supports high-speed scanners, TSS supports low-speed scanners only. Depending on the configuration, there may be anywhere from 2 to 32 low-speed scanners in an IBM 3745. Connectivity with communication lines is provided for different physical interfaces (e.g., RS-232) on various line interface couplers (LICs). With an appropriate configuration, a maximum of 896 lines can be connected to a TSS.

Some of the salient features of low-speed scanners are as follows:

- They support link-level protocols such as BSC, SDLC and Asynchronous.
- Maximum line speed for synchronous protocols (BSC and SDLC) is 256Kbps.
- Maximum line speed for asynchronous protocols is 19.2 kbps.
- They support up to 4 or 8 LICs in a LIC Unit Type 1 and up to 16 LICs in a LIC Unit Type 2. For now, suffice it to say that LIC Unit Type 1 supported LICs need external DCEs (modem or DSU/CSU) while a LIC Unit Type 2 has built-in DCEs. Type 2 LIC units have been supported recently and did not exist in old models of the IBM 3745. Out of a maximum of 896 lines, up to 416 lines can be attached to LICs with built-in DCEs.
- A 3745 LSS supports selective scanning. In other words, it only scans LICs with *active* lines rather than all the LICs. Therefore, the user may activate and deactivate lines to balance line weight for a particular scanner. In the days of the IBM 3725, all of the LICs with *installed* (even if inactive) lines were scanned. While selective scanning may be used to make more efficient use of a low-speed scanner, it increases the user responsibility to ensure that active lines do not overload a scanner. Line weight considerations will be discussed in detail in Chapter 3.
- LICs can be removed and/or replaced while the IBM 3745 is up and running. This facility, called hot pluggability, allows upgrading and repair to take place without having to bring down the communications controller.

The various components of a transmission subsystem are as follows:

1. Scanner — a microprocessor providing the necessary cycles to control various LICs for sending and receiving data. A scanner's processing power determines various line configurations as calculated by line weight considerations.
2. LIC Unit — allows for grouping of various LICs. LIC Unit Type 1 controls traditional LICs where a DCE (modem or DSU/CSU) is provided externally. LIC Unit Type 2 provides built-in DCEs and thus allows direct connectivity to a physical line.
3. LIC — LICs provide the ports which have direct interface with a DCE for Unit Type 1 and a physical line for Unit Type 2.
4. LAB, LIU, LIB — for all practical purposes, a line attachment base (LAB), LIC interface unit (LIU) and LIC interface board (LIB) refer to the same thing. While the term LAB has been used in the past, it is called LIU for Models 210/410 and LIB for Models 130/150/170.
5. Ports — a LIC contains one or more physical ports supporting different physical interfaces (e.g., RS-232) for connectivity to communication lines through a DCE or directly.

2.5.3 Token-Ring Subsystem (TRSS)

Recently, Token-Ring Networks have been playing a major role in the IBM networking architecture. When originally introduced a few years ago, their scope was limited to IBM PCs and servers on a local area network (LAN). But later on, IBM brought other hardware under its domain. Now, Token-Ring Networks provide connectivity for 9370 mid-frames, communications controllers (e.g., 3745 and 3720) and subsystem control units (e.g., 3174). Token-Ring Networks provide high-speed transmission of data among attached devices in a limited-distance environment like an office building or campus grounds. The data transmission rates supported are 4 megabits/second and 16 megabits/second.

Multistation Access Units (MAUs) form the hub of a Token-Ring's connectivity. Different devices like PC or PS/2 workstations, servers, IBM 9370s, 3174s, 3745s and 3720s may be connected to individual MAU ports. Depending upon configuration limitations, the token-ring access method will allow the high-speed exchange of data between the aforementioned devices. Before Token-Ring Networks were introduced, a cluster controller (e.g., IBM 3274 or 3174) could be connected to a communications controller through communication line ports only.

Adapters. High-end models of the IBM 3745 provide for a maximum of four token-ring adapters. Each adapter can be attached to up to two Token-Ring Networks. Thus four adapters will allow a maximum of eight token-ring networks. However, lower-end models support fewer adapters and will be discussed later. Token-Ring Networks can operate at a line speed of 4 or 16 million bits/second.

Token-Ring Interface Couplers (TICs). TICs provide the physical interface for Token-Ring Network connectivity. There are two types of TICs supported. TIC Type 1 supports only those token-rings which are operating at 4 million bits/second. TIC Type 2 supports token-rings operating at 4 or 16 million bits/second. The physical transmission media connecting a 3745 TIC to the MAU port is a shielded cable or a twisted telephone wire. However, twisted wire can only support 4 million bits/second Token-Ring Networks.

2.6 MAINTENANCE AND OPERATOR SUBSYSTEM (MOSS)

In the days of the IBM 3705, all of the communications controller functions were performed from the host using VTAM operator commands. The concept of providing certain procedures at the controller level originated with IBM 3725s. This has continued for 3720s and 3745s.

The MOSS console communicates with the controller and provides a window into the functioning of a 3745. MOSS may be used to initial program load (IPL) a communications controller or initial microcode load (IML) its components such as a scanner. It provides for concurrent maintenance while the functional components of an IBM 3745 are up and running. MOSS is one of the main sources for performing problem determination. It can perform control program (NCP) loading and is also useful for performing various dump operations on a 3745. For a LIC Unit Type 2, it can do error notification for integrated modems (for analog lines) and DSU/CSUs (for digital lines). It supports remote support facility

38 Advanced SNA Networking

(RSF), which may be used by IBM for remote logon and diagnostics for problem determination. In a nutshell, MOSS provides powerful tools and procedures for the operation and maintenance of an IBM 3745.

2.6.1 MOSS Components

Figure 2.6 shows the various architectural components of the MOSS in an IBM 3745. Note that it has a separate power supply so that its own maintenance does not interfere with normal 3745 operations.

MOSS Microprocessor. This runs independently of the central control unit (CCU). At power-on, microcode is loaded from the integrated hard disk. One megabyte of main memory is associated

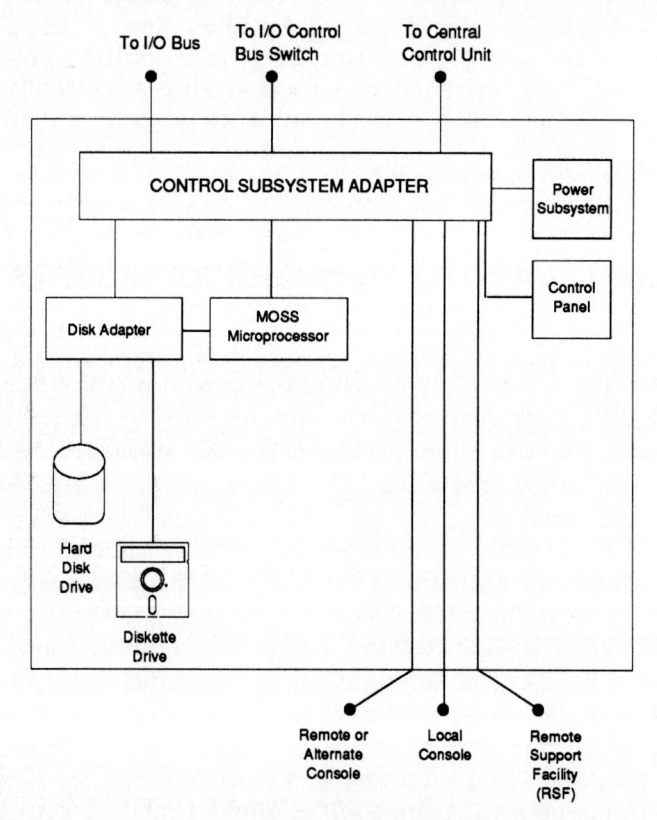

Figure 2.6 Architecture of the Maintenance and Operator Subsystem of an IBM 3745.

IBM 3745 Communications Controller - Function and Architecture   39

with the MOSS microprocessor. Power-on automatically IMLs the microprocessor. It accesses information from the hard disk and diskette via the disk adapter.

Diskette Drive. A diskette drive supports 1.2 megabyte removable diskettes. The diskette contains microcode, MOSS files and various diagnostic programs. At the time of 3745 installation, all diskette files are copied to the hard disk. Therefore, for day-to-day operations, a MOSS microprocessor accesses all the files from the hard disk only. However, under those circumstances where the hard disk becomes inoperable, a control panel provides for MOSS IML directly from the diskette.

Hard Disk Drive. A hard disk drive supports an integrated (non-removable) hard disk with a storage capacity of 72 megabytes. As we already know, it contains microcode, MOSS files and diagnostic routines which are copied to it from the diskette at installation time. It also contains scanner microcode for LSS and HSS.
  The IBM 3745 control program (NCP) can also reside on the hard disk. A program load from the hard disk is much faster than performing it over the communication lines for remote 3745s. It supports one or two control programs per CCU. In case control programs have to be dumped, it can be done quickly by writing them to the dump file on the hard disk. Later, when the 3745 has been reloaded and is operational, dump programs can be sent to the host for analysis and printing. A hard disk supports one control program dump file per CCU.
  Other dump files supported are a TIC dump file and a MOSS dump file. There is also a scanner dump file for each CCU. Trace buffer areas for a scanner are also allocated on the hard disk.
  Since the 3745 supports port swapping, this information is contained in the port swap file. Complete configuration information for a 3745 is contained in the configuration data file (CDF).

Control Panel. A control panel consists of various switches on the exterior of an IBM 3745. Although most of the control functions are performed from the MOSS console, some are activated from the control panel. The control panel supports a power-on switch and also provides a unit emergency switch for stopping the controller operation. There is also a ten-digit alphanumeric display which displays the progress of various stages during IPL. It also gives a visual display of various errors during

40 Advanced SNA Networking

initialization. The control panel is always powered on even if the controller is powered off.

2.6.2 MOSS Consoles

An IBM 3745 communications controller provides for three different console attachments:

1. Local Console.
2. Alternate Console.
3. Remote Console.

Figure 2.7 shows the different possiblities for console connectivity. A local console is mandatory. Among the alternate and remote consoles, only one may be attached at a given time. However, out of the three console types, only one may be *active* at a time. There is also a facility to let IBM have access for remote diagnostics and maintenance using the remote support facility (RSF). For RSF

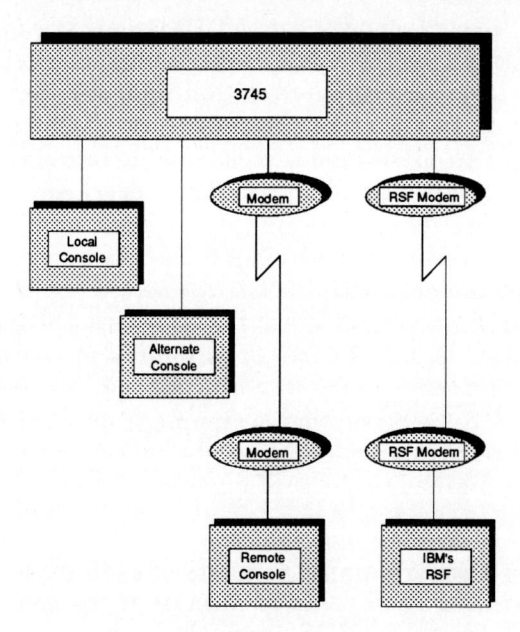

Note: 1. Either alternate console or remote console may be attached at one time.
2. Maximum distance for a local console is 23 feet. Maximum distance for an alternate console is 400 feet.

Figure 2.7 MOSS consoles supported for an IBM 3745.

access, there is a provision for customer controllable time-out to disconnect an RSF console if it has been inactive for a certain period of time. For security reasons, access to the MOSS console is password protected. There are three types of passwords; one each for local, remote and alternate console.

Local Console. A local console is mandatory and can be attached up to a maximum distance of 23 feet. It communicates with the MOSS subsystem at 2400 bps in a start-stop mode. Its physical interface is compatible with CCITTs V.24. You may use a wide variety of terminals or PCs as the local console. It supports many models of IBM 3151, 3161 and 3163 in addition to a PS/2 running IBM's OS/2 Extended Edition operating system. In almost all cases, it emulates an IBM 3101. Figure 2.8 identifies the different display stations and workstations which may be used as MOSS consoles.

Alternate Console. An alternate console is an alternate for a remote console. While an alternate console must be within 400 feet of a 3745, a remote console can be at an unlimited distance. Since they both use the same port, only one may be attached at a time. The physical interface supported is compatible with CCITT's V.24 and communicates at 2400 bps in start-stop mode. Again, Figure 2.8 itemizes the different hardware that may be used as an alternate console.

Remote Console. An alternate console and a remote console are mutually exclusive because they attach to the same port. A remote console is connected to the 3745 via a pair of modems on either end of a common carrier communication line. The modems may be compatible with Bell 212A in the U.S.A., Canada and Japan. In other countries, the DCE (modem) may be compatible with V.22 (alternative B or C) or V.22 bis (mode 4) supporting an auto-answer feature. Figure 2.8 details the different IBM display devices that may be used as remote consoles.

Console Sharing. In large installations, there may be multiple hosts and communications controllers. It would be quite cumbersome to have as many consoles as the number of controllers. Under these circumstances, console sharing provides single console support for many 3745s and 3725s. A *local console* may be shared between up to four 3745s and 3725s. An *alternate*

42 Advanced SNA Networking

Display Station/ Personal Computer	Models	Emulation Mode	Console Supported
IBM 3151	30X 40X 310 360 410 460	Native Mode (recommended) or IBM 3101	Local Remote Alternate
IBM 3161	11 12 21 22	IBM 3101	Local Remote Alternate
IBM 3163	11 12 21 22	IBM 3101	Local Remote Alternate
IBM PS/2	Any model that can run OS/2 EE	IBM 3101	Local Remote Alternate
IBM 3727	-	-	Local Alternate
IBM PC	XT AT	IBM 3101 (block mode)	Remote

Figure 2.8 Different models of IBM display stations/Personal Computers which may be used as MOSS consoles.

console may be shared between up to six 3745s and 3725s. However, the distance limitations discussed previously still apply.

To support console sharing, you need another component called an IBM 7427 Console Switching Unit. Be aware that a 7427 is an RPQ (Request for Price Quotation) from IBM.

2.6.3 Remote Support Facility (RSF)

IBM's RSF provides maintenance assistance for 3745s over communication lines. Needless to say, a modem will be required at the customer site to support a communications link. In some countries, the RSF modem is built in to the controller itself. In the U.S.A., an RSF modem is V.22 bis compatible, has an auto-answer feature (due to a switched line attachment), runs at 2400 bps and supports BSC protocol. In other countries, it is V.23 compatible and runs at 1200 bps.

2.6.4 MOSS Functions

As already mentioned, a MOSS provides communications controller management, control and diagnostic functions from its MOSS console. Some of the major functions it performs are:

1. It is helpful in configuring the controller initially. It is also used when a change in configuration is required later.
2. It is used to IPL the CCUs and the channel adapters (CAs), and IML the scanners.
3. MOSS can be used to perform a scheduled power on.
4. In an IBM 3745 Model 410, MOSS helps to fallback from a malfunctioning CCU to the second CCU.
5. It can be used to swap ports in an LSS, HSS and TRA.
6. MOSS helps to create and alter console passwords.
7. It can be used to perform wrap tests on HSS and LSS.
8. It is used to perform an automatic or manual NCP dump, CA dump, TIC dump, MOSS dump and selective scanner dump.
9. It provides utility programs to perform some essential functions like sending dumps to the host for printing, RSF for remote diagnostics, copying from a floppy diskette to the hard disk, microcode change management, display of dumps on the MOSS console and many more.
10. It performs logging of box event records (BERs) on the MOSS hard disk.
11. It generates alert messages for display at a host Netview console.

2.7 SUMMARY

The IBM 3745 communications controller plays a strategic role in an SNA network. In this chapter, we discussed the functions and the architecture of an IBM 3745 controller. We also discussed the three major architectural components — the central subsystem, the communications subsystem and the MOSS. The central subsystem consists of the central control unit (CCU), cache buffers, main storage, direct memory access (DMA), Input/Output control buses, channel adapters (CAs), and the two processor switches (TPSs). The high performance communications subsystem supports high-speed T1 lines while the transmission subsystem supports lines on a low-speed scanner (LSS). It also supports terminals, workstations and processors on a Token-Ring Network via the Token-Ring subsystem (TRSS). The maintenance and operator subsystem (MOSS) provides various control and maintenance functions through a local, alternate or remote console. Now that we know various architectural and functional aspects of a communications controller, we will learn about the different models of an IBM 3745 and their capabilities in the next chapter. Finally, we will see how to configure a controller for various line weights, line speeds, LICs and scanners.

Chapter

3

IBM 3745 Communications Controller - Types and Models

In the previous chapter, we learned about the functions and the architecture of an IBM 3745. We discussed the three subsystem components: Control, Communications and MOSS. This chapter will give detailed information about the various types and models of IBM 3745s. Also included is a discussion on the IBM expansion unit 3746 and its various models. It is important to note that the information in this chapter is time dependent. We have provided the most up-to-date specifications on the various models and their characteristics available when this book was written. As IBM comes up with new models and discontinues the existing ones, the authors will include that information in the next edition. However, there will always be a time gap, no matter how insignificant, between the two events.

3.1 TYPES AND MODELS

At the time this was written, the IBM 3745 was available in five different models — 130, 150, 170, 210 and 410. Each model is discussed giving the following characteristics:

46 Advanced SNA Networking

- Single or twin CCU capability
- Maximum and minimum memory supported
- Number of scanners and channel adapters
- External and integrated modem lines
- High speed lines
- Token-ring interfaces
- Expandability and upgradability

In *Introduction to SNA Networking*, we discussed other communications controllers like the IBM 3705, 3725 and 3720. Remember that the IBM 3720 and 3745 are the only state-of-the-art controllers at this time. Models 210 and 410 are the top of the line controllers in capabilities (and price of course!). Models 130, 150 and 170 provide capabilities which place them somewhere between a 3720 and 3745 Model 210.

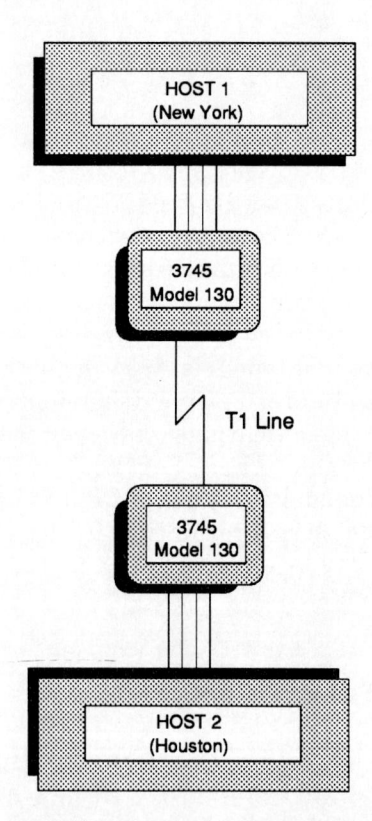

Figure 3.1 Use of 3745 Model 130 to connect two hosts, channel-to-channel, via a high-speed T1 line.

IBM 3745 Communications Controller -Types and Models   47

3.1.1 Model 130

Model 130 has a single CCU with 32K of CCU cache memory. Although Models 210 and 410 are top of the line models, their CCUs come with only 16K of cache memory. The amount of main memory supported in Model 130 is 4 megabytes.

Model 130 does not support low-speed lines. In other words, it does not have low-speed scanners. It supports a maximum of two high-speed T1 lines through its high-speed scanner. It can also support a maximum of four Token-Ring interface couplers (TICs) through its two Token-Ring adapters (TRAs). Recall from the previous chapter that each Token-Ring adapter supports two interfaces. This model can also have a maximum of four channel adapters (CAs).

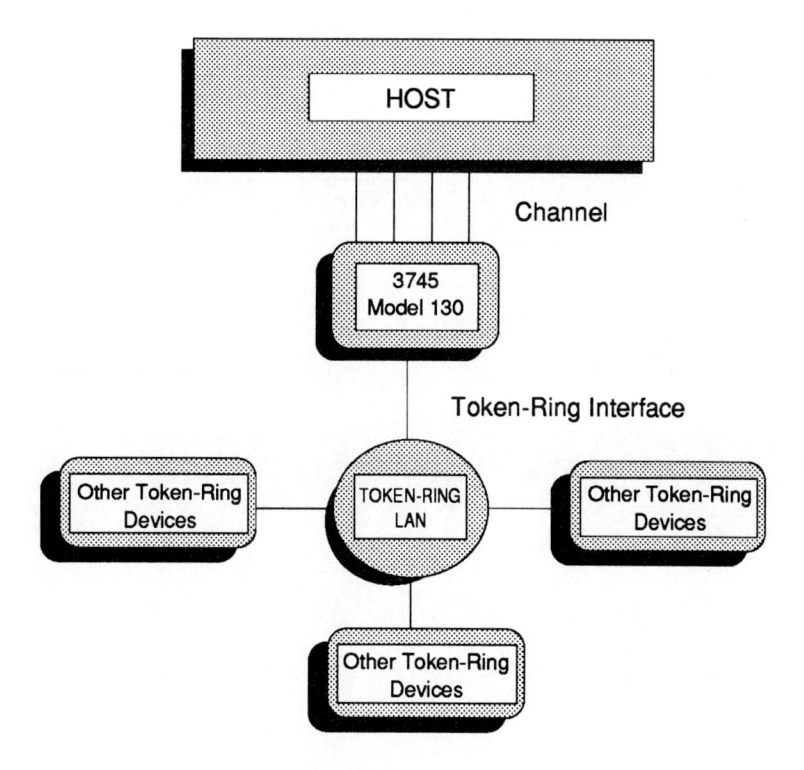

Note: "Other Token-Ring Devices" refers to any equipment that can be connected to a Token-Ring LAN and needs to communicate with other LAN devices and/or the host.

Figure 3.2 Use of 3745 Model 130 to locally connect a LAN to the host.

48 Advanced SNA Networking

Model 130 can be effectively used to connect hosts, channel-to-channel, through high-speed T1 lines (Figure 3.1). It may also be used to locally connect a local area network (LAN) to the host (Figure 3.2).

However, if the LANs are remote, they may be connected via T1 lines (Figure 3.3).

Model 130 can be upgraded in the field to a Model 170. Since Model 170 only supports one Token-Ring adapter (with two TICs), the second TRA from the 130 is removed during the upgrade. There is no expansion unit for a Model 130.

Model 130, with NCP 5.2.1 and VTAM 3.2, can support up to two NCPs on its hard disk. These two NCP load modules can be

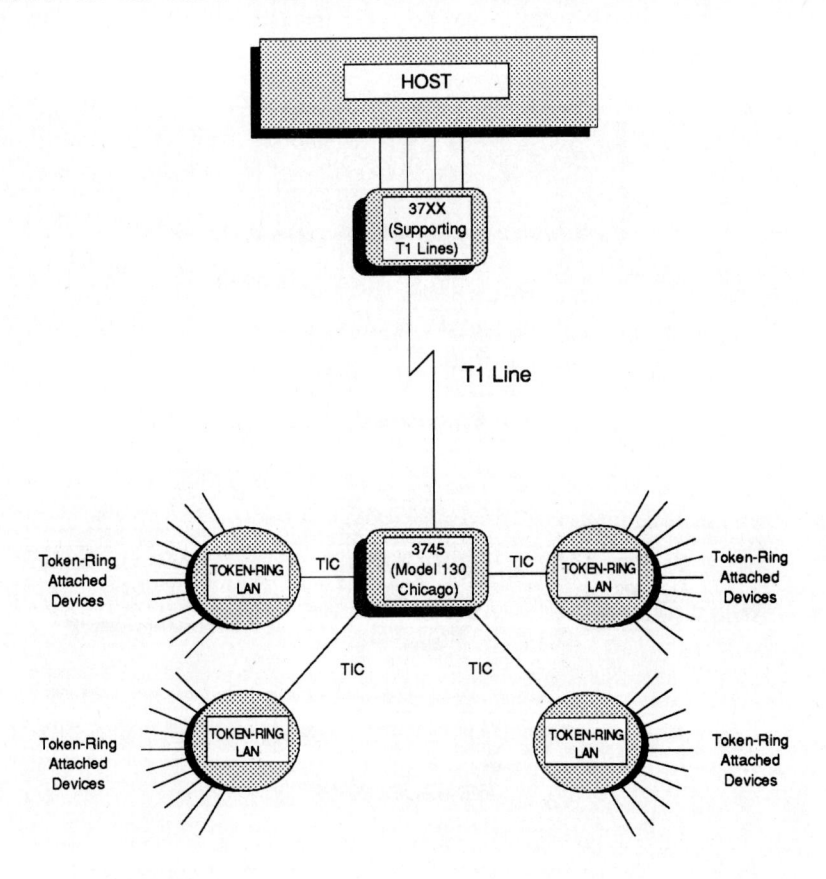

TIC = Token-Ring Interface Coupler

Figure 3.3 Use of 3745 Model 130 to remotely connect up to four Token-Ring LANs to a host via high-speed T1 lines.

IBM 3745 Communications Controller -Types and Models   49

downloaded from the host while the unit is up and running. Thus it is possible to IPL a Model 130 by loading the NCP from the hard disk rather than loading it through the telecommunications lines from the host. Obviously, loading an NCP from the hard disk is a much quicker process. You may also store an NCP dump on the hard disk and ship it to the host for printing later. Figure 3.4 summarizes the salient features of Model 130.

3.1.2 Model 150

Like Model 130, Model 150 also has a single CCU with 32K of cache. Four megabytes of main memory are supported.

Model 150 does not support channel adapters. Therefore, it may only be used as a remote communications controller. We can attach up to 16 external or integrated modem lines. In addition, it supports one T1 line on its high-speed scanner. It provides one Token-Ring adapter with two Token-Ring interface couplers for attachment to up to two Token-Ring LANs.

There is no expansion unit supported for Model 150. However, it can be upgraded in field to a Model 170. Notice that while Model 130 does not support low-speed scanners, Model 150 does not support channel adapters.

Model	130
Number of CCUs	1
Cache	32K
Low-Speed Scanners	None
High-Speed Scanners	2
Maximum Number of T1 Lines	2
Maximum Number of Token-Ring Adapters	2
Maximum Number of Token-Ring Interface Couplers	4
Maximum Number of Channel Adapters	4
Field Upgradability	Model 170

Figure 3.4 Salient features of the IBM 3745 Model 130.

50   Advanced SNA Networking

Model 150, with NCP 5.2.1 and VTAM 3.2, can support up to two NCP load modules on its hard disk. They can be downloaded to the hard disk while the controller is operational. It is possible to IPL the controller from one of the two NCPs residing on the hard disk. It is also possible to direct the NCP dump to the hard disk for subsequent shipment to the host for printing. Figure 3.5 summarizes the salient features of Model 150.

3.1.3 Model 170

Model 170 also has a single CCU with 32K of cache and 4 megabytes of main memory. Like Model 130, it supports a maximum of four channel adapters for local attachment to the host channels. It provides for a maximum of six low-speed scanners. LSSs may support a maximum of 96 external modem lines. With proper configuration, it can also have a maximum of 32 integrated modem lines. Mixing external modem and integrated modem attachments can support up to 112 lines.

You may also have up to two T1 lines supported by two high-speed scanners. One Token-Ring adapter, providing two Token-Ring interface couplers can provide connectivity to two Token-Ring LANs.

Model 170 *neither* supports any expansion units *nor* can it be field upgraded to the next higher controller like Model 210. This is

Model	150
Number of CCUs	1
Cache	32K
Low-Speed Scanners	1
Maximum Number of External or Integrated Modem Lines	16
High-Speed Scanners	1
Maximum Number of T1 Lines	1
Token-Ring Adapters	1
Maximum Number of Token-Ring Interface Couplers	2
Channel Adapters	None
Field Upgradability	Model 170

Figure 3.5 Salient features of the IBM 3745 Model 130.

IBM 3745 Communications Controller -Types and Models 51

primarily due to differences in the way Models 130/150/170 and 210 are physically packaged.

This model also supports the storage of up to two NCP load modules on its hard disk which may be used for faster IPL if need be. You may also direct the NCP dump to the hard disk for later shipment to the host for printing and analysis purposes. Figure 3.6 gives the salient features of Model 170.

3.1.4 Model 210 (base)

The Model 210 has a single CCU with 16K of cache and up to 8 megabytes of main storage. Notice that the low-end Models 130/150/170 come with 32K cache, while the high-end Model 210 supports only 16K cache.

It comes with a channel adapter board (CAB) that supports up to eight channel adapters. The base unit also has a line adapter board (LAB) which may be configured in two different ways - with or without the token-ring option. *If the token-ring option is chosen*, the LAB will support up to four Token-Ring adapters (TRAs) and up to four low-speed scanners (LSS) and high-speed scanners (HSS). The LSSs and HSSs may be mixed provided their total count does not exceed four. Also note that four TRAs will support 8 TICs, thus providing connectivity to up to 8 Token-Ring LANs.

Model	170
Number of CCUs	1
Cache	32K
Low Speed Scanners	6
Maximum Number of External Modem Lines	96
Maximum Number of Integrated Modem Lines	32
Maximum Number of External/Integrated Modem Lines	112
High Speed Scanners	2
Maximum Number of T1 Lines	2
Token-Ring Adapters	1
Maximum Number of Token-Ring Interface Couplers	2
Maximum Number of Channel Adapters	4
Field Upgradability	None

Figure 3.6 Salient features of the IBM 3745 Model 170.

If the token-ring option is not chosen, you may have a mixture of up to eight LSSs and HSSs in any combination you desire. If you choose eight HSSs only, they will support eight high-speed T1 lines. If you opted for eight LSSs, they may support up to 256 low-speed lines. The number of low-speed lines supported is a function of how you configure various line interface couplers (LICs). This will be discussed in the next chapter.

The Model 210 consists of a maximum of two line interface coupler units (LIUs). These two LIUs may be either a Unit Type 1 or a Unit Type 2. These types will be discussed in the next chapter. For now, suffice it to say that LIU Type 1 contains up to 16 LICs and requires an external DCE (modem or DSU/CSU). LIU Type 2 also contains a maximum of 16 LICs, but they have built in DCEs (modems or DSU/CSUs). LIU Type 2 eliminates the need for external modems. Thus you may connect a communication line directly into the LIC port of the controller.

Model 210 may be expanded using the expansion units discussed in the next section of this chapter. It is also field upgradable to a Model 410. Like other models, it provides for storage of the NCP load modules locally on its hard disk. Figure 3.7 gives the salient features of Model 210.

Model	210
Number of CCUs	1
Cache	16K
Maximum Main Storage	8 Mb
Maximum Low-Speed Scanners*	8
Maximum Low-Speed Lines	256
Maximum High-Speed Scanners*	8
Maximum T1 Lines (active)	8
Maximum Token-Ring Adapters*	4
Maximum Token-Ring LAN Support	8
Maximum Channel Adapters	8
Field Upgradability	Model 410

Note: This table gives the characteristics of a Model 210 base unit only and does not include expansion units.
* Maximum capacity refers to what each feature (LSS, HSS and TRA) is capable of attaining. In combination with other features, it will be a lower number, as explained in the text.

Figure 3.7 Salient features of the IBM 3745 Model 210 base unit.

3.1.5 Model 410

This model is similar to Model 210 except that it contains a second CCU. The purpose and use of the second CCU is to increase reliability and is discussed later in this chapter. The second CCU supports additional main storage of 8 megabytes, thus giving Model 410 a total of 16 megabytes of memory. The second CCU has its own 16K of cache buffer.

Like the Model 210, it can be configured with or without the token-ring support option. *If the token-ring option is chosen*, the base unit will support up to four Token-Ring adapters (TRAs) and a mixture of up to four LSSs and HSSs. Four Token-Ring adapters can provide connectivity to up to eight Token-Ring LANs.

If the token-ring option is not chosen, it is possible to have a combination of up to eight LSSs and HSSs in any ratio you wish. If you opt for eight LSSs, they may support up to 256 low-speed lines. On the other hand, HSSs (with no LSS) will support up to eight high-speed T1 lines.

Like the Model 210, the Model 410 supports LIU Type 1 as well as LIU Type 2. LIU Type 1 contains up to 16 LICs and requires external DCEs (modems or DSU/CSU). LIU Type 2 has built in DCEs and thus eliminates the need for external modems or DSU/CSUs.

Model 410 may be expanded using the expansion units discussed in the next section. Since Model 410 is the top-of-the-line model, it cannot be upgraded further. Like other models, it provides for the storage of NCP load modules on its hard disk. Figure 3.8 gives the salient features of Model 410.

3.2 EXPANSION UNITS

The IBM 3745 Models 130/150/170 come with features that may not be altered. Although Model 130 and 150 can be upgraded in the field to Model 170, none of the three models can be expanded by using an expansion unit. Expansion units have been used in the past to upgrade IBM's old 3705 and 3725 controllers. The only 3745 models that may be expanded are 210 and 410. There are five IBM 3746 expansion units to provide such enhancements. Remember that expansion units enhance the capabilities of Models 210 and 410 and do not provide any service as stand-alone equipment.

54 Advanced SNA Networking

Model	410
Number of CCUs	1
Cache per CCU	16K
Maximum Main Storage	16 Mb
Maximum Low-Speed Scanners*	8
Maximum Low-Speed Lines	256
Maximum High-Speed Scanners*	8
Maximum T1 Lines (active)	8
Maximum Token-Ring Adapters*	4
Maximum Token-Ring LAN Support	8
Maximum Channel Adapters	8
Field Upgradability	None. This is the top-of-the-line model.

Note: This table gives the characteristics of a Model 410 base unit only and does not include expansion units.
* Maximum capacity refers to what each feature (LSS, HSS and TRA) is capable of attaining. In combination with other features, it will be a lower number, as explained in the text.

Figure 3.8 Salient features of the IBM 3745 Model 410 base unit.

Notice that expansion unit models have a prefix of A or L. "A" denotes that the expansion unit will provide additional adapters (channel or line), while "L" indicates additional LIC units of Types 1 and 2.

3.2.1 3746 Model A11

This model requires that base units for the 210 and 410 be installed first. This expansion unit provides for additional channel adapters and LABs.

The second channel adapter board (CAB) provides eight additional channel adapters. Since the 210 and 410 base units already have eight CAs, this gives a total of 16 CAs for the controller.

Recall that the base unit comes with a single LAB with up to eight LSSs and HSSs in any combination (without token-ring support). This expansion unit provides a second and third LAB with up to eight LSSs each. Since this expansion unit does not support HSSs, you have to provide that capability on the base unit LAB (first LAB) if needed. Figure 3.9 gives the salient features of a Model A11.

IBM 3745 Communications Controller -Types and Models   55

3.2.2 3746 Model A12

This expansion can be installed only if a Model A11 expansion unit has already been installed on the base unit. It provides an additional LAB with up to eight LSSs. There are no provisions for HSSs, TRAs or CAs in this unit. Figure 3.9 lists the expansion features for an A12.

3.2.3 3746 Model L13

This model requires that the 210 and 410 base units be installed first. It provides up to four LIC Units Type 1 or up to four LIC Units Type 2 or any combination of four LIC Units Type 1 and Type 2. Recall that LIU Type 1 supports up to 16 LICs with *external* modems or DSU/CSUs and LIU Type 2 supports up to 16 LICs with *built-in* modems or DSU/CSUs. Figure 3.9 identifies these features.

Expansion Unit Model	Prerequisite	Additional Channel Adapters	Additional Token-Ring Adapters	Additional High-Speed Scanners	Additional Low-Speed Scanners	Additional LIC Units Types 1 & 2
A11	Base Unit 210 or 410	8	None	None	16	None
A12	Expansion Unit A11	None	None	None	8	None
L13	Base Unit 210 or 410	None	None	None	None	4
L14	Expansion Unit L13	None	None	None	None	4
L15	Expansion Unit L14	None	None	None	None	4

Figure 3.9 Salient features of the IBM 3746 Expansion Units A11, A12, L13, L14 and L15.

3.2.4 3746 Model L14

Installation of the L13 expansion unit is a prerequisite for L14. It provides four additional LIC units in any combination of LIC Units Type 1 or Type 2 depending upon whether you intend to use external modems (or DSU/CSU for digital transmission) or built-in internal modems. Figure 3.9 enumerates the features of a Model L14.

3.2.5 Model L15

Installation of Model L14 expansion unit is a prerequisite for Model L15. Since the Model L13 is a prerequisite for the L14, Models L13 and L14 must be installed before L15. This model provides four additional LIC Units. Such LIC units may be in any combination of LIC Units Type 1 or Type 2.

3.3 3745 MODEL 410 MODES OF OPERATION

All of the IBM communications controllers of the past have used a single processor (called CCU). The failure of a single component of the controller could break the communications link to the host or to other controllers. Such failing components could include the processor, its associated main memory, the software or some other essential element.

IBM introduced Model 410, available since September 1988, which has two CCUs capable of running separate NCPs. Both CCUs operate and run in the same box. Depending upon the user requirements, a Model 410 can be configured in three different ways. Various techniques provide different modes of operation which can increase the reliability of the controller.

3.3.1 Twin-Dual Mode

In this mode, each CCU acts as a separate communications controller. Therefore, you can run two independent NCPs with two different subareas. It's just like having two separate Model 210 controllers standing side by side. Each CCU has its own main memory and each NCP interacts with its own communication ports. It is important to know that the two NCPs in a Model 410 have no

IBM 3745 Communications Controller -Types and Models 57

internal link. For them to communicate with each other requires an *external* connectivity aid such as a channel adapter or a communication link.

Remember that this configuration has no provision for backup. There is no switching in case of failure. Under normal circumstances, each CCU runs a separate NCP. In case of failure, one NCP is inoperative while the other one is still operational, as diagrammed in Figure 3.10.

3.3.2 Twin-Standby Mode

In this case, there is one active NCP while the second one is in standby mode. The second NCP takes over only if the first NCP has problems. This allows quick recovery from storage-related failures and from a CCU's hardware check. Note that the idle CCU is totally inactive unless a failure is detected. This mode is not

A) Both CCUs are operational.

3745 Model 410

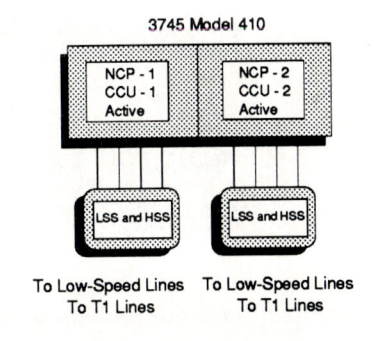

NCP - 1	NCP - 2
CCU - 1	CCU - 2
Active	Active

LSS and HSS   LSS and HSS

To Low-Speed Lines   To Low-Speed Lines
To T1 Lines   To T1 Lines

B) CCU - 2 has problems; CCU - 1 is still active.

3745 Model 410

NCP - 1	CCU - 2
CCU - 1	Failure
Active	

Inoperative

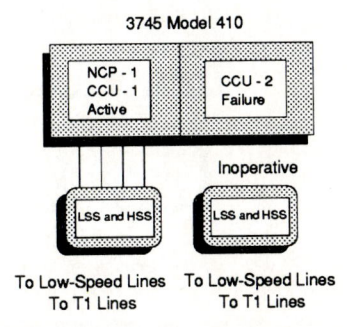

LSS and HSS   LSS and HSS

To Low-Speed Lines   To Low-Speed Lines
To T1 Lines   To T1 Lines

Figure 3.10 3745 Model 410 operating in twin-dual mode. A) Both CCUs are operational. B) One CCU has problems.

58 Advanced SNA Networking

very cost effective because you are paying for the second CCU and its associated paraphernalia while not using it all the time. However, for networks requiring high availability, this mode is the recommended one. Figure 3.11 shows twin-standby mode under normal circumstances and when failure is detected. The fallback procedure is executed as follows:

1. MOSS detects failure of an active CCU.
2. Adapters from the failing CCU are disconnected and are connected to the standby CCU.
3. An automatic IPL is executed on the standby CCU.
4. User activates the switched network resources.

A) CCU - 1 is active; CCU - 2 is in Standby Mode.

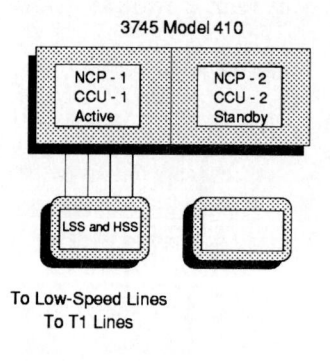

3745 Model 410

```
NCP - 1      NCP - 2
CCU - 1      CCU - 2
Active       Standby
```

LSS and HSS

To Low-Speed Lines
To T1 Lines

B) CCU - 1 has a failure; CCU - 2 takes over.

3745 Model 410

```
CCU - 1      NCP - 2
Failure      CCU - 2
             Active
```

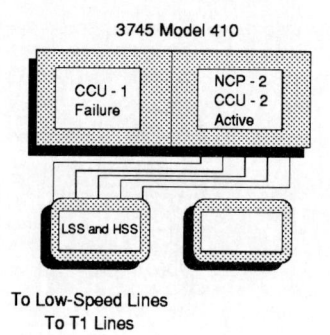

LSS and HSS

To Low-Speed Lines
To T1 Lines

Figure 3.11 3745 Model 410 operating in twin-standby mode. A) CCU-1 is operational while CCU-2 is in a standby mode. B) CCU-1 has had a failure and CCU-2 has taken control of its network.

IBM 3745 Communications Controller - Types and Models

Notice that the IPL component is a time consuming procedure. If you have NCP 5.2.1 or a later release, you can set up for the *fast fallback* capability. In this expedited procedure, the standby CCU is already loaded with a copy of the NCP. Thus the switch over takes less time than what was described in a *regular fallback* situation. To qualify for a fast fallback, you must also ensure that there is an active NCP load module on the hard disk and that there is no NCP dump on that disk.

3.3.3 Twin-Backup Mode

In this mode, each CCU controls approximately half of the network. It is like having two IBM 3745 Model 210s running one-half of the network load. If one CCU fails, the other CCU can assume

A) CCU-1 and CCU-2 are both active; Each one controls one-half of the network.

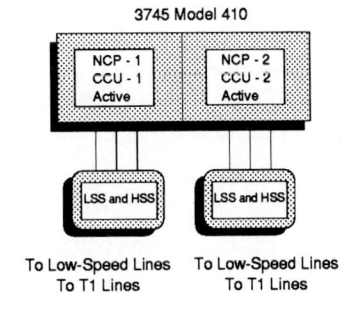

3745 Model 410

NCP-1 / CCU-1 / Active   NCP-2 / CCU-2 / Active

LSS and HSS   LSS and HSS

To Low-Speed Lines   To Low-Speed Lines
To T1 Lines   To T1 Lines

B) CCU-1 has a failure; CCU-2 takes over CCU 1's network.

3745 Model 410

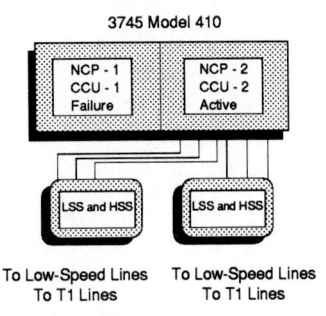

NCP-1 / CCU-1 / Failure   NCP-2 / CCU-2 / Active

LSS and HSS   LSS and HSS

To Low-Speed Lines   To Low-Speed Lines
To T1 Lines   To T1 Lines

Figure 3.12 IBM 3745 Model 410 operating in twin-backup mode. A) CCU-1 and CCU-2 are both active, controlling approximately one-half of the network each. B) CCU-1 has had a failure and CCU-2 has taken control of CCU-1's network while also taking care of its own network.

the load of the failed CCU. Since that CCU has an increased network load, operations will obviously be degraded. This mode provides for easy recovery from storage-related failures and a CCU's hardware check. The switching operation is done by MOSS as explained in the previous subsection. However, the reactivation of the switched-over resources is done by the user. Figure 3.12 shows a switch-over from a failing CCU in twin-backup mode.

3.4 SUMMARY

In this chapter, we learned about the different models of an IBM 3745. Five different models, named 130, 150, 170, 210 and 410, provide different features and capabilities regarding the number of CCUs, main memory, channel adapters, LSSs, HSSs, TRAs, and modes of operation. Models 210 and 410 can also be enhanced with the help of expansion units. Models A11 and A12 provide expansions for the channel and line adapters. Models L13, L14 and L15 provide expansions for LIC Units Type 1 and 2. IBM 3745 Model 410 can operate in three different models — Twin-Dual Mode, Twin-Standby Mode and Twin-Backup Mode. The latter two modes enhance availability of the network in case of malfunctions and failures.

Chapter

4

IBM 3745 Communications Controller - Configuration

In the previous two chapters, we learned about IBM 3745 functions, architecture, various models, expansion units and modes of operation. In this chapter, you will learn how to configure a 3745 for various line speeds, communications ports, line weight considerations and communications protocols. We will see that the port configurations of a 3745 are determined by a set of simple but mandatory rules. In Chapter 2 you were introduced to a lot of acronyms like LICs, LABs, LIUs and many more. But once you finish reading this chapter, you will feel quite comfortable with the nomenclature as well as its use.

4.1 COMMUNICATIONS COMPONENTS

A myriad of communications components, called by similar sounding acronyms, comprise the transmission subsystem (TSS) of an IBM 3745. These components, such as scanners, LABs, LIBs, LICs and LIUs are interconnected in a not too easy to understand fashion. Some of these names, such as LIBs and LIUs, did not exist before the IBM 3745 was introduced. We will try to demystify their purpose and use and their interdependency on other related components.

4.1.1 Scanners

As the name suggests, a scanner scans the incoming and outgoing bits of data. There are usually many scanners in a communications controller. A scanner contains a microprocessor called a Communications Scanner Processor (CSP). The speed of the CSP determines how much of a load of input/output communication lines can be placed on various components attached to the scanner. A scanner interfaces with the controller's main processor via a Line Attachment Base (LAB). Usually, a LAB interacts with one or two scanners, a factor which determines the LAB type.

A scanner interfaces with the physical communication lines via Line Interface Coupler (LIC) panels. LIC panels have ports which connect to DCEs (modems or DSU/CSU) or the physical lines directly. A CSP also provides an integrated clock controller (ICC) for a LAB. An ICC is required for direct attachment to non-clocking modems, (e.g., asynchronous modems). An ICC, when used with a special cable, acts as a modem eliminator.

A low-speed scanner (LSS) has an aggregate scanning capability of up to 307,200 bits of data per second. A high-speed scanner (HSS), which usually interfaces with up to one active T1 line, can handle much faster data traffic. In the U.S.A, Canada and Japan, a T1 line delivers a digital data rate of 1.544 megabits/second, while in Europe such lines (called CEPT) can communicate at up to 2.048 megabits/second.

A fully configured IBM 3745 can support a maximum of up to 32 low-speed scanners or up to 8 high-speed scanners. The maximum allowable number will be less when you mix and match low and high-speed scanners in the same box. In addition, a 3745 also supports up to four token-ring adapters.

Scanners of older models of communications controllers like the IBM 3725 used to scan active as well as inactive LICs. However, an IBM 3745's scanners only scan the active LICs. In other words, if a line has been varied inactive, a scanner will not waste its machine cycles to scan that line. This creates a responsibility for the operator to see that the total line weight of all the active lines does not exceed 100. More on this later.

4.1.2 Line Attachment Base (LAB) / Double Multiplexers (DMUX)

A LAB provides an interface between the controller's processor and the scanners. Depending upon its type, a LAB can interface with one or two scanners. A LAB also supports multiple LICs. In the next section, we will learn that LIC ports are the ones which have a direct physical interface with the communication lines. Basically, you are aware of LABs and LICs while scanners are invisible entities.

Although many communications systems programmers still use the terminology of LAB, the correct name for it in an IBM 3745 is Double Multiplexer (DMUX). While it was called a LAB in the IBM 3725, it is called a DMUX in a 3745. Like a 3725 LAB, a DMUX can connect to one or two scanners.

If a DMUX goes to two scanners, the first scanner scans LICs 1 to 4 and the second scanner scans LICs 5 to 8. For the same line speed, the line weight of single scanner DMUX is more than the line weight of two scanner DMUX.

4.1.3 Hierarchy of Components

In a 3745, LICs are packaged in LIC units. Further more, each LIC unit consists of four LIC areas. A LIC area, depending upon LIC type, can have a maximum of up to four LICs. A LIC may attach a maximum of four lines. Thus, a LIC unit can have a maximum of 64 lines. Since a base unit of an IBM 3745 can have up to eight LIC units, they may provide connectivity to 512 lines. Figure 4.1 shows the relationship between a DMUX, a LIC unit, a LIC area and LICs.

To understand this concept in a different manner, review the following:

- A base 3745 provides for up to 32 LSSs.
- A base 3745 also provides for up to 8 LIC units.
- Thus, each LIC unit has four LSSs assigned to it.
- Each set of two LSSs controls a DMUX, thus, there are 2 DMUXs in a LIC unit.
- Each LIC unit has four LIC areas.
- Each LIC area may have up to four LICs.
- Each LIC unit provides connectivity for up to 64 lines and a base 3745 provides for up to 512 lines.

64 Advanced SNA Networking

4.1.4 Line Interface Coupler (LIC)

While a single DMUX supports multiple LICs, a single LIC may support one or more communication lines. Based on the position of the LIC unit, each port has a fixed address. An LSS can connect to one LIC area or a LIC area pair (Figure 4.1). If it is attached to a pair, it must be an odd/even pair. LICs in an IBM 3745 have an internal clock function. An internal clock supports 110 bits/second to up to T1 line speeds. A MOSS console may be used, on a port by port basis, to set the speed for each port. In addition to supporting traditional LIC types, the IBM 3745 has introduced two new types called LIC Type 5 and LIC Type 6.

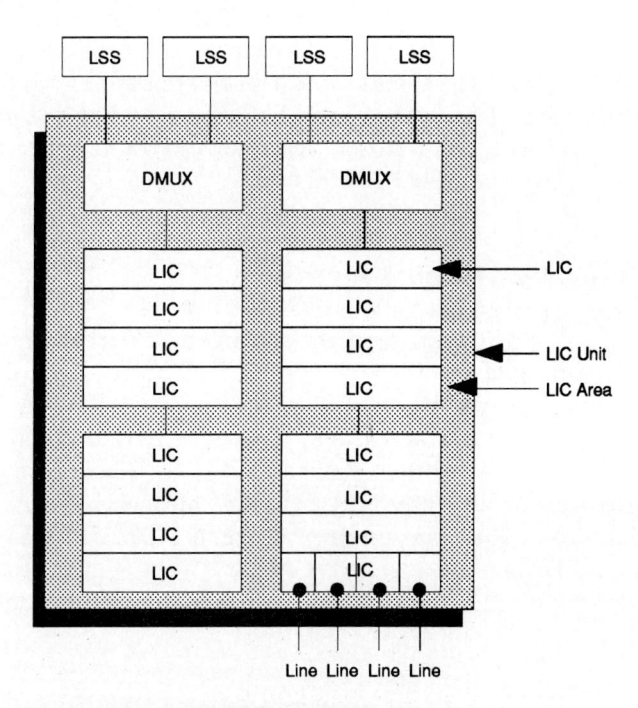

- Each DMUX has two Low-Speed Scanners (LSSs)
- Each DMUX controls two LIC areas
- Each LIC area has a maximum of four LICs
- Each LIC may have up to four lines
- Whole configuration is a LIC unit with four LIC areas, up to 16 LICs and up to 64 lines

Figure 4.1 Relationships between LSS, DMUX, LIC unit, LIC areas, LICs and lines.

IBM 3745 Communications Controller - Configuration

The capabilities and features of various LIC types are described as follows:

LIC Type 1: This LIC type supports a maximum line speed of 19.2 Kbps. The line level protocols can be asynchronous, SDLC or BSC. The interfaces may be EIA 232D or CCITT V.24. For autocall support their interfaces can be EIA RS-366 or CCITT V.25. In addition, it supports X.20 bis or X.21 bis. In case these interfaces read like Greek to you, please refer to Chapter 3 of *Introduction to SNA Networking* where these terminologies were introduced. A DMUX can support up to eight LICs of this type. Figure 4.2 tabulates these features for easy reference.

LIC TYPE	PHYSICAL INTERFACE	MAXIMUM LINE SPEED (KBPS)	NUMBER OF PORTS	PROTOCOL
LIC 1	RS232 / V.24 RS366/V.25 X.21 BIS Direct	19.2 19.2	4	SDLC BSC ASYNC
LIC 2	Wideband for 8801, 8803 or 8751 Service	64 (BSC) 230.4 (SDLC)	1	SDLC BSC
LIC 3	V.35 Direct	256 240	1	SDLC BSC
LIC 4A	X.21 Direct	9.6 9.6	4	SDLC
LIC 4B	X.21 Direct	64 56	1	SDLC
LIC 5	Nonswitched 4-wire telephone line	14.4	2	SDLC BSC
LIC 6	Digital Data Service (DDS)	9.6 56	1	SDLC BSC

Figure 4.2 Characteristics of various types of LICs for IBM 3745.

LIC Type 2: LIC Type 2 is available in the IBM 3745 via Request for Price Quotation (RPQ) only.

LIC Type 3: A LIC may support only one port for LIC Type 3. While supporting a physical interface of V.35, it can support line speeds from 56 kbps to 256 Kbps.

LIC Type 4A: This LIC type is not available in the U.S.A. due to a lack of support for X.21. It can support a line speed of up to 9.6 Kbps and is an equivalent of a LIC Type 1 in some respects.

LIC Type 4B: Again, this LIC is not available in the U.S.A. due to a lack of support for X.21.

LIC Type 5: This LIC combines the functions of a modem and a LIC. In other words, you do not need an external modem with this LIC type. It can attach directly to a telephone line. Up to two telephone lines, with a maximum speed of up to 14.4 Kbps each, are supported. The line has to be a nonswitched (leased) 4-wire telephone line. It supports point-to-point as well as multi-point modes.

LIC Type 6: While LIC Type 5 supports analog (voice) lines, LIC Type 6 supports digital transmission lines. The equivalent of a built in modem in this LIC type is called DSU/CSU. Therefore, it can attach directly to a digital transmission line. In the U.S.A. and Canada, a Digital Data Service (DDS) network provides the digital service. It supports point-to-point as well as multi-point mode.

4.1.5 LIC Unit (LIU)

Please refer back to Figure 4.1. A LIC unit consists of four LIC areas with each LIC area supporting up to four LICs. Each LIC can support up to four lines. Thus, a LIC Unit can support up to a maximum of 64 communication lines.

On the other hand, a LIC unit has two DMUXs (called LABs in pre-IBM 3745 hardware) with each DMUX controlled by up to two low-speed scanners (LSSs).

An IBM 3745 has a maximum of up to 8 LIC units. With each LIC unit supporting a maximum of up to 64 lines, an IBM 3745 can support up to 512 communications links in all.

4.1.6 Line Interface Base (LIB)

We already know that up to four LICs are housed in a LIC area and up to two LIC areas are controlled by a DMUX (Figure 4.1). These two LIC areas put together are called a LIC Base or a LIB. There are three types of LIBs as follows:

LIB Type 1: This LIB supports only LIC1, LIC2, and LIC3. Recall that these LIC types need an external modem (or DSU/CSU for digital lines). Thus LIB Type 1 is not meant for LIC5 and LIC6 which have built-in modems and DSU/CSUs support. This LIB supports a maximum of up to 32 communication lines.

LIB Type 2: LIB Type 2 supports LIC Type 5 and LIC Type 6 only. Since LIC Type 5 has built-in modem support and LIC Type 6 has built in DSU/CSU support, they do not need external DCE equipment. It supports a maximum of 16 external modem lines.

LIB Type 3: This LIB is only for an IBM 3745 Model 150. It is one-half of a LIB Type 1. Therefore, instead of supporting up to 32 external modem lines, it only supports up to 16. The LIC types can be 1, 3, or 4.

4.2 LINE WEIGHT CONSIDERATIONS

IBM 3725s and 3705s were configured using LIC weight considerations. If you are still using this hardware, refer to Chapter 2 of *Introduction to SNA Networking*. While configuring an IBM 3725/3705, we took the maximum LIC weight value from each LIC and added them up for a specific LAB. We made sure that the total weight does not exceed 100 for a single scanner LAB and 200 for a dual scanner LAB. Configuration rules have changed for IBM 3745s and 3720s. Before we get into the rules, let's understand an important concept called Selective Scanning.

4.2.1 Selective Scanning

In an IBM 3705 and an IBM 3725, all the LICs with installed ports were scanned. Thus, those LICs whose ports were not active (though installed) contributed to the load on the scanner. Installations whose daytime and nighttime line activity was different (e.g., interactive traffic versus bulk data transfer) had to live with under-utilized scanner capacity when lines were not active. This has changed in the IBM 3745/3720s. Only those LICs that have activated lines are scanned. This has been made possible by a fundamental change in the scanning design.

4.2.2 Maximum Line Configurations

Figure 4.3 gives line weights based upon line speed, link-level protocols, and scanner considerations. While configuring an IBM 3745, line weights are considered to have a cumulative effect.

PROTOCOL	LINE SPEED (BPS)	LINE WEIGHT
SDLC (FDX)	256000**	100
	64000**	25
	57000**	22.3
	19200**	7.5
	19200	10 / 12.5*
	14400	7.5 / 9.4*
	9600	5 / 6.2*
	4800	2.5 / 3.1*
SDLC (HDX) and BSC EBCDIC	256000**	60
	64000**	15
	57000**	13.5
	19200**	4.5
	19200	5.6 / 6.2*
	14400	4.2 / 4.7*
	9600	2.8 / 3.1*
	4800	1.4 / 1.6*
	2400	0.7 / 0.8*

HDX = Half Duplex
FDX = Full Duplex
* Lower Line Weights are for Double Scanner LIBs and the Higher Line Weights are for Single Scanner LIBs.
** One Port LICs.

Figure 4.3 Table showing relationships between line weight, line speed and link-level protocols used for an IBM 3745. This table is also applicable to an IBM 3720.

IBM 3745 Communications Controller - Configuration   69

Thus, you would add up the line weights for each active port on a LIC and add up the cumulative line weights of each LIC within a LIB. Notice that the line weights have two values in certain columns of Figure 4.3. The lower figures are for a double scanner LIB (e.g., Type 1 and 2). The higher figures are for a single scanner LIB (e.g., Type 3).

Example 1: Figure 4.4 shows a LIB with eight LICs. LIC1 has 4 ports, each having an SDLC/FDX line at 9.6 Kbps. Thus each port has a line weight of 5 with a cumulative line weight of 20 for LIC number 1.

LIC2 has two ports, each having a BSC/HDX at 19.2 Kbps. Each port has a line weight of 5.6 with a cumulative LIC weight of 11.2 for LIC number 2.

LIC3 has three lines of SDLC/FDX at 19.2 Kbps with individual line weights of 10 each and a cumulative line weight of 30. Similarly, LIC4 and LIC5 have cumulative line weights of 10 and 13.5 respectively. Our total line weight for the entire LIB is 84.7. Notice that we have used only five LICs out of a maximum of eight. In examples 2 and 3 we will explain the possibilities of using LIC Type 6 and find out how it may cause problems for us. Keep in

| Port | Double Scanner DMUX ||||||||
	LIC 1	LIC 2	LIC 3	LIC 4	LIC 5	LIC 6	LIC 7	LIC 8
1	5	5.6	10	2.5	13.5			
2	5	5.6	10	2.5				
3	5		10	2.5				
4	5			2.5				
Total	20	11.2	30	10	13.5			

Grand Total: 20 + 11.2 + 30 + 10 + 13.5 = 84.7

Specifications:
LIC 1 - SDLC/Full Duplex at 9.6 Kbps, LIC Weight 5
LIC 2 - BSC/Half Duplex at 19.2 Kbps, LIC Weight 5.6
LIC 3 - SDLC/Full Duplex at 19.2 Kbps, LIC Weight 10
LIC 4 - SDLC/Full Duplex at 4.8 Kbps, LIC Weight 2.5
LIC 5 - SDLC/Half Duplex at 56 Kbps, LIC Weight 13.5

Figure 4.4 An example of determining the line weight for a LIB in an IBM 3745.

mind that we took the lower line weights from the table in Figure 4.3 because LIB Type 1 is a double scanner LIB.

4.3 CONFIGURATION RULES

The line weight consideration rules are summed up as follows:

Rule 1: The total line weight of the active lines on a scanner cannot exceed 100. Since the line speed of an IBM 3745 can be changed from a MOSS console, you could inadvertently exceed the line weight limit. Be extra careful.

Rule 2: The maximum line speed for a particular port must meet the following criterion:

$$MLS = \frac{307200}{NAL * NAP}$$

where:

MLS = Maximum line speed

NAL = Total number of active LICs

NAP = Number of ports on that LIC

The constant value of 307,200 is the maximum scanner speed (307.2 Kbps).

Now let's apply rules #1 and #2 to our configuration in Example 1. Since the total line weight on the LIB is 84.7 (Figure 4.4), it satisfies rule #1.

Rule #2 is a little more complicated to understand. Suppose we have activated all 14 lines on the LIB under consideration. Notice that the value of NAL will be five because there are a total of five active LICs. The total number of ports on LIC1 is four. Let's substitute these values in the above formula:

$$MLS = \frac{307200}{5 * 4} = 15,360$$

Note that the installed line speed of 9600 bps is less than the calculated maximum line speed of 15,360. Hence, the conditions of rule #2 are satisfied.

Similarly, if you calculate the value of MLS by substituting the values of NAL and NAP in the formula for the other four LICs, you will see that we are well within the limits of safety.

4.4 OVERLOADING SCANNERS

We will consider two examples to determine the effect of some minor changes to our LIC line configurations.

Example 2: Let's see if we can alter the line configuration for LIC5 by changing its line speed from 56 Kbps to 64 Kbps. The line weight for LIC5 will increase from 13.5 to 15. Thus, the total line weight for the entire LIB will increase by a value of 1.5. In other words, the total line weight will be 86.2 instead of 84.7. It's still lower than 100, so it does not violate the conditions in Rule #1. Now let's apply the values in the formula in rule #2.

$$MLS = \frac{307200}{5 * 1} = 61,450$$

We can see that the scanner cannot support a line speed of more than 61,450 bps on LIC5 ports. Since 64000 bps is more than this value, we can not support this line speed. Notice that you may not have more than four active LICs to support a 64 Kbps line speed.

Example 3: In this example we have a requirement to put a 2400 bps BSC/HDX line on the same LIB. Let's say that we decide to put it on LIC6, which is an unused LIC. From Figure 4.3 we determine that such a line will increase the line weight by 0.7. Therefore, the total line weight for the entire LIB will be 84.7 + 0.7 or 85.4. Since this is less than 100, it satisfies the requirements of Rule #1 mentioned in the previous section. However, calculating the value of MLS tells us that we are not within the limits for LIC3 and LIC5 as per the rule. This is due to the fact that the value of NAL has increased from 5 to 6, which reduces the value of MLS as calculated in the formula. One solution would be to ensure that we don't activate more than 5 LICs at a time. However, another alternative solution would be to move the new line to one of the free ports on LIC2, thus satisfying the requirements imposed by both rules.

4.5 SUMMARY

In this chapter we learned how to configure a 3745 communications controller. Configuring a 3745/3720 is different from configuring a 3705/3725. While a 3705/3725 takes into account LIC weight limitations, a 3745/3720 requires line weight considerations. We learned how to apply two rules to determine the validity of a configuration. Line weight considerations for active lines impose considerable responsibility on the operator. Activating more lines than a scanner can handle will violate the provisions of Rule #1 and/or Rule #2 and will create problems.

Now that we have learned about the IBM 3174 and the IBM 3745 in detail, we are ready to move on to the VTAM and NCP definition for multi-domain and SNI networks.

Part 2

Beyond Single Domain

Chapter

5

Multi-Domain VTAM Definitions

For many computer installations, the need for several host computers is necessary due to the large number of end users and/or the applications that execute on the computer to meet the company's data processing objectives. VTAM must be present in each host for end-users to communicate with the applications, and for the applications to communicate with the end-users.

Each VTAM has defined network addressable units (NAUs). These resources make up VTAM's domain. A domain can be defined as the resources that are under the control of the SSCP within that VTAM host. All the PUs, LUs, link stations, and applications that can be activated or inactivated by VTAM are in VTAM's domain. In a multiple domain network, two or more VTAM domains may communicate with each other by using the Multi-System Networking Facility (MSNF) of VTAM.

In Figure 5.1 we see an example of a multi-domain network. HOST01 has a channel-attached front-end processor labeled FEP11. HOST02 also has a channel-attached front-end processor labeled FEP21. Each front-end processor has two links that connect to the other FEP. Both FEP11 and FEP21 have a link to FEP12, which is a remote IBM 37X5 communications controller. The domain for HOST01 consists of FEP11 and the remote clusters defined in the NCP residing in FEP11. The domain for HOST02 consists of

76 Advanced SNA Networking

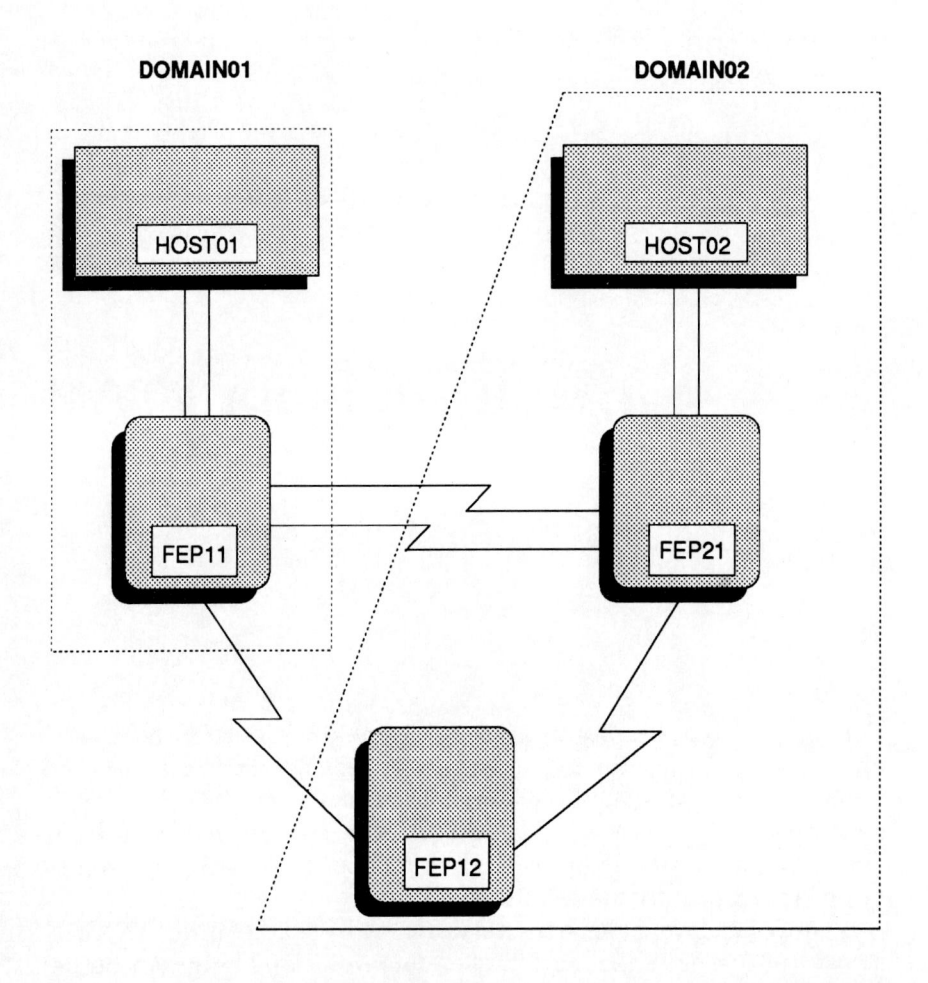

DOMAIN01   **DOMAIN02**

Figure 5.1 CDRM naming assignments.

FEP21 and the remote clusters defined in the NCP that reside in the FEP, along with FEP12 and its associated remote clusters. In order for the domains to communicate, we must establish cross-domain communication. Cross-domain communication is managed by the Cross-Domain Resource Manager (CDRM). The CDRM is responsible for establishing cross-domain sessions and resource requests for LUs to or from an external domain. These external domain resources are called Cross-Domain Resources (CDRSC). The CDRSCs may be explicitly or dynamically defined to the presiding CDRM. By explicitly defining the CDRSC, you must know the owning CDRM for the resource. In large multi-domain networks, this proves to be a substantial project in itself. But, by using dynamic definitions and the use of an Adjacent SSCP (ADJSSCP) table, the task of CDRM ownership is diminished significantly.

The question of ownership and backup of VTAM is addressed by the PCCU macro that resides in the NCP. The operands of the macro allow you to pre-define which VTAM has ownership of the NCP and which VTAM can act as a backup in case the owning VTAM fails.

Finally, for this cross-domain communication to work, we need to define the routes of communication between the domains by coding new PATH statements in both VTAMs and all the NCPs.

5.1 CROSS-DOMAIN RESOURCE MANAGER (CDRM)

The CDRM is a function of the system services control point (SSCP) of VTAM and manages cross-domain sessions. The CDRM is defined in a VTAM major node. There must be a CDRM defined for each domain that will have sessions with this domain. In our example, DOMAIN01 must have a CDRM defined for DOMAIN02 and likewise, DOMAIN02 must have a CDRM defined for DOMAIN01. Each domain must also have its own CDRM defined. Therefore, in DOMAIN01, a CDRM definition statement is needed for HOST01's VTAM as well as HOST02's VTAM. The same is needed for DOMAIN02. The CDRM definitions may be defined in separate major nodes for greater control or they can be defined in the same major node.

5.1.1 VBUILD Statement for CDRM

In our previous book, *Introduction to SNA Networking*, we discussed the use of major and minor nodes in VTAM and how they can affect your ability to reconfigure the network. Although it may be easier to define all of the CDRMs under one CDRM major node, it does not facilitate effective cross-domain management. In your career, you will find many instances where you will have to inactivate the CDRM major node to correct a network problem for one CDRM minor node. By having a CDRM major node for each CDRM minor node, inappropriate inactivation of CDRMs that are trouble

```
DOMAIN01:
    MAJOR NODE:      HOST01
                     HOST01      VBUILD      TYPE=CDRM
DOMAIN02:
    MAJOR NODE:      HOST02
                     HOST02      VBUILD      TYPE=CDRM
```

Figure 5.2 CDRM Major Node statements for DOMAIN01 and DOMAIN02.

free can be avoided. Therefore, we will code two major nodes for each of the domains in our example.

Since we are defining two major nodes for each domain involved in our cross-domain example, two VBUILD statements are needed. They are shown in Figure 5.2, one statement for each major node. You will see that the full definitions of one domain can also be used on the external domains VTAMLST. This simplifies the coding involved for large multi-domain networks because the major nodes need no modifications between domains.

5.1.2 CDRM Definition Statement

The cross-domain manager is defined to VTAM by using the CDRM definition statement. The format of this statement is found in Figure 5.3.

The name assigned to the CDRM being defined is determined by the value coded for the cdrmname operand. The name follows the standard naming rules for VTAM resources. Be careful not to use the name you assigned to the major node for this CDRM. This will

```
cdrmname         CDRM     [CDRDYN=YES|NO]
                          [,CDRSC=OPT|REQ]
                          [,ELEMENT=n|1]
                          [,ISTATUS=ACTIVE|INACTIVE]
                          [,RECOVERY=YES|NO]
                          [,SPAN=(NCCF or NETVIEW spanname)
                          [,SUBAREA=n]
                          [,VPACING=n|0|63]
```

Figure 5.3 CDRM definition statement format.

Multi-Domain Network Definitions for VTAM

```
DOMAIN01:
  MAJOR NODE:    HOST01
  MINOR NODE:    HOST01    VBUILD    TYPE=CDRM
                 VTAM01    CDRM      CDRDYN=YES,CDRSC=OPT,
                                     SUBAREA=1
DOMAIN02:
  MAJOR NODE:    HOST02
  MINOR NODE:    HOST02    VBUILD    TYPE=CDRM
                 VTAM02    CDRM      CDRDYN=YES,CDRSC=OPT,
                                     SUBAREA=2
```

Figure 5.4 CDRM Major Nodes as coded for DOMAIN01 and DOMAIN02.

cause duplicate resource names in the same network and the minor node will never be activated. For our example, the CDRM for HOST01 will be named VTAM01. The CDRM for HOST02 will be called VTAM02. Figure 5.4 shows the coded CDRM Major Nodes that will be used for DOMAIN01 and DOMAIN02.

The CDRDYN operand defines to VTAM whether this CDRM is authorized to dynamically define cross-domain resources during session requests from the CDRM that manages that cross-domain resource. By allowing the default of NO to take effect, all cross-domain session requests will fail because the cross-domain resource is not defined to the receiving CDRM. So, if the value used is NO, then you must define cross-domain resources explicitly to this domain's VTAM. This is not the preferable definition. Instead we will use the YES parameter. This parameter authorizes this CDRM to create cross-domain resource entries dynamically during a session request. This eliminates, to a large degree, the tedious coding necessary to define all the cross-domain resources to the CDRM. But this dynamic definition is also dependent on the CDRSC operand value of the requesting CDRM. This dynamic definition holds for both the originating and destination LUs in an MVS, VSE or VM operating system environment running VTAM V3.1.1 or higher. However, VTAM V3.1 under VM only supports dynamic definition for origin LUs.

The CDRSC operand provides information to VTAM as to whether this CDRM's owned resources can be dynamically defined when a session request is received from or sent to another domain. The OPT parameter tells VTAM that this CDRM is authorized to build VTAM control blocks when a CDINIT command is transmitted between the CDRMs. The REQ parameter specifies that a

80 Advanced SNA Networking

CDRSC entry is required to establish a cross-domain session. Since we want dynamic definitions, we have coded CDRSC=OPT.

The RECOVERY parameter is set to YES to allow automatic session establishment between CDRMs if their session has been broken by some type of network outage, such as an NCP inactivation. This CDRM session is known as an SSCP-SSCP session. You must have this session for a cross-domain resource to have a cross-domain session. The RECOVERY operand, in most cases, is defaulted to YES. In VM under VTAM V3.1, this operand is ignored.

The SUBAREA operand value is equal to the HOSTSA value that is coded in the ATCSTR00 start list of VTAM for this CDRM. In our example start list, the operand HOSTSA is set to 1. Therefore, the value for the CDRM residing in HOST01 will be SUBAREA=1. For HOST02 it will be SUBAREA=2. Figure 5.5 depicts the CDRM naming assignments.

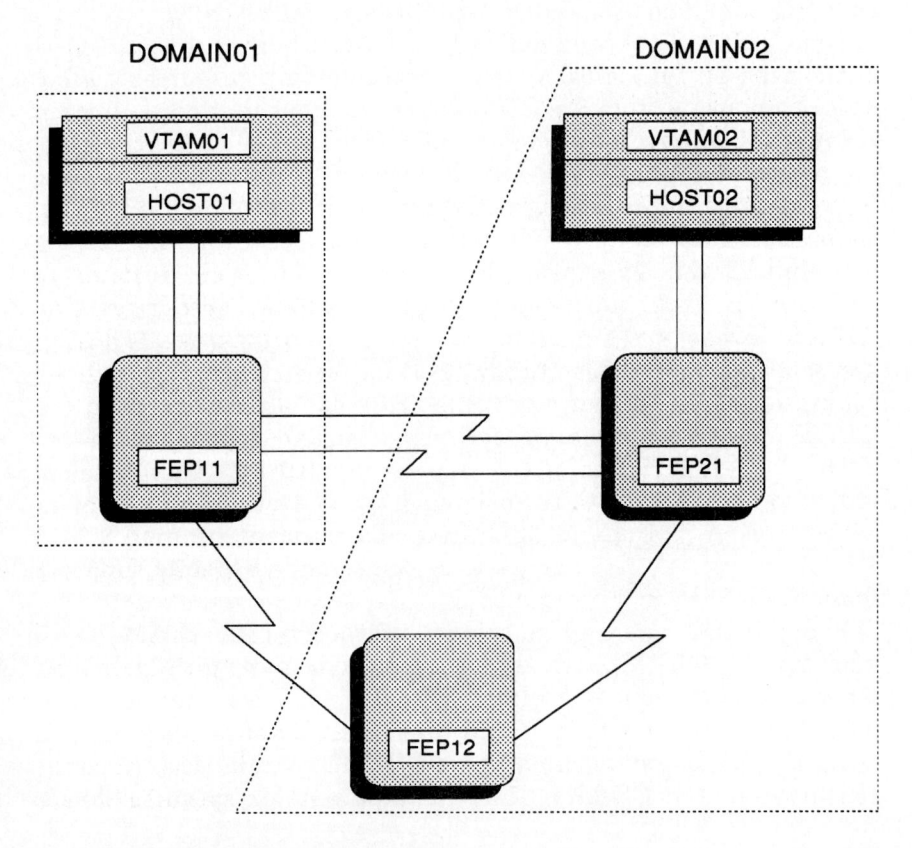

Figure 5.5 CDRM naming assignments

```
DOMAIN01:
            MAJOR NODE:     H02PRTS
                            H02PRTS     VBUILD    TYPE=CDRSC
            MAJOR NODE:     H02APPLS
                            H02APPLS    VBUILD    TYPE=CDRSC
DOMAIN02:
            MAJOR NODE:     H01PRTS
                            H01PRTS     VBUILD    TYPE=CDRSC
            MAJOR NODE:     H01APPLS
                            H01APPLS    VBUILD    TYPE=CDRSC
```

Figure 5.6 CDRSC Major Node statements for DOMAIN01 and DOMAIN02.

5.2 CROSS-DOMAIN RESOURCES (CDRSC)

For CDRSCs, it is not a recommended practice to create a major node for each CDRSC. However, it is recommended that you group the CDRSC entries into a logical category. This grouping may be according to domain, LU type, or application. We have chosen to group our sample cross-domain resources according to LU type and application.

5.2.1 VBUILD Statement for CDRSC

The TYPE operand defines to VTAM that this major node contains cross-domain resource minor nodes by specifying TYPE=CDRSC. Note from Figure 5.6 that the major nodes for DOMAIN01 define resources owned by DOMAIN02 and that DOMAIN02 defines resources for DOMAIN01.

5.2.2 CDRSC Definition Statement

Although we have stressed the use of dynamic definitions for cross-domain resources, there are some instances where a CDRSC entry is either required or useful to decrease session establishment time. Figure 5.7 outlines the format of the CDRSC definition statement.

The cross-domain resource name associated with the CDRSC entry is coded for the cdrscname operand. The name coded here is the actual name of the resource as it is known to the owning CDRM

```
cdrscname    CDRSC         [CDRM=cdrmname]
                           [,ISTATUS=ACTIVE|INACTIVE]
                           [,SPAN=(NCCF or NETVIEW spanname)]
```

Figure 5.7 CDRSC definition statement format.

of that resource. In our sample network, we will code printer LU names and application names.

In CICS, many application transactions involve printing information at a location remote from the host. Usually, CICS will not have a session with that printer until the print transaction is called to start printing. CICS will then issue a VTAM ACQUIRE command to take control of the printer. Because that printer is unknown to the CICS's owning VTAM, the printer name is included as a CDRSC. In the next section on ADJSSCP tables, we will discuss how to avoid defining CDRSCs for all SNA resources.

For applications, use the application name and not the ACB-name that is assigned to the application. When defining the application to VTAM, we suggest that the same value be used for the application name and the ACBname. Here is an instance where the suggestion helps to avoid the confusion of what name to use for the application name.

The CDRM operand defines to VTAM the controlling cross-domain resource manager for this CDRSC. This operand is optional and for a good reason. Ownership and control of a network resource is very dynamic in an SNA network. An LU may be under the control of VTAM01, for example, for 10 hours and then VTAM01 inactivates the controlling PU of the LU. VTAM02 then issues an activate to the LU. Now, the LU is under the control of VTAM02. If the CDRMname was coded on the CDRSC statement, it would be in error because VTAM02 now controls the LU. Normally, as in our scenario, VTAM02 would not generate an error for the LU because VTAM's search for resource reconciliation starts with its own domain resource list before searching the CDRSC entries. However, if we had a VTAM03 that had coded the LU as a CDRSC under VTAM01, then an error on VTAM03 and VTAM02 would occur if a session request were attempted between the LU in VTAM02 and an application in VTAM03. Because of this dynamic ownership ability in SNA networks, the rule of thumb is to not code the CDRM operand. In this case, the Adjacent SSCP table search routine is invoked to locate the owning SSCP. Figure 5.8 shows a sample of our network CDRSC definitions.

5.3 ADJACENT SSCP TABLE (ADJSSCP)

The ADJSSCP table provides a list of SSCPs that may participate in an SSCP-SSCP session with this VTAM. This list is used to locate the owning SSCP of an undefined cross-domain destination LU. The list is searched from the first entry to the last — a top-down search. By using an ADJSSCP table, it is not necessary to code CDRSCs for resources in other domains. Let's look at an example.

In Figure 5.8 we coded some of the applications that reside on VTAM02 as cross-domain resources for VTAM01. Let's assume that a new CICS test region is implemented on VTAM02 for end-users of VTAM01 to access. What information must be provided to VTAM in order for a terminal on VTAM01 to access the new CICS region CICSP02 on VTAM02? If we analyze the route of information from the end user to the CICS test region on VTAM02 the answer becomes clear.

Look at Figure 5.9. How do end-users enter CICS requests from the terminal? They type 'CICSP02'. This unformatted request must be included on the USSTAB that is defined for this terminal.

```
DOMAIN01:
        MAJOR NODE:     H02PRTS
        MINOR NODE:     H02PRTS     VBUILD      TYPE=CDSRC
                        F21C2P16    CDRSC
                        F21C2P15    CDRSC
        MAJOR NODE:     H02APPLS
        MINOR NODE:     H02APPLS    VBUILD      TYPE=CDRSC
                        TSO02       CDRSC       CDRM=VTAM02
                        CICSP02     CDRSC       CDRM=VTAM02
                        IMST02      CDRSC       CDRM=VTAM02
DOMAIN02:
        MAJOR NODE:     H01PRTS
        MINOR NODE:     H01PRTS     VBUILD      TYPE=CDSRC
                        F11C2P16    CDRSC
                        F11C2P15    CDRSC
        MAJOR NODE:     H01APPLS
                        H01APPLS    VBUILD      TYPE=CDRSC
                        TSO01       CDRSC       CDRM=VTAM01
                        CICSP01     CDRSC       CDRM=VTAM01
                        IMSP02      CDRSC       CDRM=VTAM01
```

Figure 5.8 CDRSC Major Nodes as defined in DOMAIN01 and DOMAIN02.

84 Advanced SNA Networking

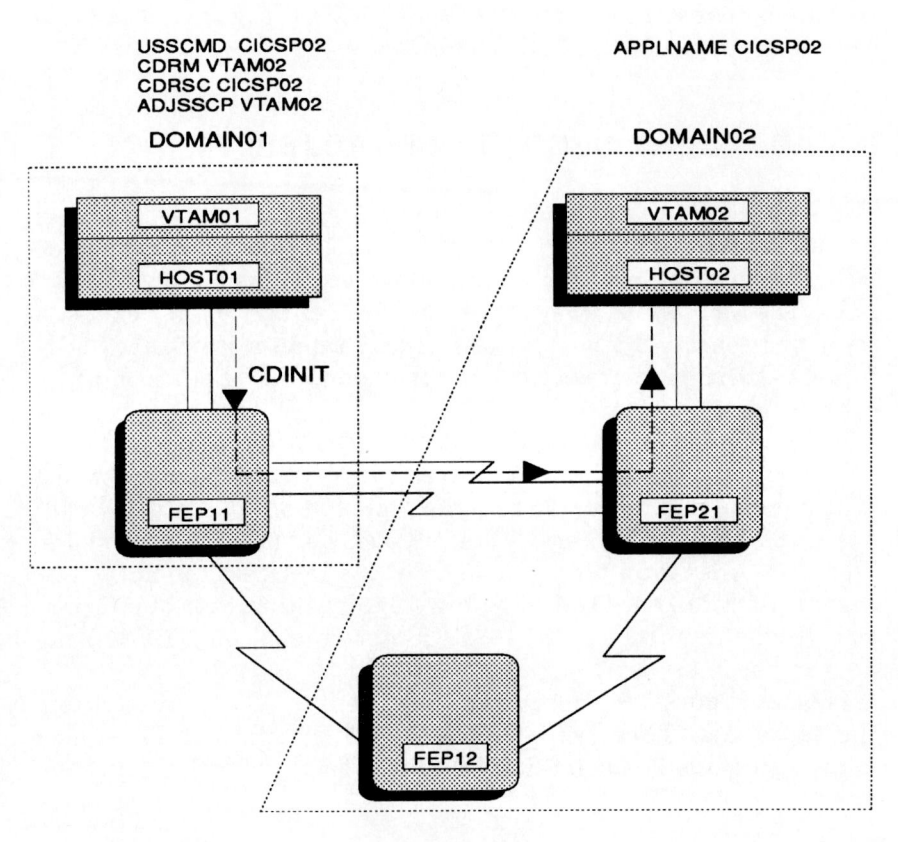

```
USSCMD CICSP02                          APPLNAME CICSP02
CDRM VTAM02
CDRSC CICSP02
ADJSSCP VTAM02
    DOMAIN01                                DOMAIN02
```

Figure 5.9 Preparing for cross-domain sessions.

The request is sent to VTAM01. VTAM01 scans the list of open ACBnames and finds there is no entry for CICSP02. But before sending a session unavailable error, VTAM01 checks for any SSCP-SSCP sessions. If SSCP-SSCP sessions exist, then VTAM01 finds his CDRSC entry table and searches for CICSP02. But again CICSP02 is not found. All this is done prior to accessing the ADJSSCP. Once the CDRSC entry table is searched, the last attempt is to locate the ADJSSCP table. If the table exists, VTAM01 begins trial-and-error routing to the SSCPs that are in the ADJSSCP table.

The routing is accomplished by using the cross-domain initiate request command (CDINIT). The CDINIT command asks each SSCP in the table, as they are ordered, to establish a cross-domain session for CICSP02. This is performed until the owner of the

CDRSC is found or the ADJSSCP table is exhausted. The CDINIT request may have been routed to an SSCP that also has an ADJSSCP table, but as long as that SSCP resides in the same network, the request will not be rerouted through the second ADJSSCP table. This example illustrates the use of the CDRSC definition in conjunction with the ADJSSCP table. However, we could have just as well not defined a CDRSC definition. In this case, VTAM would have gone immediately to the ADJSSCP table, since no CDRSC table exists.

5.3.1 ADJSSCP Start List Options

As you have seen, the setup time for a session request is lengthy when the requested resource is unknown. This session setup time can be increased dramatically in large networks that have several VTAMs. The larger the network, the longer the trial and error search through the ADJSSCP table.

To provide optimum performance and reliability for session set up, VTAM employs the following algorithms. When a session initiation request is received from an SSCP that is not in the ADJSSCP table, VTAM will add that requesting SSCP CDRM name to the end of the table dynamically. This function is controlled by the Start List Option SSCPDYN. During a sesssion initiate request from VTAM, the ADJSSCP is searched in priority order, with preference given to the SSCPs with the most recent successful session initiate request. This search is controlled by the Start List Option SSCPORD. The default values for these options are SSCPDYN=YES and SSCPORD=PRIORITY. These options will provide you with the best search time. They are not applicable for a VM operating system using VTAM V3.1.

In contrast, specifying SSCPDYN=YES and SSCPORD=DEFINED changes the search algorithm. In this instance, VTAM begins each search from the top of the ADJSSCP table list with no priority to the most recent successful session initiate request. The CDRM name of a requesting SSCP is added to the bottom of the ADJSSCP table list This definition in the start list increases the setup time and diminishes the flexibility of the table.

The pairing of SSCPDYN=NO and SSCPORD=PRIORITY limits the number of available paths to route requests. No entries will be added to the ADJSSCP table list unless the owner of the CDRSC is explicitly defined by the CDRM keyword of the CDRSC statement. This severely degrades the reliability of session initiate requests.

```
name           VBUILD      TYPE=ADJSSCP
cdrmname       ADJCDRM
```

Figure 5.10 ADJCDRM definition statement.

You may also need to define additional ADJSSCP tables to provide VTAM with optional routes to send session initiate requests.

The final combination of SSCPDYN=NO and SSCPORD=DEFINED increases session initiation setup time and limits the number of available routes for the request. There are no dynamic entries added to the ADJSSCP table, except if the CDRSC owner is explicitly defined on the CDRSC statement by the CDRM keyword. The order of the search is not prioritized, which limits the search to the defined order. This combination reduces performance and reliability.

5.3.2 ADJCDRM Definition Statement

Although the use of the ADJSSCP table is involved, especially for larger networks, the actual coding for the table is simple. Figure 5.10 outlines the format of the ADJCDRM definition statement.

As you can see, the format for the ADJCDRM statement has one operand. The cdrmname operand value is the name assigned to the CDRM of an adjacent SSCP. The ADJCDRM statement must be preceded by a VBUILD statement with the TYPE operand equal to ADJSSCP.

In Figure 5.11 we see the completed code for our sample network. Since our sample is small, it might be better not to use the ADJSSCP table. But we have included it for reference in a later chapter.

```
DOMAIN01:
              MAJOR NODE:    ADJ01TAB
                             ADJ01TAB    VBUILD     TYPE=ADJSSCP
                             VTAM02      ADJCDRM
DOMAIN02:
              MAJOR NODE:    ADJ02TAB
                             ADJ02TAB    VBUILD     TYPE=ADJSSCP
                             VTAM01      ADJCDRM
```

Figure 5.11 ADJSSCP tables for DOMAIN01 and DOMAIN02.

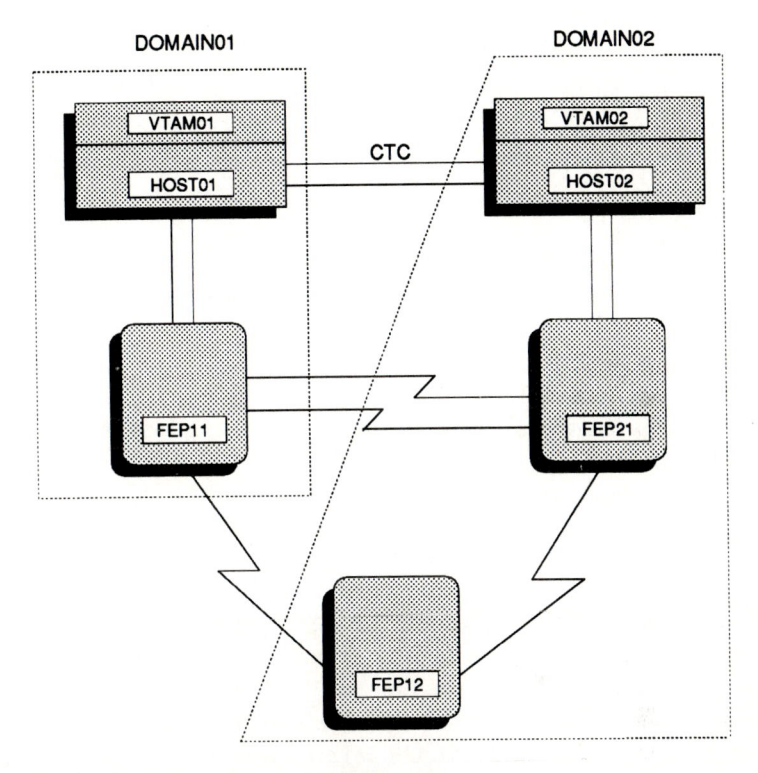

Figure 5.12 Channel-to-channel configuration.

5.4 CHANNEL-TO-CHANNEL ATTACHMENT

In many computer data centers, information is exchanged between host systems within the same computer room or building. So far we have discussed using the NCP as a means of sending information between hosts. But there is another method called Channel-to-Channel Attachment (CTCA), as diagramed in Figure 5.12. This method alleviates the use of the NCP and allows the hosts to communicate to each other through I/O channels, a direct link between the computers with no intervening front-end processor. This provides faster transmission time since the channel I/O rate approaches 3 megabytes per second and above. The coding for a CTCA is similar to that of an NCP line. The major node has four statements: the VBUILD statement, the GROUP statement, the LINE statement and the PU statement.

88 Advanced SNA Networking

```
[name] VBUILD      TYPE=CA
                   [,CONFGDS=name] [,CONFGPW=password]
name    GROUP      LNCTL=CTCA
                   [,MIH=YES|NO]
                   [,REPLYTO=time|3.0]
                   [,SPAN=(NCCF or NETVIEW spanname)]
```

Figure 5.13 GROUP statement for CTCA Major Node.

5.4.1 CTCA GROUP Definition Statement

The GROUP definition statement for a CTCA has one required operand. This statement defines the type of links that follow the GROUP definition statement. Figure 5.13 outlines the GROUP definition operands.

The name operand of the GROUP statement is the assigned minor node name for this line group represented by this GROUP definition statement. It is required. LNCTL=CTCA is also a required operand. This operand defines the links in this group as channel-to-channel attachment links. The MIH operand is optional and determines if the link should become inoperative if a Start I/O timeout occurs because the receiving host is disabled. The default is NO, but to automate the recovery we suggest YES as the MIH value. The REPLYTO operand determines the wait time for completing a start channel program command. The default is more than adequate and is usually taken.

5.4.2 CTCA LINE Definition Statement

The LINE definition statement defines the characteristics of the link adapter end of this VTAM. One LINE definition statement may be coded for each channel-to-channel attachment used by this VTAM. Figure 5.14 outlines the format of the LINE definition statement.

```
name    LINE       [,ADDRESS=channel unit address]
                   [,MIH=YES|NO]
                   [,MAXBFRU=) [norm|10] [,max|norm]
                   [,ISTATUS=ACTIVE|INACTIVE]
                   [,SPAN=(NCCF or NETVIEW spanname)]
```

Figure 5.14 LINE statement for CTCA Major Node.

Multi-Domain Network Definitions for VTAM 89

```
IODEVICE    UNIT=CTC,ADDRESS=(500,1),FEATURE=370
```

Figure 5.15 Sample I/O GEN statement for a channel-to-channel attachment for an MVS operating system.

The *name* operand of the LINE statement is the assigned minor node name for the link being defined by this statement. It is a required operand. The ADDRESS operand is optional The value used here is the address assigned to the CTC according to the I/O generation. The format of the I/O GEN for a CTC is in Figure 5.15. If the ADDRESS operand is not specified on the LINE statement, the operator must supply the channel unit address using the U operand of the VARY ACT command. The MAXBFRU operand defines the number of IO buffers VTAM will allocate during the start of a normal channel program. The norm value should be set larger than the actual normal data transfer. The value however should not be exceedingly large so that it will not waste buffer storage. The max value is used to define the number of buffers to allocate for the largest PIU that will be transmitted over the CTC. This value is also used when the PIU is larger than the norm value. In the latest release and maintenance levels of VTAM, the norm value is coded large enough to support the largest PIU. The max value is ignored.

5.4.3 CTCA PU Definition Statement

The PU definition statement defines the link station for the adjacent host processor. One PU definition is required for each line defined in this major node. The format of the PU definition statement is outlined in Figure 5.16.

The *name* operand of the PU statement is the assigned minor node name for the physical unit that represents the link station. The DELAY operand is the time interval VTAM will wait before

```
name    PU      [DELAY=time|0|.100]
                [,PUTYPE=4]
                [,ISTATUS=ACTIVE|INACTIVE]
                [,SPAN=(NCCF or NETVIEW spanname)]
```

Figure 5.16 PU statement for CTCA Major Node.

sending normal data flow to the other VTAM. This delay allows VTAM to queue more messages destined for the other VTAM. The value should be set as high as possible to take full advantage of efficient use of the channel IO rate. For maximum transmission speed, the 0 value can be used. The value range is from 0 to 9.999. The PUTYPE=4 operand is the only possible PUTYPE that can be used for a CTCA. This operand defines the link station as having PU type 4 characteristics even though the communication is directly between VTAMs. Figure 5.17 shows the completed CTCA Major Node for both domains in our sample network.

5.5 VTAM PATH TABLE CONSIDERATIONS

With the addition of DOMAIN02 to our sample network, the PATH table from a single domain network becomes complex. Let's look at the configuration in Figure 5.18 and analyze the routes.

The questions you should ask yourself when coding PATH statements are:

1. Where is the originating subarea?
2. Through which subarea adjacent to the originating subarea can we route information to reach the destination subarea? Or simply, 'How can I get there from here?'

We have added two channel connections to the configuration, one channel per FEP. This allows each VTAM to communicate directly with either FEP. For each VTAM there are four possible destination subareas. VTAM01 must be able to communicate with VTAM02, FEP11, FEP21, and FEP12. VTAM02 needs to communicate with VTAM01, FEP21, FEP12, and FEP11. For each VTAM

```
DOMAIN01:
           MAJOR NODE:    CTC01
                          CTC01      VBUILD    TYPE=CA
           MINOR NODES:   CTC01501   GROUP     LNCTL=CTC
                          CTCL501    LINE      ADDRESS=501
                          CTCP501    PU
DOMAIN02:
           MAJOR NODE:    CTC02
                          CTC02      VBUILD    TYPE=CA
           MINOR NODES:   CTC02502   GROUP     LNCTL=CTC
                          CTCL502    LINE      ADDRESS=502
                          CTCP502    PU
```

Figure 5.17 CTCA Major Node definitions for DOMAIN01 and DOMAIN02.

there are several different combinations of origin:adjacent:destination subarea routes to take. Our job is to provide the shortest possible path. Now let's start asking those questions we mentioned above.

5.5.1 Defining the Multi-Domain PATH Table

From the perspective of VTAM01, we need to communicate with VTAM02 and the three NCP subarea nodes. How do we get there from here? Well, we know the destination subarea for VTAM02 is 02. That's the subarea number that was assigned to VTAM in DOMAIN02. We can also see from Figure 5.18 that there are 3 adjacent subareas that can lead us to our destination subarea. Of the 3 adjacent subareas, the most direct route is to go to VTAM02 directly using the CTC attachment that we defined in the previous section. Along with the selection of the adjacent subarea is the Explicit Route (ER) number, the Virtual Route (VR) number and

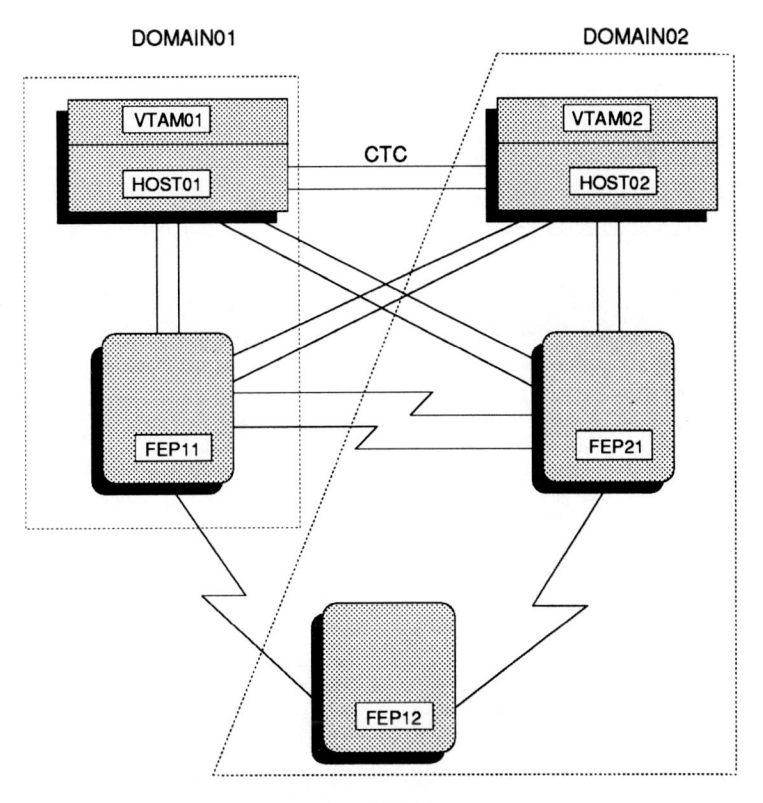

Figure 5.18 Full multi-domain network configuration.

the Transmission Group (TG) number. Recall that for each origin:destination subarea pair there can be 8 ERs (16 in VTAM V3R2 and NCP V4R3.1/V5R2.1) mapped to 8 VRs. So, in this configuration we can have a maximum of 32 ERs (8x4) defined for each subarea in pre-VTAM V3R2 and 64 ERs (16x4) in VTAM V3R2.

In the following figures, we have detailed the selected path table for each of the 5 subareas shown in Figure 5.18. Note that in Figures 5.19 and 5.20, the charts reflect "Where am I?", "Where do I want to go?" and "Where can I first go to get to my final destination?".

Figure 5.19 details the question and answer scenario between VTAM01 and the other four subareas in the network. Figure 5.20 details the same question and answer scenario between VTAM02 and the other four subareas. Note that in all cases, ER0 has been

OSA	DSA	ADJSA	TG	ER	VR
1	2	2	1	0	0
		11	1	2	2
		21	1	1	1
		21	1	3	3
		11	1	4	4
		2	1	5	5
	11	11	1	0	0
		21	1	1	1
		2	1	2	2
		2	1	3	3
	21	21	1	0	0
		11	1	1	1
		2	1	3	3
		21	1	5	5
		11	1	4	4
	12	11	1	0	0
		21	1	1	1
		11	1	2	2
		21	1	3	3

Figure 5.19 Complete path table for VTAM01 to all subareas in the network.

Multi-Domain Network Definitions for VTAM 93

OSA	DSA	ADJSA	TG	ER	VR
2	1	1	1	0	0
		11	1	4	4
		21	1	6	6
		11	1	2	2
		21	1	3	3
		11	1	1	1
		2	1	5	5
	11	11	1	2	2
		21	1	3	3
		1	1	0	0
		21	1	4	4
	21	21	1	0	1
		21	11	3	3
		11	1	2	2
		1	1	5	5
		1	1	1	1
	12	21	1	0	0
		11	1	1	1
		21	1	3	3
		11	1	2	3

Figure 5.20 Complete path table for VTAM02.

used as the primary direct route between VTAM01 and the other subareas for each origin:destination subarea path. One other note: VTAM decides on which route to use for sessions by this table. The COS table entry specified in the logon mode table entry for the LU determines which of the VRs, and consequently ERs, are selected for the session. Sessions that exist between VTAMs must ride on the same VR number. For example, any session in our network that begins and ends within VTAM will ride on VR0. The VR must be the same in both VTAM definitions for complete communication to take place. Figure 5.21 defines the net and VTAM definitions for the path tables detailed in Figures 5.19 and 5.20.

5.6 PARALLEL TRANSMISSION GROUPS

Up to this point we have discussed channel connections between a VTAM host computer and a channel-attached NCP communications controller through transmission group number 1 and a single channel connection between the two. The potential for multiple channel connections has always been inherent in the hardware but not provided by the software. VTAM V3R3 and NCP V5R3 resolve this problem by allowing multiple single-link transmission groups,

```
VTAM01:
    PATH TABLE:
        PATH0102    PATH    DESTSA=02,ER0=(2,1),ER2=(11,1),
                            ER1=(21,1),ER3=(21,1),ER4=(11,1)
                            ER5(2,1),VR0=0,VR2=2,VR1=1,
                            VR3=3,VR4=4,VR5=5

        PATH0111    PATH    DESTSA=11,ER0=(11,1),ER1=(21,1),
                            ER2=(2,1),ER3=(2,1),VR0=0,VR2=2,
                            VR1=1,VR3=3

        PATH0121    PATH    DESTSA=21,
                            ER0=(21,1),ER1=(11,1),ER3=(2,1),
                            ER5=(21,1),ER4=(11,1),VR0=0,
                            VR1=1,VR3=3,VR4=4,VR5=5

        PATH0112    PATH    DESTSA=12,ER0=(11,1),ER1=(21,1),
                            ER2=(11,1),ER3=(21,1),VR2=2,
                            VR1=1,VR3=3,VR0=0
VTAM02:
    PATH TABLE:
        PATH0201    PATH    DESTSA=01,ER0=(1,1),ER4=(11,1),
                            ER6=(21,1),ER2=(11,1),ER3=(21,1),
                            ER1=(11,1),ER5=(2,1),VR2=2,
                            VR1=1,VR3=3,VR4=4,VR5=5,VR0=0

        PATH0211    PATH    DESTSA=11,ER2=(11,1),ER3=(21,1),
                            ER0=(1,1),ER4=(21,1),VR2=2,
                            VR0=0,VR3=3,VR4=4

        PATH0221    PATH    DESTSA=21,ER0=(21,1),ER3=(21,1),
                            ER2=(11,1),ER5(1,1),ER1=(1,1),
                            VR1=1,VR2=2,VR3=3,VR5=5, VR0=0

        PATH0212    PATH    DESTSA=12,ER0=(21,1),ER1=(11,1),
                            ER3=(21,1),ER2=(11,1),VR1=1,
                            VR2=2,VR3=3,VR0=0
```

Figure 5.21 VTAM path table definitions for VTAM01 and VTAM02

using different transmission group numbers, to be active concurrently. This new capability between channel-attached subareas is known as parallel transmission groups.

The concept of parallel tranmission groups is not new. It has been in use, connecting NCP subareas together, for quite some time. But it is new for connections between two channel-attached VTAMs or between VTAM and a channel-attached NCP.

This improvement provides more channel bandwidth, improving availability and the flexibility to adjust transmission priorities based on virtual routes. The impetus behind this functionality is based on the rapid expansion of high-speed links and Token-Ring Networks. These facilities can have data rates from 1.54Mbps (T1) to 16Mbps for token-ring networking. In the near future, data rates will reach 100Mbps using FDDI technology. Line speeds like these can cause a potential bottle neck at the channel level because an IBM 3745 has a maximum data rate of 2.08 megabytes per second. Simple mathematics will tell you that a T1 connection to your IBM 3745 has the potential of transmitting 192,500 bytes per second whereas a Token-Ring Network operating at 16 Mbps has the potential of sending 2 megabytes per second and the 100 Mbps FDDI connection has the potential of transmitting 12.5 megabytes per second. You can see as technology marches on, so does the size of the available bandwidth. The pace at which these technologies are being implemented is rapidly out-growing the available channel-bandwidth. Increasing the amount of channel bandwidth to support high-speed facilities and utilizing SNA's virtual route capabilities will allow you to equalize the flow of data between the SNA channel-attached subareas.

5.6.1 Defining Parallel Transmission Groups

The configuration in Figure 5.22 demonstrates the connection of a VTAM host channel-attached to an IBM 3745 using parallel transmission groups. The VTAM is V3R3 and the NCP is V5R3. The transmission groups are defined as TG1 and TG2. We could have chosen any numbers from 1 to 255 for these transmission groups. Both channels are concurrently active to the IBM 3745. Using the class of service table we can differentiate the types of users over the two channels and provide for virtual route backup.

The definition of parallel transmission groups with VTAM V3R3 requires the addition of a channel-attached major node for the non-primary channels. Figure 5.23 details the definitions required for defining parallel transmission groups to VTAM and the NCP. The PCCU definition statement in the NCP identifies to VTAM which channel unit address (CUA) to use to load or dump the NCP into/from the IBM 3745. The first PCCU definition statement encountered by VTAM during the load or activate process is the primary channel. In our scenario, the primary channel is C10 and the secondary channel is 810. Note also on these PCCU definitions, that the SUBAREA keyword for both specifies the same value. In fact, the two PCCU definitions are identical with the exception of the CUADDR keyword.

Another keyword is added to the PCCU definition statement for parallel transmission groups. This is the TGN keyword. We have seen this keyword before when defining NCP transmission groups and defining channel-to-channel attached VTAMs. Recall that transmission groups are identified by two subarea addresses and a transmission group number. Each link in a TG must have a transmission group number assigned to it either explicitly by coding a value from 1 to 255 or by coding the parameter of ANY. Coding TGN=ANY actually assigns a value of zero to the transmission group. The actual transmission group number used is determined at subarea contact time. During this procedure, at least one subarea must have a transmission group number explicitly defined or the contact will fail. For this reason, the TGN value must be explicitly coded for parallel transmission groups on either the

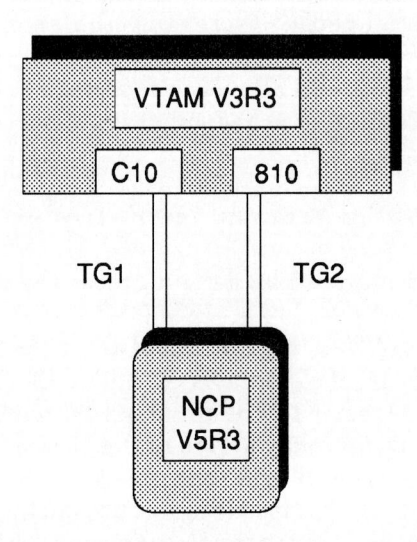

Figure 5.22 Diagram depicting parallel transmission groups between VTAM and a channel-attached NCP.

Multi-Domain Network Definitions for VTAM

```
In VTAM:
    CA MAJOR NODE:
            PTG          VBUILD      TYPE=CA
            PTGGRP       GROUP       LNCTL=NCP,ISTATUS=ACTIVE
            PTGLINE      LINE        ADDRESS=810,ISTATUS=ACTIVE,
                                     MAXBFRU=16
In NCP:
    PCCU Definitions:
            VTAMC10      PCCU        CUADDDR=C10,MAXDATA=5000,
                                     OWNER=CDRM01,SUBAREA=01,
                                     VFYLM=YES,TGN=ANY

            VTAM810      PCCU        CUADDR=810,MAXDATA=5000,
                                     OWNER=CDRM01,SUBAREA=01,
                                     VFYLM=YES,TGN=ANY

                         . . . .
Host Definition:         . . . .
            VTAM01       HOST        INBFRS=10,MAXBFRU=34
                                     UNITSZ=152,BFRPAD=0,
                                     SUBAREA=01

                         . . . .
                         . . . .
Channel Link Definitions:
            CAGROUP      GROUP       LNCTL=CA,ISTATUS=INACTIVE
            LC10CA6      LINE        ADDRESS=01,CASDL=120,
                                     DELAY=0.0,TIMEOUT=120,
                                     CA=TYPE6
            PUC10CA6     PU          PUTYPE=5,TGN=1
            L810CA4      LINE        ADRESS=11,CA=TYPE6,CASDL=120,
                                     TIMEOUT=120,DELAY=0.0
            PU810CA4     PU          PUTYPE=5,TGN=2
```

Figure 5.23 Definitions for parallel transmission groups.

PCCU or the channel-link PU definition. It is recommended that TGN=ANY be specified on all the PCCU definitions. This will allow you to load the NCP and activate the communications controller using any of the parallel transmission groups.

5.7 SUMMARY

In this chapter we learned how a single domain SNA network can become a multiple domain network. VTAM residing on one host computer can be connected to another VTAM in one of two ways: over an SSCP-SSCP session using intermediate networking nodes in the NCPs, or directly attached to the other VTAM host computer through a channel-to-channel attachement. We also learned of the ability of VTAM V3R3 and NCPV5R3 to allow us to define multiple transmission groups between channel-attached subareas. Each transmission group has a unique transmission group number so that all transmission groups can be concurrently active to the channel-attached subarea.

Chapter

6

Multiple Domain Definitions for an NCP

When defining an NCP that is to participate in a multi-domain configuration, it is important to evaluate whether the NCP will function as a Boundary Network Node (BNN), an Intermediate Network Node (INN) or both. Functioning as a BNN, the NCP is concerned with the transmission of data to its peripheral nodes (e.g., PUs and LUs). If the NCP receives data that is not destined for the NCP's subarea, then using the routing information defined in the PATH statements, the NCP will pass the data to the next subarea for routing. The NCP is said to be an INN when functioning in this manner. Therefore, NCPs can act as an INN in a single-domain network that is comprised of one VTAM and multiple NCPs or in a multiple domain network that is comprised of multiple VTAMs and multiple NCPs. See Figure 6.1 for a diagram of BNN and INN functionality.

As you can see from the diagram, a major consideration for a multi-domain NCP configuration is the PATH statements used for the routing of data. But, there are some other nuances in an NCP that need attention for a multi-domain environment.

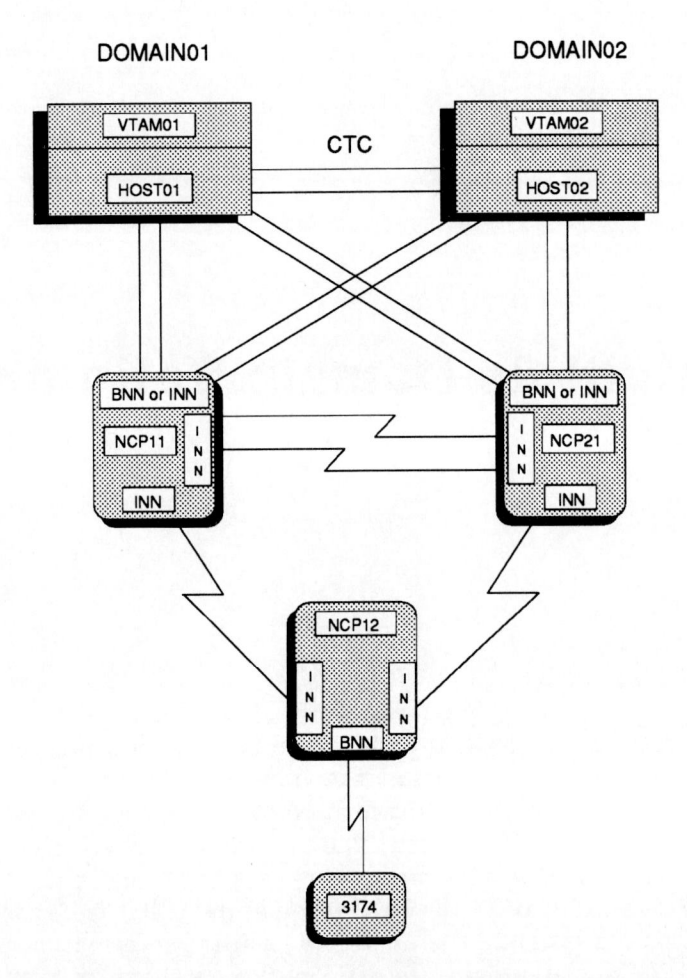

Figure 6.1 Sample multi-domain network depicting BNN and INN functions.

6.1 PCCU DEFINITION STATEMENT FOR ADDITIONAL HOSTS

If an NCP can be loaded into the FEP and activated by more than one VTAM host, than a PCCU definition statement is used for each host that is given this capability. Each host must have a copy of the NCP source and an NCP load module. The source and load module must have the same name in each host. We will discuss the implications of some of the operands in a multi-domain NCP.

Multiple Domain Definitions for an NCP

```
         VTAM01      PCCU     CUADDR=A01,            X
                              AUTODMP=YES,           X
                              AUTOIPL=YES,           X
                              AUTOSYN=YES,           X
                              DUMPDS=NCPDUMP,        X
                              MAXDATA=4096,          X
                              SUBAREA=01,            X
                              VFYLM=YES,             X
                              LOADSTA=A01-S,         X
                              INITEST=YES,           X
                              DUMPSTA=A01-S
         VTAM02      PCCU     CUADDR=B01,            X
                              AUTODMP=NO,            X
                              AUTOIPL=NO,            X
                              AUTOSYN=YES,           X
                              DUMPDS=NCPDUMP,        X
                              MAXDATA=4096,          X
                              SUBAREA=02,            X
                              VFYLM=YES,             X
                              LOADSTA=B01-S,         X
                              INITEST=NO,            X
                              DUMPSTA=B01-S
```

Figure 6.2 Example of PCCU statements in a multi-domain NCP.

In Figure 6.2 there are two PCCU definition statements defined for this NCP. VTAM01 and VTAM02 represent the VTAMs that reside in HOST01 and HOST02 respectively. VTAM01 was already present in the NCP when we defined the single-domain environment in Chapter 17 of *Introduction to SNA Networking*. VTAM02 has been added to create a multi-domain network. In the PCCU definition statement for VTAM02, the HOST communicates to NCP11 by using the I/O Channel B01 as defined in the CUADDR operand. Notice that the AUTODMP, AUTOIPL and INITEST operands all specify NO. We do this because we want VTAM01 to have control over dumping and initializing the communications controller storage. As a safeguard against VTAM02 loading a new NCP into the communications controller, the AUTOSYN and VFYLM modules both indicate to VTAM02 that it is to use the NCP that is present in the communications controller before allowing a load from VTAM02. This provides safety for sessions that are currently using NCP11 when VTAM02 activates the NCP.

6.2 BUILD DEFINITION STATEMENT CONSIDERATIONS FOR MULTIPLE DOMAINS

Operands of the BUILD definition statement that affect a multi-domain network are the MAXSUBA, NCPCA, NUMHSAS, VRPOOL, MAXSSCP and the TRANSFR operands. With the exception of TRANSFR, these operands define to the NCP the number of VTAMs that can communicate with the NCP concurrently. The TRANSFR operand defines the amount of data that can pass between the NCP and the VTAM host.

The MAXSUBA value must be used in a network that is pre-ENA or in an ENA network that includes pre-ENA nodes. Again, this value must equal the MAXSUBA value specified throughout the network. If VTAM02 does not equal this value, an error will occur during activation of the NCP.

The NCPCA operand defines the status of the channel adapters installed in the communications controller at the time of activation of the NCP. Be sure to verify that this operand defines the channel adapter addressed by the new VTAM host (in this case VTAM02) as being active. Otherwise, VTAM02 will never activate the NCP over this channel adapter interface.

```
NCP11BLD    BUILD   MODEL=3725,  concontroller type          X
                    MEMSIZE=1024, installed memory           X
                    CA=(TYPE5,TYPE5-TPS), CA types           X
                    NCPCA=(ACTIVE,ACTIVE), active CAs        X
                    DELAY=(.2),  delay attn signal           X
                    TIMEOUT=420.0, default timeout/          X
                    host
                    BFRS=128,    NCP data buffer size        X
                    TRANSFR=32,  # of BFRS xfrd to           X
                    host
                    MAXSUBA=15,  maximum subareas            X
                    SUBAREA=11,  Subarea of NCP              X
                    MAXSSCP=2,   Concurrent SSCP-PU          X
                    NUMHSAS=2,   # of Host subareas          X
                    VRPOOL=2,    # of VR                     X
                    TYPSYS=MVS,  host operating system       X
                    TYPGEN=NCP,                              X
                    VERSION=V4R2, version of NCP             X
                    NEWNAME=NCP11 NCP load module name
```

Figure 6.3 BUILD definition statement for a multi-domain NCP.

The NUMHSAS, MAXSSCP and VRPOOL operands all define the number of VTAMs that can communicate with this NCP concurrently. You may code more than needed, but this uses valuable buffer space in the NCP. It is best to code the exact number of SSCPs that are attached to this NCP. In Figure 6.3 we increased this value by 1 from the BUILD coded in the single-domain NCP for NCP11 in Chapter 15 of *Introduction to SNA Networking*.

6.3 HOST DEFINITION STATEMENT FOR A MULTI-DOMAIN NCP

Remember there must be one HOST definition statement for each VTAM that communicates with this NCP over a channel. Since VTAM02 is also channel connected to NCP11 through the second channel adapter of the communications controller, a HOST definition defining the transfer of data between NCP11 and VTAM02 is required. Remote NCPs do not require a HOST definition statement since they do not have a channel-attached host processor.

Notice that in Figure 6.4, the HOST definitions for the two VTAMs are identical except for the SUBAREA operand. This allows for ease of implementation and eliminates the concern for sending and receiving more data than can be handled by the NCP or VTAM. However, analysis of your system will assist you in determining the MAXBFRU, UNITSZ and INBFRS operand values. For information on defining the HOST definition statement to VTAM V3R2 and NCP V4R3/V5R2 consult Chapter 15 of *Introduction to SNA Networking*.

```
HOST01      HOST     INBFRS=10,                X
                     MAXBFRU=16,               X
                     UNITSZ=256,               X
                     BFRPAD=0,                 X
                     SUBAREA=1
HOST02      HOST     INBFRS=10,                X
                     MAXBFRU=16,               X
                     UNITSZ=256,               X
                     BFRPAD=0,                 X
                     SUBAREA=2
```

Figure 6.4 HOST definition statement for a multi-domain in NCP.

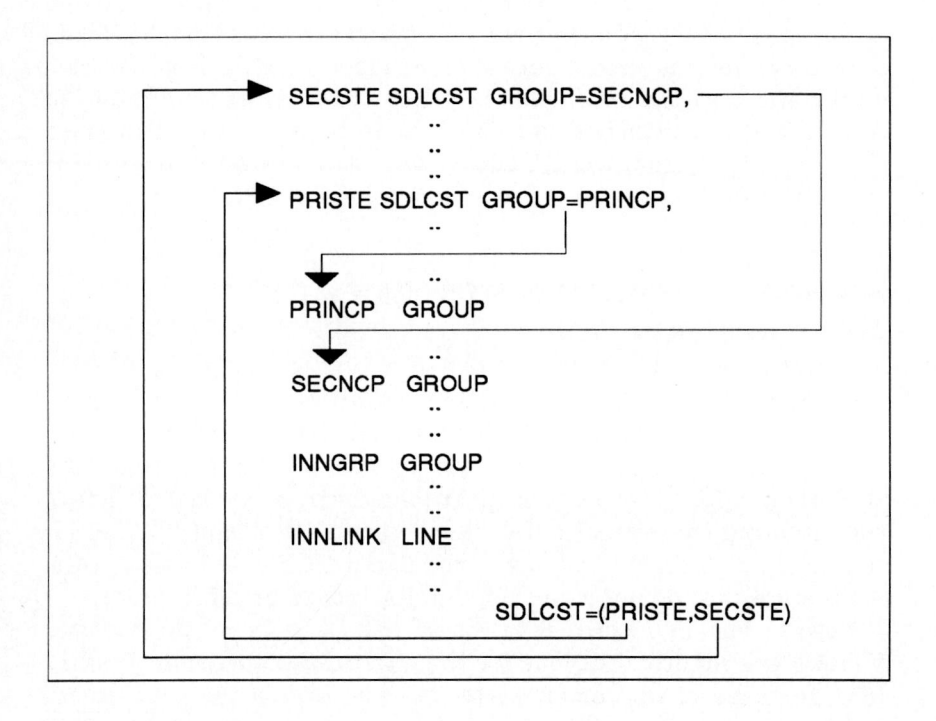

```
          ┌──▶ SECSTE SDLCST  GROUP=SECNCP, ──┐
          │         ..                         │
          │         ..                         │
          │         ..                         │
          │  ┌──▶ PRISTE SDLCST  GROUP=PRINCP, │
          │  │        ..                       │
          │  │        ..                       │
          │  ▼                                 │
          │ PRINCP   GROUP                     │
          │  ▼        ..                       │
          │ SECNCP   GROUP                     │
          │           ..                       │
          │           ..                       │
          │ INNGRP   GROUP                     │
          │           ..                       │
          │           ..                       │
          │ INNLINK  LINE                      │
          │           ..                       │
          │           ..                       │
          │          SDLCST=(PRISTE,SECSTE) ───┘
          └────────────────────────────────────
```

Figure 6.5 Diagram outlining the use of the SDLCST definition statement.

6.4 SDLCST DEFINITION STATEMENT FOR A MULTI-DOMAIN NCP

In a multi-domain network, it is not uncommon for NCP subareas to be connected by an SDLC link. In fact, most large networks have several SDLC subarea links between NCPs. This configuration allows for multiple paths between subareas. When these paths are activated, the NCPs must determine their roles and the subarea links characteristics according to their roles. The role and link characteristics are determined by the SDLCST definition statement. The SDLCST definition statement must appear in the NCP source before any GROUP definition statement.

As you can see from Figure 6.6, there are only two operands required in the SDLCST definition statement. The *name* operand is coded as any valid assembler language symbol and is used by the

```
          name      SDLCST  GROUP=group name,                    X
                            [,MAXOUT=n|71]                       X
                            [,MODE=PRI|SEC]                      X
                            [,PASSLIM=n|254]                     X
                            [,RETRIES=NONE|(m[,t[,n]])]          X
                            [,SERVLIM=n|4]                       X
                            [,TADDR=chars]
```

Figure 6.6 SDLCST definition statement format.

SDLCST operand of the LINE definition statement that defines the SDLC subarea link.

The GROUP operand of the SDLCST definition statement is also required. The value coded here identifies the GROUP definition statement that defines the subarea link parameters associated with this SDLC selection table (SDLCST) definition.

The MAXOUT operand specifies the number of SDLC frames the NCP can receive on the line before issuing a response. This is specific to the NCP when operating in secondary mode. The MAXOUT value specified on the PU definition statement for this subarea link is the value that the primary mode NCP will use for sending frames to the secondary mode NCP before requesting an acknowledgement. The value for MAXOUT is determined by the modules being enforced by the NCPs. If MODULO 128 is in use then MAXOUT can range from 8 to 127. For NCP V4R3/V5R2, the valid range is 1 to 127. If the lines are operating in MODULO 8, specify 1 to 7, if they are in MODULO 128 specify 8 to 127.

The MODE operand specifies if this SDLCST definition describes functional characteristics for the NCP when it is in primary (polling responsibility and error recovery) or secondary mode. The value coded here must be the same as the MODE operand of the associated GROUP definition statement pointed to by the GROUP operand of this SDLCST definition statement. Figure 6.7 outlines the procedure for determining which NCP of a subarea link is to act in primary or secondary mode.

The PASSLIM operand is functionally equivalent to the PASSLIM operand discussed for the SDLC LINE definition in Chapter 15 of *Introduction of SNA Networking,* except here in the SDLCST, definition of the PASSLIM value can affect the mode of transmission on the subarea link (e.g., full or half-duplex). Usually, SDLC subarea links are defined with a send and receive address on the LINE definition statement to facilitate the trans-

106 Advanced SNA Networking

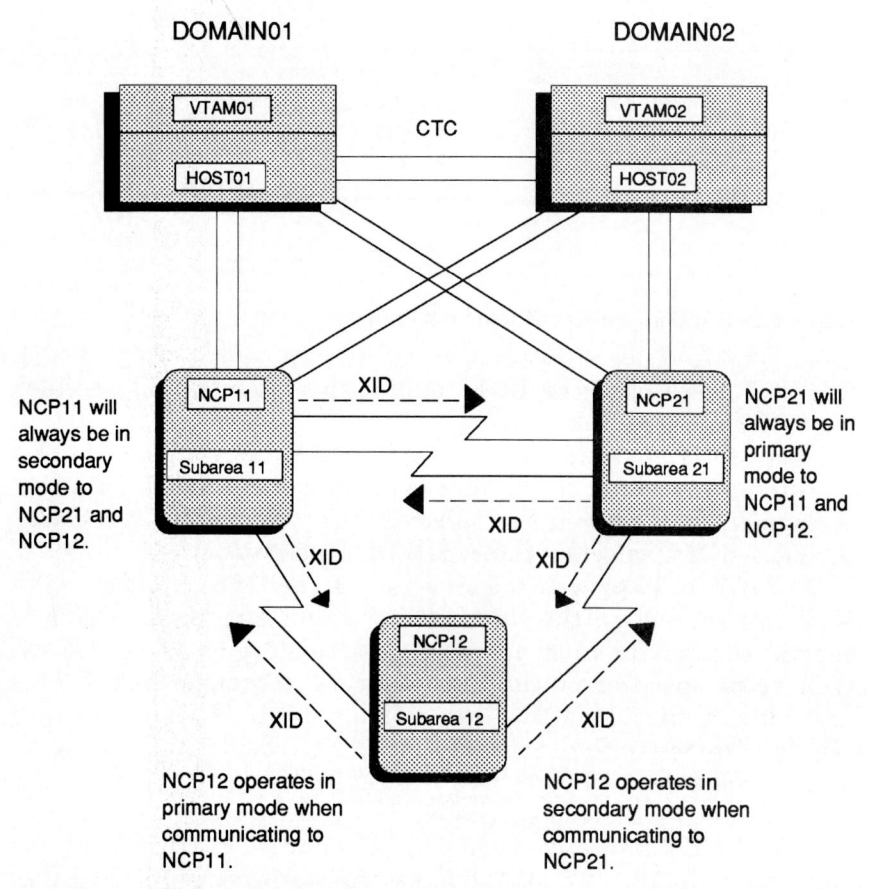

DOMAIN01 — VTAM01 / HOST01
DOMAIN02 — VTAM02 / HOST02
CTC

NCP11 (Subarea 11)
NCP21 (Subarea 21)
NCP12 (Subarea 12)

NCP11 will always be in secondary mode to NCP21 and NCP12.

NCP21 will always be in primary mode to NCP11 and NCP12.

NCP12 operates in primary mode when communicating to NCP11.

NCP12 operates in secondary mode when communicating to NCP21.

Figure 6.7 Primary mode is determined by the higher subarea number during exchange of identification (XID) between NCPs.

mission of data in both directions. If, however, the PASSLIM value specified for the SDLCST definition is less than the MAXOUT value specified for this SDLCST definition, then the line will operate in half-duplex transmission mode. When the LINE definition for the subarea link is assigned two addresses, it is best to take the default for this operand to ensure full duplex transmission.

The RETRIES operand acts in the same manner as the RETRIES operand for error recovery to peripheral nodes. However, ample time should be given to allow a link-attached NCP subarea to access its dump data sets on disk. Therefore, we suggest a minimum retry time for the RETRIES and REPLYTO values of 60 seconds. For more information on how the RETRIES operand functions, refer to Chapter 15 of *Introduction to SNA Networking*.

Multiple Domain Definitions for an NCP 107

The SERVLIM operand also functions in the same manner as the SERVLIM operand of the LINE definition statement. Remember that the SERVLIM value determines the number of scans through the service order table (SOT) to complete normal service for the resources on the link before performing special services for the resources. That is, activation and deactivation or status requests from the SSCP for a resource on the link. The value for SERVLIM is dependent upon the number of status commands and activation and deactivation of devices on this link. If the commands are frequent, then a low SERVLIM value is justifiable to avoid queuing of the status commands. However, for an SDLC subarea link, few status commands should traverse the link. And in most cases, the subarea link is point-to-point and not multi-point, so the SERVLIM value can be set to 254 for optimal service to the INN link.

Finally, the TADDR operand of the SDLCST definition statement specifies a unique SDLC station address for the NCP operating in secondary mode and may be specified on the SDLCST definition describing secondary mode. The default is the hexadecimal representation of the NCP's subarea address. The following figure (Figure 6.8) shows the SDLCST definitions for NCP11.

```
PRISTE    SDLCST    GROUP=PRINCP,    NCP IN PRIMARY MODE      X
                    MAXOUT=127,      USING MODULO128          X
                    MODE=PRI,        PRIMARY MODE             X
                    PASSLIM=254,     ENSURE FULL DUPLEX       X
                    SERVLIM=254      MAX SERVICE FOR INN
                                     LINK
SECSTE    SDLCST    GROUP=SECNCP,    NCP IN SECONDARY MODE    X
                    MAXOUT=127,      USING MODULO128          X
                    MODE=SEC,        PRIMARY MODE             X
                    PASSLIM=254,     ENSURE FULL DUPLEX       X
                    SERVLIM=254      MAX SERVICE FOR INN
                                     LINK
```

Figure 6.8 SDLCST Definitions for multi-domain NCP NCP11.

6.5 GROUP DEFINITION STATEMENTS FOR MULTI-DOMAIN NCP

Two GROUP definition statements must be defined for an SDLC subarea link when using the SDLCST definition statement. One group will specify the characteristics of the link during primary operation mode and the second will define the characteristics of the link during the secondary mode of operation. A GROUP definition statement must still be defined just before the LINE definition statement that defines the actual SDLC subarea link. All in all, three GROUP definition statements must be defined for one SDLC subarea link.

However, the GROUP definition statements that reflect the mode of operation identified by the SDLCST definition statement for primary and secondary modes need only be defined once. Let's look at the coded example of the GROUP definition statements for the SDLC subarea links between NCP11 and NCP21 in Figure 6.9.

In Figure 6.9, we have defined the LINE characteristics that will be enforced by the NCP when the SDLC subarea link is operating in primary and secondary modes. It is these values, and not those defined on the GROUP, LINE and PU definitions for the SDLC subarea link, that will be used.

```
PRINCP     GROUP    MODE=PRI,              NCP IN PRIMARY MODE        X
                    LNCTL=SDLC,            SDLC LINE CONTROL          X
                    TYPE=NCP,              NETWORK CONTROL MODE       X
                    DIAL=NO,               DEDICATED LINK             X
                    REPLYTO=(,60),         60 SECOND REPLY TIME       X
                                           OUT
                    TEXTTO=3               3 SECONDS TEXT TIME
                                           OUT
SECNCP     GROUP    MODE=SEC,              NCP IN SECONDARY MODE      X
                    LNCTL=SDLC,            SDLC LINE CONTROL          X
                    TYPE=NCP,              NETWORK CONTROL MODE       X
                    DIAL=NO,               DEDICATED LINK             X
                    REPLYTO=(NONE,NONE),                              X
                    TEXTTO=NONE,           NO TEXT TIME OUT           X
                    ACTIVTO=420.0          TIME BETWEEN I-FRAMES
```

Figure 6.9 GROUP definition statements for primary and secondary modes.

Multiple Domain Definitions for an NCP 109

The first GROUP definition statement defines the characteristics of the SDLC subarea link when the NCP is in the primary state. The name PRINCP is the same name defined in the SDLCST definition statement operand GROUP of the statement that defines the primary mode of operation. The MODE operand of the GROUP statement in Figure 6.9 tells the NCP that the operands defined here are to be used when the NCP is in a primary mode of operation with the SDLC subarea link.

The LNCTL, TYPE and DIAL operand values are all typical for a dedicated SDLC link. The LNCTL operand specifies the use of SDLC as the link protocol. The TYPE operand specifies that the lines in this group operate in network control mode. The DIAL operand identifies this link as a dedicated nonswitched line.

The REPLYTO operand of the PRINCP group specifies the number of seconds the primary NCP will wait for a response to a poll, selection or message text that was sent to the secondary NCP before issuing a timeout error for the secondary NCP. The range is .1 second to 60 for a link in network control mode. The comma before the 60 value of the REPLYTO operand indicates that the default for SDLC links, MODULO8, is taken, 1 second. The 60 indicates that for SDLC links in MODULO128 mode, 60 seconds must expire between receipt of a response to a poll from the secondary NCP before issuing a timeout error.

The TEXTTO operand defines the amount of time, in seconds that the primary NCP will wait between receipt of text messages from the secondary NCP before issuing a text timeout error. Barring problems with the link, a value of 3 seconds is sufficient for this type of condition. For more information on timeout values, see Chapter 15 of *Introduction to SNA Networking*.

The group that defines the secondary mode characteristics for SDLC subarea links in this NCP is labeled SECNCP. Again, this must match the GROUP operand of the SDLCST definition statement that defines the link characteristics for the NCP operating in secondary mode. The MODE operand of the GROUP definition statement SECNCP identifies this group for use in defining the link characteristics when the NCP is in a secondary mode of operation.

The LNCTL, TYPE and DIAL operands have the same meaning here as in the definition for the PRINCP group. The timeout operands are defined differently and we have added a new timeout value called ACTIVTO.

The REPLYTO value for the SECNCP group specifies that the NCP will not keep elapsed time counts on this link. This prevents the link from becoming inoperative by the secondary NCP due to an error on the link from the primary NCP. The value REPLYTO=(NONE,NONE) is required when the group being defined describes a secondary mode of operation (e.g., MODE=SEC).

The same logic can be applied to the TEXTTO operand of the group SECNCP. In fact, if MODE=SEC for an SDLC subarea link group definition, then the TEXTTO value must be equal to NONE. This makes sense because the NCP in secondary mode is acting in a passive state and the primary NCP controls error recovery on the link.

The ACTIVTO operand is pertinent to the NCP in secondary mode only. It specifies the timeout value, in tenths of a second, that the secondary NCP will wait for a response from the primary NCP before entering shutdown mode. The range is from 60 to 420 seconds. The default, if ACTIVTO is not specified, is 60 seconds in a 3725 or 3720, for both MODULO 8 and MODULO 128 links. The 3705 defaults to 420 seconds. You do not want to have to go through the process of reactivating NCPs and subarea links if ACTIVTO has been reached and the secondary NCP goes into shutdown mode. Therefore, it is to your advantage to have the secondary NCP wait as long as possible for communication to be re-established by the primary NCP. Hence, we have coded the maximum value of 420.0 seconds.

6.6 GROUP, LINE AND PU DEFINITION STATEMENTS FOR SDLC SUBAREA LINKS

The LINE definition statements for an NCP SDLC subarea link are the same as those for peripheral line definitions. There are, however, three operands that are specific to an SDLC subarea link. They are the:

1. SDLCST operand.
2. MONLINK operand.
3. MODULO operand.

Figure 6.10 contains the GROUP, LINE and PU definitions for the SDLC subarea links in NCP11. For each subarea link defined, we have specified the same values for the SDLCST, MONLINK and MODULO operands on the LINE definition statement. For subarea links, the SDLCST operand on the LINE definition statement tells the NCP which SDLCST definition to use when the NCP is in

Multiple Domain Definitions for an NCP

primary or secondary mode. The first parameter specifies the name of the primary mode definitions. In this case, we have the NCP reading the parameters specified on the SDLCST statement labeled PRISTE. The second parameter tells the NCP to use the characteristics identified in the SDLCST statement defined for secondary mode. In this instance, the parameter points to the label that identifies the SDLCST definitions for secondary mode SECSTE. Using the SDLCST operand of the LINE definition statement places the link stations in a configurable state. The primary and secondary link station roles are determined during the XID between the NCP subareas. The NCP with the higher subarea number becomes the primary link station. In NCP

```
SALINKS    GROUP   LNCTL=SDLC,             SDLC IS LINE PROTOCOL         X
                   CLOCKING=EXT,           MODEMS DO CLOCKING            X
                   NRZI=NO,                NO NON-RETURN TO ZERO         X
                   PAUSE=0,                DO NOT WAIT TO POLL           X
                   SERVLIM=254,            MAXIMIZE SERVICE TO LINKS     X
                   SPEED=56000,            LINE SPEED IS 56KPS           X
                   ISTATUS=ACTIVE
SA113221   LINE    ADDRESS=(32,FULL),      SEND/RECEIVE XMIT             X
                   ATTACH=MODEM,           MODEM ATTACHES LINK           X
                   SDLCST=(PRISTE,SECSTE), PRI & SEC SDLCST              X
                   MONLINK=NO,             MONITOR FOR ACTPU             X
                   MODULO=128              USE MODULUS 128
PU2132     PU      PUTYPE=4,               PU T.4 DEVICE (NCP)           X
                   MAXOUT=127,             USE MODULUS 128               X
                   TGN=21,                 TG NUMBER FOR LINK            X
                   ANS=CONTINUE            KEEP  X-DOMAIN SESSIONS
SA113421   LINE    ADDRESS=(34,FULL),      SEND/RECEIVE XMIT             X
                   ATTACH=MODEM,           MODEM ATTACHES LINK           X
                   SDLCST=(PRISTE,SECSTE), PRI & SEC SDLCST              X
                   MONLINK=NO,             MONITOR FOR ACTPU             X
                   MODULO=128              USE MODULUS 128               X
PU2134     PU      PUTYPE=4,               PU T.4 DEVICE (NCP)           X
                   MAXOUT=127,             USE MODULES 128               X
                   TGN=21,                 tG NUMBER FOR LINK            X
                   ANS=CONTINUE            KEEP X-DOMAIN SESSIONS
SA113612   LINE    ADDRESS=(36,FULL),      SEND/RECEIVE XMIT             X
                   ATTACH=MODEM,           MODEM ATTACHES LINK           X
                   SDLCST=(PRISTE,
                   SECSTE),                PRI & SEC SDLCST              X
                   MONLINK=NO,             MONITOR FOR ACTPU             X
                   MODULO=128              USE MODULES 128
PU1236     PU      PUTYPE=4,               PU T.4 DEVICE (NCP)           X
                   MAXOUT=127,             USE MODULUS 128               X
                   TGN=21,                 TG NUMBER FOR LINK            X
                   ANS=CONTINUE            KEEP X-DOMAIN SESSIONS
```

Figure 6.10 GROUP, LINE and PU definitions for SDLC subarea links in NCP11.

V4R3/V5R2, the SDLCST operand can now specify just one of the selection table entries defined by the SDLCST definition statement. Used in this fashion, the link stations are said to be predefined. This predefined configuration will take precedence over the previously described method for determining primary and secondary link station roles. For instance, changing the SDLCST operand of line SA113421 from SDLCST=(PRISTE,SECSTE) to SDLCST=(PRISTE), in Figure 6.10, forces the XID to indicate that this link will only operate as a primary link station. This puts a requirement on the opposite link station which must either be configurable or be predefined as a secondary link station. The reverse would be true if we had coded SDLCST=(,SECSTE).

The MONLINK operand is used on subarea link definitions by the NCP to actively monitor the link address for an ACTPU command from an SSCP when the NCP is not in session with an SSCP on this link. The code in Figure 6.10 is for the channel-attached NCP11, and therefore, the SSCP-PU session is established via the channel and not the defined subarea links. For NCPs such as NCP12 in Figure 6.1, remotely loaded and activated NCPs should have MONLINK=YES specified on all their SDLC subarea links to turn the activation process around quickly. However, if NCP11 were defined to be activated by VTAM01 through NCP21, then MONLINK=YES should also be specified. The default value for MONLINK is NO if the TYPGEN operand of the BUILD definition statement is equal to NCP (channel-attached). If the TYPGEN operand of the BUILD definition statement specifies NCP-R then the MONLINK operand defaults to YES (link-attached).

The MODULO operand of the LINE definition statement specifies the use of Modulus 8 or Modulus 128. Since we stated on the SDLCST definitions that MAXOUT=127, we must code MODULO=128 to enable the NCP to handle the number of frames that the link-attached subarea can send or receive. Remember that the equivalent definition on the attached NCP must also specify MODULO=128.

The PU definitions under each subarea link define the link station in the attached NCP. PU2132 defines the characteristics of the link station for the subarea link that terminates in NCP21. The PUTYPE operand identifies the PU at the end of this link as a PU T.4 device. Again, the MAXOUT operand defines the number of frames that can be sent before a response is requested. It is best for both documentation and implementation purposes that this value match the MAXOUT value specified on the MAXOUT operand of the SDLCST definition statement.

Multiple Domain Definitions for an NCP 113

The TGN operand identifies the transmission group number assigned to the subarea link. This number is used in correlation with the PATH statements when defining explicit routes to the link-attached NCPs.

The ANS operand tells the NCP whether or not to keep active cross-domain sessions enabled if the NCP loses contact with the owning SSCP. For the most part, ANS=CONTINUE is always coded to avoid a complete session outage.

6.7 GROUP, LINE AND PU DEFINITIONS FOR MULTI-POINT SUBAREA LINKS

Suppose we reconfigure our network picture from that in Figure 6.6 to that in Figure 6.11. VTAM02, NCP21, NCP12 and L24C1 are all attached to NCP11 via a multi-point SDLC leased line.

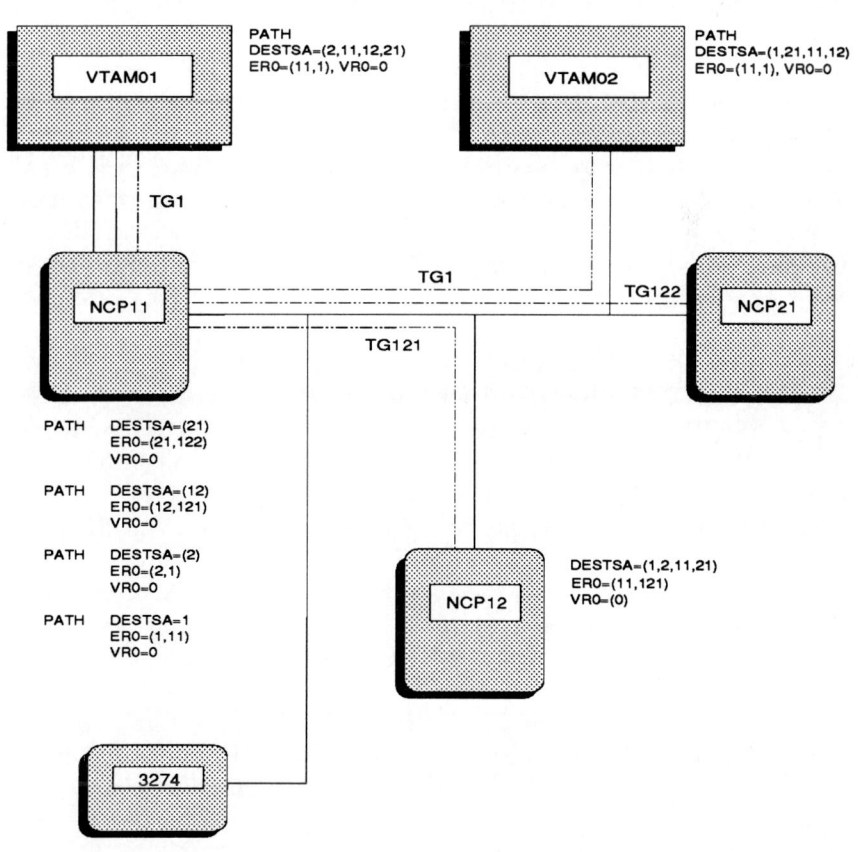

Figure 6.11 Multi-point configuration with multiple PU types.

Using the predefined configuration as described above, the primary and secondary link station roles are predetermined. There can be only one primary link station on a multi-point link and it must reside in an NCP. We have selected NCP11 as the primary link station. Note that on the multi-point link we can now mix PU types. VTAM02 is representing PU Type 5, NCP21 and NCP12 are representing PU Type 4 and L24C1 is representing PU Type 2. In this type of configuration, only the primary NCP (NCP11) may load or dump the secondary NCPs (NCP21 and NCP12). To support a multi-point subarea link, VTAM V3R2 and NCP V4R3/V5R2 are required.

Figure 6.11 shows both the physical and logical connections between the resources. Note that the connection to a PU Type 5 from NCP11 is still required to be defined as Transmission Group Number 1 (TG1). In the multi-point configuration for a subarea link, all communication must pass through the primary link station. The primary NCP acts as an intermediate routing node. In our scenario, communications between any of the subareas must pass through NCP11. This is denoted by the PATH statements included in Figure 6.11. Each of the secondary subareas must have an ER specified to the adjacent primary NCP (NCP11). So, even if VTAM02 owns resources on NCP21, all sessions (SSCP-PU, SSCP-LU, LU-LU) between VTAM02 and NCP21 resources must pass through NCP11. In fact, in order for VTAM02 to load NCP21, the path must still go through NCP11. Once this configuration is operable it remains static. That is, PU Type 4 resources cannot be dynamically added or deleted. However, PU Type 2 or Type 1 resources may be dynamically reconfigured.

In Figure 6.12, the definitions for NCP11 have been detailed. The GROUP definition statement must specify GROUP=PRI for this NCP to act as the primary link station on this multi-point link. This operand does not refer back to a previously defined SDLCST definition. For multi-point subarea links, the SDLCST definition and its corresponding SDLCST operand on the LINE definition statement is not coded. There are no special operands to a LINE definition for a multi-point subarea link. However, it is recommended that you specify FULL on the ADDRESS and DUPLEX parameters.

The SERVICE statement does not support the MAXLST operand for a multi-point subarea link. Instead, the NCP takes the default for MAXLST, which is the number of PUs defined in the service order table.

Multiple Domain Definitions for an NCP

```
NCP11 Definitions
    MPTGROUP    GROUP     MOD=PRI,LNCTL=SDLC,DIAL=NO,TYPE=NCP
    N11L24      LINE      ADDRESS=(24,FULL),DUPLEX=FULL,
                          MONLINK=YES
                SERVICE   ORDER=(L24T502,L24T421,L24T412,L24C1)
    L24T502     PU        PUTYPE=4,ADDR=02,MODULO=8,TGN=1
    L24T421     PU        PUTYPE=4,ADDR=21,MODULO=128,TGN=122
    L24T412     PU        PUTYPE=4,ADDR=12,MODULO=8,TGN=121
    L24C1       PU        PUTYPE=2,MAXDATA=265
    L24C1T00    PU        LOCADDR=2
```

Figure 6.12 NCP11 definitions for a multi-point subarea link.

In our definitions, L24T502 defines the PU for VTAM02. Note that even though this is a PU Type 5, the PUTYPE operand indicates that the PU is PU Type 4. This is because currently, only PU Type 5 hosts supporting the Integrated Communications Adapter (ICA) are supported on a multi-point link. Hosts that support the ICA are typically the IBM 9370/4300 computers. The valid values for PUTYPE in a multi-point configuration are 1, 2 and 4. In our example, we have defined one host (L24T502) PU Type 5, two NCPs (L24T421 and L24T412) PU Type 4 and one cluster controller (L24C1) PU Type 2.

The ADDR operand specifies the polling address of the PUs. In a point-to-point subarea link, the NCP issues a broadcast station address (X'FF'). Here, in a multi-point configuration, the primary NCP will issue unique polling addresses for each PU defined on the link. This is no different than multi-point polling for multi-point links that have multiple PU Type 2 devices attached.

The MODULO operand can now be coded on the PU definition statement rather than on the LINE definition statement. For NCP-NCP communication the modulus can be 8 or 128. In communication between NCP-VTAM, the modulus must be specified as 8. Communication between the primary NCP and the PU Type 2 is dependent on the PU Type 2 support for modulus 8 or 128.

The DATMODE operand of the PU definition statement is not applicable to multi-point subarea links. Full-duplex versus half-duplex data transmission is exchanged in the XID. In the NCP, the specification of ADDRESS=(nn,FULL) on the LINE definition statement sets the two-way simultaneous indicator in the XID. If the parameter is defined as ADDRESS=(nn,HALF), the NCP sets the two-way alternate indicator in the XID. The full-duplex mode

```
NCP12 Definitions
    N12MPT       GROUP      MOD=SEC,LNCTL=SDLC,DIAL=NO,TYPE=NCP
    N12L18       LINE       ADDRESS=(18,FULL),DUPLEX=FULL,
                            TADDR=12,IPL=YES
    L18T411      PU         PUTYPE=4,,MODULO=8,TGN=121
NCP21 Definitions
    N21MPT       GROUP      MOD=SEC,LNCTL=SDLC,DIAL=NO,TYPE=NCP
    N21L48       LINE       ADDRESS=(48,FULL),DUPLEX=FULL,
                            TADDR=21,IPL=YES
    L48T411      PU         PUTYPE=4,,MODULO=128,TGN=ANY
```

Figure 6.13 NCP12 and NCP21 definitions for a multi-point subarea link.

is used only if both NCPs have ADDRESS=(nn,FULL) specified. Otherwise, half-duplex is used. VTAM always sets the two-way alternate indicator. This determination of transmission modes allows for mixed modes on the multi-point subarea link (Figure 6.13).

The TGN operand specifies which tranmission group number will be used for communicating to its respective PU. In a multi-point subarea link, one line can be associated with several transmission groups. This is clearly diagrammed in Figure 6.11.

For the secondary NCPs on the multi-point subarea link, the definitions are quite similar to a normal point-to-point subarea link. In the GROUP definition statement, the MODE operand must specify SEC to indicate that the NCP will operate in secondary mode. Again, the SDLCST operand of the LINE definition statement is not coded. The key assignments are the DUPLEX and TADDR operands.

The DUPLEX operand of a secondary NCP must specify HALF. This disables the Ready-To-Send (RTS) signal on the link from this NCP. This must be done so that other PUs on the link can send to

```
VTAM02 Major Node Definitions:
                 VBUILD     TYPE=CA
    CAMPT        GROUP      LNCTL=SDLC,DIAL=NO
    V02L400      LINE       ADDRESS=400
    L40011       PU         PUTYPE=4,MAXOUT=7,SUBAREA=11,
                            TADDR=02
```

Figure 6.14 VTAM02 definitions for a multi-point subarea link.

the primary NCP when they are polled. If DUPLEX=FULL were coded, indicating that RTS is permanently on, only one of the secondary NCPs will be allowed to send, since the others will never be able to turn RTS on.

The value of the TADDR operand for this NCP must be the same as the ADDR operand of the PU definition statement in the primary NCP. Recall that the ADDR operand of the PU statement identifies the polling address of the secondary NCP. The TADDR value can range from X'00' to X'FF'.

The IPL operand of the LINE definition statement indicates to the secondary NCP that it may load or dump over the address specified in the TADDR operand. The IPL ports table in MOSS on the communications controller must have an SDLC controller address equal to the TADDR value.

In VTAM02, as shown in Figure 6.14, we must define the secondary channel adapter for the multi-point subarea link. The definition is the standard channel-attached major node definition with minor adjustments. The TADDR operand on the PU definition statement defines the polling address this VTAM will respond to when receiving a poll from the primary link station at subarea 11. VTAM is always the secondary link station on a non-switched subarea link to an NCP.

6.8 SWITCHED SUBAREA LINKS

The use of switched subarea support (Figure 6.15) provides increased connectivity between subareas in the network. The sup-

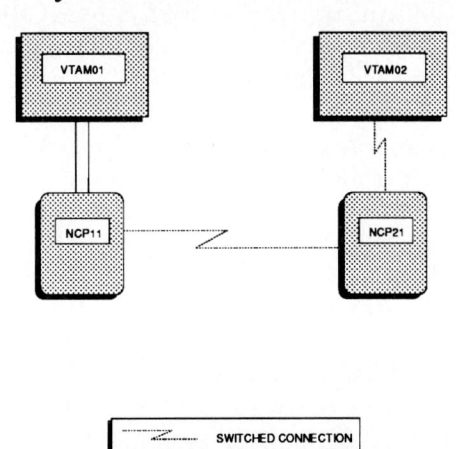

Figure 6.15 Switched subarea connectivity.

port can be used for either subarea link backup or for frequent access to other subareas. Switched subarea support allows for dial up connection between NCP-NCP, NCP-VTAM or VTAM-VTAM. Multiple switched subarea links may be combined into a single tranmission group. They can also be included with leased lines to form a multilink transmission group. These two configurations are only applicable to NCP-NCP subarea links.

To make the connection, the calling subarea node requires an Auto Calling Unit (ACU), the call cannot be manual. Once the connection is established, the primary and secondary link station modes can be determined through the XID. You can use either configurable or predefined. It is recommended that you use configurable since this gives you the most flexibility.

To define a switched subarea link, we need to code a "dummy" PU and a switched major node in VTAM. The "dummy" PU is coded in Figure 6.16 along with the other definition statements used for point-to-point subarea links. We have highlighted those parameters that pertain to the switched subarea link support. In the group labeled SALINK, the DIAL, PUTYPE and ACTIVTO parameters are highlighted. The DIAL parameter is specified as YES to indicate that the following line in this group requires switched line control procedures. The PUTYPE parameter identifies to the NCP that this group is defining a switched subarea link. It is required to be in the GROUP definition statement in order for the NCP to prepare for switched subarea support. Finally, the ACTIVTO parameter specifies the number of seconds allowed between receipt of I-frames before disconnecting the link with an error.

In the LINE definition, the ANSWER operand tells VTAM to accept dial-in PUs from this NCP. The AUTO operand specifies the address of the auto call unit in the NCP. This address must be different from the address specified for the LINE ADDRESS operand. The CALL operand indicates that incoming and outgoing calls may be made through this switched link.

The PU definition statement specifies the BRKCON operand. This operand tells the NCP how to break the connection when ACTIVTO had been reached. The default is NONE, meaning that the connection will stay alive. Two other options are CONNECTO and NOWNERTO. The CONNECTO tells the NCP to start checking for time ACTIVTO at connect time. Coding NOWNERTO starts time out activity when the owning SSCP begins automatic network shutdown (ANS).

Multiple Domain Definitions for an NCP

PRISTE	SDLCST	GROUP=PRINCP,	NCP IN PRIMARY MODE	X
		MAXOUT=7,	USING MODULO8	X
		MODE=PRI,	PRIMARY MODE	X
		PASSLIM=254,	ENSURE FULL DUPLEX	X
		SERVLIM=254	MAX SERVICE FOR INN LINK	
SECSTE	SDLCST	GROUP=SECNCP,	NCP IN SECONDARY MODE	X
		MAXOUT=7,	USING MODULO8	X
		MODE=SEC,	PRIMARY MODE	X
		PASSLIM=254,	ENSURE FULL DUPLEX	X
PRINCP	GROUP	MODE=PRI,	NCP IN PRIMARY MODE	X
		LNCTL=SDLC,	SDLC LINE CONTROL	X
		TYPE=NCP,	NETWORK CONTROL MODE	X
		DIAL=YES,	DEDICATED LINK	X
		TEXTTO=3	3 SECONDS TEXT TIME OUT	
SECNCP	GROUP	MODE=SEC,	NCP IN SECONDARY MODE	X
		LNCTL=SDLC,	SDLC LINE CONTROL	X
		TYPE=NCP,	NETWORK CONTROL MODE	X
		DIAL=YES,	DEDICATEDLINK	X
		TEXTTO=NONE,	NO TEXT TIME OUT	X
		ACTIVO=420.0,	TIME BETWEEN I-FRAMES	X
		SERVLIM=254	MAX SERVICE FOR INN LINK	
SALINK	GROUP	LNCTL=SDLC,	SDLC IS LINE PROTOCOL	X
		NRZI=NO,	NO NON-RETURN TO ZERO	X
		PAUSE=0,	DONOT WAIT TO POLL	X
		SERVLIM=254,	MAXIMIZE SERVICE FOR INN LINK	X
		SPEED=4800,	LINE SPEED IS 4800BPS	X
		DIAL=YES,	SUPPORT DIAL UP	X
		PUTYPE=4,	INDICATES SUBAREA DIAL-UP	X
		ACTIVTO=120.0,	TIME BETWEEN I-FRAMES	X
		ISTATUS=ACTIVE		
SA113221	LINE	ADDRESS=(32,HALF),	SEND/RECEIVE XMIT	X
		ATTACH=MODEM,	MODEM ATTACHES LINK	X
		SDLCST=(PRISTE,SECSTE),	PRI & SEC SDLCST	X
		MONLINK=NO,	MONITOR FOR ACTPU	X
		ANSWER=ON,	ANSWER STATE OF LINE	X
		AUTO=33,	ADDRESS OF ACU	X
		CALL=INOUT,	RECV/INIT CALLS	X
		MODULO=128	USE MODULUS 128	X
PU2132	PU	BRKCON=NONE		

Figure 6.16 Sample NCP switched subarea link definition.

A switched major node in VTAM is used to merge with the "dummy" PU definition found in the calling NCP or VTAM. The definition in Figure 6.17 is your basic switched major node. The differences are the inclusion of the PUTYPE, TGN and SUBAREA operands. These are needed to tell VTAM that this switched major node is supporting switched subarea links. This example shows the definition for a PU Type 4 dial connection by the specification of PUTYPE=4. The TGN operand indicates which transmission

```
VTAM02 Switched Major Node:
    SWNODE1      VBUILD    TYPE=SWNET
    SWNCP11      PU        PUTYPE=4,TGN=ANY,ANS=CONT,
                           NETID=NETA,IDNUM=FFE00,SUBAREA=11
                 PATH      DIALNO=201|555|1212,GID=1,PID=1,
                           GRPNM=SALINK,REDIAL=3,USE=YES
    SWVTAM2      PU        PUTYPE=5,TGN=ANY,ANS=CONT,
                           NETID=NETA,IDNUM=FFE00,SUBAREA=02
                 PATH      DIALNO=201|555|1212,GID=1,PID=1,
                           GRPNM=SALINK,REDIAL=3,USE=YES
```

Figure 6.17 Sample switched major node in VTAM for switched subarea links.

group is to be used. The specification of ANY makes this connection totally flexible in this regard. The SUBAREA operand value must match the subarea of the switched connected subarea. In this example, the calling NCP has a subarea address of 11. The PU labeled SWVTAM02 is the code for accepting a dial connection with VTAM02 in Figure 6.15.

For VTAM to perform a switched subarea link connection, it too needs a "dummy" PU definition. This type of connection is currently supported by the IBM 4361 with the Integrated Communications Adapter and the IBM 9370 with the Transmission Subsystem Controller (TSC). The definition in Figure 6.18 can be used to dial both PU Type 4 and PU Type 5 subareas. The SUBADIAL operand identifies this channel-attachment major node as supporting switched subarea links. The AUTO operand specifies the same address as the ADDRESS operand on the LINE definition statement. This is required for making outgoing calls. The function of calling is actually provided by the microcode of the ICA and the TSC. Figures 6.19, 6.20 and 6.21 provide routing charts for NCP11 and NCP12 and PATH statements for each NCP in the sample network.

```
VTAM02 "dummy" Definitions:
                 VBUILD    TYPE=CA
    SWGRP        GROUP     LNCTL=SDLC,DIAL=YES,SUBADIAL=YES
    SWLINE       LINE      ADDRESS=420,AUTO=420,CALL=INOUT,
                           ANSWER=ON
    SWDMY        PU
```

Figure 6.18 Sample "dummy" PU definition for switched subarea link in VTAM.

6.9 PATH STATEMENT UPDATES FOR A MULTI-DOMAIN NCP

The final, and probably the most confusing step, is the definition of the routes between the NCP subareas. Again we go back to that old question, "How can I get there from here?". For each row in each of the charts in Figures 6.19, 6.20 and 6.21, ask yourself the question and see if it helps you understand the path defined. Then, when you have completed that, look at Figure 6.22 for the completed PATH statements for each of the three NCPs.

It is important to remember that when defining path tables in the NCP, the order in which you define the ERs for each DESTSA denotes the hierarchical search that is performed. Note that only in NCP12 did we combine DESTSAs for the PATH statements. This is because both DESTSAs share the same primary route for the destination of the data. However, this was not true for NCP11 and NCP21. In those path tables, we defined each DESTSA with its own PATH statement. This allows for direct path selection for each destination subarea defined.

OSA	DSA	ADJSA	TG	ER	VR
11	1	1	1	0	0
		21	11	1	1
		2	1	2	2
		21	11	3	3
		1	1	4	4
		1	1	5	5
		21	11	6	6
	2	2	1	2	2
		2	1	3	3
		12	12	4	4
		21	11	1	1
		1	1	0	0
		1	1	5	5
	21	21	11	1	1
		21	11	2	2
		12	12	4	4
	12	12	12	0	0
		21	11	2	2
		12	12	3	3
		12	12	1	1

Figure 6.19 Routing chart for NCP11 paths to other subareas.

122 Advanced SNA Networking

OSA	DSA	ADJSA	TG	ER	VR
21	1	1	1	1	1
		2	1	3	3
		1	1	0	0
		11	11	4	4
		12	21	5	5
		1	1	6	6
	2	2	1	0	0
		2	1	1	1
		11	11	3	3
		2	1	4	4
		11	11	2	2
		11	11	5	5
	11	11	11	1	1
		11	11	3	3
		12	21	4	4
	12	12	21	1	1
		12	21	2	2
		11	11	3	3
		12	21	0	0

Figure 6.20 Routing chart for NCP21 paths to other subareas.

OSA	DSA	ADJSA	TG	ER	VR
12	1	11	12	5	5
		11	12	0	0
		21	21	1	1
		21	21	4	4
		11	12	6	6
	2	21	21	4	4
		11	12	2	2
		11	12	1	1
		21	21	3	3
	11	11	12	0	0
		11	12	4	4
	21	21	21	4	4

Figure 6.21 Routing chart for NCP12 paths to other subareas.

Multiple Domain Definitions for an NCP

```
NCP11:
   PATH TABLE:
         PATH1101      PATH     DESTSA=01,ER0=(1,1),ER1=(21,1),
                                ER2=(2,1),ER3=(21,11),ER4=(1,1),
                                ER5=(1,1),ER6=(21,11),VR0=0,VR2=2,
                                VR1=1,VR3=3,VR4=4,VR5=5,VR6=6
         PATH1102      PATH     DESTSA=02,ER2=(2,1),ER3=(2,1),
                                ER4=(12,21),ER1=(21,11),ER5=(1,1),
                                VR0=0,VR2=2,VR1=1,VR3=3,VR4=4,VR5=5
         PATH1121      PATH     DESTSA=21,ER1=(21,11),ER2=(21,11),
                                ER4=(12,12),VR1=1,VR2=2,VR4=4
         PATH1112      PATH     DESTSA=12,ER0=(12,12),ER2=(21,11),
                                ER3=(12,12),ER1=(12,12),VR2=2,VR1=1,VR3=3,VR0=0

NCP21:
   PATH TABLE:
         PATH2101      PATH     DESTSA=01,ER1=(1,1),ER3=(2,1),
                                ER0=(1,1),ER4=(11,11),ER5=(12,21),
                                ER6=(1,1),VR1=1,VR3=3,VR0=0,VR4=4,VR5=5,VR6=6
         PATH2102      PATH     DESTSA=02,ER0=(2,1),ER1=(2,1),
                                ER3=(11,11),ER4=(2,1),ER2=(11,11),
                                ER5=(11,11),VR2=2,VR0=0,VR3=3,VR4=4,VR1=1,VR5=5
         PATH2111      PATH     DESTSA=11,ER1=(11,11),ER3=(11,11),
                                ER4=(12,21),VR1=1,VR3=3,VR4=4
         PATH2112      PATH     DESTSA=12,ER1=(12,21),ER2=(12,21),
                                ER3=(11,11),ER0=(12,21),VR1=1,
                                VR2=2,VR3=3,VR0=0

NCP12:
   PATH TABLE:
         PATH1201      PATH     DESTSA=01,ER5=(11,12),ER0=(11,12),
                                ER1=(21,21),ER4=(21,21),ER6=(11,12),VR0=0,
                                VR1=1,VR4=4,VR5=5,VR6=6
         PATH1202      PATH     DESTSA=02,ER4=(21,21),ER2=(11,12),
                                ER1=(11,12),ER3=(21,21),VR4=4,VR2=2,VR1=1,VR3=3
         PATH1211      PATH     DESTSA=11,ER0=(11,12),ER4=(11,12),VR0=0,VR4=4
         PATH1221      PATH     DESTSA=21,ER4=(21,21),VR4=4
```

Figure 6.22 PATH statements for each NCP in the sample network.

6.10 SUMMARY

In this chapter, we detailed the necessary changes needed in an NCP to support a multi-domain configuration. We learned that a PCCU definition statement is needed in the NCP for each VTAM host that will participate in an SSCP-PU session with the NCP. We also explained the use of the SDLCST definition statement and its role in determining an NCP's characteristics when the NCP is a primary or secondary link station, and how to define these characteristics as predefined or configurable. Lastly, we explored some of the new NCP subarea link configurations using switched and multi-point connections.

Chapter

7

SNI - Single Gateway for VTAM

In the early 1980's, corporate America realized that the age of information had begun. Around the world, corporations started expanding their services to the general public and to other businesses. The dawning of the Automatic Teller Machine (ATM) is one example. For the first time, bank customers could query their accounts for balances, make transfers, and withdraw money at hundreds of locations around the country. Businesses can now verify credit cards and checks electronically for approval world wide. Point-of- Sale (POS) operations for supermarkets and department stores increase inventory tracking, augment buying patterns and provide greater price control. These services, and more, required intricate networking strategies to support hundreds of thousands of end-users world wide. Corporate America looked to expanding their markets. Networking provided the vehicle.

Coinciding with the birth of the information age came the age of acquisition. Corporate mergers and acquisitions during the early 1980's reached all time highs. Huge conglomerates increased their market holdings or ventured into new market areas for which they were not known. General Electric's acquisition of RCA is just one example. One of the priorities after merger or acquisition is to create a communications environment for the flow and exchange of information between totally independent networks. This is the function of SNI.

The principal idea is to allow each network to remain autonomous from the other(s). Minimal or no impact on the end user community is desirable. The massive network reconfiguration that is required, e.g., subarea addressing, duplicate network resource names and application names, is reduced to a finite set of communications operands for VTAM and the NCP.

7.1 INTERCONNECTION CONSIDERATIONS

The tasks involved in merging two or more independent networks into one large network may seem immeasurable. The coordination of naming conventions, user ids, application names, addressing and security, not to mention the new network connectivity configuration, creates a project of monumental proportions that may take years to accomplish. The use of SNI helps reduce the risks and time frames involved in merging these networks by providing a gateway to the other networks.

This gateway is a combination of hardware and software that provides SSCP rerouting, address translation and name translation between independent networks' communications with each other under SNA. This communication between independent SNA networks is called cross-network communications. Cross-network communications, therefore, provides the means for cross-network sessions.

The level of software that is needed to provide this gateway capability is critical. VTAM must be at V2R2 or later and the NCP must be at V3 or later. When VTAM is providing SNI functions it is known as the gateway VTAM, gateway SSCP or gateway host. All are synonymous. The NCP is known simply as the gateway NCP.

The gateway VTAM provides the routing of initiation and termination requests for cross-network sessions, session outage notification and network takedown. When the gateway SSCP is in session with the gateway NCP, the two work together to provide network name translation and alias network addressing. The gateway NCP must be channel-attached or link-attached to the gateway SSCP and have an active session with the gateway SSCP.

The use of SNI has created two more terms that need definition. Native and non-native network resources. Native network resources are those resources that are attached to the gateway NCP and are defined by that NCP as resources of that NCP. Non-native network resources are resources of any network attached to the

SNI - Single Gateway for VTAM 127

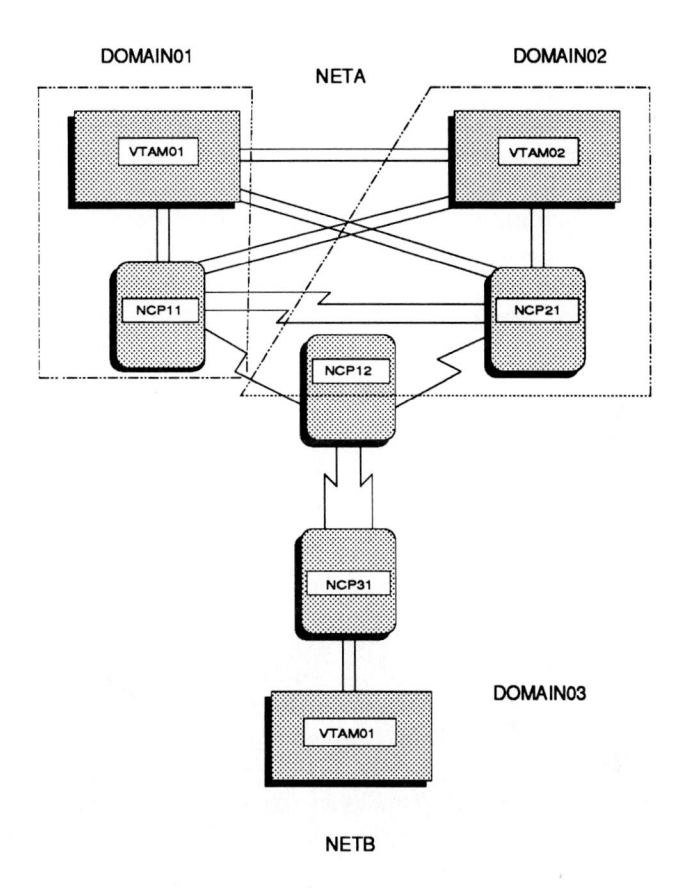

Figure 7.1 SNI sample configuration.

gateway NCP but they are not defined to that gateway NCP. Look at Figure 7.1. NETA is comprised of DOMAIN01 and DOMAIN02. The resources that reside off of NCP12 are native network resources. NETB has one domain DOMAIN03. The resources of DOMAIN03 are considered non-native network resources to NCP12 and NETA.

7.1.1 Determine Gateway Location

The actual location of the gateway is twofold. A gateway consists of a VTAM gateway and an NCP gateway. The minimum software levels for the gateway must be adhered to. VTAM must be at V2R2 or later for MVS and VSE operating systems and VTAM V3R1.1 for VM operating systems. The NCP levels must be at NCP V3 or later for compatibility with the SNI facility support with VTAM. So the software levels of your network must be reviewed. Next, the physical location of the gateways must be determined. One approach is to review performance statistics on the VTAM hosts that are possible candidates for supporting the host gateway function. Is it important to you, management or the end-users to have the cross-network session set up as quickly as possible or can the initial session setup take longer than the accepted average response time? If quick response to session setup is important, then select a host that is not burdened with a large end-user base for interactive applications. Likewise with the NCP. Select an NCP whose transaction volume is suitable for managing SNI sessions.

There is another factor in the selection of the NCP gateway and that is money. Management may not opt for your request of a new communications controller to support SNI. Not that a new FEP is necessary to support SNI, but if your performance data indicates that SNI sessions may be hindered by flowing through FEPs that are processing at peak performance levels daily, you may want to offload some of this volume to a new FEP. However, in many companies the bottom line is the final decision maker. In our scenario, NCP12 is selected as the gateway NCP. Since, gateway NCPs connect to the other network's NCP, telecommunications links must be acquired. In this example, the communication links are seen by management as a more cost effective solution to interconnect the two networks. For our scenario, VTAM02 is the gateway VTAM and NCP12 will act as the gateway NCP.

7.1.2 Establish Physical Connectivity

As was previously stated, the interconnection of SNA networks requires a minimum of one telecommunications link to an FEP of the non-native network. The speed of the links is optional. All speeds supported by the IBM 37x5 communications controller are supported for SNI links. The only restriction is that the protocol for the link must be SDLC. In our example, we will be coding two 56 kilobits per second links between the gateway NCP and the non-gateway NCP of NETB. Figure 7.2 diagrams this configuration for a single-gateway configuration.

SNI - Single Gateway for VTAM   129

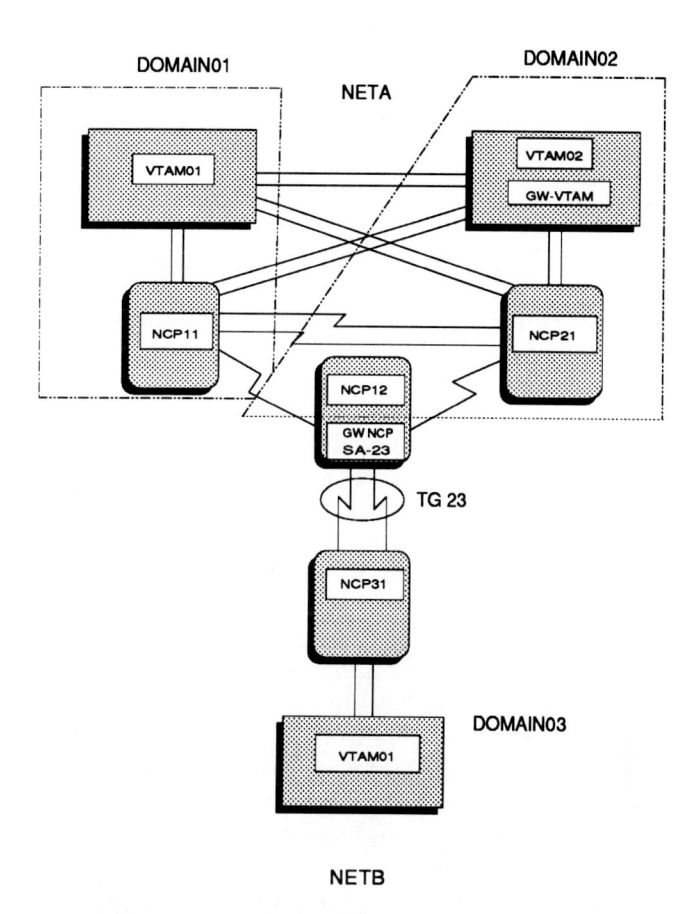

Figure 7.2 Single-gateway configuration.

7.1.3 Assign Gateway NCP Subarea

The non-native interconnected network, NETB, must assign a subarea to the gateway NCP that resides in the native network, NETA. Before assigning a subarea address, determine an available subarea address in NETB. Even if ENA is being used in NETB, the gateway NCP subarea address must be unique within NETB's network. In Figure 7.2 you can see that we have assigned subarea 23 to the gateway NCP. This is the subarea address that NETB will use to interface to NETA. The element addresses assigned in this subarea will represent cross-network resources. NETA, however, need not assign a new subarea address for the gateway NCP since only the NCP's function is changing and not its addressing. NETA will still address NCP12 with subarea 12. Subarea 12 will also be the subarea address used by NETA for resources in NETB. The gateway NCP is logical and resides in both networks.

7.1.4 Define Gateway to VTAM

Definitions on both the gateway and non-gateway VTAMs must be coded. The SSCPID parameter in the ATCSTR00 start list options for both gateway and non-gateway VTAMs in the native and non-native networks must be unique. This includes uniqueness throughout all interconnected networks. The SSCPNAME is required by all gateway VTAMs. Like the SSCPID, the SSCPNAME must be unique from any VTAM that is to have a session with the gateway VTAM. Prior to VTAM V3R2, this parameter of the start options list is optional for non-gateway VTAMs. However, it is highly recommended because it assists in identifying resource ownership and aids in debugging problems. Common to both VTAMs, a new CDRM statement that defines the cross-domain manager of the interconnecting network must be defined in a CDRM major node and specified in the ADJSSCP table. However, if you use CDRSCs, then the CDRSC name must be unique in both networks. Unlike resource names, logon mode table entries and class of service table entries must have corresponding names in the interconnected networks. The final addition to the non-gateway VTAM in NETB is a new PATH statement for providing the logical connection to NCP23 the gateway NCP. The gateway VTAM in NETA does not need a new path coded since it will be relating all NETB resources to NCP12.

Specific to the gateway VTAM are the additional parameters and definition statements that enable the SNI function. In the start options list, the NETID and SSCPNAME options must be coded for a gateway VTAM. In the gateway VTAM CDRM definitions, a NETWORK definition statement precedes the cross-network CDRM definition statement for NETB. We will discuss these statements in greater detail in Section 7.2 of this chapter.

7.1.5 Define Gateway to NCP

Non-gateway NCPs that are the interconnection point for a network are defined as if they are connecting to a host in the same network. In Figure 7.2 the non-gateway NCP, NCP31 in NETB, defines a link to NETA as an MSNF link. Remember that MSNF links are communication lines that connect two FEPs in the same network but of different domains. For example, the two links between NCP11 and NCP21 of NETA are MSNF links connecting DOMAIN01 and DOMAIN02 of NETA. However, in SNI, a link between two independent networks is referred to as an SNI link. A new link must be defined from the non-gateway NCP NCP31, a GROUP macro is needed to define the SNI link. Each SNI link defined must have a corresponding LINE, SERVICE and PU macro specified.

Since the link is being defined as if it were connecting to another host in NETB, a new PATH statement that defines the ER to use to route information to the gateway NCP NCP12 in NETA must be added to NCP31.

One final note on the non-gateway NCP, NCP31. The BUILD macro has two operands that may be affected by the SNI link. The NUMHSAS and the VRPOOL operands. The NUMHSAS defines to the non-gateway NCP the number of host and NCP subareas that have VRs ending in this NCP. The VRPOOL operand should have a value that equals the number of VRs that end in this NCP. We will discuss the implications of these operands in the later sections of this chapter.

Updating the non-gateway NCP, NCP31, is not out of the ordinary when connecting to a new host via an MSNF link. However, the gateway NCP, NCP12, must have specific SNI macros and operands in order for it to function as a gateway. Existing macros, PCCU, BUILD, HOST and the PU macros of the SNI line definition, all have new operands that must be added to define SNI.

The PCCU macro has two new operands that must be added. They are the network identification operand, NETID, and the gateway control operand, GWCTL. You will notice that the NETID operand is used on many of the other macros as we define the gateway.

The BUILD macro has two operands that must be added, two operands that are optional, and two operands that may need updating. The NETID operand and the half-session block pool operand, HSBPOOL, must be added to the BUILD macro. The class of service table operand, COSTAB, and the channel-attached network identifier operand, CANETID, are optional. Additional optional operands that may affect the resources of the gateway NCP are the NETLIM, SESSLIM. One other small but important operand of the BUILD macro is the virtual route activate operand, VRACT. You will read later that the gateway NCP has the ability to activate VRs in the non-native network. Finally, as with the non-gateway NCP, NCP31, the NUMHSAS and VRPOOL operand values should be reviewed.

The HOST macro and the PU macro of the SNI line definition in the gateway NCP NCP12 should have the NETID operand defined.

All of the above mentioned operands define SNI capabilities to the gateway NCP. These definitions are aimed at the native network NETA. The following additional macros and operands define what we call the pseudo-SSCP that resides in the gateway NCP. The one exception is the GWNAU macro.

The gateway network addressable unit macro, GWNAU, is used in three instances in the gateway NCP. The first use is to reserve a pool of element addresses that will be used by NETA for NETB resources. These addresses can be referred to as alias addresses. For this use, the GWNAU is positional and must follow the SYSCNTRL macro in the NCP source. The second use for the GWNAU macro is to assign an alias address for the gateway VTAM. This is the address that will be used by the non-native network in NETB. This GWNAU macro must follow the NETWORK macro. Thirdly, the GWNAU macro is coded again following the GWNAU macro for the gateway host. This time it is used to define alias element addresses that will be used by NETB to address resources in NETA.

The NETWORK macro is used in the gateway NCP to define the actual gateway NCP subarea. The macro must follow all of the native network resource definitions. It is important to remember that the gateway NCP functions as a pseudo-SSCP. The gateway NCP assists the gateway host in element addressing, session set up and activation of virtual routes.

Keeping in mind that a gateway NCP has some of the functions of a PU-TYPE5, additional PATH statements are coded prior to the GENEND macro in the NCP source just after the last GWNAU macro definition. These PATH statements differ from the normal NCP PATH statements in that they also define virtual routes. This is a requirement for a gateway NCP. These PATH statements define the cross-network paths that may be used by the gateway NCP for session setup. The virtual routes supplied in the path statements are used in the order mapped by the class of service table defined on the NCP NETWORK defintion statement.

7.1.6 Network Autonomy

One of the key concerns for network interconnection for the communications systems programmer is the duplication of network resource names. SNA requires that all network resource names be unique. In an SNI configuration, the resource names of logical units and other network resources frequently have the same names assigned to them in both independent networks. Attempts at establishing a cross-network session by one of these LUs will fail due to duplicate LU names in the network. The LU that establishes the session first will lock out the other LU, preventing it from establishing a session until the established session is released.

There is, however, a question that remains to be asked. Does SNI truly provide autonomy between the interconnected SNA networks? To answer this question we need to view the interconnection from different perspectives.

From the point of view of the end-user, establishing a session with an application in the non-native network starts at the entry into the network. A new USS command will be entered to notify VTAM of the end-user's request to establish a session with an application in the interconnected network. Once the session has been established, the end-user can access the application just as he/she would in his/her own network. So, from where the end-user stands, access to the interconnected network is simplistic. That simplicity for the end-user is, of course, one of the objectives of using SNI. But, is that session establishment as simple as entering a new USS command? Let's look at the other side of the story.

Somehow, transparently to the end-user, the correct information of the end-user's request must be passed to the destination logical unit. The destination logical unit in the previous example is an application. The originating logical unit has an LUname of LS320T02. Prior to any SNI connectivity, the communications systems programmer must review the naming conventions of the interconnected networks to identify any duplicate resource names. The OLU LS320T02 just happens to be a valid LU name on the native and non-native networks. To circumvent duplicate resource names, VTAM has an alias name translation facility. An IBM-supplied application for alias name translation is provided by the Network Control Command Facility (NCCF). The alias name translation facility allows the gateway VTAM to assign alias resource names to all resources in the SNI configuration. Let's look at the session request further.

Along with the request for the application, the logon mode table entry and a class of service table entry is passed to the DLU's VTAM. These table entries must be present in the DLU's host or the session request will fail. Here again, research must be performed to determine if the entry names already exist or if alias names must be assigned to provide existing names in the DLU's VTAM logon mode table and class of service tables.

More complications arise for applications that use LUnames. For instance, CICS has a Terminal Control Table (TCT) that defines all of the terminals and printers that can access the CICS region. In interconnecting networks, this table may grow to incredible proportions due to the additional alias LUnames that are needed to allow the interconnected resources access to the CICS region. The same holds true for other applications such as VTAM printing subsystems and RJE applications that directly access LUs by their network names.

As you can see, network autonomy is not as simple as it appears to be. Extensive research into the interconnected networks' compositions is required. Analysis of cross-network session requirements will help in determining the extent of keeping each network independent from the other as much as possible. You may be thinking that this doesn't appear to be creating truly independent networks, but there is always a price for freedom.

7.2 SINGLE GATEWAY DEFINITION FOR VTAM

A single gateway provides connectivity between two or more SNA networks by means of one gateway NCP. Figure 7.3 is a sample single-gateway configuration. This figure illustrates the effective changes that are described in the following sections. Contrast Figure 7.3 to Figure 7.1 to compare the changes.

In our sample configuration in Figure 7.3, two independent networks will communicate using SNI. NETA will be referred to as the native network. NETA is comprised of DOMAIN01 and DOMAIN02. The gateway VTAM is located in DOMAIN02 of NETA. The gateway NCP for the configuration is NCP12. This gateway NCP is link-attached to the gateway VTAM via NCP21 of DOMAIN02 or NCP11 of DOMAIN01. NETA will be referred to as the native network. The interconnected network is NETB. It is comprised of a single domain labeled DOMAIN03. The two networks are connected via two SNI links of 56Kbps. The links are physically connected between NETB's NCP31 and NETA's NCP12. The gateway NCP subarea address assigned in NCP12 is subarea 23. Logically, this subarea resides in NETB DOMAIN03.

SNI - Single Gateway for VTAM   135

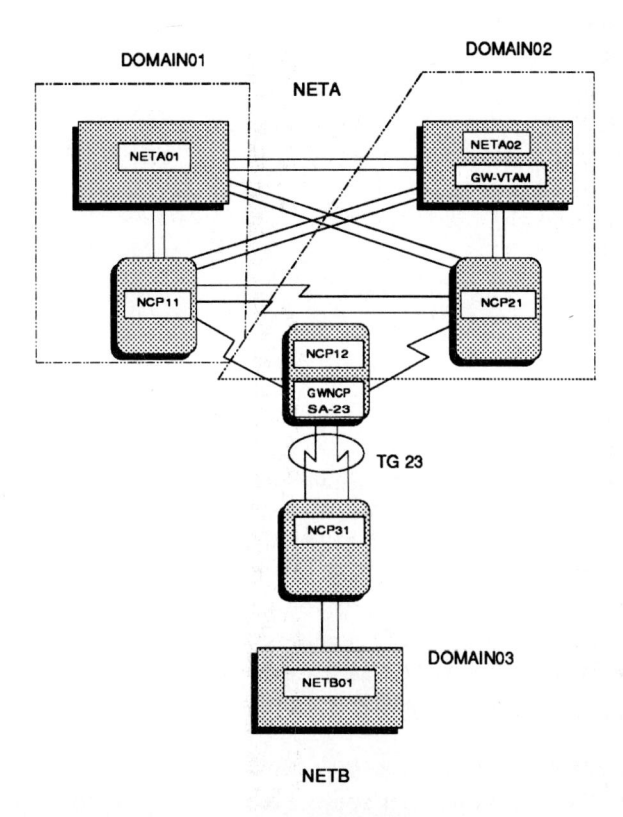

Figure 7.3 SNI gateway configuration used for text example.

7.2.1 Non-Gateway VTAM Definition

As discussed in the previous section of this chapter, updates to the ATCSTR00 start options list in VTAMLST are advisable as long as the VTAM level is V2R2 or later. The start options list in VTAM01 of DOMAIN03 in NETB will be coded as shown in Figure 7.4.

```
MAJOR NODE:      ATCSTR00
                 MODIFICATIONS:    SSCPID=03
                 ADDITIONS:        SSCPNAME=NETB01,
                                   NETID=NETB,
                                   HOSTPU=NETBPU01
```

Figure 7.4 ATCSTR00 updates for the non-gateway VTAM of DOMAIN03 in NETB.

136 Advanced SNA Networking

```
MAJOR NODE: NETBCDRM
            NETBCDRM   VBUILD     TYPE=CDRM
                       NETWORK    NETID=NETB
            NETB01     CDRM       SUBAREA=01,CDRYN=YES,      X
                                  CDRSC=OPT, ELEMENT=1,      X
                                  ISTATUS=ACTIVE
                       NETWORK    NETID=NETA
            NETA02     CDRM       SUBAREA=23,CDRYN=YES,      X
                                  CDRSC=OPT,ELEMENT=1,       X
                                  ISTATUS=INACTIVE
```

Figure 7.5 The CDRM Major Node for the non-gateway VTAM in DOMAIN03 of NETB.

After reviewing the start options list, the SSCPID option was changed to 03 so that it is unique throughout the interconnected networks. The additions to the start options list are not required, but they supply meaningful names that will prove useful for debugging and tracing sessions between the networks.

A CDRM Major Node in VTAM01 of DOMAIN03 in NETB must be created and have the CDRM name of the gateway VTAM defined. Figure 7.5 depicts the major node for this non-gateway VTAM.

The coding of the CDRM Major Node for the SNI connection is very similar to the standard coding for MSNF. Both CDRMs support dynamic allocation of CDRSCs, eliminating the need to code CDRSC definitions for terminals and printers that reside in NETB. The important difference in this CDRM definition is the subarea operand for the gateway VTAM CDRM definition. Notice that the subarea number is not the true location of the gateway VTAM. As you can see from Figure 7.3, the actual subarea address for the gateway VTAM is 02. The subarea address of 23 is coded in the non-gateway VTAM because in the gateway NCP definitions, NETB will address NETA by using the CDRM name of NETA02 with the subarea address 23. The subarea address of the gateway NCP is the alias network address for the CDRM in the gateway VTAM of NETA.

At this point in the definitions of the non-gateway VTAM in NETB, the only CDRM that is known to NETB for cross-network session establishment is NETA02. However, NETA has a second domain with applications that end users of NETB may need to access. To take full advantage of SNI, it behooves us to use the ADJSSCP table in the non-gateway VTAM. Although the table

```
MAJOR NODE:   ADJSSCPB
              ADJSSCPB    VBUILD      TYPE=ADJSSCP
                          NETWORK     NETID=NETA
              NETA02      ADJCDRM
```

Figure 7.6 The ADJSSCP Major Node for the non-gateway VTAM in DOMAIN03 of NETB.

itself will presently have one entry, its importance is seen during cross-network session establishment. Figure 7.6 shows the ADJSSCP table that is coded for VTAM01 in DOMAIN03 of NETB.

The final update needed for the non-gateway VTAM in NETB is the addition of a PATH statement. This PATH statement defines the route NETB01 will use to communicate to the gateway VTAM in NETA. Figure 7.7 shows the new PATH table for the non-gateway VTAM in NETB.

The PATH table defines the route to the gateway VTAM from VTAM01 in NETB. Either ER0 or ER1 can be used by the non-gateway VTAM. The explicit routes are mapped to VR0 and VR1 respectively. Note that the only destination subarea for the interconnected network from NETB is the gateway subarea 23. This is because the destination of all resources outside of the control of NETB is the SNI gateway.

7.2.2 Gateway VTAM Definition

The definitions for the gateway VTAM in DOMAIN02 of NETA are more involved than the definitions for the non-gateway VTAM.

```
TABLE:    PATHSNI
          PATH          DESTA=(31,23),        X
                        ER0=(31,1),           X
                        ER1=(31,1),           X
                        VR0=0,                X
                        VR1=1
```

Figure 7.7 The PATH table for the non-gateway VTAM in DOMAIN03 of NETB.

138 Advanced SNA Networking

```
SSCPID=2,                                                *
IOBUF=(32,256,4,F,16,8),                                 *
CONFIG=01,CSALIMIT=512,CSA24=0,HOSTPU=VTAM01,            *
HOSTSA=01,ITLIM=0,PPOLOG=YES,PROMPT,                     *
TNSTAT,CNSL,TIME=60
```

Figure 7.8 ATCSTR00 for VTAM01 in NETA.

Let's review the start options list that is already coded for VTAM02 in DOMAIN02 of NETA.

In Figure 7.8 is the current ATCSTR00 start options list for VTAM01 NETA. The start options list for VTAM02 is identical except for the HOSTSA and HOSTPU options. VTAM02 has HOSTSA=02 and HOSTPU=VTAM02. A quick glance at the options tells us that some chosen naming conventions should be changed for SNI. The naming convention for the SSCPNAME and HOSTPU options should be more descriptive of the owning network and the subarea address for this VTAM. Figure 7.9 shows the three options that have been updated for SNI.

The changes made to the start options list for the gateway VTAM in NETA follow the naming convention that was chosen for the non-gateway VTAM in NETB. These names can now indicate to the network operator which network is in control of a resource and which SSCP in the controlling network owns the resource. To follow up on this change in naming conventions, a similar change is made to VTAM01 in DOMAIN01 of NETA. Figure 7.10 shows the updated version of the ATCSTR00 start options list for the non-gateway VTAM in DOMAIN01 NETA. Note that these changes are practically identical to the updates for VTAM01 in DOMAIN03 NETB. The only difference is the network identifier key of "A".

Next in line for updating are the CDRM Major Nodes. Since we have elected to change the naming convention for the SSCPNAME,

```
MAJOR NODE:        ATCSTR00
MODIFICATIONS:     SSCPNAME=NETA02
                   NETID=NETA,
                   HOSTPU=NETAPU02
```

Figure 7.9 ATCSTR00 updates for the gateway VTAM of DOMAIN02 in NETA.

```
MAJOR NODE:     ATCSTR00
MODIFICATIONS:  SSCPNAME=NETA01
                NETID=NETA,
                HOSTPU=NETAPU01
```

Figure 7.10 ATCSTR00 updates for the non-gateway VTAM of DOMAIN01 in NETA.

it is advisable to follow suit by changing the CDRM names. Figure 7.11 contains the updated version of the CDRM Major Nodes for the existing VTAMLSTs in VTAM02 DOMAIN02 NETA and VTAM01 DOMAIN01 NETA. These changes would not be made if we choose to keep the old naming convention. But, we think you will agree that following the new naming convention will lead to less confusion.

For the gateway VTAM, one more CDRM Major Node must be defined. This CDRM Major Node defines the non-native network CDRM to the gateway VTAM in NETA. Here we introduce the use of the NETWORK and GWPATH definition statements.

Figure 7.12, the NETWORK statement, precedes any CDRM definition statements. All CDRM definition statements that follow a NETWORK statement are said to be residing in the network that is identified by the NETWORK statement. This is true until another NETWORK statement is encountered in the major node definition. In our example, there is only one NETWORK statement and the CDRM defined under it resides in that network. Note that the only change in defining a CDRM for an SNI gateway is the omission of the SUBAREA operand. It is optional for a cross-network CDRM. The CDRM is located by the GWPATH statement.

```
MAJOR NODE:     CDRM01
                CDRM01      VBUILD    TYPE=CDRM
                NETA01      CDRM      CDRDYN=YES,CDRSC=OPT,
                                      SUBAREA=1,ISTATUS=ACTIVE
MAJOR NODE:     CDRM02
                CDRM02      VBUILD    TYPE=CDRM
                NETA02      CDRM      CDRDYN=YES,CDRSC=OPT,
                                      SUBAREA=2,ISTATUS=ACTIVE
```

Figure 7.11 The CDRM Major Nodes for the non-gateway VTAM and gateway VTAM in NETA.

```
MAJOR NODE: CDRMB1
            CDRMB1      VBUILD      TYPE=CDRM
            NETB        NETWORK     NETID=NETB
            NETB01      CDRM        CDRDYN=YES,CDRSC=OPT,
                                    ISTATUS=INACTIVE
                        GWPATH      SUBAREA=12,                 X
                                    ADJNET=NETB,                X
                                    ADJNETSA=1,                 X
                                    ADJNETEL=1
```

Figure 7.12 The CDRM Major Node that defines the non-gateway VTAM of NETB to the gateway VTAM of NETA.

The GWPATH statement follows each cross-network CDRM definition. There may be more than one GWPATH to a cross-network CDRM. The gateway path statement defines the NCP this gateway VTAM is to use as the gateway NCP for cross-network sessions that concern this cross-network CDRM. The SUBAREA operand of the GWPATH statement defines the subarea of the gateway NCP to use for cross-network sessions. Another operand, GWN, the gateway name operand, can also be used for this purpose. This operand supplies the name of the gateway NCP rather than the subarea of the gateway NCP. We chose the SUBAREA operand because in most shops the NCP name changes frequently and the use of the GWN operand would require an update any time a new gateway NCP has been generated. The ADJNET operand defines the network identifier for the adjacent network to use for cross-network sessions. This operand should match the NETID operand of the NETWORK statement. The real subarea address and network element address of the cross-network CDRM, as it is known in its own network, are defined by the ADJNETSA operand and the ADJNETEL operand, respectively.

Now that we have defined the cross-network CDRM, the adjacent SSCP table in NETB02 must be reviewed. The cross-network CDRM should be added to the table to allow full dynamic resource allocation for cross-network sessions. The CDRM name for the cross-network CDRM is added to the ADJSSCP list. See Figure 7.13. A NETWORK statement may be added to the list, but, it is used only when the NETID of the resource is known. In our example, all network resource allocation is dynamic. Therefore, no CDRSC Major Nodes have been defined, so, owning CDRMs and NETIDs are unknown.

```
MAJOR NODE:       ADJSSCP2
MODIFICATIONS:    ADJSSCP2    VBUILD      TYPE=ADJSSCP
                  NETA01      ADJCDRM
                  NETB01      ADJCDRM
```

Figure 7.13 The ADJSSCP table for the gateway VTAM in NETA.

Notice that we have also updated the CDRM name for the ADJCDRM for the non-gateway VTAM in DOMAIN01 NETA. The ADJSSCP table in VTAM01 DOMAIN01 NETA must also reflect the new CDRM name for the gateway VTAM in DOMAIN02 NETA. However, the cross-network CDRM is not included in the table because the gateway VTAM, NETA02, will reroute requests to NETB01 on behalf of NETA01. The routes for both VTAMs in NETA do not change. They remain the same since they are already defined to route to the gateway NCP at subarea 12.

7.2.3 Alias Name Translation

During session establishment between LUs, three pieces of data are passed between the interconnected networks. The LU name, the COS entry, and the MODE entry names. The LU name must be unique or the potential to lock out a native network resource exists. However, the COS and MODE entries for the logon must be found on the DLU's VTAM. In the first instance we must create an alias name. For the second instance, we must create a real name that is found in the COS and MODE tables of the DLU's VTAM.

Figure 7.14 diagrams the use of the alias name translation table. All translations will be performed at VTAM NETA02. The Network Control Command Facility or NetView must be available to use the alias name translation facility. To use the facility, an APPL definition statement must be defined as follows for VTAM NETA02:

```
ALIASAPL   APPL AUTH=CNM
```

Consult the NCCF or NetView IBM manuals for a full description of this APPL statement. A member named DSIDMN in the NCCF initialization parameter library must have a TASK statement coded as follows:

```
TASK MOD=DSIZDST, TSKID=ALIASAPL,MEM=ALIASNETA,
INIT=Y, PRI=1
```

142 Advanced SNA Networking

ALIAS NAME TRANSLATION

ORIGNET NETB
LU LS320T02,NETA,AS320T02
COS INTERACT,NETA,ONLINE
MODE S3270X,NETA,LS3270
ORIGNET NETA
LU LS320T02,NETB,BS320T02
COS ONLINE,NETB,INTERACT
MODE LS3270,NETB,S3270X

CROSS-NETWORK LUNAME TRANSMITTED TO NETB01 IS AS320T02.

CROSS-NETWORK COS ENTRY TRANSMITTED TO NETB01 IS ONLINE.

CROSS-NETWORK LOGON MODE ENTRY IS LS3270.

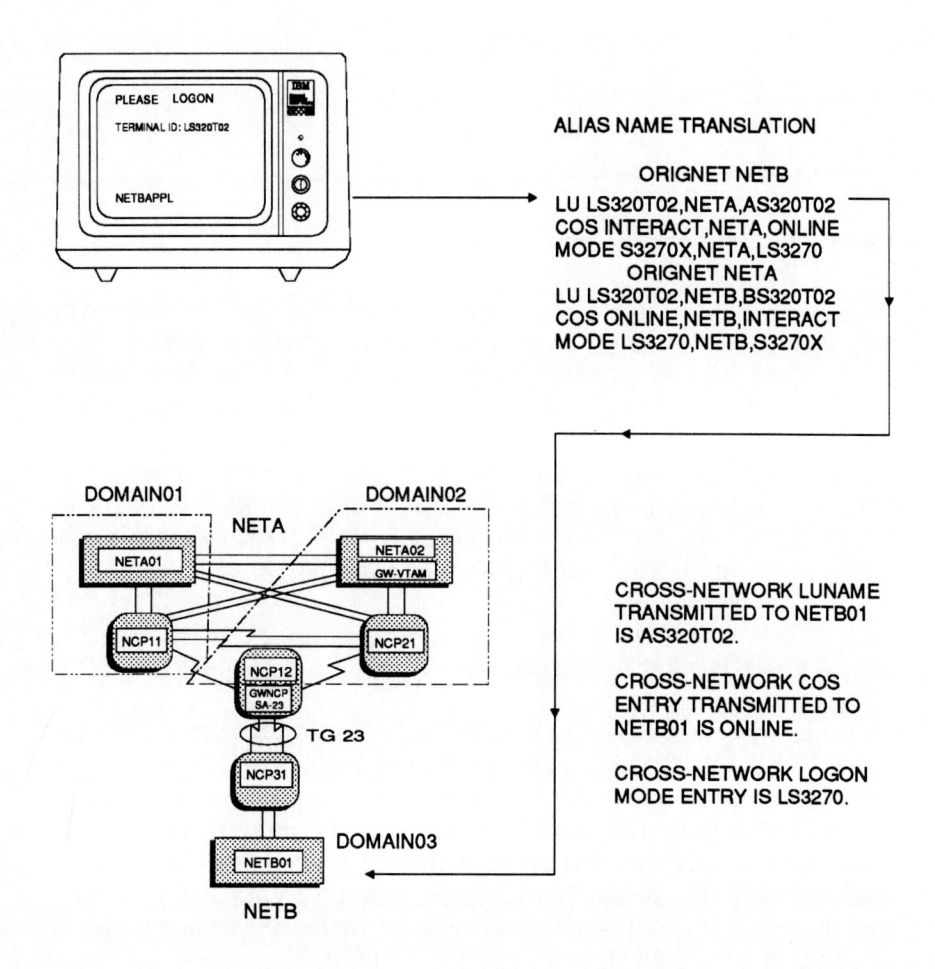

Figure 7.14 Using alias name translation in SNI.

The MEM operand defines the name of the member that contains the Data Services Task initialization (DSTINIT) parameters and the ALIASMEM statement. The ALIASMEM statement identifies the name of the alias name translation table. These statements are coded as follows:

```
ALIAS DSTINIT FUNCT=CNMI, UNSOL=DSIACNMP, DSIAINIT
ALIASMEM ANTLST02
```

The table specified on the ALIASMEM statement is the core of the alias name translation facility. Let's analyze Figure 7.14 to understand just how this facility works.

From Figure 7.14 we can determine the alias names used in both networks. Prior to establishing a requested LU-LU cross-network session, the gateway VTAM, NETA02, determines if an alias name translation facility exists. The gateway VTAM examines the originating LU (OLU) name for possible translation in the translation table. In our example, LU LS320T02 in NETA is requesting a cross-network session with an application in NETB. The gateway VTAM, NETA02, determines the COS and MODE table entries from the parameters coded for this LU definition. In this case, the MODE entry is S32702X. This is the name defined on the DLOGMOD operand of the LU definition statement. From the MODE entry, the COS entry name INTERACT is determined from the COS operand of the MODEENT macro in the logon mode table.

Viewing the translation table, the gateway VTAM, NETA02, determines which ORIGNET statement to use by analyzing the destination network. NETB is the destination for the request, so NETB must be supplied with alias names. While scanning the table, the gateway VTAM matches the LU name with an entry in the table. This name is then propagated to the destination network for a session request. The gateway VTAM then establishes the cross-network session using the alias LU name. The COS and MODE table entry alias name translation outcome is, in fact, the opposite of an LU name. Instead of creating an alias name in the destination network, the object of the translation is to provide an existing COS and MODE table entry name. The translation table is searched for the requested COS and MODE table entry names and assigned an alias that matches a table entry in the destination network.

The same logic holds for cross-network session requests from NETB to NETA. This is because NETA performs all cross-network session establishment requests. Instead of using the ORIGNET NETB table, the ORIGNET NETA table is shown in Figure 7.15.

ORIGNET	netid alias is known
LU	real name, native netid, alias name
MODE	real name, native netid, alias name
COS	real name, native netid, alias name

Figure 7.15 The alias name translation table format.

The ORIGNET statement supplies the *netid* of the non-native network that will use the *alias name* for the cross-network LU, COS or MODE real names. The *real name* is the name found in the requesting VTAM's network. The *native netid* is the network identifier of the *real name*'s owning network. The *alias name* is the name that the ORIGNET will know the *real name* by.

In following chapters you will see how the translation table can grow when more than two independent networks interconnect using SNI.

7.3 SUMMARY

In this chapter we reviewed the need of businesses to interconnect independent SNA networks. We discussed the process of determining the effectiveness of SNI and the considerations that need attention when implementing an SNI network. We also detailed the definitions necessary in VTAM and the NCP for identifying a gateway VTAM and a gateway NCP. The next chapter takes the concepts learned here and expands them for a single SNI gateway configuration.

Chapter

8

SNI - Single Gateway for NCP

As we discussed in Chapter 7, changes to the non-gateway and gateway NCPs are appropriate under certain circumstances. We will analyze the native and non-native networks to determine if any updates are necessary.

8.1 NON-GATEWAY NCP DEFINITION

The example single gateway diagram in Figure 8.1 shows one gateway NCP, NCP12, and three non-gateway NCPs. The native network contains non-gateways NCP11 and NCP21. The non-native network contains the non-gateway NCP31.

Since the non-gateway NCPs in NETA are not directly involved in providing SNI capabilities, there are no updates to consider. The BUILD statement operands of NUMHSAS and VRPOOL are not affected because no new host connections and or virtual routes end in these NCPs. The PATH table for each NCP also goes unaltered because NETA addresses all NETB cross-network resources through the same PATHs that exist for routing to NCP12 from both NCP11 and NCP21. However, NCP31 in NETB has updates that can directly affect SNI.

In NCP31, the BUILD macro operands NUMHSAS and VRPOOL must be increased. Currently, the value for the NUMHSAS is set to 1. This means that only one subarea has virtual routes that end in this NCP. With the inception of SNI, NCP31 now has a connection

145

146 Advanced SNA Networking

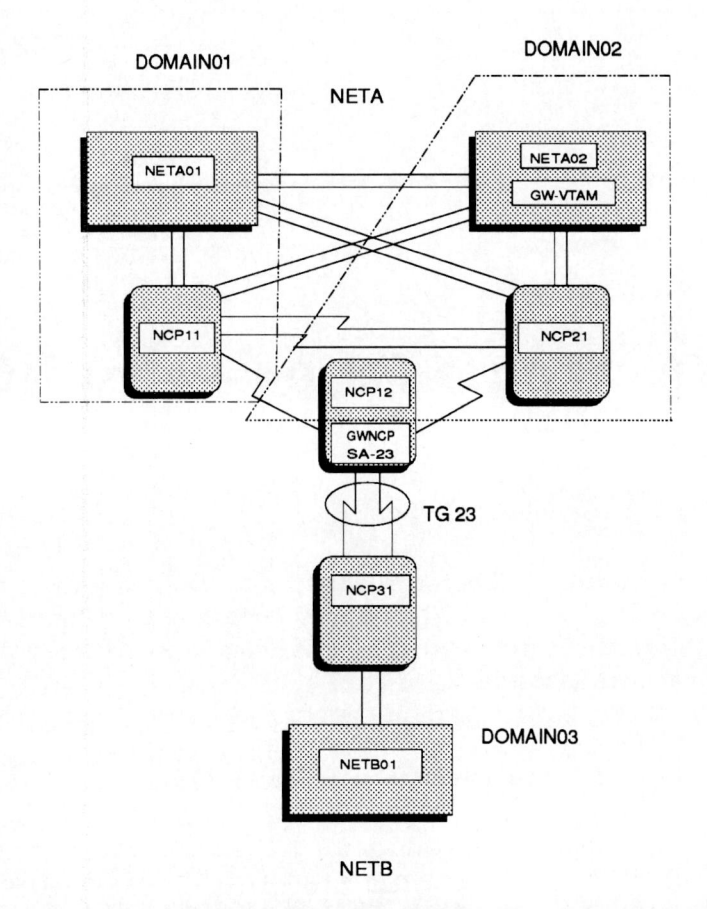

Figure 8.1 Single-gateway configuration for NCP.

to the gateway NCP. Gateway NCPs contain virtual routes, therefore the NUMHSAS should be increased by 1.

The VRPOOL operand of the BUILD macro in NCP31 must also be increased. This operand should equal the number of virtual routes that end in this non-gateway NCP. At present, the VTAM PATH table for NETB01 has VR0 and VR1 defined for routes to NCP31. The gateway NCP in NETA will have two virtual routes defined to the non-gateway NCP. So, the value for VRPOOL should be increased from 2 to 4 to compensate for the added VRs from the gateway NCP in NETA.

As you can see from the diagram in Figure 8.1, we have two SDLC links between the non-gateway NCP in NETB and the gate-

SNI - Single Gateway for NCP 147

```
*  *  *  *  *  *  *  *  *  *  *  *  *  *  *  *  *  *  *  *  *  *  *  *  *  *  *  *  *  *
*          GROUP DEFINITION FOR SNI LINKS TO SUBAREA 23         *
*  *  *  *  *  *  *  *  *  *  *  *  *  *  *  *  *  *  *  *  *  *  *  *  *  *  *  *  *  *
NETBSNI         GROUP         LNCTL=SDLC,                       *
                              ANS=CONTINUE,                     *
                              NRZI=NO,                          *
                              PAUSE=0.2,                        *
                              SDLCST=(PRI,SEC)
*
L56NETB         LINE          ADDRESS=(56,FULL),                *
                              SPEED=56000,                      *
                              CLOCKING=EXT,                     *
                              DUPLEX=FULL,                      *
                              ATTACH=MODEM, PRE-NCP 4.3         *
                              ISTATUS=ACTIVE
*
                SERVICE       ORDER=(PU56NETB)
*
PU56NETB        PU            PUTYPE=4, TGN=ANY
*
L58NETB         LINE          ADDRESS=(58,FULL),                *
                              SPEED=56000,                      *
                              CLOCKING=EXT,                     *
                              DUPLEX=FULL,                      *
                              ATTACH=MODEM, PRE-NCP 4.3         *
                              ISTATUS=ACTIVE
*
                SERVICE       ORDER=(PU58NETB)
*
PU58NET         PU            PUTYPE=4, TGN=ANY
```

Figure 8.2 SNI link definitions for non-gateway NCP31.

way NCP in NETA. Figure 8.2 outlines the NCP code necessary to define these SDLC links to NCP31.

The macros and operands used to define the SNI links in the non-gateway NCP are coded just as if they are defining MSNF links in the same network. The only operand that we need to discuss here is the TGN operand. In the code we have specified TGN=ANY. The value ANY tells the NCP that the NCP on the other side of this link will define the transmission group number for the lines. Now that we have the physical connections defined

```
*****************************************
*              SNI PATH TABLE DEFINITIONS              *
*****************************************
PATH        DESTSA=01,ER0=(1,1),ER1=(1,1)
*
PATH        DESTSA=23,ER0=(23,23),ER1=(23,23)
```

Figure 8.3 Non-gateway NCP31 PATH table definitions for SNI.

from the non-gateway NCP to the gateway NCP we should review the NCP PATH table for NCP31.

Before interconnection, the NCP PATH table defined the routes between NCP31 and NETB01. Figure 8.3 contains the new PATH table in NCP31 that incorporates the routes to the gateway NCP.

The existing PATH to NETB01 from NCP31 is not disturbed. The second PATH statement defines the route NCP31 is to use for communicating to the gateway VTAM. Notice that the destination subarea is 23 and not 12. This is because the gateway NCP is defined in the NCP definitions as subarea 23. All communications to NETA are routed to subarea 23 regardless of the final subarea destination. As you will read in the next section, this is due to the gateway NCP's ability to add alias addresses to native and non-native resources.

8.2 GATEWAY NCP DEFINITION

In defining a gateway NCP, several macros have additional operands that must be included to support SNI. In fact, there are several new macros that must be coded to provide SNI functionality in NCP12.

The PCCU macro has two operands that directly relate to SNI. These VTAM operands are GWCTL and NETID. The gateway control (GWCTL) operand of the PCCU macro specifies if other gateway SSCPs can share cross-network session initiation functions in this gateway NCP. The NETID operand identifies the network of the host that this PCCU macro defines.

In this NCP, there are two PCCU macros — one that defines the non-gateway VTAM and one that defines the gateway VTAM. The PCCU macro that defines the gateway VTAM must be updated, but no changes are necessary for the non-gateway VTAM in NETA. In

SNI - Single Gateway for NCP 149

our example, the PCCU macro labeled VTAM02 represents the gateway VTAM. Figure 8.4 outlines the SNI updates for the gateway VTAM PCCU macro.

GWCTL=ONLY tells VTAM that the gateway VTAM will assume total responsibility for cross-network session establishment between LUs. Since there is only one gateway VTAM in this example this value is practical. We will discuss the SHR value that may also be coded for this GWCTL operand in the section that deals with multiple gateways.

There are four rules to follow when coding the GWCTL operand. The first rule is that the value ONLY may be coded for only one PCCU macro in the gateway NCP. The second rule is pertinent if the session setup path crosses two gateway SSCPs within a single gateway NCP. The GWCTL=ONLY operand must be coded on one of the PCCU macros. The third rule defines the use of the GWCTL operand when three gateway SSCPs are involved in the session setup path. In this arrangement, the center gateway must be appointed as the sole controller of the LU-LU session set up during cross-network session establishment. The fourth rule is in effect when three or more gateway SSCPs are crossed during session setup. In this case, all of the PCCU macros that define the gateway SSCPs must specify GWCTL=SHR.

The NETID operand identifies the name of the network to the gateway VTAM during NCP activation. This operand, along with the SUBAREA operand, allows VTAM to determine which PCCU macro the gateway VTAM should process.

The BUILD macro (Figure 8.5) of the gateway NCP has several SNI operands. The NUMHSAS and VRPOOL of the gateway NCP should be increased as described in Section 8.1.1 for the non-gateway NCP in NETB. The NETID operand must be coded on the BUILD macro if this NCP is to be considered a gateway NCP. If the NETID operand value is the same as the gateway SSCP's NETID start option value, then the gateway SSCP and all other resources in the gateway NCP, up until the first NETWORK definition statement is encountered, are the same network. All these resource definitions are said to be in the native network.

```
VTAM02      PCCU        . . . .
*                       . . . .
                        GWCTL=ONLY, NETID=NETA
```

Figure 8.4 Gateway NCP PCCU macro updates.

```
BUILD     . . . . . , . . . . . . . . . . . . . . . . . . . .   *
          . . . . . , . . . . . . . . . . . . . . . . . . . .   *
          NETID=NETA,                                           *
          COSTAB=NETACOS,                                       *
          HSBPOOL=1518,                                         *
          NETLIM=500,                                           *
          SESSLIM=255,                                          *
          VRACT=YES
```

Figure 8.5 BUILD macro updates for a single link-attached gateway NCP.

The COSTAB operand specifies the name of the class of service table for the network identified by the NETID operand. This name is used by VTAM to locate and load a COS table that is used to resolve class of service names for cross-network sessions. This only occurs when the primary logical unit is assigned an alias address in the gateway NCP.

The Half Session Control Blocks operand (HSBPOOL) defines the number of half session control blocks that will be pooled for all attached networks to use. Each session consists of two half sessions, a primary and a secondary. The value for this operand can be calculated in the following way. Determine the number of terminals and printers that may have a cross-network session through this NCP from the attached networks defined:

NETA = 300 TERMINALS + 20 PRINTERS
+ NETB = 200 TERMINALS + 5 PRINTERS
TOTAL = 500 TERMINALS + 25 PRINTERS = 525 LUs

Add to this the total number of CDRMs in the SNI network and multiply this by a factor of 25% for growth:

525 LUs + 2 (NETA CDRMs) + 1 (NETB CDRMs) = 528

528 x 1.25 = 660 total alias addresses required

This value should be used for the NUMADDR operand of the GWNAU macro, which is discussed later. Now, take this value and multiply it by 2 to allow two HSCBs per session. A rule of thumb is to increase this value by 15% to allow for session setup requirements by applications like TSO:

660 x 2 = 1320 + 15% = 1518 HSCBs

The NETLIM operand limits the number of HSCBs that can be used by the native network at any time. This prevents networks from monopolizing the HSCB pool. The SESSLIM operand specifies the upper limit of the number of HSCBs that can be assigned to a single address in the native network. The single address may be TSO, CICS or IMS, for example. This value does not limit the number of sessions an application can have, but the number of HSCBs. Under TSO, each cross-network LU will have its own TSO address space. But an additional HSCB is needed for TSO to establish the cross-network session. So the HSCB value cannot be set to only 1. CICS and IMS can be represented to multiple users by one alias address space, so they require multiple HSCBs for their address space. All in all, it is best to take the default value of 255 at first, then, after cross-network session analysis, a more accurate number for SESSLIM can be determined.

Finally, the VRACT operand of the BUILD macro determines whether this NCP can activate virtual routes in the native network. The value specified here must be YES for a gateway NCP. The VRACT operand is not coded for NCP 4.2 or higher. These NCPs will automatically activate virtual routes when these routes are needed.

The gateway network addressable unit (GWNAU) macro has three uses it:

1. Reserves a pool of alias element addresses for the native network.
2. Assigns a specific alias element address to the gateway host.
3. Reserves a pool of alias element addresses that reside in the non-native network.

The macro must be coded as described. Since it is positional, we will discuss the three usages as they appear in a gateway NCP.

In the first usage, the GWNAU macro assigns the number of reserved element addresses for the native network. The value is determined as we described previously for the HSBPOOL operand of the BUILD macro. The macro is coded as:

```
SYSCNTRL    .....
GWNAU       NUMADDR=660
```

These alias element addresses are used to address non-native network resources. In our example, these addresses will represent resources that reside in NETB. The GWNAU macro must follow

152 Advanced SNA Networking

the SYSCNTRL macro for the reserved pool to be created. Otherwise, no alias element addresses will exist for non-native network resources.

The NETWORK macro identifies each adjacent network that is to be interconnected. It must follow the definition for the last native network device in the NCP generation. Figure 8.6 shows the NETWORK macro and its operands.

The NETID operand of the NETWORK macro identifies the network to which this NETWORK macro applies. This is the non-native network to the gateway NCP.

The ACTPU operand specifies whether a VTAM in the non-native network can activate the gateway NCP. Usually, control of the activation of the gateway NCP is performed at the gateway VTAM, hence NO is coded.

The COSTAB operand has the same function here as the COSTAB operand on the BUILD macro. However, here the operand specifies a COS table that resolves COS names in the non-native network. It will be used to select and activate virtual routes in the non-native network. The table resides on the gateway VTAM load library.

The NETLIM and SESSLIM operands also are used for the same purpose as they are in the BUILD macro. Again, however, they represent limits on the non-native network that is being defined by this NETWORK macro.

The NUMHSAS operand specifies the number of subareas in the non-native network that can have concurrent communications with this NCP. The value for our example is 2.

The SUBAREA operand on the NETWORK macro supplies the subarea address that is used by the non-native network to address this NCP. This subarea number must match the subarea number that is defined in the non-native network's CDRM definition for the native network. Review section 7.2 for a more detailed discus-

```
NETWORK    NETID=NETBA,                      *
           ACTPU=NO,                         *
           COSTAB=NETBCOS,                   *
           NETLIM=500,                       *
           SESSLIM=255,                      *
           NUMHASAS=02,                      *
           SUBAREA=23
```

Figure 8.6 NETWORK macro for gateway NCP.

sion of the subarea number and its relation to the CDRM definitions.

The second use of the GWNAU appears here. Following the NETWORK macro, a GWNAU macro is used to define the reserved alias element address for the gateway SSCP. Figure 8.7 details the macro.

The NAME operand identifies the name of the SSCP to which this definition applies. This must match the SSCPNAME assigned to the gateway SSCP in the ATCSTR00 start options list of the gateway VTAM. Also, this name should equal the CDRM name that was assigned to the gateway VTAM.

The ELEMENT operand assigns the alias element address for the SSCP named by the NAME operand. This value must match the ELEMENT operand of the CDRM definition in the non-native network for this SSCP. Recall that the definition of the non-native CDRM major node, that NETA02 is defined to be addressed by subarea 23 element 1.

The NETID operand supplies the network identifier for the SSCP specified on the NAME operand. In our example, the SSCP resides in NETA.

The NUMSESS operand should equal the NUMHSAS operand of the NETWORK macro. This operand specifies the number of HSCBs that are permanently assigned to this SSCP. The values supplied by this GWNAU macro allow the gateway NCP to map alias and real addresses. During initial session establishment with the NCP, the gateway VTAM sends the SSCPNAME to the NCP. This enables the NCP to select the corresponding GWNAU definition for the gateway SSCP to be represented in the non-native network.

The third use of the GWNAU macro reserves a pool of element addresses that are used by the non-native network. This time the GWNAU macro must follow the GWNAU macro that defines the gateway host alias element address. It is coded as follows:

GWNAU NUMADDR=660

This reserves 660 element addresses in subarea 23 of the gateway NCP for use by the non-native network. These addresses will

```
GWNAU       NAME=NETA02,         *
            ELEMENT=1,           *
            NETID=NETA,          *
            NUMSESS=2
```

Figure 8.7 GWNAU macro usage for defining the gateway SSCP alias element.

```
    PATH        DESTA=(1,31),                    *
                ER0=(31,23),                     *
                ER1=(31,23),                     *
                VR0=0,                           *
                VR1=1
```

Figure 8.8 Cross-network PATH statement for gateway NCP.

represent native network resources to the non-native VTAMs. In our example, the alias element addresses reserved by this macro are used to represent resources of NETA to NETB.

The final update to any gateway NCP is the cross-network path statements. These PATH statements appear after the last GWNAU macro in the NCP generation and just before the GENEND macro. Figure 8.8 outlines the cross-network PATH definitions.

8.3 SUMMARY

In our sample single gateway configuration, there are two destination subareas, the non-native VTAM in NETB and the NCP in NETB. Note that we have placed VR operands in the PATH definitions. VRs are a requirement for cross-network paths. The gateway NCP has the ability to activate VRs when setting up cross-network sessions. The gateway NCP is supplied with a list of VRs that it can use to establish the session. The list comes from the COS table named in the COSTAB operand of the NETWORK macro. Each VR listed for the COS entry specified by the session parameter is activated. If activation of the first VR fails, the second VR listed is activated. If the list of VRs is exhausted, the session is not established. Notification of VR activation failure for the session is sent to VTAM. If, however, a VR becomes active, then the session is established over that VR.

Now that we have the basics of all SNI gateway configurations defined, we can discuss more complex gateway interfaces. The following chapter will discuss multiple and back-to-back gateway configurations. You will notice that a majority of the coding has been accomplished by defining a single gateway.

Chapter

9

SNI - Multiple Gateways and Back-to-Back Gateways

Multiple-gateway configurations occur when two or more gateway NCPs are used for SNI. You can see in Figure 9.1 that we have added another host and FEP to NETB. We have done this to increase your awareness of the complexity of large network configurations. The addition of the new host and FEP is not a requirement at NETB for multiple gateway configurations. In fact, the second gateway will reside in NETA. But we have introduced the second host and FEP in NETB to help illustrate some points for using gateway-capable hosts for SNI.

The sample multiple-gateway configuration in Figure 9.1 shows NETB04 as a gateway-capable host. This means that the VTAM software level is V2.2 or higher and that the appropriate SNI statements have been defined to VTAM for SNI. The gateway-capable VTAM in NETB can reroute session setup requests and take advantage of using the GWPATH statements for gaining access to the gateway host in NETA.

We will not go over all of the major nodes of the gateway-capable host. By now you should understand our naming conventions and you can identify a resource by its name. But, we will show the code necessary to implement SNI for the multiple-gateway configuration on both networks.

156 Advanced SNA Networking

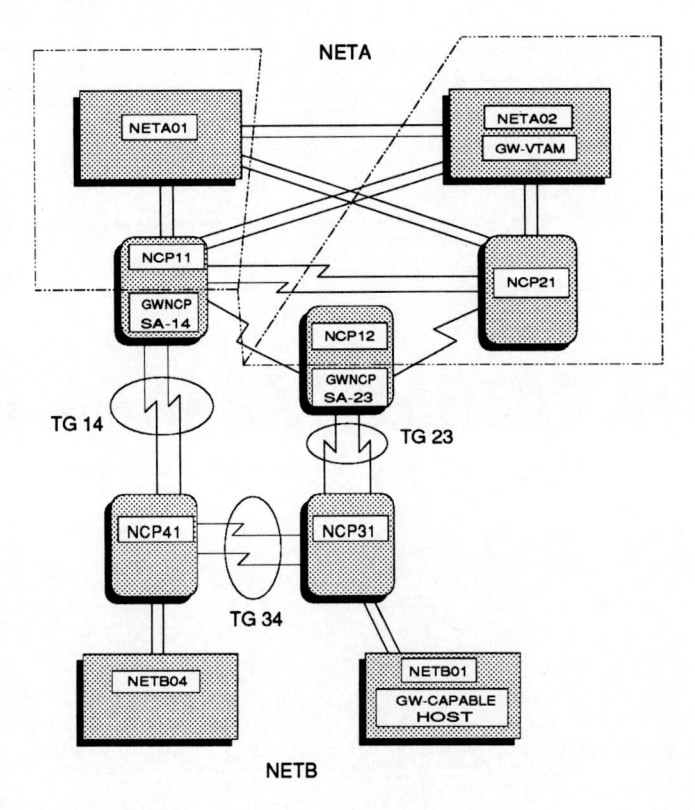

Figure 9.1 Single-gateway configuration for the NCP.

9.1 GATEWAY-CAPABLE VTAM DEFINITION

An immediate illustration of providing a gateway-capable host can be seen in our example from Figure 9.1. Previously, all cross-network sessions passed through the gateway NCP, NCP12, in NETA. In turn, the CDRM definition for the gateway VTAM, NETA02 in NETA, is defined in NETB as subarea 23. With the addition of a new gateway NCP in NETA, an alternate path to the gateway VTAM now exists. A gateway-capable VTAM can take advantage of two gateway NCPs by utilizing the GWPATH statement when defining the CDRM for the gateway NCP.

In Figure 9.2, we can see how the addition of the gateway-capable functions affect the CDRM definitions. These definitions now define two gateway paths to reach the gateway host in NETA. The route for cross-network session establishment is clearly outlined. The first path is for NETB01 to try to establish the session through

```
MAJOR NODE:   NETBCDRM
              CDRMB1      VBUILD     TYPE=CDRM
              NETB        NETWORK    NETID=NETB
              NETB01      CDRM       CDRDYN=YES,           X
                                     CDRSC=OPT,            X
                                     SUBAREA=1
              NETB04      CDRM       CDRDYN=YES,           X
                                     CDRSC=OPT,            X
                                     SUBAREA=4
              NETA        NETWORK    NETID=NETA
              NETA02      CDRM       CDRDYN=YES,           X
                                     CDRSC=OPT,            X
                                     ISTATUS=INACTIVE
                          GWPATH     SUBAREA=23,           X
                                     ADJNET=NETA,          X
                                     ELEMENT=1
                          GWPATH     SUBAREA=14,           X
                                     ADJNET=NETA,          X
                                     ELEMENT=1
```

Figure 9.2 The CDRM Major Node for NETB, NETB01, to support a multiple-gateway configuration.

the gateway NCP, NCP12, of NETA. If establishment through this gateway fails, then the next path will be tried. The second gateway path specifies that the route is to NCP11 of NETA. As diagrammed in Figure 9.1, the actual route taken is NETB01-NCP31-NCP41-NCP11. You will see this with more clarity when we discuss the PATH table changes.

The changes to the CDRM Major Node for NETB01 are similar to those coded for the CDRM Major Node in NETA01. Here we have added the new host CDRM definition. Also notice that the definition for the CDRM in NETA02 does not specify a subarea value. This is because the value is specified in the gateway NCP under the NETWORK macro. The start options list in NETB04 is similar to the definitions in NETB01. The differences, of course, are the names used for the HOST PU keyword. However, the CDRM Major Node can be coded exactly the same as NETB01.

The adjacent SSCP table in NETB01 must be updated to reflect the presence of NETB04, as shown in Figure 9.3. Now that NETB01 is a gateway-capable VTAM, it can reroute a cross-network request from NETA to NETB04 if the destination LU in the request is not in NETB01's domain. Prior to being gateway-capable, this would not have happened. We have not coded a NETWORK statement in

```
MAJOR NODE:    ADJSSCPB
               ADJSSCPB      VBUILD TYPE=ADJSSCP
               NETB04        ADJCDRM
               NETA02        ADJCDRM
```

Figure 9.3 The ADJSSCP Major Node for the gateway-capable VTAM, NETB01.

this ADJSSCP Major Node because we are not using CDRSC definitions. Remember, the ADJCDRM statements that follow a NETWORK statement are accessed only when the destination LU's NETID is known.

The updated PATH table in Figure 9.4 shows that NETB01 can reach the gateway NCP, NCP11, in NETA via NCP41 in NETB. The same path table is used in NETB04. However, the final path statement, which defines the route to the other VTAM in NETB will show a DESTSA value of 01.

From the previous discussion, you probably realized that creating a gateway-capable host enhances the dynamic capabilities of VTAM. But, remember that the level of VTAM must be V2.2 or

```
TABLE:       PATHSNI
             PATH          DESTSA=(31,23),         X
                           ER0=(31,1),             X
                           ER1=(31,1),             X
                           VR0=0,                  X
                           VR1=1
             PATH          DESTSA=(41,14),         X
                           ER0=(31,1),             X
                           ER1=(31,1),             X
                           ER2=(41,1),             X
                           ER3=(41,1),             X
                           VR0=0,                  X
                           VR1=1,                  X
                           VR2=2,                  X
                           VR3=3
             PATH          DESTSA=(04),            X
                           ER0=(31,1),             X
                           ER2=(41,1),             X
                           VR0=0,                  X
                           VR2=2
```

Figure 9.4 The PATH table for the gateway-capable VTAM, NETB01.

SNI - Multiple Gateways and Back-to-Back Gateways

higher, and the path tables must be updated to ensure the proper routing of cross-network sessions.

9.2 GATEWAY VTAM DEFINITION UPDATES

As for the gateway VTAM, very little coding is required to handle the second gateway NCP. Actually, there is only one update to be considered, and that is the addition of a new GWPATH statement to the CDRM Major Node in NETA02.

Just as the CDRM Major Node definition of the gateway-capable host in NETB, the CDRM Major Node definitions for NETB CDRMs in NETA have an added GWPATH statement. Again, this statement provides the gateway VTAM with an alternative route to establish cross-network sessions. Notice that the subareas defined in the GWPATH statements of Figure 9.5 reflect the subarea address of the gateway NCP as seen from NETA.

```
MAJOR NODE:  CDRMB1
             CDRMB1    VBUILD     TYPE=CDRM
             NETB      NETWORK    NETID=NETB
             NETB01    CDRM       CDRDYN=YES,              X
                                  CDRSC=OPT,               X
                                  ISTATUS=INACTIVE
                       GWPATH     SUBAREA=12,              X
                                  ADJNET=NETB,             X
                                  ADJNETSA=1,              X
                                  ADJNETEL=1
                       GWPATH     SUBAREA=11,              X
                                  ADJNET=NETB,             X
                                  ADJNETSA=1,              X
                                  ADJNETEL=1
             NETA04    CDRM       CDRDYN=YES,              X
                                  CDRSC=OPT,               X
                                  ISTATUS=INACTIVE
                       GWPATH     SUBAREA=11,              X
                                  ADJNET=NETB,             X
                                  ADJNETSA=4,              X
                                  ADJNETEL=1
                       GWPATH     SUBAREA=12,              X
                                  ADJNET=NETB,             X
                                  ADJNETSA=4,              X
                                  ADJNETEL=1
```

Figure 9.5 The CDRM Major Node for NETA02 that defines the gateway paths to NETB.

160 Advanced SNA Networking

```
NETWORK      NETID=NETB,                    *
             ACTPU=NO,                      *
             COSTAB=NETBCOS,                *
             NETLIM=500,                    *
             SESSLIM=255,                   *
             NUMHSAS=04,                    *
             SUBAREA=14
```

Figure 9.6 NETWORK macro for the gateway NCP, NCP11.

No other updates are necessary since paths and routes to the new gateway NCP are already defined in the existing PATH table.

9.3 MULTIPLE GATEWAY DEFINITION FOR NCP

Updates to the gateway and non-gateway NCP are basically the same as the requirements for creating the initial gateway. A new gateway NCP generation is performed much like the generation executed for NCP12.

9.3.1 Gateway NCP Definition Updates

The new gateway NCP can be cloned from the existing gateway NCP, NCP12. The HSBPOOL, NUMSESS, NUMHSAS and VRPOOL operands must be reevaluated for NCP11 since it now contains a gateway NCP and a connection to a non-gateway' NCP in NETB. The major updates to this NCP are the additional SNI macros and statements.

As mentioned in a previous section, line definitions that define SNI links are defined like normal SNA links. The NETID operand on the PU macro of the line definition determines if this link is connecting a gateway NCP.

In Figure 9.6, we can see how close the coding is between the NCP12 and NCP11 gateway NCPs. In fact, after updating the

```
GWNAU        NAME=NETA02,                   *
             ELEMENT=1,                     *
             NETID=NETA,                    *
             NUMSESS=3
```

Figure 9.7 GWNAU macro for the gateway NCP11.

```
PATH      DESTSA=(1,4,31,41),           *
          ER2=(41,14),                  *
          ER3=(41,14),                  *
          VR2=2,                        *
          VR3=3
```

Figure 9.8 Cross-network PATH statement for the gateway NCP, NCP11.

NETWORK macro in NCP12 to reflect the additional gateway NCP in the network, the only difference is the SUBAREA operand. In this case, NETB will address NETA through this gateway NCP as subarea 14.

The GWNAU macro in NCP11 (Figure 9.7) is identical to the code for NCP12. Both define an element address of 1 for the SSCP named NETA02.

Notice in Figure 9.8 that the gateway PATH table for NCP11 is defining all cross-network paths that this gateway NCP will use to establish cross-network sessions. The adjacent subarea is the new non-gateway NCP in NETB. For NCP11, subarea 41 in NETB is the entrance to NETB for NETA from the gateway NCP, NCP11. The gateway PATH table in NCP12 will also need updating to provide paths to NETB subareas 04 and 41.

9.3.2 Non-Gateway NCP Definition Updates

The non-gateway NCPs in NETB concern the routing of cross-network session requests. For NCP31, PATH statements to route traffic to the gateway NCP, NCP14, through NCP41 must be included. Figure 9.9 contains these statements. Note that we cannot route traffic to gateway NCP, NCP11 through gateway NCP,

```
***********************************************
*                 SNI PATH TABLE DEFINITIONS                  *
***********************************************
          PATH      DESTSA=01,ER0=(1,1),ER1=(1,1)
          PATH      DESTSA=23,ER0=(23,23),ER1=(23,23)
          PATH      DESTSA=41,ER0=(41,34),ER1=(41,34)
          PATH      DESTSA=14,ER0=(41,34),ER1=(41,34)
          PATH      DESTSA=04,ER0=(41,34),ER1=(41,34)
```

Figure 9.9 Non-gateway NCP31 PATH table definitions for SNI.

NCP12 from NCP31. This is because the link that connects NCP11 and NCP12 is defined in NETA. If we were to include a NETID=NETB on the respective PU definitions for these links, then traffic could be routed in this manner.

The existing PATH table in NCP31 has been updated to provide routes to the new VTAM host subarea 4, the new NCP subarea 41 and the new gateway NCP subarea 14. Likewise, the PATH statements in Figure 9.10 outline the paths for NCP41 to route traffic to NCP31, NETB01 and the gateway NCPs, NCP12 and NCP11.

9.4 BACK-TO-BACK GATEWAY DEFINITION FOR VTAM

A back-to-back gateway is sometimes called a null network. This is due to the fact that two independent networks are communicating through the use of two gateway VTAMs and two or more gateway NCPs. Figure 9.11 illustrates the null network configuration. The null network lies between the gateway NCPs.

This type of configuration increases a network's independence, reducing the amount of network configuration information exchanged between the interconnecting networks. This allows changes to occur in the independent networks without a major coordination effort. In addition, the PATH definitions are simplified because all cross-network session requests are terminated in the gateway NCP. The disadvantage to a null network configuration is the time required to establish a cross-network session. However, once the session is established, performance should resemble cross-domain session response times.

```
*************************************************
*              SNI PATH TABLE DEFINITIONS        *
*************************************************
         PATH     DESTSA=01,ER0=(1,1),ER1=(1,1)
         PATH     DESTSA=23,ER0=(23,23),ER1=(23,23)
         PATH     DESTSA=41,ER0=(41,34),ER1=(41,34)
         PATH     DESTSA=14,ER0=(41,34),ER1=(41,34)
         PATH     DESTSA=04,ER0=(41,34),ER1=(41,34)
```

Figure 9.10 Non-gateway NCP41 PATH table definitions for SNI.

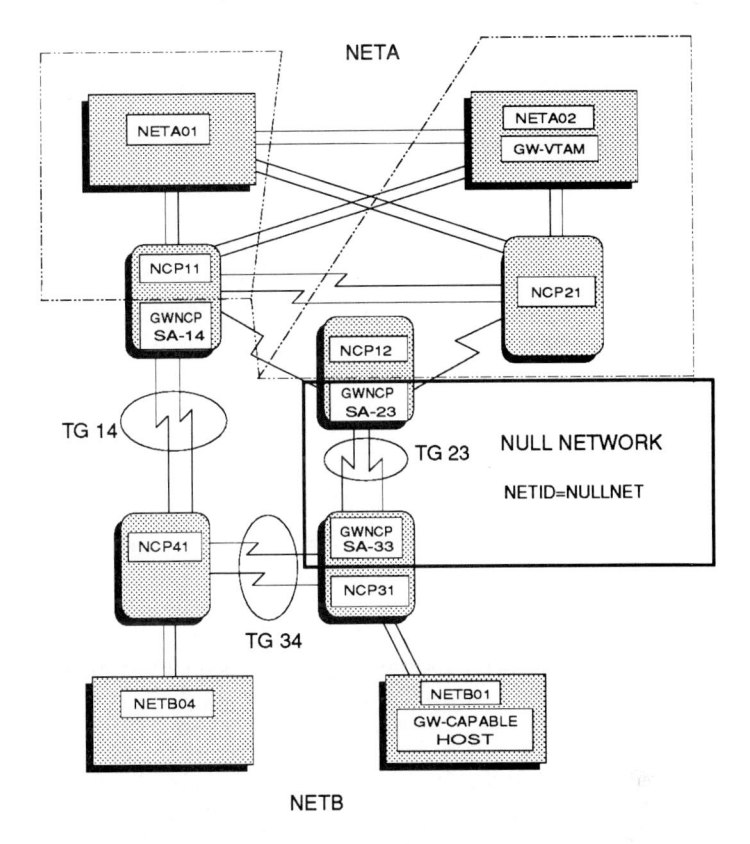

SNI - Multiple Gateways and Back-to-Back Gateways   163

Figure 9.11 Back-to-back gateway configuration using a null network.

9.4.1 Non-Gateway VTAM Definition Updates

By using a null network configuration, NETB04 can no longer have a CDRM-CDRM session with NETA02. This is because the new configuration creates nonadjacent networks. The null network is assigned a network identifier and, therefore, acts as an intermediary network between NETA and NETB.

9.4.2 Gateway-Capable VTAM Definition Updates

In the previous section we defined NETB01 as a gateway-capable VTAM. This section will be concerned with establishing NETB01 as a gateway VTAM.

NETB01, acting as NETB's gateway host, will have cross-network SSCP-SSCP sessions. The NETA gateway VTAM CDRM definition in NETB01's CDRM Major Node must be modified. The only modification necessary is the ADJNET operand of the GWPATH statements.

Since we have stated that NETB04 is the latest VTAM version and release available, we have defined the start options list with gateway-capable options. In our configuration NETB01 is the gateway SSCP for NETB. Whenever NETB04 requests a cross-network session with a resource in NETA, the request is routed to NETB01. With this in mind, the CDRM definition for NETA02 can be deleted from NETB04's CDRM definitions. The CDRM Major Node now contains the CDRM definitions for NETB04 and NETB01. See Figure 9.12.

In a back-to-back gateway configuration, only the gateway NCPs define cross-network paths. Therefore, NETB01 and NETB04 can remove their path definitions to subareas 14 and 23.

The ADJNET operand identifies the name that will be associated with the null network. The ADJNETSA must match the SUBAREA operand of the NETWORK macro in the two gateway NCPs that reside in NETA. The ADJNETEL operand must match the

```
MAJOR NODE:     NETBCDRM
                CDRMB1        VBUILD        TYPE=CDRM
                NETB          NETWORK       NETID=NETB
                NETB01        CDRM          CDRDYN=YES,            X
                                            CDRSC=OPT,             X
                                            SUBAREA=1
                NETB04        CDRM          CDRDYN=YES,            X
                                            CDRSC=OPT,             X
                                            SUBAREA=4
                NETA          NETWORK       NETID=NETA
                NETA02        CDRM          CDRDYN=YES,            X
                                            CDRSC=OPT,             X
                                            ISTATUS=INACTIVE
                              GWPATH        SUBAREA=31,            X
                                            ADJNET=NULLNET,        X
                                            ADJNETEL=1,            X
                                            ADJNETSA=23
                              GWPATH        SUBAREA=31,            X
                                            ADJNET=NULLNET,        X
                                            ADJNETEL=1,            X
                                            ADJNETSA=14
```

Figure 9.12 The CDRM Major Node for NETB, NETB01 to support a null network.

ELEMENT operand of the GWNAU macro for NETA02 in the gateway NCPs.

As was stated for the NETB04 non-gateway host in NETB, the VTAM PATH statements that were defined to route traffic to the gateway NCP subareas 14 and 23 can be deleted for the back-to-back configuration.

9.4.3 Gateway VTAM Definition Updates

For the original gateway VTAM NETA02, a minor coding modification is required to provide the back-to-back gateway connectivity. The update occurs in the CDRM definitions for NETB.

You'll notice that in Figure 9.13, the CDRM definition for NETB01 has been deleted from the CDRM Major Node in NETA02. This is because a back-to-back gateway configuration does not necessitate an SSCP-SSCP session between the gateway VTAMs. In turn, NETB01 is also deleted from the ADJSSCP table in NETA02.

Since NULLNET is an additional network in the configuration, a new COS table must be coded and linked into VTAM's executable load library on NETA02 and NETB01. The new COS table is needed to define routes within the null network. The table can be a copy of NETA's COS table renamed for documentation purposes. The new table name, XNETCOS, must be included on the COSTAB operand of the NETWORK macro that defines the network NULLNET in all of the gateway NCPs.

```
MAJOR NODE:    NETBCDRM
               CDRMB1     VBUILD     TYPE=CDRM
               NETB       NETWORK    NETID=NETB
               NETA04     CDRM       CDRDYN=YES,            X
                                     CDRSC=OPT,             X
                                     ISTATUS=INACTIVE
                          GWPATH     SUBAREA=12             X
                                     ADJNET=NULLNET,        X
                                     ADJNETEL=33,           X
                                     ADJNETSA=1
                          GWPATH     SUBAREA=11,            X
                                     ADJNET=NULLNET,        X
                                     ADJNETEL=33,           X
                                     ADJNETSA=1
```

Figure 9.13 The CDRM Major Node for NETA02 to support a null network configuration.

9.5 BACK-TO-BACK GATEWAY DEFINITION FOR AN NCP

The conversion of NCP31 to a gateway NCP is the same as we discussed in Chapter 8, Section 8.2 (Gateway NCP Definition). In that section we reviewed the various macros, operands and parameters needed to produce a gateway NCP. Here we will concentrate on the macros, operands, and parameters that directly influence the back-to-back gateway configuration.

9.5.1 Gateway NCP Definition Updates

The first change in the gateway NCPs affects the PU definition statement of the SNI links between NCP12 and NCP31. Prior to the null network configuration, these links were defined like all other SDLC links. By adding the null network, we must define the link stations that are represented by the PU statements as belonging to the null network. This is done by coding the NETID operand on the PU statements for the SNI links. The value for the operand should be NULLNET. The operand looks like:

```
SNIL1    PU   PUTYPE=4,TGN=ANY,NETID=NULLNET
```

The next macro to discuss is the NETWORK macro. Remember that all NETWORK macros must follow the last regular device definition of the NCP's native network. The operands we are primarily concerned with are the NETID, COSTAB and SUBAREA operands.

As you can see from Figure 9.14, the difference between this NETWORK macro and the one used for the multiple gateway definition is the name of the NETID and the COSTAB. Both of these names refer to the null network for identification and routing. The

```
NETWORK      NETID=NULLNET,              *
             ACTPU=NO,                   *
             COSTAB=XNETCOS,             *
             NETLIM=500,                 *
             SESSLIM=255,                *
             NUMHSAS=04,                 *
             SUBAREA=23
```

Figure 9.14 NETWORK macro for gateway NCP, NCP12.

SNI - Multiple Gateways and Back-to-Back Gateways

```
NETWORK        NETID=NULLNET,              *
               ACTPU=NO,                   *
               COSTAB=XNETCOS,             *
               NETLIM=500,                 *
               SESSLIM=255,                *
               NUMHSAS=04,                 *
               SUBAREA=33
```

Figure 9.15 NETWORK macro for the gateway NCP, NCP31.

NETWORK macro for NCP31 is identical except for the SUBAREA operand. In this case, the SUBAREA operand denotes the null network subarea as seen from NETB. Figure 9.15 details the NETWORK macro for NCP31.

The GWNAU macro in both of the gateway NCPs is updated to reflect the change in NETB's status as an SNI gateway. Following the NETWORK macro in NCP31, a GWNAU macro is coded to define an alias element address for NETB01, the controlling gateway host for this gateway NCP. Remember this definition is defining the CDRM to the null network NULLNET. Figure 9.16 contains the code for the GWNAU in NCP31 that follows the NETWORK macro.

The GWNAU macro that follows this macro defines a pool of addresses that are reserved for resources in the NULLNET side of the gateway NCP, NCP31 (Figure 9.16). The statement is coded as follows:

GWNAU NUMADDR=55

In NETA NCP12, a GWNAU macro should be coded to follow the SYSCNTRL statement. This GWNAU macro defines the reserved element address for the gateway host NETB01 in NETB. Figure 9.17 illustrates the code. Note that the code here is exactly the same code that was coded for the GWNAU macro in NCP31 that

```
GWNAU          NAME=NETB01,                *
               ELEMENT=1,                  *
               NETID=NETB,                 *
               NUMSESS=3
```

Figure 9.16 GWNAU macro for the gateway NCP, NCP31.

```
SYSCNTRL      . . . . . . . . . , . . . . . . . , . . . . .
GWNAU         NAME=NETB01,                                    *
              ELEMENT=1,                                      *
              NETID=NETB,                                     *
              NUMSESS=3                                       *
```

Figure 9.17 GWNAU macro for gateway NCP12 that follows the SYSCNTRL statement.

follows the NETWORK macro describing the null network NULLNET.

The final modifications to the gateway NCPs are the cross-network path tables. In NCP31 (Figure 9.18), prior to being a gateway NCP, all cross-network paths were coded within the native network of the NCP. Now that this is a gateway NCP, all the cross-network path statements are moved to the path table that follows the last GWNAU macro in the NCP source deck.

The final update is the cross-network path table for NCP12. Previously, the destination subareas were the hosts and front ends in NETB. However, since we are using a null network, all destination subareas to NETB are routed to the NULLNET subarea 33 in NCP31. Figure 9.19 outlines the code.

This concludes our discussion of SNA network interconnection. We have tried to provide you with some explicit examples of interconnecting networks. Hopefully we have made what appears to be a complex subject a little easier to comprehend. The examples provided should give you a good basis for creating your own SNI network.

```
NETWORK       . . . . , . . . . , . . . .
GWNAU         . . . . , . . . . , . . . .
GWNAU         . . . . . . .
PATH          DESTSA=23,    ROUTE TO NULLNET GW-NCP         X
              ER0=(23,23),  ER FROM GW-NCP TO NULLNET       X
              VR0=0
```

Figure 9.18 Cross-network path statements for NCP31.

```
PATH    DESTSA=33,                  *
        ER2=(33,23),                *
        ER3=(33,23),                *
        VR0=0,                      *
        VR1=1
```

Figure 9.19 Cross-network PATH statement for gateway NCP NCP12.

9.6 SUMMARY

In this chapter we discussed the multiple gateway and back-to-back gateway configurations for an SNI network. We identified the use of a gateway-capable VTAM, and the necessary updates to the gateway VTAM for a multiple gateway and a back-to-back gateway. We introduced the concept of a NULL network in a back-to-back SNI configuration and the role of the GWNAU defintion statement. This concludes our discussion on SNI. In the next chapter we will describe the SNA protocols used by VTAM and the NCP for network activation and de-activation.

Chapter

10

VTAM Initialization

So far we have discussed how to define an SNA network to VTAM. By using VTAM definition statements, operands and parameters, the communications systems programmer relates the physical network to a logical representation which is understood by VTAM. In this chapter, we will explore the interpretation process VTAM uses to map the physical to the logical network as defined in VTAMLST and the NCP.

10.1 ATCSTR00 START OPTIONS

When VTAM is started by the computer operator, the start options list is accessed by VTAM. The start options list provides VTAM with an initial environmental setup for VTAM under the operating system.

The parameters found in the start list are used as the starting point for network definition. Most of the initial values may change during the course of operation, but some of the values remain static. The SSCPID operand is one example of a static value. In fact, you may recall it is the only required operand in the start options list. The SSCPID value provides VTAM with a unique identifier for this domain.

The storage area on the host processor for VTAM components is defined in the start options list and used by VTAM's Storage Management Services (SMS) routines. These SMS routines, in conjunction with the operating system's storage management routines, allocate the storage area required in the host for VTAM components. The buffer pool specifications in the start options list provides the SMS routines with the amount of storage needed to build the initial I/O buffer pools. In addition, values for the expansion of these pools are also provided to the SMS routines.

The CSALIMIT and CSA24 operands in the start options list also provide storage management information to the SMS routines. These operands may, in fact, impose a limit on the storage space available to VTAM. In the storage area acquired by SMS, VTAM builds its cornerstone control block and the initial configuration table used at start up prior to assigning buffer pool address allocation.

10.2 VTAM MAJOR NODE CONFIGURATION TABLE (ATCCON00)

Upon successful initialization of the ATCVT and CONFT tables, VTAM reads the initial network configuration list provided by the suffix value for the CONFIG operands in the start list options member of VTAMLST. The configuration list provides VTAM with the names of the major nodes to activate during initialization of the network. If the DDname of the reconfiguration data set had been coded instead of a suffix for the configuration list member ATCCONxx in VTAMLST, VTAM would initialize the status of all network resources according to the reconfiguration data set during the activation of the Resource Definition Table.

10.3 RESOURCE DEFINITION TABLE (RDT)

The RDT allows VTAM to keep up-to-date with the network configuration status. The RDT itself is composed of several other tables. Each of these tables is called a segment (RDTS). The resource definition table segment is broken down into entries. The header entry contains the type and name of the major node. The resource entry contains information on the type of resource or minor node associated with the major node this RDTS represents. Figure 10.1 details the relationship between the ATCCON00 configuration list and the mapping into the RDT.

In the brief example shown in Figure 10.1, you can see how the code from VTAMLST is used in the RDT segments. Included in each segment are the operands coded for the resource. For in-

VTAM Initialization

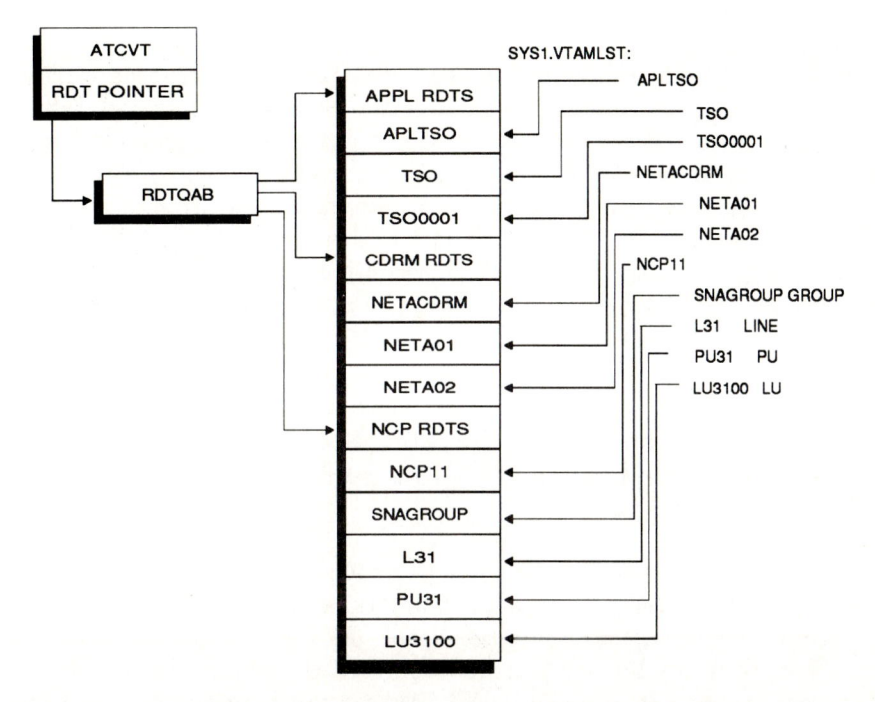

Figure 10.1 Example of mapping network resources defined in VTAMLST to the Resource Definition Table (RDT) segments and entries in VTAM control blocks.

stance, in the RDTS that describes the NCP Major Node, all the parameters entered for each macro are represented in the RDT entries that describe the resource. The PU RDT entry for PU31 not only contains the name and type of physical unit, but all of the other characteristics such as the maximum RU size for the PU, the SDLC station address of the PU, and the number of LUs associated with this PU. In fact, all of the parameters that define each network resource are used in the RDT entries that describe the resource.

There are ten possible RDT segment formats. An application program segment, local non-SNA segment, local SNA segment, host PU segment, switched SNA segment, CDRM segment, CDRSC segment, VTAM segment, communications controller segment and a channel-attached (CA) segment. At the end of each RDT segment is a suffix table. The suffix table may contain the names of the logon mode table, USS tables, COS tables and the interpret logon table that is used by the resources for this segment.

10.4 SYMBOL RESOLUTION TABLE (SRT)

The final VTAM table that we will discuss that is created during the initialization of the network is the Symbol Resolution Table. Though we are discussing this table last, it does not mean it is not important. It may be the most important table used by VTAM for the network operator and the communications systems programmer. It is the use of this table that allows us to assign a meaningful symbolic name to a network resource rather than a numeric address. The SRT entries contain the symbolic node name of the resource as it is known to VTAM. An SRT entry can be used to:

1. Point to RDT entries for network resources.
2. Point to tables, e.g., COS, USSTAB.
3. Resolve application program names to SNA logical unit addresses.

A complex algorithm is used to process the network resource name when VTAM either adds or deletes or searches for a network resource by using the symbolic name.

Now that we have discussed some of the initialization procedures and processes used by VTAM, we will turn our attention to the sequence of VTAM and SNA commands for activation and deactivation of some network resources.

10.5 ACTIVATION OF THE HOST NODE

The activation of the host node involves the receipt of a network address for a designated link to a channel-attached subarea, namely an NCP subarea. This is depicted in Figure 10.2. The network address for the link station is received after the SSCP, named SSCPA01, issues the SNA command ADDLINK to VTAM's PU, named PUA01. The ADDLINK command is a function of the SNA Network Services (NS) configuration. The Response Unit returned to SSCPA01 from PUA01 contains the network address that is assigned by PUA01 for the requested link. This exchange of information sets up the host node environment for activation of the channel between the NCP and VTAM. Let us now examine the activation of the channel between the host and the NCP.

VTAM Initialization

NETA01

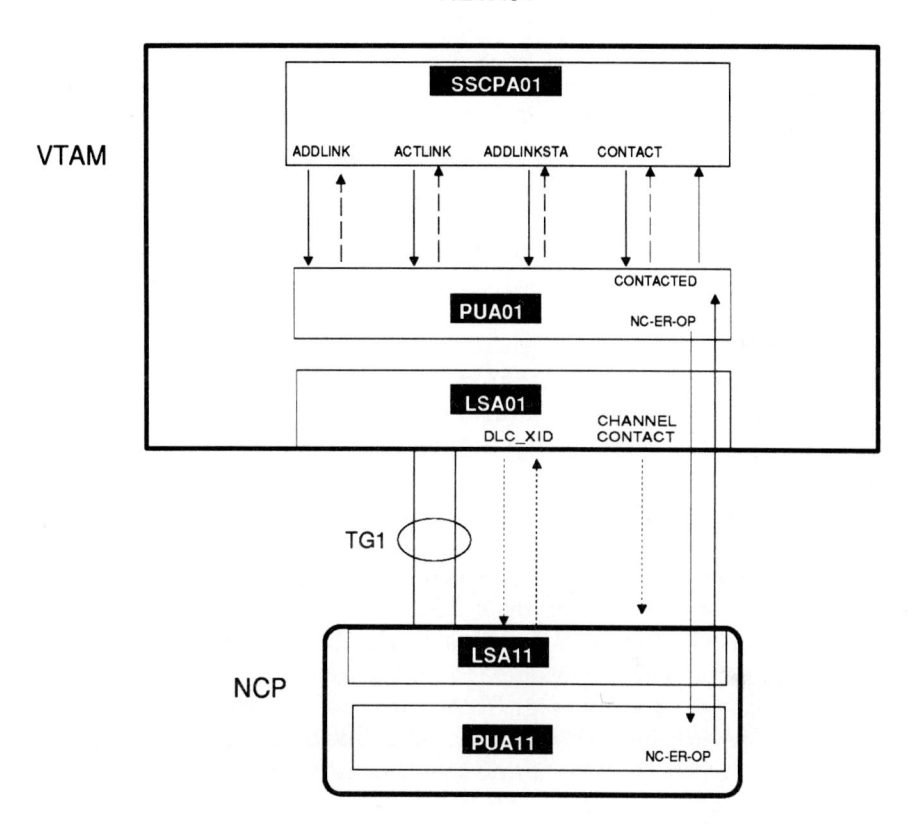

Figure 10.2 Diagram for activating a host node, channel-attached subarea and the channel.

10.5.1 Activating the Channel Between the Host and the NCP

Now that the SSCP has a network address for its link station, it requests PUA01 to begin a protocol procedure by issuing the ACTLINK command to the PU. The ACTLINK command directs the PU to send and receive data link control commands for the link attached to the host node link station. The host link station named LSA01 has been assigned a network address from the issuance of the ADDLINK command. Likewise, the ADDLINKSTA command is issued from the SSCP to the PU in the host node to assign a network address for the adjacent link station at the end of the channel that attaches the host node with the NCP subarea node. The actual channel address that is used by the host node for communicating with the NCP subarea is determined by the CUADDR operand of the PCCU macro that is found in the NCP Resource Resolution Table that is used by VTAM when activating the NCP.

The PU PUA01 returns a network address that is assigned to LSA11 in Figure 10.2. In response to the network address assignment of LSA11, SSCPA01 requests PUA01 to begin the data link control procedure for contacting the adjacent link station. This directive is provided by the CONTACT command. The data link control level must be performed before any type of data information is transmitted between the subareas.

The host node PU sends information about the host node to NCP PU PUA11. This information is carried to the NCP subarea by the exchange ID (XID) data link control command. The XID contains pertinent information about SSCPA01 that PUA11 should know. The XID from PUA01 to PUA11 tells PUA11 the subarea address of the host node, the maximum sized PIU that can be transmitted and the address of link station LSA01. Upon receiving the XID from PUA01, PUA11 determines if the information received is acceptable and then proceeds to construct and send an XID to PUA01. This XID will notify PUA01 if the XID describing the host node was acceptable or not. It will also inform the host node if the NCP load module is present and whether it is the same as specified in the XID received from PUA01. The XID from PUA11 will also contain parameters from the HOST macro of the NCP that correspond to this host node. After accepting the exchanged information from the NCP subarea PUA11, the host node completes the activation of the channel.

Once the data link control procedure performed by the PU in the host node has completed successfully, PUA01 notifies SSCPA01 that messages can be sent to PUA11 through link station LSA01.

The final operation is the exchange of path information between the host node and the NCP subarea node. Using the Network Control request unit, NC-ER-OP, PUA01 notifies PUA11 of which subareas can be reached through this host node and which explicit routes are used to reach them. In return, PUA11 notifies PUA01 of which subareas can be reached through this NCP and what explicit routes can be used to reach them. This exchange of route information causes the explicit routes involved to be marked operational.

10.6 ACTIVATING AN NCP SUBAREA

In the previous discussion, we talked about the initial exchange of information between the host subarea node and the channel-attached NCP subarea node. What we did not discuss was the actual activation of the NCP subarea. In Section 10.5.1, we assumed that the NCP load module was already present in the communications controller that was contacted over the channel-attached link. This section will provide examples of activating the channel-attached NCP and the procedure for loading and activating a remote link-attached NCP.

10.6.1 Activating a Channel-Attached NCP

In Figure 10.3 we see a channel-attached NCP configuration with a link-attached 3274 cluster controller off of the NCP subarea.

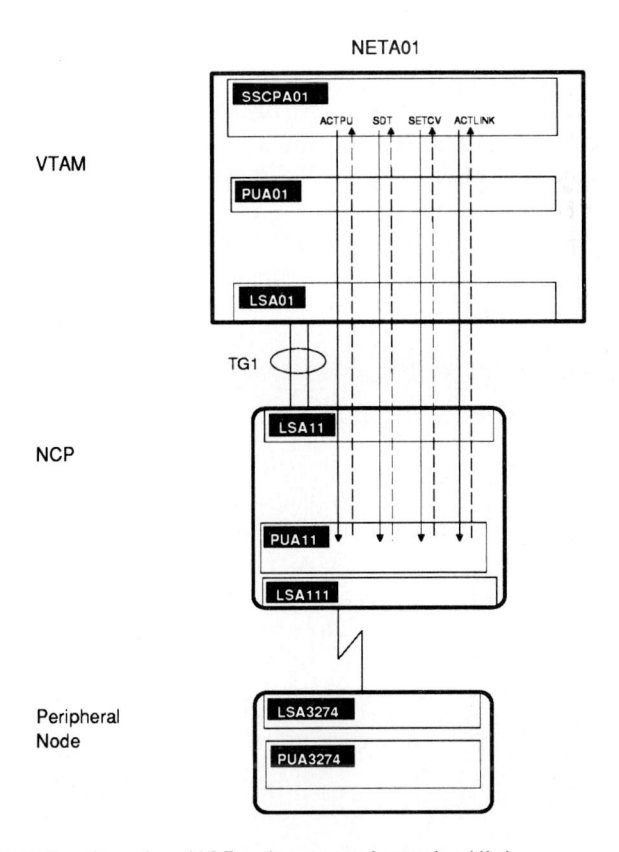

Figure 10.3 Activation of an NCP subarea and attached links.

Before users on the remote 3274 cluster controller can access an application residing on the host, the host node SSCP must establish an SSCP-PU session with the physical unit of the channel-attached NCP, PUA11.

After the NCP load module has been loaded into the communications controller, SSCPA01 issues an activate physical unit (ACTPU) command to gain control of PUA11. PUA11 responds to the ACTPU command with the name of the NCP load module that is present in the communications controller.

Once the SSCP-PU session is active, the SSCP in the host node enables the flow of PIUs on the SSCP-PU session by issuing the start data traffic command (SDT). To synchronize the NCP subarea intensive mode recording functions, the SSCP sends the set control vector command (SETCV) to the NCP PU. This command sets the date and time in the NCP to the date and time in the host node. This SETCV is issued by each SSCP that shares ownership of an NCP. It is important to note that the date and time in the NCP is set according to the last SSCP-PU session that issued the SETCV command.

Finally, during the initial stages of NCP activation, the SSCP identifies which peripheral links attached to the NCP have an initial status of active or inactive. The SSCP will issue an ACTLINK request to the NCP PU for each link that has an initial status as active.

10.6.2 Activating Routes to a Channel-Attached NCP

Once the activation of the NCP is completed and an SSCP-PU session is established, the explicit and virtual routes between the host node subarea and the NCP subarea must be made active to establish a session.

The route ER1 over TG1 in Figure 10.4 has been marked as operative during the activation of the channel and link stations between the host and NCP. PUA01 in the host node sends a network control explicit route activation request (NC-ER-ACT) to PUA11 residing in the NCP. This request delivers the number of the explicit route, the subarea of the sender responsible for the activation request and the maximum PIU length that can be transferred across this ER.

The NCP PU, PUA11, replies with the network control-explicit route activation reply request unit (NC-ER-ACT-REPLY). This RU

VTAM Initialization

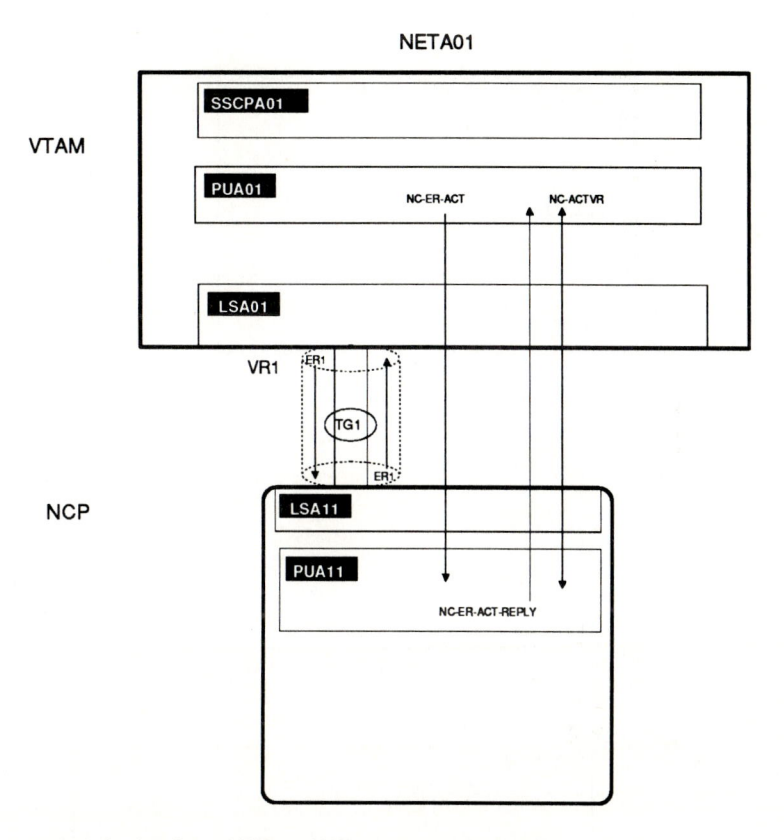

Figure 10.4 Activation of ER and VR routes to the NCP.

specifies the reverse ER used. In our example, ER1 from the NCP to the host node is also used.

Session activation in SNA requires a virtual route as well as explicit routes. PUA01 activates the virtual route that is mapped to the explicit route ER1 from the VTAM PATH tables with the destination subarea of 11. PUA11 is subarea 11. The activation is issued by the NC-ACTVR command from PUA01 to PUA11.

10.6.3 Loading a Remote NCP

Up to now we have discussed the activation of channels, link stations, peripheral links and the NCP. All this cannot happen,

180 Advanced SNA Networking

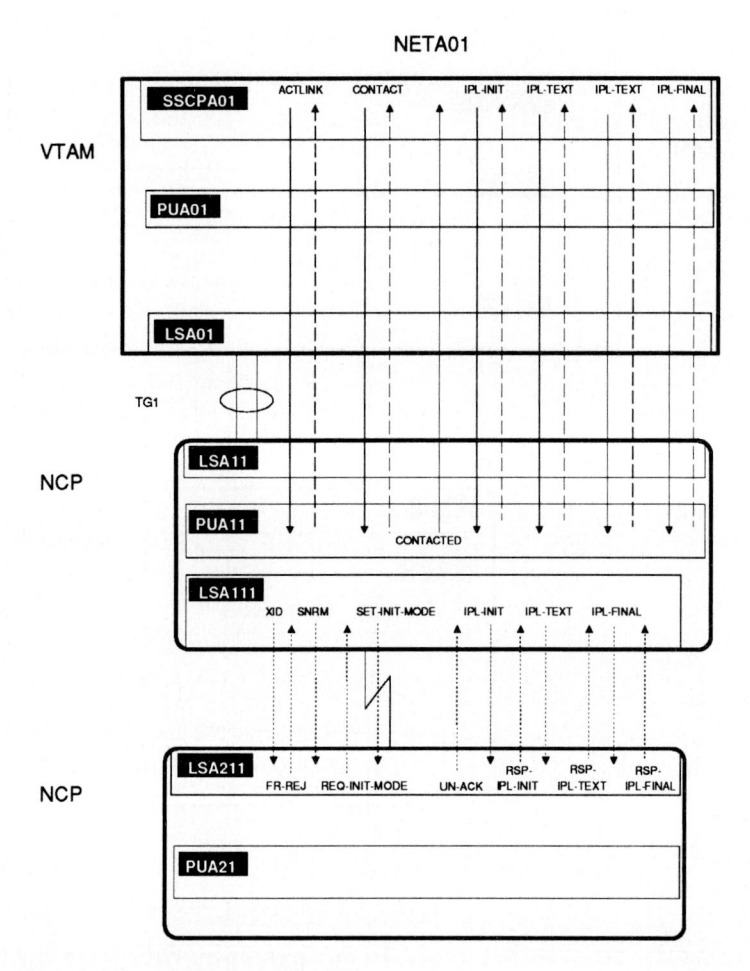

Figure 10.5 Activating a remote NCP.

however, unless the NCP executable load module is present in the communications control unit. Figure 10.5 details the process.

When the operator issues the VARY NET,ACT,ID=NCP21 command to activate the remote NCP represented by PUA21 in Figure 10.5, the host SSCP sends an ACTLINK request to PUA11 to contact the link station LSA211 residing in the remote NCP. The host knows of the link station name because of the RNAME operand specified on the PCCU macro for the NCP. PUA11 returns the network address of LSA211 to the SSCP. The address is known in the NCP of PUA11 through the link station name (PU name) of the

VTAM Initialization

LINE definition statement that defines the link between the two NCPs.

Just as in the channel activation in Section 10.5.1, an XID is used to identify the requesting PU. In this case, the remote NCP has not been loaded and the link station rejects the XID request by issuing a frame reject (FR-REJ) command.

To set up receipt of an NCP load module, link station LSA111 sends a set normal response mode (SNRM) command to link station LSA211 of the remote NCP communications controller. LSA211 sends a request for initialization mode. The PU, PUA11, sends the CONTACTED request back to the SSCP SSCPA01. This request informs the SSCP that contact has been made but that the communications control unit does not contain an NCP load module.

The SSCP sends the initial program load initialization (IPLINIT) information for the link station LSA111 to PUA01. The data link control level protocol started from the IPLINIT command tells LSA111 to set initialization mode (SET-INIT-MODE). LSA111 responds with an unnumbered acknowledgement (UNACK). The data link-level control protocol then forwards the IPLINIT request and LSA111 responds. This response is sent back to SSCPA01.

The SSCP begins to send the NCP load module to the remote communications controller with the IPLTEXT request unit. This RU flows until the end of the load module has been successfully loaded into the remote communications control unit. The final request is the IPLFINAL request unit. This request notifies LSA111 that all of the NCP load module data has been processed and forwarded. Now the SSCP can begin activation of the NCP and its resources as described in Section 10.6.1.

10.6.4 Activating Routes to a Remote NCP

As in the activation of explicit and virtual routes of the channel-attached NCP, the remote NCP must have its routes activated for session establishment of its resources. As shown in Figure 10.6, the intermediate NCP forwards the request from the host node to the designated remote node identified in the request. The commands generated by PUA01 for the activation of the remote NCP explicit routes and virtual routes are the same. If you like, you can refresh your memory by reviewing Section 10.6.2 in this chapter.

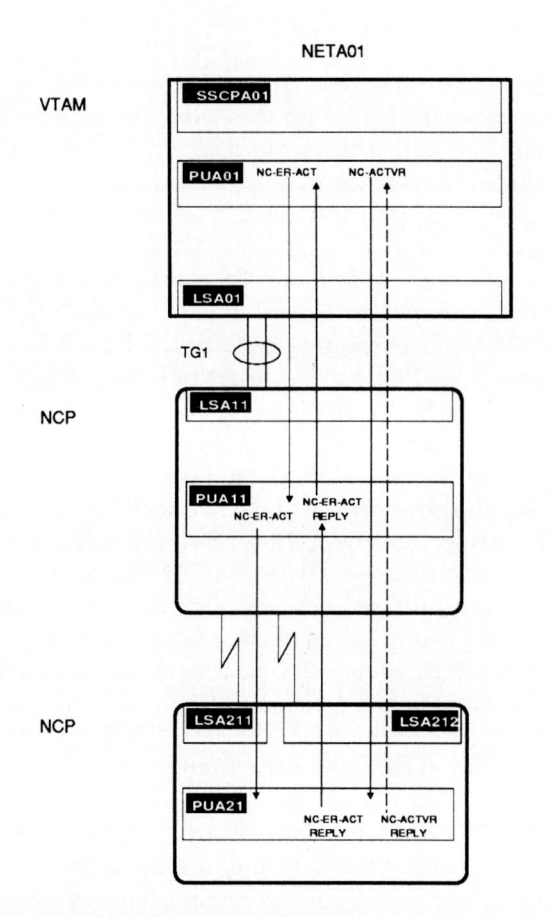

Figure 10.6 Activating routes to a remote NCP.

10.7 ACTIVATING NONSWITCHED SDLC NODES

SDLC nodes are physical units that are found at the end of an SDLC link-attached to an NCP communications controller. In our example we will be using a remote 3274 cluster controller as the nonswitched SDLC node.

The activation process occurs whenever a VARY NET,ACT command is issued for a PU and an LU, or if the ISTATUS operand of the PU or LU definition statement specifies ACTIVE.

VTAM Initialization   183

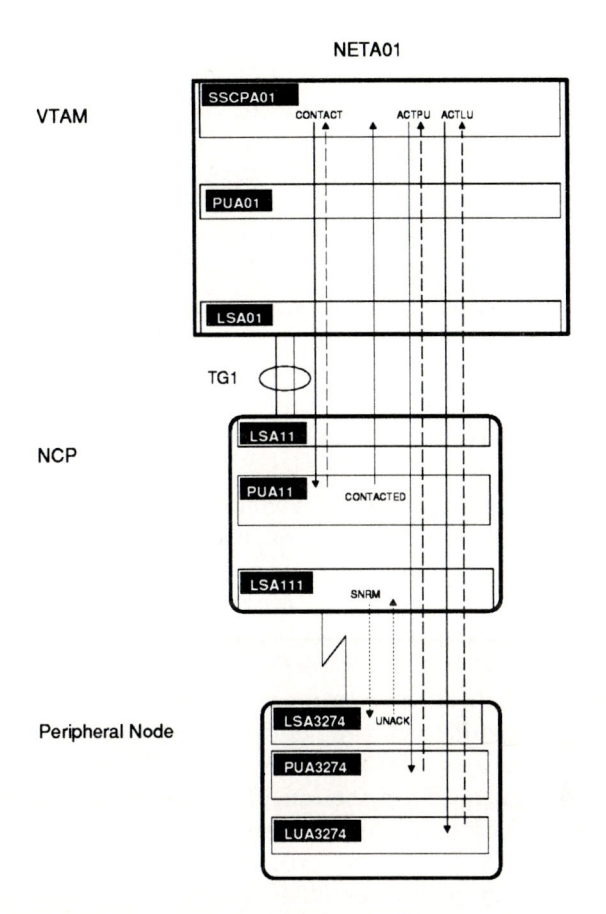

Figure 10.7   Activation of nonswitched SDLC nodes.

10.7.1 Establishing a Nonswitched SDLC Node SSCP-PU Session

At this point in the session establishment, the SSCP issues an ACTPU command to activate the 3274 physical unit control point. The network address of the PU is known from the NCP resource resolution table for the NCP. The PU responds favorably to the ACTPU command. In so doing, the network operator will notice that the PU is now active from a VTAM message displayed on the operator's console. This exchange is diagrammed in Figure 10.7.

10.7.2 Establishing a Nonswitched SDLC Node SSCP-LU Session

The ACTLU command is issued by the SSCP as depicted in Figure 10.7. This command will provide the LU designated as the recipient of the request with information about the requesting SSCP. In reply, the LU returns its PU station address, the maximum RU size that it can accept from a half-session partner, and its address as known by the PU. The network operator will notice that the LU is now active from a VTAM message displayed on the operator's console.

10.8 ACTIVATING SWITCHED SDLC NODES

When a dial-up connection to a network resource is used, the sequence of events to establish sessions is altered from that of a nonswitched SDLC node. This is because the definition of the switched node resources are defined on the host and not in the NCP. These definitions reside in the switched major node found in VTAMLST. The NCP contains definitions to support the dynamic allocation of the switched resources.

Some of the parameters that define the switched line, such as, the DIAL, CALL, and ANSWER directly influence the SSCP during the initial phase of connection. Depending on how these NCP parameters are coded, along with the definitions in the switched major node, VTAM will issue either a connect out (CONNOUT) request or notify the PU in the NCP to accept incoming calls.

The CONNOUT procedure is used when the CALL=OUT or CALL=INOUT operand in the NCP is coded along with the PATH definition in the switched major node. The PATH definition in the switched major node will supply the CONNOUT procedure with the phone number that is used to make the connection. The ACTCONNIN procedure is invoked when the CALL=IN or CALL=INOUT operand is coded in the NCP. The protocol for establishing a switched connection is detailed in Figure 10.8.

Once PUA11 has established a physical connection, it sends the switched resource node information about its PU characteristics with the XID. Likewise, PUA3274 responds with an XID that informs the NCP PU of the cluster's characteristics, including the type of SNA node this cluster represents and the maximum RU size that it can accept from the NCP.

VTAM Initialization

The PU in the NCP then notifies the SSCP with the request contact (REQCONT) command that connection to the SDLC node has been established. The REQCONT request unit sends the assigned network address of the switched PU and informational data the PU received from the switched PU in the XID to the SSCP. This is the same information that was received by the NCP PU. This XID information is parsed for the specific block identification and identification number. The values received must match the BLKID and IDNUM values specified in the PU definition of the switched major node for this switched PU. If the values do not match, the connection is broken and the operator is informed of the mismatch.

Using the SETCV request unit, the SSCP sends the SDLC station address of the switched PU as it is coded in the switched major

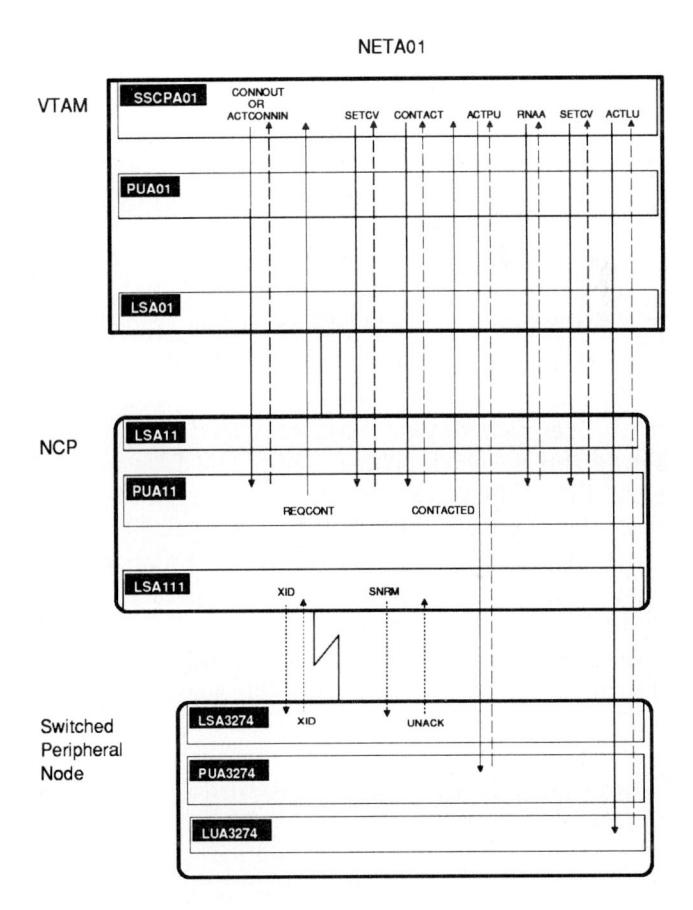

Figure 10.8 Activating a switched cluster controller.

node. SSCPA01 issues a CONTACT request unit to NCP PUA11 for contact procedures to begin for the link station in the cluster controller LSA3274. The data link control level protocol is initiated and the NCP link station LSA111 sends a set normal response mode (SNRM) command to LSA3274. LSA3274 responds with the unnumbered acknowledgement (UNACK) information data link control level message.

10.8.1 Activating Switched SSCP-PU Sessions

Once the link station LSA3274 has been contacted, PUA11 informs SSCPA01 via the CONTACTED RU, that the link is ready for the transmission of messages. The SSCP then prepares and sends the ACTPU RU to the PU residing in the 3274 switched cluster controller PUA3274. The SSCP identifies itself to the cluster and assumes control of PUA3274. The SSCP-PU session is established upon receipt of the ACTPU reply from the cluster controller PU. This is shown in Figure 10.8.

10.8.2 Activating Switched SSCP-LU Sessions

Prior to the issuance of the ACTLU request unit, VTAM must obtain the network address it will use for the LUs associated with the switched PU from the NCP, as seen in Figure 10.9. SSCPA01 sends the local addresses (LOCADDR) defined for the LUs on the LU definition statement in the switched major node to the NCP PU PUA11 in the request network address assignment RU (RNAA). PUA11 sends the network addresses of the LUs associated with the switched PU. VTAM now sends information to PUA11 on how to control each LU with the SETCV RU for each LU defined for the switched PU. The SETCV RU will contain the maximum RU size the LU can receive and the LU's service priority. The service priority is determined by the value coded on the BATCH operand of the LU definition statement. This information tells the NCP PU if the LU is used for interactive or batch sessions. The NCP will place the LU on the corresponding dispatching queue. Finally, the SSCP identifies itself to the LUs on the switched PU as per the ISTATUS operand coded for each LU definition statement, and an SSCP-LU session is established.

10.9 ACTIVATING AN SSCP-SSCP SESSION

For cross-domain and cross-network sessions to occur we must have an SSCP-SSCP session. The activation sequence is simple and is used for both cross-domain and cross-network SSCP-SSCP sessions. The difference in the cross-network session is that the requests are passed through a gateway NCP rather than directly to the designated SSCP.

In Figure 10.9, SSCPA01 is requesting an SSCP-SSCP session with SSCPA02 over a channel-to-channel attachment link. SSCPA01 issues the ACTCDRM request to SSCPA02. The ACTCDRM RU contains a control vector that specifies SSCPA01's receive capabilities and functions. These capabilities include the SSCP's ability to allocate cross-domain resources dynamically. In turn, SSCPA02 responds with its capability information for

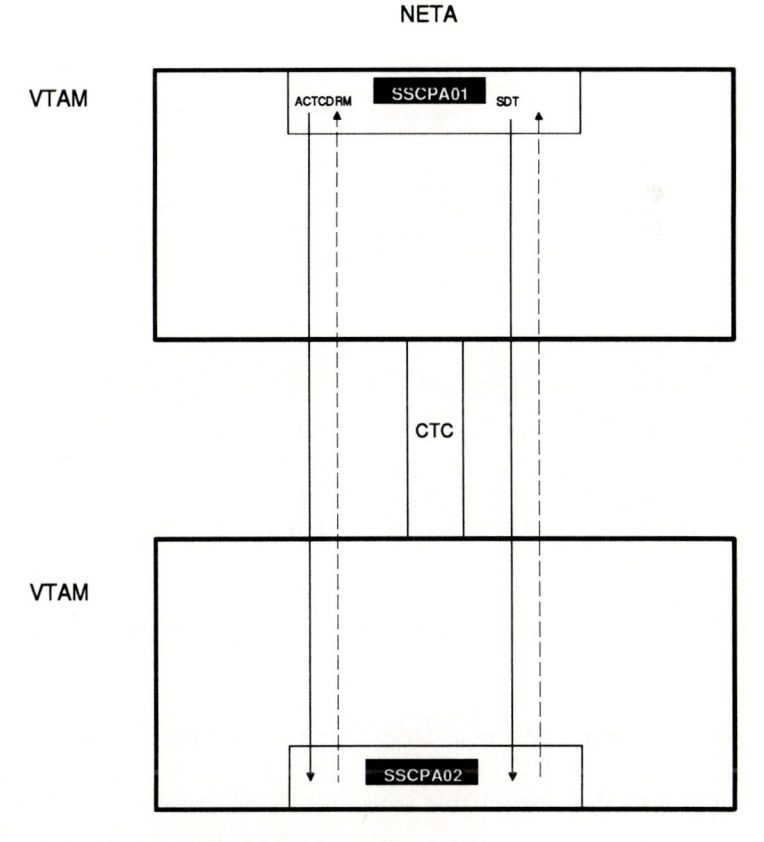

Figure 10.9 Establishing an SSCP-SSCP session.

188 Advanced SNA Networking

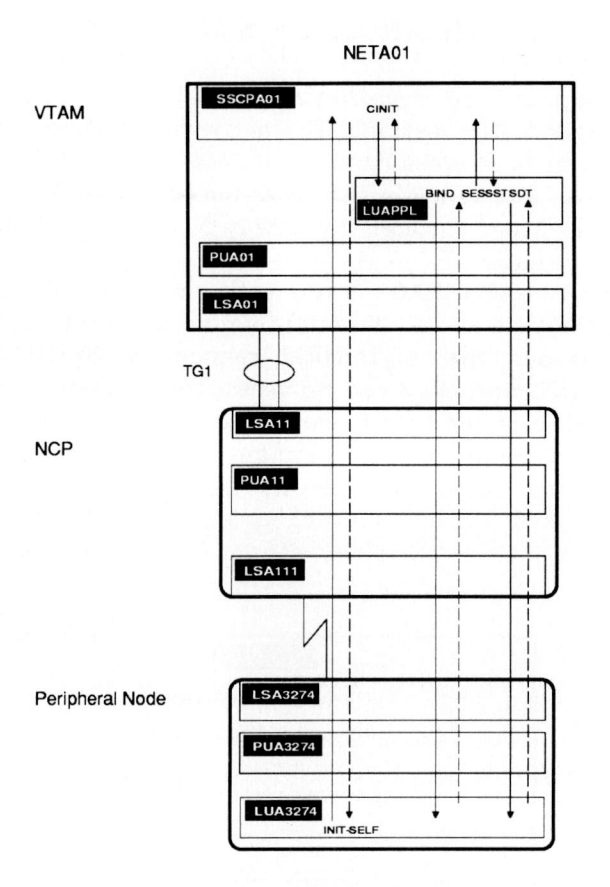

Figure 10.10 An LU-LU same domain session activation.

SSCPA01 to note. Once the capabilities and functions of both SSCPs has been determined, SSCPA01 starts the SSCP-SSCP session by issuing the start data traffic (SDT) RU to SSCPA02. This will enable the flow of PIUs for cross-domain sessions.

10.10 ESTABLISHING A SINGLE-DOMAIN LU-LU SESSION

When an end-user enters a USS logon for a specific application, the process of LU-LU session establishment has begun. Figure 10.10 outlines the flow of this session establishment in a single or same domain.

The LU LUA3274 sends an initiate self (INIT-SELF) request unit to its controlling SSCP. This RU asks the SSCP for assistance in establishing the LU-LU session on behalf of the requesting LU. The INIT-SELF RU contains session specific data. This data includes the name of the application that is the destination LU for the request, the logon mode name, and the class of service entry name. The destination LU name is, in fact, the value specified for an APPLNAME in VTAMLST. The logon mode name comes from the DLOGMOD operand of either the USSCMD statement that defines the application logon command, or the DLOGMOD operand of the LU definition statement, or the DLOGMOD operand of the APPL definition statement.

After receiving the INIT-SELF RU from LUA3274, SSCPA01 forwards a control initiate (CINIT) request to the destination LU. The CINIT informs the application LUAPPL that it is to act as a primary logical unit (PLU) and attempt to activate an LU-LU session with LUA3274. The logon mode entry supplies the PLU with the session parameters that are passed to the secondary LU (SLU) LUA3274 to establish an LU-LU session. The SLU replies with a favorable response and the PLU notifies the SSCP that a session has started (SESSST). LUAPPL enables the flow of data by issuing the start data traffic (SDT) request to the SLU LUA3274.

10.11 ESTABLISHING A CROSS-DOMAIN LU-LU SESSION

In Figure 10.11, a user residing on LUL3274 requests a logon to an application in host SSCPA01. This SSCP, however, is in another domain of the network and the controlling SSCP of LUL3274, SSCPA02, must first establish that he does not own the destination logical unit imbedded in the request. The INIT-SELF RU issued as a result of the end-user's logon has requested a cross-domain application. SSCPA02 in response to the RU, assists LUL3274 in establishing the session on its behalf.

SSCPA02 forwards a cross-domain initiate request (CDINIT) to SSCPA01 for assistance in establishing the LU-LU session between the domains. The CDINIT request unit contains some of the necessary information from the INIT-SELF RU that is pertinent to session establishment. Specifically, this includes the name of the originating LU (LUL3274), the requesting LU's network address,

190 Advanced SNA Networking

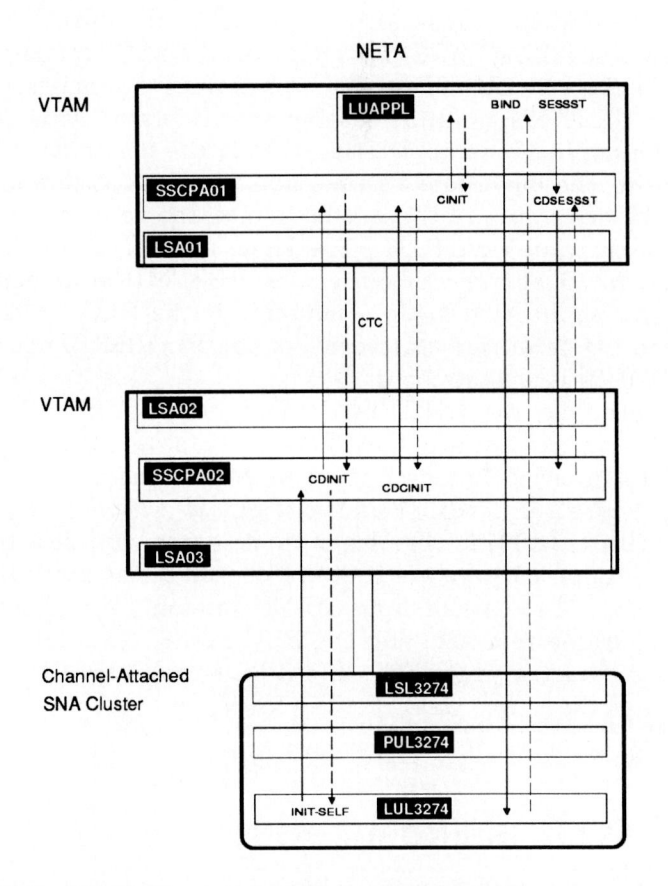

Figure 10.11 Establishing a cross-domain LU-LU session.

the logon mode entry to use for the BIND image, and the name of the PLU that is the target of the session request.

SSCPA01 replies to SSCPA02's CDINIT request by informing SSCPA02 of the status of the destination logical unit found in the CDINIT RU. If the destination logical unit is active and controlled by SSCPA01, SSCPA02 sends to SSCPA01 a cross-domain control initiate request (CDCINIT). This request actually passes the session parameters that are to be used by the PLU LUAPPL in SSCPA01 for an LU-LU session with LUL3274. The session parameters are passed to the PLU in the CINIT request in SSCPA01 allowing LUAPPL to issue the BIND request to the secondary LU LUL3274. After receipt of a positive response from the SLU, LUAPPL notifies SSCPA01 that the session has started (SESSST).

VTAM Initialization 191

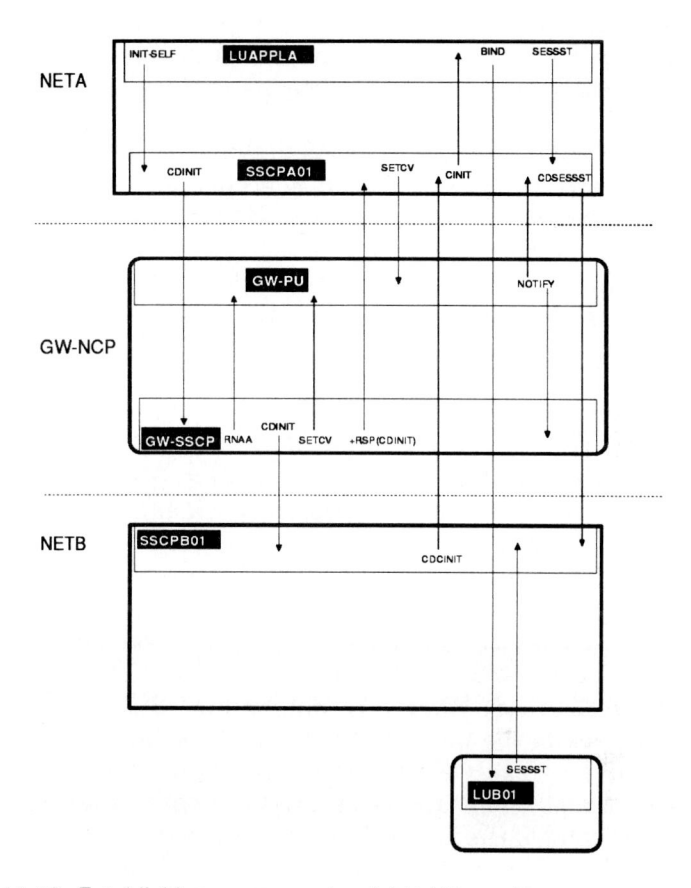

Figure 10.12 Establishing a cross-network LU-LU session.

Notification of the successful establishment of a cross-domain LU-LU session between SSCPA02 and SSCPA01 is conveyed in the cross-domain session started (CDSESSST) RU that flows from SSCPA01 to SSCPA02.

10.12 ESTABLISHING A CROSS-NETWORK LU-LU SESSION

For the cross-network scenario depicted in Figure 10.12, an application in NETA, LUAPPLA, begins establishing a cross-network LU-LU session with LUB01 in NETB by issuing the INIT-SELF RU to SSCPA01. SSCPA01 is also a gateway VTAM in this case, and

192 Advanced SNA Networking

performs some gateway functions on the request. The gateway VTAM determines if the destination LU is in this network or an adjacent network and any alias name translation needed for both LUs.

The cross-domain initiate (CDINIT) request containing the originating network ID and the destination network ID is sent to the gateway SSCP residing in the gateway NCP. Recall that the gateway SSCP in the gateway NCP is established by the NETWORK definition statement coded for the network control program. After determining which of the adjacent networks is to receive the CDINIT request from SSCPA01, the gateway SSCP in the GW-NCP requests network address assignments (RNAA) from the GW-PU in the GW-NCP. The addresses returned supply the alias addresses for the originating LU in NETA and the destination LU in NETB. The GW-SSCP in the GW-NCP forwards the CDINIT RU from SSCPA01 to SSCPB01 with the network addresses that were assigned by the GW-PU.

The reply from the CDINIT to SSCPB01 provides the real address of the LU LUL3274 as it is known in NETB. The GW-SSCP sends this address to the GW-PU in a set control vector RU (SETCV). The GW-SSCP also propagates the CDINIT response from SSCPB01 to SSCPA01. At this point, SSCPA01, using the SETCV RU, sends the name of the COS entry LUAPPLA will use for this session. The COS name is the resolved name from the alias name translation facility or the COS table specified in the COSTAB operand of the network control program.

SSCPB02 sends a cross-domain control initiate (CDCINIT) request to SSCPA01 to supply SSCPA01 with the session parameters defined in NETB for LUB01. SSCPA01 sends a control initiate RU (CINIT) to LUAPPLA to establish the session with the session parameters supplied from SSCPB01. LUAPPLA issues the BIND RU to LUB01 with the corresponding session parameters. Upon receipt and acceptance of the bind image, the cross-network LU-LU session is established.

LUB01 sends notification of the session establishment to its controlling SSCP with the session started (SESSST) request unit. The GW-PU notifies all gateway SSCPs of the LU-LU session with the NOTIFY RU. After receiving a positive response from the BIND RU, LUAPPLA informs SSCPA01 of the session with the SESSST RU. Finally, SSCPA01 issues the cross-domain session started (CDSESSST) RU to SSCPB01. Data between the LUs can now flow uninterrupted on an LU-LU session.

10.13 DEACTIVATING A HOST NODE

Deactivation of a host node involves actually taking down VTAM. The operator may issue the command HALT NET,QUICK which directs VTAM to end all sessions immediately. This causes VTAM to go into termination mode. The following scenarios cover some of the major events that take place during VTAM and NCP termination.

10.14 DEACTIVATING A CROSS-DOMAIN SESSION

Hopefully, prior to issuing the HALT command the operator has notified all of the active end-users on the network that VTAM will be terminated shortly. The end-user will notify VTAM of his intent to end the session by logging off of the application he is in session with.

This LOGOFF procedure creates a terminate self (TERM-SELF) request to the LU's controlling SSCP as shown in Figure 10.13. SSCPA02 reads the request and forwards a cross-domain terminate RU (CDTERM) to SSCPA01. This RU informs SSCPA0 that the session between LUAPPL and LUL3274 is to be terminated. The controlling SSCP of the application, LUAPPL, notifies the application to begin termination of the session with LUL3274 by the control terminate (CTERM) request unit.

The termination of the session is conveyed to the secondary LU, LUL3274, by the UNBIND request unit. LUL3274 responds to the unbind request and LUAPPL informs SSCPA01 that the cross-domain session has ended with the session end RU (SESSEND). SSCPA01 notifies SSCPA02 of the deactivation of the session with the cross-domain session ended RU (CDSESSEND).

This sequence of events for cross-domain deactivation of LU-LU sessions also occurs for cross-network sessions. However, the gateway NCP is used to resolve any of the addresses used for the session.

10.15 DEACTIVATING A SAME DOMAIN SESSION

In Figure 10.14, the deactivation sequence you see has a close similarity with the deactivation of a cross-domain LU-LU session. The basic difference is the absence of the CDTERM and

194 Advanced SNA Networking

CDSESSEND RUs used for the cross-domain deactivation sequence.

The secondary LU, LUA3274, initiates the session termination by issuing the TERM-SELF RU. The TERM-SELF RU identifies the primary LU, LUAPPL, as the LU to receive this termination request. SSCPA01 receives the RU and assists the SLU, LUA3274, in its request by directing LUAPPL to deactivate the session. The control terminate (CTERM) identifies the LU requesting the termination to LUAPPL. LUAPPL issues an UNBIND request to the SLU. Both LUAPPL and LUA3274 inform SSCPA01 of the terminated session. The SESSEND that describes the termination on behalf of LUA3274 is actually sent by the NCP.

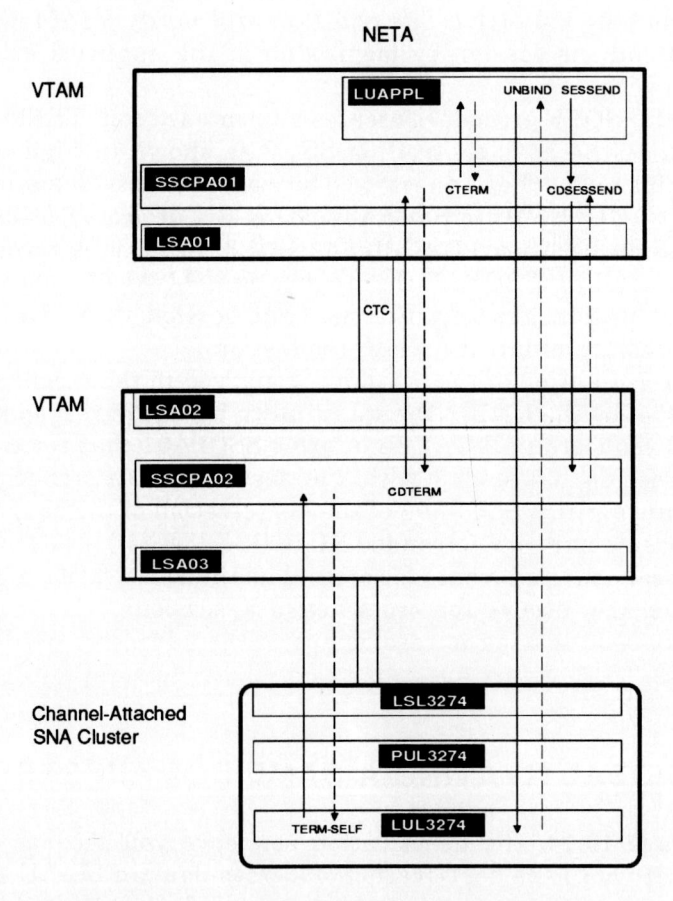

Figure 10.13 Deactivating a cross-domain LU-LU session.

VTAM Initialization

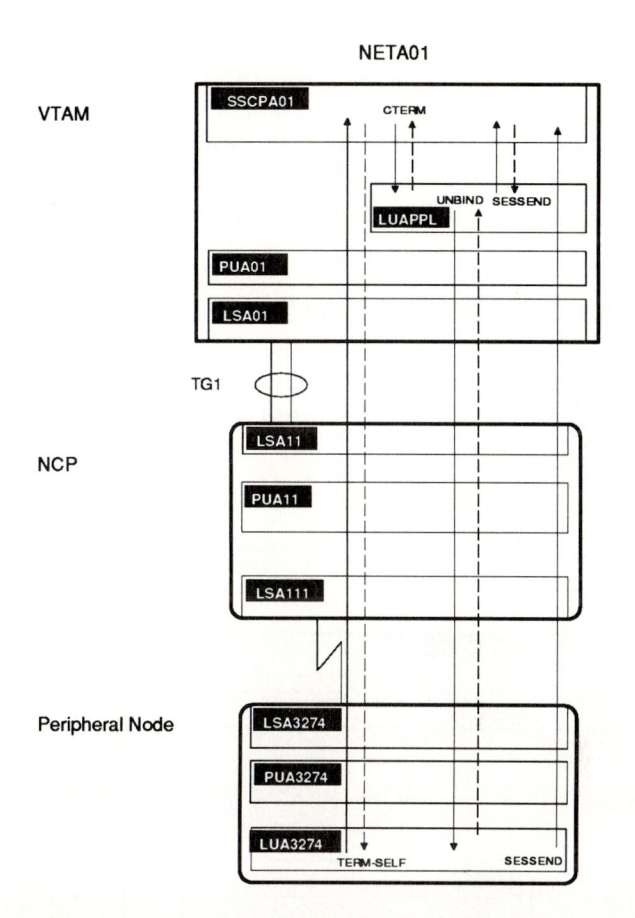

Figure 10.14 Deactivating a same-domain LU-LU session.

10.16 DEACTIVATING AN SSCP-SSCP SESSION

When the VARY NET,INACT,ID=CDRMname command is issued, any SSCP-SSCP session that the specified CDRMname has is deactivated. The SSCP goes into takedown mode, which causes all active cross-domain LU-LU sessions to be terminated.

The takedown procedure begins with the cross-domain takedown (CDTAKED) request unit passing between the SSCPs that are in session with the terminating CDRM. This is depicted in Figure 10.15. The cross-domain LU-LU session deactivation sequence discussed in Section 10.14 occurs. Additionally, the termination proceeds on both of the SSCPs through the issuance of the control

196 Advanced SNA Networking

terminate (CTERM) RU for each cross-domain session between SSCPA01 and SSCPA02.

Deactivation of all cross-domain LU-LU sessions causes the SSCPs to send a cross-domain takedown complete (CDTAKEDC) RU to each other to verify the activities of the other SSCP during takedown mode. To deactivate the SSCP-SSCP session, SSCPA01 sends the deactivate CDRM (DACTCDRM) request to SSCPA02.

10.17 DEACTIVATING SWITCHED SDLC NODES

The deactivation of a switched SDLC node and its resources involves freeing allocated network addresses that were created dur-

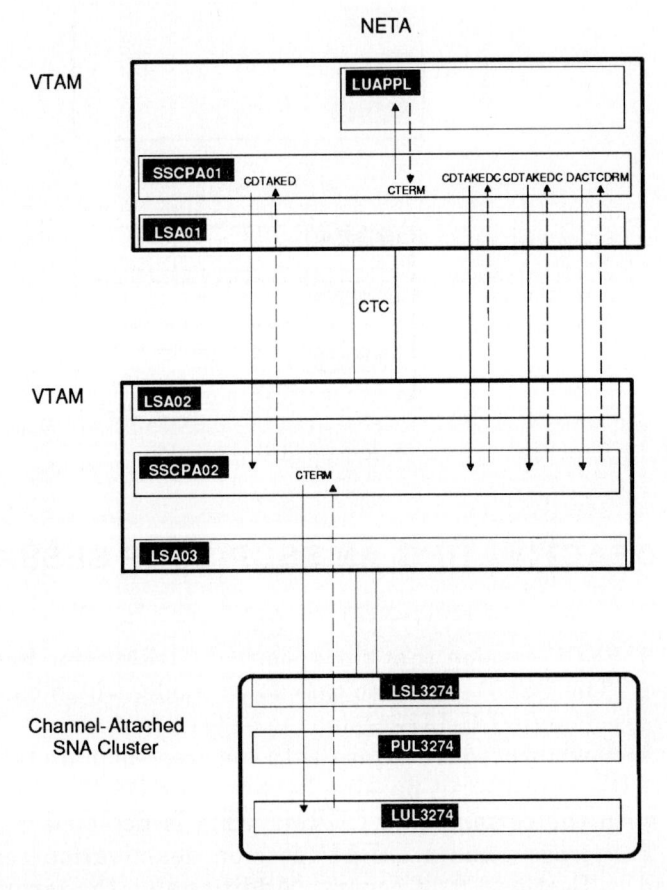

Figure 10.15 Deactivating an SSCP-SSCP session and all active cross-domain sessions.

VTAM Initialization 197

ing the activation of the switched SLDC node. Figure 10.16 illustrates the deactivation of the switched node.

10.17.1 Deactivating a Switched SSCP-LU Session

In the process of deactivating the host node thus far, VTAM has deactivated all LU-LU sessions. Now, the SSCP begins an orderly deactivation of network resources.

In Figure 10.16, VTAM sends a deactivate LU (DACTLU) request to all of the switched LUs of the switched SDLC node that have an SSCP-LU session. SSCPA01 informs the NCP, PU, PUA11 via the free network address (FNA) RU that the session is deactivated and that the address assigned to the LU should be returned to the address pool for reassignment at a later time.

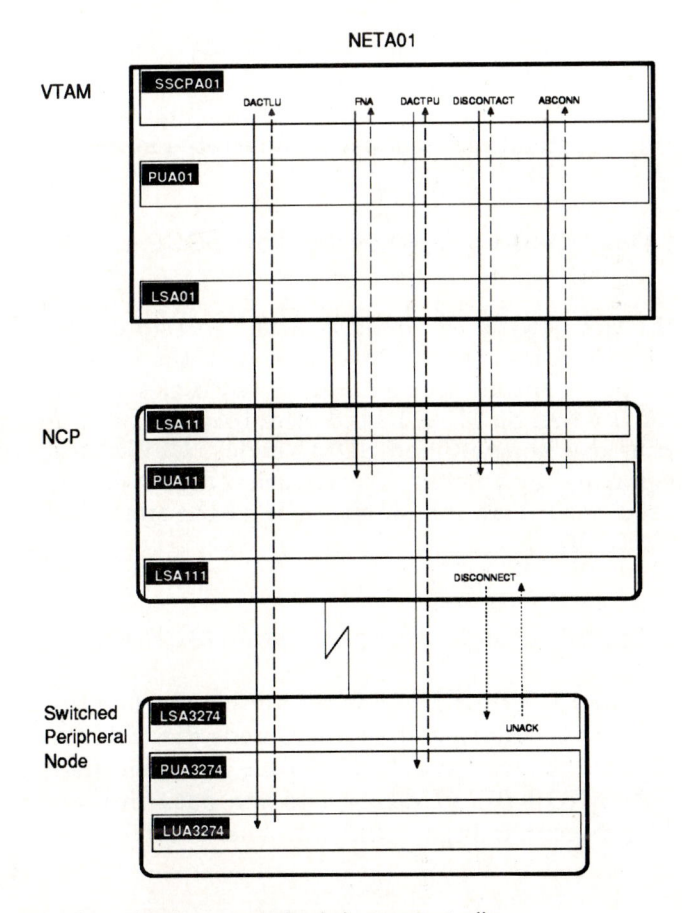

Figure 10.16 Deactivating a switched cluster controller.

10.17.2 Deactivating a Switched SSCP-PU Session

Control of the switched PU is removed by the SSCP when the deactivate PU (DACTPU) RU is sent to PUA3274. SSCPA01 directs NCP PUA11 to break the logical connection with link station LSA3274 by issuing the DISCONTACT RU to PUA11. This causes the data link control level protocol to be initiated for disconnection between LSA111 and LSA3274. After receiving the disconnection response, SSCPA01 tells PUA11 to disconnect the actual physical connection with the abandon connection request (ABCONN). In essence, it says hang up the phone.

10.18 DEACTIVATING NONSWITCHED SDLC NODES

For a nonswitched SDLC node, the deactivation sequence parallels switched deactivation with the exception of freeing network addresses and the physical disconnection of the link. The nonswitched SDLC node deactivation sequence is illustrated in Figure 10.17.

10.18.1 Deactivating a Nonswitched SSCP-LU Session

As with the switched deactivation example, VTAM will deactivate the LUs prior to deactivation of the owning PU when network deactivation occurs. The SSCP-LU session is broken for each LU when SSCPA01 sends the DACTLU command to all the LUs of the nonswitched SDLC node. Unlike the switched node scenario, no freeing of network addresses occurs since these resources are defined in the NCP at the time of generation, not dynamically.

10.18.2 Deactivating a Nonswitched SSCP-PU Session

Control of the PU by the SSCP is relinquished when the DACTPU RU is issued to the nonswitched SDLC node PU. SSCPA01 sends a DISCONTACT RU to the NCP PU that owns the peripheral resource. The NCP PU PUA11 starts the data link control level protocol for disconnecting the link stations.

VTAM Initialization   199

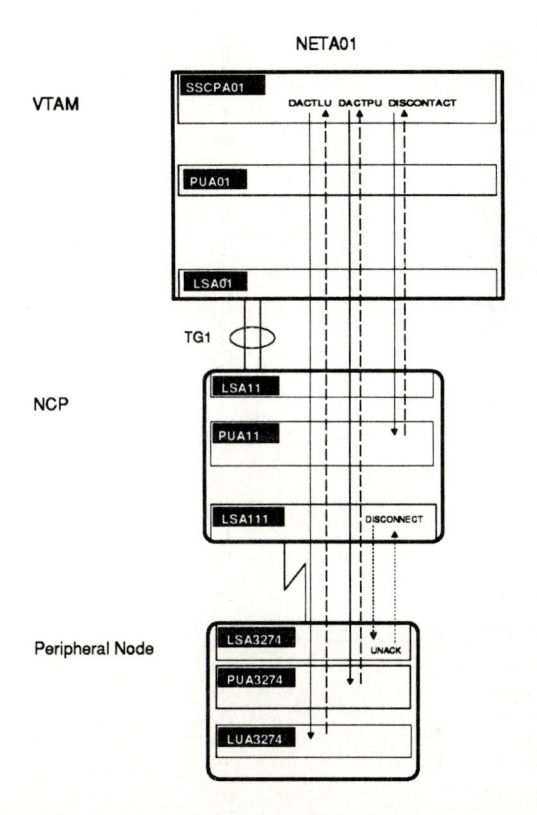

Figure 10.17 Deactivating a nonswitched SDLC cluster controller.

10.19 DEACTIVATING ROUTES TO A REMOTE NCP

The completion of all session deactivations during a controlled takedown procedure by VTAM allows for the deactivation of explicit and virtual routes to all subareas. In this section we will be discussing the protocol for the deactivation of routes to a remote NCP.

The deactivation of explicit routes is combined with the deactivation of virtual routes. VTAM issues the network control request for virtual route deactivation (NC-DACTVR). In Figure 10.18 we see that the request is destined for the remote NCP PU, PUA21. PUA21 responds and the SSCP issues the DISCONTACT request to PUA11 to initiate the data link control level protocol of disconnecting the link stations between PUA21 and PUA11. Now that

200 Advanced SNA Networking

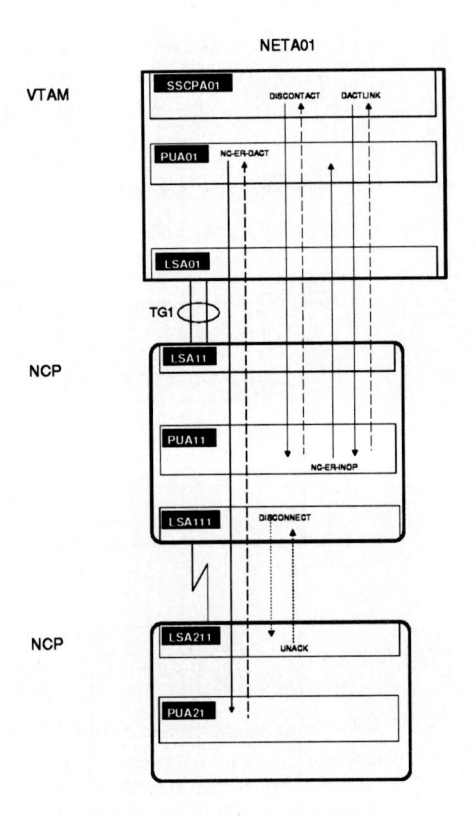

Figure 10.18 Deactivating routes to a remote NCP.

the link is down, PUA11 informs PUA01 that explicit routes assigned to the virtual route have become inoperative with the NC-ER-INOP request unit. SSCPA01 directs NCP PU PUA11 to deactivate the link for link station LSA111 by using the DACTLINK request.

10.20 DEACTIVATING A CHANNEL-ATTACHED NCP SUBAREA

The final phase in a clean takedown of VTAM is the deactivation of the channel-attached NCP subarea and the links to the associated peripheral nodes. Following the deactivation of the NCPs and local nodes, VTAM will close all of the ACBs of active applications in its domain.

VTAM Initialization 201

NETA01

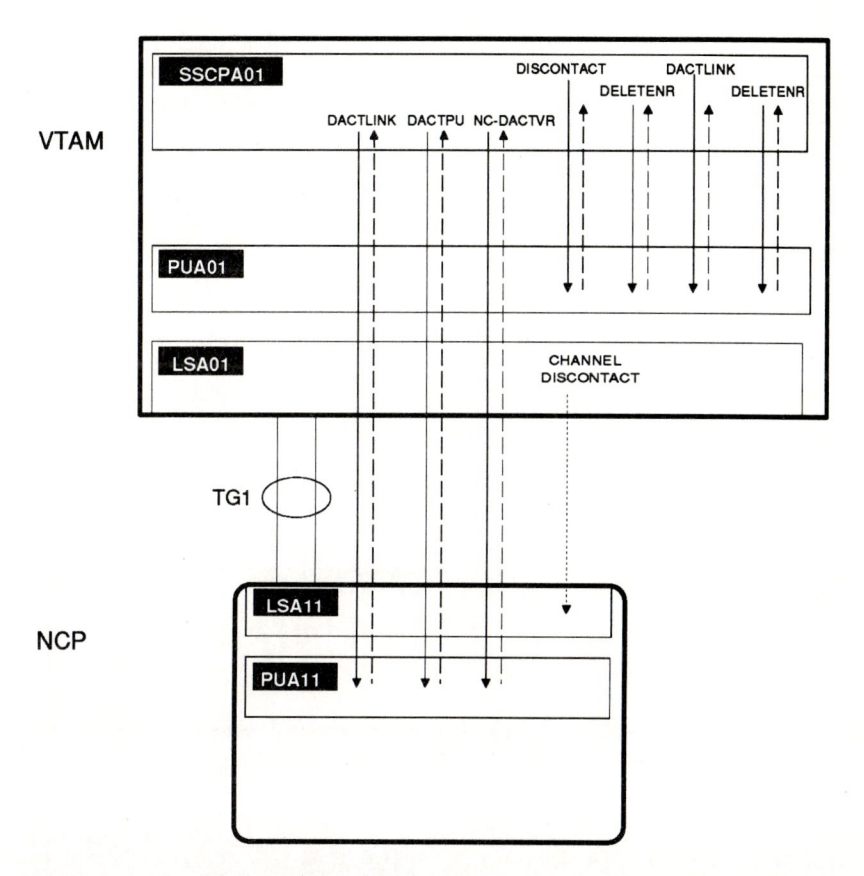

Figure 10.19 Deactivation of the host node, channel-attached NCP subarea, and its associated resource links.

Before deactivating the NCP itself, VTAM issues deactivate link requests to the NCP PU (DACTLINK) for each link to a peripheral node off of the NCP subarea This is illustrated in Figure 10.19. Following the successful deactivation of all the links, VTAM issues a deactivate PU (DACTPU) request to the NCP PU to end the SSCP-PU session between VTAM and the NCP. Now that the SSCP-PU session has ended, PUA01 executes the deactivate virtual route request (DACTVR) for the virtual route that was mapped to the NCP subarea just inactivated.

The link station in the NCP subarea, LSA11, loses contact with the link station in the host when VTAM issues the DISCONTACT request to PUA01 to break the contact between LSA01 and LSA11. The link station address is returned to VTAM for reassignment by virtue of the delete network resource (DELETNR) request unit. The data link control level protocol procedure had been started prior to the DELETENR RU to perform a Channel Discontact. Finally, the link is rendered inactive by the DACTLINK RU sent from the SSCP to the PU in VTAM and the network address associated with the channel link is returned to VTAM for reassignment.

10.21 SNA NODE T2.1 ACTIVATION

In Low Entry Networking (LEN), the LEN/VTAM, along with the LEN/NCP are viewed as a composite T2.1 node. As such, during the activation of a T2.1 node attached to an LEN/NCP, a new activation sequence was devised. The basis of the new flow is the XID Type 3 (XID3) and is depicted in Figure 10.20.

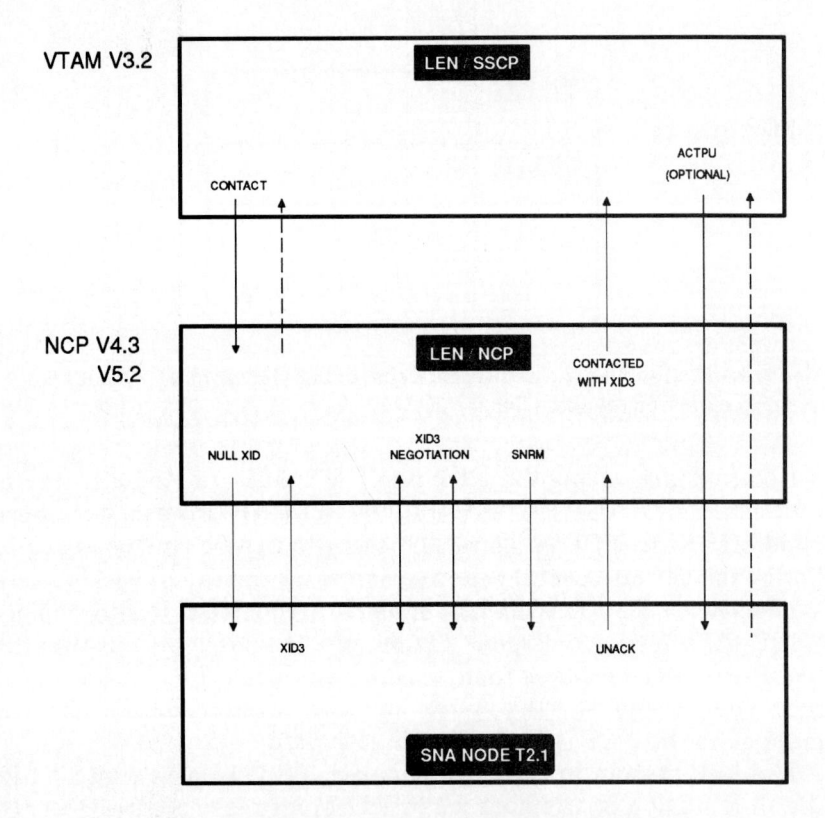

Figure 10.20 Low Entry Networking activation of SNA Node T2.1.

During activation, the LEN/SSCP issues a CONTACT command to the LEN/NCP. The LEN/NCP responds and sends a NULL XID to the T2.1 node. The LEN/NCP definition for this node has XID=YES defined. This definition tells the LEN/NCP to bypass normal activation procedures, as described previously for T2.0 nodes, and to issue the NULL XID. The T2.1 node responds with an XID3. The LEN/NCP and the T2.1 node then negotiate by exchanging several XID3 formats until both partners agree or one partner ends the negotiation. Once information has been agreed upon, the LEN/NCP sends an SNRM to the T2.1 node. As in the T2.0 activation, the T2.1 node responds to the SNRM with an unnumbered acknowledgement (UA). After receiving the UA, the LEN/NCP indicates to the LEN/SSCP that contact has been made with the XID3 format. It is at this point that the T2.1 node is considered to be owned by the LEN/SSCP.

If the LEN/NCP had received a negative response to the NULL XID, it would have determined that the node is not a T2.1 node. The LEN/NCP would then proceed to activate the node by an SNRM as is done for non-T2.1 nodes.

The LEN/SSCP may send an ACTPU request to the T2.1 node if the negotiation between the LEN/NCP yielded an SSCP-PU session request by the T2.1 node. In theory, T2.1 nodes do not need an SSCP-PU session to exist since they have many of the capabilities of an SSCP. However, if the T2.1 node is supporting dependent LUs (DLU), then it requests the SSCP-PU session for DLU support only.

A point to remember about LEN. During successful contact between a LEN/NCP and the T2.1 node, the LEN/NCP will always be the primary link station (PLS) and the T2.1 node will always be the secondary link station (SLS). In this way, the LEN/NCP can protect the subarea network from being overloaded with T2.1 data, since a PLS controls which partner can send/receive data at any given instant.

10.22 CROSS-DOMAIN T2.1 ILU SESSIONS

In LEN T2.1, nodes utilize an extended BIND to initiate sessions. This BIND image is delivered from the T2.1 node, VTAM has no participation in the original makeup of the BIND image. The extended BIND includes the fully-qualified network names of the primary LU (PLU) requesting a session and requested secondary LU (SLU) partner.

204 Advanced SNA Networking

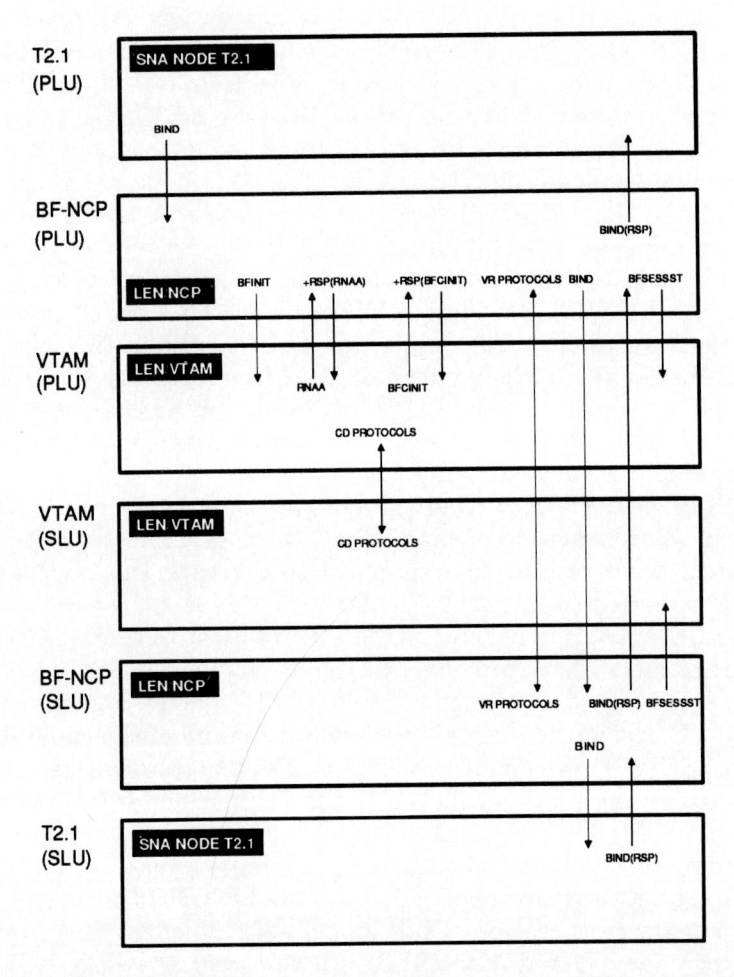

Figure 10.21 Cross-domain ILU session initiation using Low Entry Networking.

The LEN/NCP receives the extended BIND and issues a new command, Boundary_Function_Initiate (BFINIT) to VTAM on behalf of the T2.1 node This is seen in Figure 10.21. The LEN/SSCP then requests an address to use for the T2.1 ILU from the LEN/NCP. The Request_Network_Address_Assignment (RNAA) response is filled with an available address from the auxiliary address pool in the LEN/NCP. The number of addresses available in this pool is specified by the AUXADDR parameter of the BUILD definition statement.

Since the PLU's SSCP does not own the requested SLU, it begins normal cross-domain protocols for LU-LU session set up. At this time, the PLU's SSCP sends a Boundary_Function_Control_Initiate (BFCINIT) to the PLU LEN/NCP. This BFCINIT will contain a modified version of the original bind image. This new bind image indicates the virtual route that will be used for this LU-LU session. The virtual route was selected from the PLU's bind image defined in LEN/VTAM's logmode table. The entry in the table was derived from the PLU definition found in the PLU's LEN/NCP.

The PLU LEN/NCP responds to the BFCINIT and starts the virtual route specified in the BFCINIT to the SLU LEN/NCP. The boundary function of the PLU LEN/NCP then sends the bind image to the SLU LEN/NCP. The SLU LEN/NCP issues the FID2 with the bind image to the SLU T2.1 node. A positive response from the SLU T2.1 node is transmitted from the SLU LEN/NCP to the PLU LEN/NCP to the PLU T2.1 node. The SLU LEN/NCP sends a Boundary_Function_Session_Start (BFSESSST) to the SLU LEN/VTAM. Likewise, the PLU LEN/NCP sends a BFSESSST to the PLU's LEN/VTAM. The ILU-ILU session establishment is complete.

10.23 SUMMARY

This concludes our discussion of VTAM Initialization. As you can see from reading this chapter, the protocols used for activation and deactivation of an SNA network are quite complex. We could have gone into greater detail and described the actual data found in each of the vectors sent with the commands, however, we felt that this would be too detailed for this type of text. If you are interested in exploring the details, you may want to consult the IBM manual *SNA Formats and Protocol SC30-3112*. We have tried to show you the relation between the SNA network protocols and how VTAM and the NCP utilize them. By analyzing some of the activation and deactivation scenarios that take place during normal operations, you can see how your VTAM and NCP network definitions affect SNA protocols.

Part 3

Network and Performance Management

Chapter

11

Network Management and Problem Analysis

In the earlier days of communications network management (CNM), an application managed the network using BTAM. As SNA and VTAM/NCP became the dominant players in data networking, the role of CNM migrated from the responsibility of the application to that of the telecommunications access method. VTAM has become the central point for managing the network.

Until the importance of network management became a reality, the VTAM operator used a rudimentary character-text interface to manage the network. The VTAM messages displayed for network operators were, and by many are still, considered to be cryptic. Evidence of this can be found in the sudden surge in well-defined network management applications that enhance the interface between the network operator and VTAM.

The specification of VTAM operands on VTAM and NCP definition statements allows the communications system programmer to not only define the network's initial configuration, but also to:

1. Define network resource application ownership.
2. Define domains.
3. Prepare for backup and recovery of the network in anticipation of faults.

During the early stages of planning for your network you should consider the network management functions. Identify the options available to you through VTAM for designing your network with backup, recovery and reconfiguration facilities and how these possibilities can affect network management for your installation.

In this chapter we will discuss some of the more commonly used approaches to managing the network through VTAM and some of the four tools available to assist you in problem determination.

11.1 MANAGING THE NETWORK WITH VTAM

Although centralizing the network management responsibility is of value, the interface VTAM provides is rather primitive. Each operator message presented on the VTAM console is accompanied by a VTAM message identifier to assist the VTAM operator in determining the meaning and perhaps the severity of the message. Moreover, the network operator is concerned with responding to recovery and backup procedures that should be well documented by the communications systems programmer.

The well-versed communications systems programmer may elect to use the VTAM operator USSTAB to simplify VTAM messages presented to the operator. By redefining the VTAM message, we can improve the interface to the network operator by descriptive text rather than keyword displays. The communications systems programmer can explicitly define resource ownership and recovery by effective use of the OWNER, BACKUP and LOGAPPL VTAM operands. By using Dynamic Reconfiguration, Communication Management Configuration and the Extended Recovery Facility, you can further enhance the capabilities of VTAM to manage the network.

11.1.1 VTAM Operator USSTAB

As we discussed in *Introduction to SNA Networking*, the Unformatted System Services (USS) table is used to facilitate the end-user's interface with VTAM. Likewise, USS can be used to assist the VTAM operator in managing the network. A USSTAB module can be defined to alter VTAM messages before they appear on the operator's console. Additionally, a USSTAB can be defined to modify the VTAM commands a VTAM operator can enter from the console.

Network Management and Problem Analysis   211

Using the USS table in this manner affects the operational level of VTAM command processing. The process described in Chapter 11 of *Introduction to SNA Networking* outlines the session-level command processing used by end-users. In this chapter we will describe the use of operation-level command processing. IBM supplies a default operation-level USS table named ISTINCNO. This table contains VTAM command and message definitions. Under the MVS and VSE operating systems, the default IBM operation-level USS table contains the operands and defaults for all DISPLAY and MODIFY commands and the VARY TERM command. In the VM environment, this same table contains the operands and defaults for the DISPLAY NCPSTOR, DISPLAY STATIONS, DISPLAY PATHTAB, DISPLAY ROUTE, all MODIFY commands and the VARY TERM command.

The operation-level USS table is coded, assembled and link-edited. However, a translation table is not required here. You associate the operation-level USS table with VTAM by defining your user-coded USS table on the VTAM start option parameter USSTAB. Defining your USS table here will affect all VTAM messages displayed and VTAM operator commands entered on every operator's console. A CNM application such as NetView, can have a user-defined USS table for operator commands and messages assigned to it by using the USSTAB and SSCPFM operands of the APPL definition statement. This way, only those users of the CNM application will be affected by the new command and message formats. The operation-level table uses the same USS statements as the session-level USS table. Only the USSMSG statement is altered.

Figure 11.1 details the format of the USSMSG statement used when redefining VTAM messages. The name is an optional symbol used to identify the USSMSG statement. The MSG operand is

```
[name]    USSMSG    MSG=n|(n1,n2,...)
                    [,DESC=(desc-code)]
                    [,MCSFLAG=(value)]
                    [,OPT=option]
                    [,SUPP=class]
                    [,ROUTCDE=(route-code)]
                    [,TEXT='message text']
```

Figure 11.1 Format of USSMSG statement for redefining VTAM messages.

required and identifies the exact VTAM message(s) that will be redefined by this USSMSG statement. For the MVS and VM environments, the VTAM message identifier begins with the characters IST followed by the values 001I through 999I. An example is IST450I. Prior to VTAM V3R2, under the VSE environment, the VTAM message identifier range from 5A01I through 5I99I for pre-VTAM V3.3. Each VTAM message identifier specified on the MSG operand of this USSMSG statement will be redefined to the value specified on the TEXT operand of this USSMSG statement. If you plan to use the operation-level USS table, it is advisable to define a USSMSG statement for each VTAM message identifier that you plan to redefine.

The DESC, MCSFLAG and ROUTCDE operands are specific to the MVS environment. These fields are specified exactly like those used on the MVS WTO and WTOR macro instructions. The DESC (description-code) operand is used for message presentation on the console. Depending on the description-code, the message may be highlighted in a specific color according to the severity of the message, made non-erasable, or even require a response. The MCSFLAG operand identifies which system consoles are to receive the message. Values specified here indicate if the message should be broadcasted to all active consoles, queued for hardcopy and if a response is required immediately. The ROUTCDE operand values indicate which system consoles will receive the message, i.e., the master system console, the teleprocessing console or a user-defined console. For more detailed information on the values for these operands, consult the IBM System Programming Library Supervisor manual for a description of the Write-To-Operator (WTO) and the Write-To-Operator-Reply (WTOR) macro instructions.

The OPT operand value defines the use of compressing two or more consecutive blanks into one blank character for display. Coding BLKSUP performs this function. Specifying NOBLKSUP leaves the message as is for display on the console.

The SUPP operand specifies the class of message suppression for the message defined by this USSMSG statement. ALWAYS dictates that the message should never be written regardless of the message severity. INFO identifies this message as "informational". NEVER means that this message is always written, overriding any message suppression that may be in effect. NORM places this message in the "normal" class. SER specifies that this message belongs to the "serious" class. WARN means that this is a "warning" message.

Network Management and Problem Analysis 213

```
USERUSS USSTAB
ST097I  USSMSG  MSG=IST097I,SUPP=ALWAYS
*   REMOVES SYNTAX ACCEPTED MESSAGE FOR ALL COMMANDS
IST486I USSMSG MSG=IST486I, SUPP=INFO, OPT=BLKSUP,          X
TEXT= 'THE NODE NAMED %(1) IS CURRENTLY %(2)                X
                    AFTER AN %(3) REQUEST.'
*  IST486I NAME=  CDRM01, STATUS= INACT, DESIRED STATE= ACTIV
*          %(1)       %(2)        %(3)
           USSEND
```
Displayed on the VTAM console:
```
IST486I  THE NODE NAMED CDRM01 IS CURRENTLY INACT AFTER AN
         ACTIV REQUEST
```

Figure 11.2 Sample use of a user-defined operation-level USS table to redefine VTAM operator messages.

The TEXT operand specifies the actual message text that is to be used to replace the VTAM message identified in the MSG operand of this USSMSG statement. This message follows the rules outlined in Chapter 11 where we discussed the use of the TEXT operand for the session-level USS table. Figure 11.2 details a sample of an operation-level USS table and its use.

Redefining VTAM operator commands is a bit more difficult than redefining VTAM operator messages. Each command consists of three parts. The first part is the command verb (e.g., DISPLAY, VARY, MODIFY). The second is the required positional parameter for VTAM (NET). The remaining part consists of the keyword parameters for the command (e.g., ID=, LOAD=, LOGMODE=). Take a look at Figure 11.3. Here we have defined a USS table that modifies the operator's VTAM command DISPLAY NET, NCPSTOR. Common with this command are parameters to identify the NCP, storage location and length of the storage that is to be displayed on the operator's console. But not every operator knows either the syntax of the command or the values for the starting address and the length of data that is needed by the communications systems programmer. Well, the communications systems programmer can supply defaults for the command by including default values for the keywords in the user-coded operation-level USS table. In this way, both parties are assured a successful display.

```
USERUSS USSTAB
NCPSTOR USSCMD CMD=NCPSTOR,FORMAT=BAL
USSPARM PARM=ID,DEFAULT=NCPTEST
USSPARM PARM=ADDR,DEFAULT=0
USSPARM PARM=LENGTH,DEFAULT=256
USSEND

Operator enters command on console as:

D NET,NCPSTOR

VTAM interprets the command as:

D NET,NCPSTOR,ID=NCPTEST,ADDR=0,LENGTH=256
```

Figure 11.3 Sample use of a user-defined operation-level USS table to simplify operator commands.

11.2 Managing Resource Ownership and Recovery

In SNA, the sharing of resources in the network is a primary characteristic. Large multi-domain environments have enhanced the need for managing the ownership of these networked resources. In *Introduction to SNA Networking* we discussed how an NCP can be shared by up to eight SSCPs concurrently and that the resources in the NCP can also be shared. Here we will discuss the necessity to initially obtain resource ownership to supplement the management of the network resources.

11.2.1 LOGAPPL Operand

The TERM and LU definition statements used by VTAM can define a controlling application for this device by specifying the LOGAPPL operand. This controlling application program is also known as the controlling PLU (primary logical unit). LU activation by the SSCP (SSCP-LU session) causes VTAM to automatically attempt to initiate a session between the LU and the application name identified on the LOGAPPL operand. Examine the use of the LOGAPPL operand to establish application ownership of a terminal in Figure 11.4.

Network Management and Problem Analysis

The application identified by the LOGAPPL operand may be the sole controlling application for this LU or it can be an intermediary application that passes control to another application. However, once the user ends the session with the application, VTAM will initiate a session between the controlling application program and the LU. This approach is commonly used by applications that replace the USS of VTAM. In this way, the application can present the end-user with more detailed information about available applications, interactive logon assistance and notification of planned system outages. For the communications systems programmer the application can be used to dynamically manage end-user accessibility to applications in the network and provide detailed analysis of application usage, uptime, accounting, and availability of both the LU and the application. Some applications available today that perform some or all of these management facilities are:

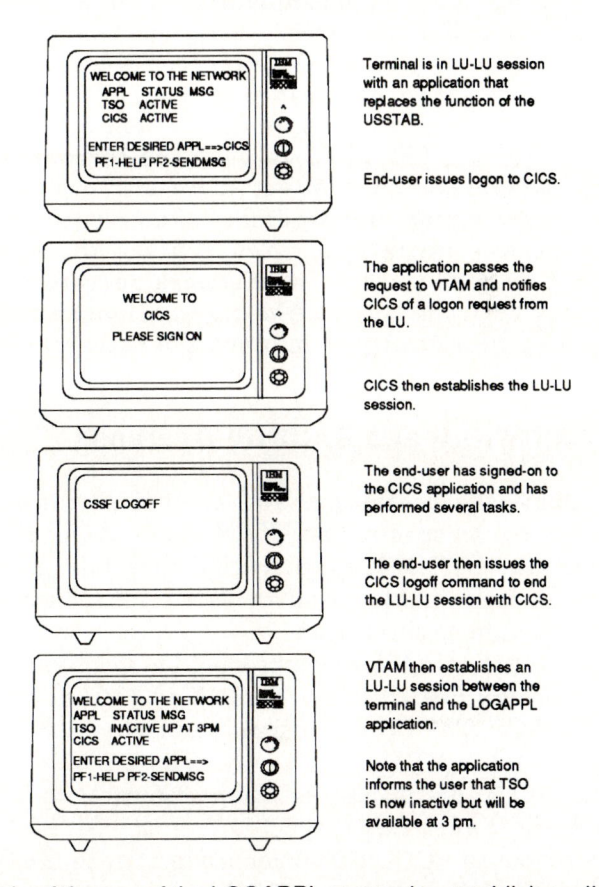

```
WELCOME TO THE NETWORK
APPL   STATUS  MSG
TSO    ACTIVE
CICS   ACTIVE

ENTER DESIRED APPL==>CICS
PF1-HELP PF2-SENDMSG
```
Terminal is in LU-LU session with an application that replaces the function of the USSTAB.

End-user issues logon to CICS.

```
WELCOME TO
   CICS
PLEASE SIGN ON
```
The application passes the request to VTAM and notifies CICS of a logon request from the LU.

CICS then establishes the LU-LU session.

```
CSSF LOGOFF
```
The end-user has signed-on to the CICS application and has performed several tasks.

The end-user then issues the CICS logoff command to end the LU-LU session with CICS.

```
WELCOME TO THE NETWORK
APPL   STATUS  MSG
TSO    INACTIVE UP AT 3PM
CICS   ACTIVE

ENTER DESIRED APPL==>
PF1-HELP PF2-SENDMSG
```
VTAM then establishes an LU-LU session between the terminal and the LOGAPPL application.

Note that the application informs the user that TSO is now inactive but will be available at 3 pm.

Figure 11.4 Example of the use of the LOGAPPL operand to establish application ownership of a terminal.

1. Net/Master EASINET by Systems Center.
2. CL-MENU by Candle.
3. SAMON by IBM.

11.2.2 ISTATUS Operand

Throughout the book we have discussed the ISTATUS operand and its use in defining the initial status of the resource to the SSCP. Recall that when VTAM activates an NCP it will activate the NCP resources according to the ISTATUS value coded for each resource and that resource's higher-node ISTATUS value (e.g., a PU is the higher-node to an LU). Up to eight SSCPs can activate an NCP. Consequently, each SSCP will contend to activate the NCP resources. Only one SSCP can own a PU T.1 or PU T.2 and its associated LUs for SNA devices. For non-SNA BSC devices, the ownership of the LINE that serves those devices determines the owner of the non-SNA resources on that line. When the ISTATUS value or the current status of a device is INACTive, the subsequent successful activate request by an SSCP may change the ownership of a resource from the time the network was initialized. You can see the havoc that can be created by such a scenario. Network operators that had control of a device from one VTAM may no longer have that control, reducing their ability to manage the resources on the network.

11.2.3 OWNER and BACKUP Operands

To reduce the contention and confusion of ownership between SSCPs, we can specify two VTAM operands for NCP resource definitions: the OWNER and BACKUP operands. Proper use of these operands will enable resource partitioning between VTAMs in a multi-domain environment.

The partitioning is accomplished by specifying the OWNER operand on the PCCU, GROUP LINE and PU definition statements for the NCP. The PU definition statement with the OWNER operand is valid in VTAM V32R only. The OWNER operand specified on the PCCU definition statement indicates to VTAM that it is to match the owner name specified on the OWNER operand of the corresponding PCCU definition statement to the OWNER operand of the GROUP, LINE and PU definition statements in the NCP. This is performed so that the SSCP can assume ownership of the

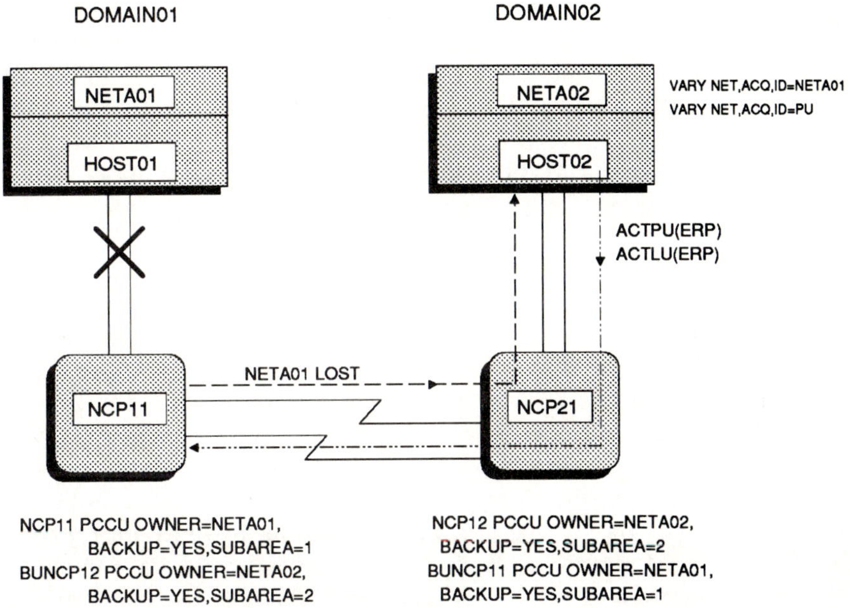

Network Management and Problem Analysis 217

```
       DOMAIN01                    DOMAIN02
                                                    VARY NET,ACQ,ID=NETA01
        [NETA01]                    [NETA02]        VARY NET,ACQ,ID=PU

        [HOST01]                    [HOST02]
                                       ↑
                                       ┊  ACTPU(ERP)
            ╳                          ↓  ACTLU(ERP)

                    NETA01 LOST
        [NCP11]    - - - - - - →    [NCP21]
                ←- - - - - - -
```

NCP11 PCCU OWNER=NETA01,   NCP12 PCCU OWNER=NETA02,
   BACKUP=YES,SUBAREA=1   BACKUP=YES,SUBAREA=2
BUNCP12 PCCU OWNER=NETA02,   BUNCP11 PCCU OWNER=NETA01,
   BACKUP=YES,SUBAREA=2   BACKUP=YES,SUBAREA=1

Figure 11.5 Example of using OWNER and BACKUP operands.

LINEs, PUs and LUs associated with the GROUP, LINE and PU definition statements. Couple this with the BACKUP operand on the PCCU definition statement defined as BACKUP=YES, and we have created a non-disruptive backup and recovery procedure.

Take a look at Figure 11.5. In this example, NETA01 and NETA02 are in session with both NCP11 and NCP21. NETA01 owns all of the resources on NCP11, while NETA02 owns all of the resources on NCP21. NETA01 is defined as the backup SSCP for NETA02 and NETA02 is defined as the backup for NETA01. Suppose the channel connection between NETA01 and NCP11 is disabled. NCP11 will notify NETA02 that the SSCP-PU session with NETA01 was lost. However, the network operator at NETA02 may elect not to take over the unowned NCP11 resources until further messages indicate a true outage. In this scenario, the network operator waits to see if the SSCP-SSCP session between NETA01 and NETA02 has also been lost. During the automatic network shutdown procedure for NCP11, all LU-LU sessions between network resources and applications on NETA01 are lost. However, cross-domain resources from NCP11 NAUs and applications on NETA02 still function. The network operator on NETA02 issues the VARY NET,ACQ,ID=NCP11 to obtain ownership of the NCP and its lines. However, the same command must be issued for all physical units in NCP11. The associated LUs for each PU can also be acquired from the VARY ACQ command issued for the PU. The PU must support the ACTPU(ERP) SNA request to avoid a disruptive takeover for the PU's associated LU-LU sessions. In turn, the LUs associated with the PU must support their ACTLU(ERP) SNA request to avoid a disruptive takeover. If any of these LUs were previously known to the backup SSCP as cross-domain resources, the SSCP updates the new configuration and treats these LUs as same-domain resources.

Enhancements in VTAM V3R2 reduce the time needed by NETA02 to recover NETA01 resources. The VARY ACQuire command has been enhanced with the addition of the PUSUB parameter. The command would now be specified as VARY NET,ACQ, ID=NCP11,PUSUB. The result of this command would be that the NCP, all the PUs and their associated LUs would be owned by NETA02. Note that in this case, only one VARY ACQuire command had to be issued to gain ownership of all of the NCP11 resources.

11.3 ADVANCED CONFIGURATION FACILITIES

The rapid growth of network dependency for corporate needs has generated the need for more management capabilities within VTAM. We will discuss three advanced configuration facilities used by VTAM. The first is Dynamic Reconfiguration (DR). The second is the Communication Management Configuration (CMC) and the third is specific to MVS, the Extended Recovery Facility (XRF). In addition, we will discuss Dynamic Path Update and Dynamic Table Replacement. Both are enhanced features of VTAM V3R2.

11.3.1 Using Dynamic Reconfiguration

The purpose of dynamic reconfiguration is to allow the deletion, addition and modification of NCP SNA resources without requiring an NCP generation process. This allows for the addition and

Network Management and Problem Analysis 219

deletion of PUs to or from lines and LUs to or from PUs, all without disturbing existing resources in the NCP. Another advantage is the ability to test resource definitions dynamically. However, a problem does occur for versions of VTAM prior to VTAM V3R2 and NCP V4R3/V5R2. To illustrate this problem let's use the following example.

Let's look at Figure 11.6. Here we see a configuration consisting of two host processors and channel-attached communications controllers, an SDLC link, a PU and an LU. Because of SDLC station address changes in the PU, we have elected to use dynamic reconfiguration to define the changes in NCP11. The original station address of the PU is found in the naming convention. The 'C1' in both the PU name and the LU name denotes the PU's SDLC station address assigned on the ADDR operand of the PU definition

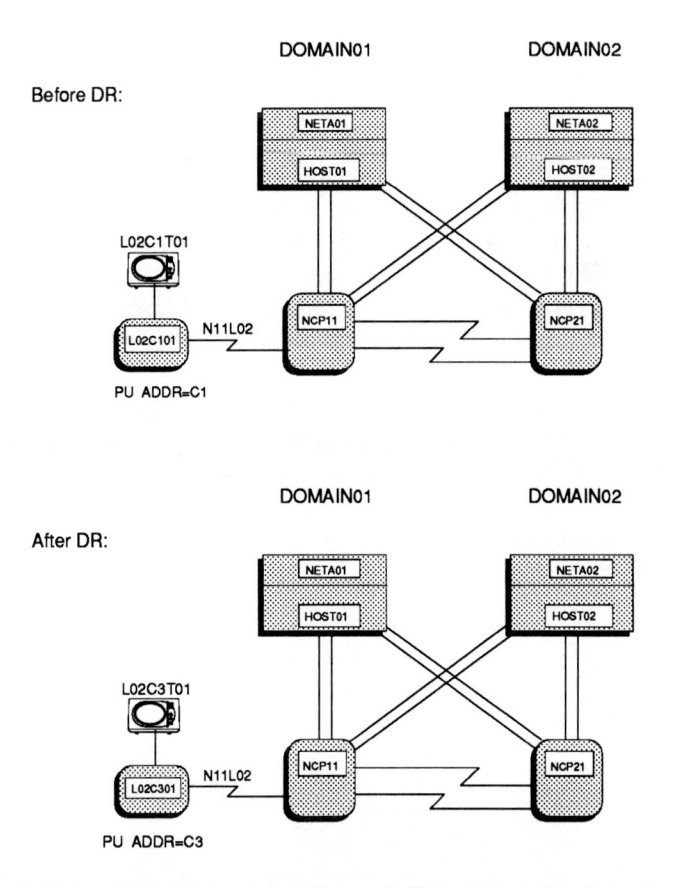

Figure 11.6 Example of using explicit Dynamic Reconfiguration Data Set (DRDS) member in VTAMLST.

220 Advanced SNA Networking

statement. The PU's cluster controller was reconfigured with an SDLC station address of 'C3', hence the name of the PU and the LU must change to be consistent with the networks naming convention.

To invoke the change we must first code a dynamic reconfiguration data set (DRDS) member in VTAMLST. Figure 11.7 contains the DRDS definitions that will be processed when the following command is entered by the network operator:

VARY NET,DRDS,ID=C1C3DR

Prior to invoking the command, the PU and LUs must be inactive. The ID parameter identifies the dynamic reconfiguration data set name in VTAMLST to use for this VARY DRDS command. The statements found in this DRDS will delete PU L02C101 and its LUs from line N11L02 and then add PU L02C301 and the LU L02C3T01 to line N11L02. This delete and add function is really modifying the current definition of the PU and LU.

This process of deletion and addition uses predefined entries in VTAM and the NCP resource tables. Figure 11.8 illustrates the use of the resource tables. In VTAM, the Resource Definition Table (RDT) contains the names and network addresses of resources in the NCP. Likewise, a Resource Vector Table (RVT) resides in the NCP for attached resources. Before the DR takes place, the PU L02C101 and the LU L02C1T01 contain entries in the RDT and RVT. Each entry is assigned a network address. The RVT is created during NCP generation. The number of DR entries supplied in the RVT is the sum of the PUDRPOOL, LUDRPOOL and RESOEXT values specified. It is this sum that determines the number of entries added to the end of the RVT, with each entry pointing to a DR pool control block. After the reconfiguration, we can see that the network address for L02C301 and L02C3T01 is

```
VTAMLST DRDS:  C1C3DR
               VBUILD    TYPE=DR
               DELETE    FROM=N11L02
     L02C101   PU
               ADD       TO=N11L02
     L02C301   PU        ADDR=C3,PUTYPE=2,ISTATUS=ACTIVE
     L02C3T01  LU        LOCADDR=02,USSTAB=USSSNA,              X
                         DLOGMOD=S3270,LOGAPPL=IMSP01,          X
                         ISTATUS=ACTIVE
```

Figure 11.7 DR statements for deleting and adding a PU and LU.

different from the original definition in both the RDT and the RVT. In fact, the original addresses are no longer valid and may not be used until the NCP is re-loaded into the front-end. An excessive number of dynamic reconfigurations for this NCP may result in a loss of available DR element addresses.

Enhancements to dynamic reconfiguration provided by VTAM V3R2 and NCP V4R3/V5R2 alleviate this shortage of DR element addresses. The depletion of DR element addresses has been cleared by simply allowing the NCP and VTAM to reuse the element addresses. Instead of the RDT and RVT entries being marked unavailable, they are now marked available for use.

Additionally, dynamic reconfiguration under VTAM V3R2 and NCP V4R3/V5R2 has been defined into two types, dynamic reconfiguration that is explicit and DR that is implicit. Explicit DR uses

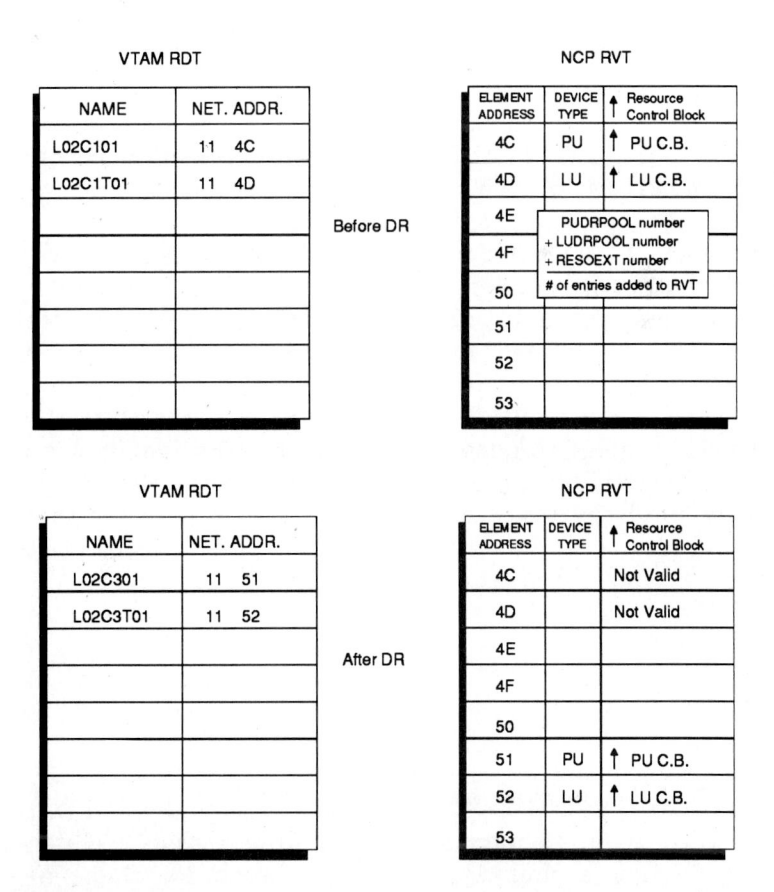

VTAM RDT

NAME	NET. ADDR.
L02C101	11 4C
L02C1T01	11 4D

Before DR

NCP RVT

ELEMENT ADDRESS	DEVICE TYPE	Resource Control Block
4C	PU	PU C.B.
4D	LU	LU C.B.
4E		
4F	PUDRPOOL number + LUDRPOOL number + RESOEXT number	
50	# of entries added to RVT	
51		
52		
53		

VTAM RDT

NAME	NET. ADDR.
L02C301	11 51
L02C3T01	11 52

After DR

NCP RVT

ELEMENT ADDRESS	DEVICE TYPE	Resource Control Block
4C		Not Valid
4D		Not Valid
4E		
4F		
50		
51	PU	PU C.B.
52	LU	LU C.B.
53		

Figure 11.8 Pre-VTAM V3R2 and pre-NCP V4R3 dynamic reconfiguration pool considerations.

222 Advanced SNA Networking

the VARY NET, DRDS and MODIFY DR, TYPE=MOVE | DELETE VTAM operator commands. The implicit DR allows changes to the NCP source statements that are reconciled at NCP activation. These two enhancements provide fuller functionality to dynamic reconfiguration.

Explicit DR is provided by the older format of a VARY NET,DRDS operator command and the new MODIFY DR,TYPE=MOVE | DELETE command. The VARY NET,DRDS command can still be used and may be preferable when changing resource names as in the above example, adding resources, or moving a resource from one NCP to another NCP. The new MODIFY DR, TYPE=MOVE | DELETE command facilitates deletes and adds within the same NCP. An advantage to using the new command is that it relieves the communications systems programmer from having to code all the necessary parameters of a PU and an LU when the DR is within the same NCP. These paramaters (e.g., USSTAB, DLOGMOD, LOGAPPL, ISTATUS) are carried with the new definition. It also allows for adding multiple resources to a line that was previously defined as a point-to-point configuration, assuming that the MAXPU operand of the LINE definition and the MAXLST operand of the SERVICE definition statement were coded to support more than one PU.

In Figure 11.9, we see a typical example of moving a PU from one line to another within the same NCP. There are two explicit DR methods available to us. To use the pre-VTAM V3R2 method, a DRDS must be defined and specified in VTAMLST. Remember that typical cluster controllers have 16 to 32 LU definitions. Each LU has specific needs defined by the various parameters specified in the NCP. Using this method, the communications systems programmer would have to recreate the definitions in the DRDS or all the original definitions would be lost, defaulting to the IBM supplied defaults. In a recovery situation, this time to code the DRDS is unacceptable. With the new MODIFY DR,TYPE=MOVE command, the resources can not only be recovered quickly, but all the existing definitions move with the resources. After a successful move, the ACTIVATE=YES parameter tells VTAM to activate the resource and all its subordinate resources that originally had ISTATUS=ACTIVE defined.

There is a drawback to the new command. When using the MODIFY DR,TYPE=MOVE command to change the SDLC station address, the resource names must remain unchanged. This would have gone against naming convention standards. But, since the SDLC station address change may have occurred without prior

Network Management and Problem Analysis 223

knowledge, the unconventional name for the resource may be acceptable for a short period of time.

People will often make changes to the production NCP source definition statements rather than copy the production NCP source. This update will be read by VTAM when the operator enters the VARY NET,ACT,ID=NCPname command. If the NCP is not already active to VTAM, these NCP source changes will cause the VTAM messages IST339I and IST072I to appear on the operator console. Essentially these messages are telling the operator that the NCP source statements and the NCP load module do not

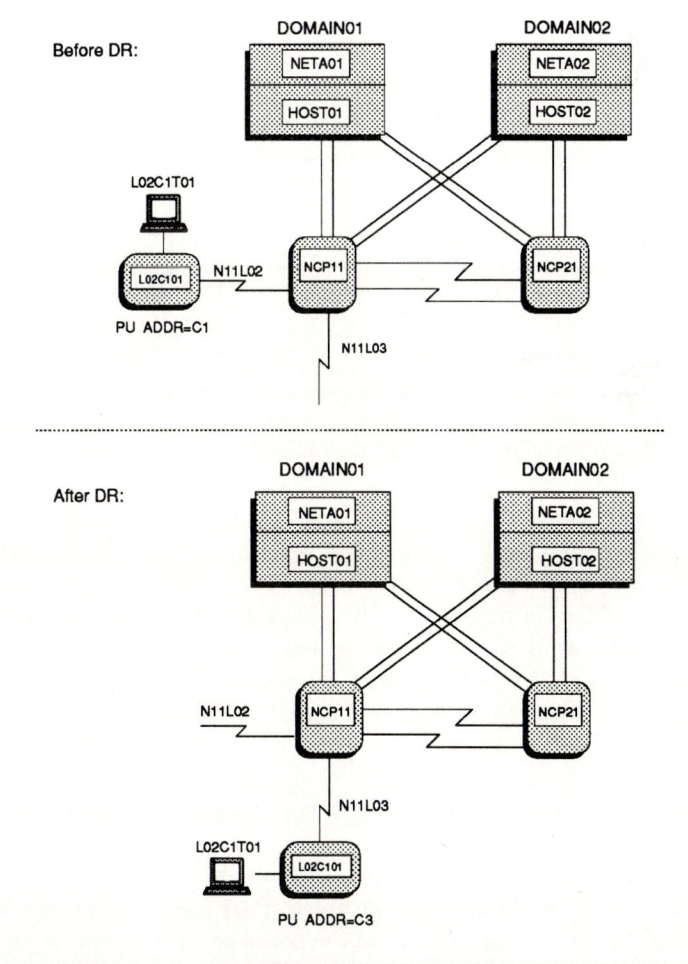

Figure 11.9 Example of using VTAM V3R2 MODIFY DR,TYPE=MOVE dynamic reconfiguration operator command.

NCP STATEMENT	OPERAND(S)	USE
BUILD	RESOEXT	Provides network addresses for generated devices which can be deleted and inserted into the DR pool.
	DR3270	Defines DR support for SDLC 3270 Type 1 devices models 11 and 12.
PUDRPOOL		Adds the executable code into the NCP load module to support dynamic reconfiguration.
	NUMBER	Specifies the number of DR PUs supported.
	MAXLU	Specifies the maximum number of DR LUs to any DR PU defined in this NCP.
LUDRPOOL	NUMTYP1	Specifies the total number of DR LUs for Type 1 PUs in this NCP.
	NUMTYP2	Specifies the total number of DR LUs for Type 2 PUs in this NCP.
	NUMILU	Specfies the total number of DR independent LUs for Type 2.1 PUs in this NCP.
LINE	MAXPU	Specifies the maximum number of PUs that can be defined for this line. Dynamic and actual.
SERVICE	MAXLIST	Maximum number of PUs defined in the sevice order table. Should match the MAXPU.
PU	MAXLU	Maximum number of actual and dynamic LUs that can be associated with this PU.
	PUDR	Specifies DR eligibility for this PU.
LU	LUDR	Specifies DR eligibilty for this LU.

Figure 11.10 NCP definition statements and their operands that affect dynamic reconfiguration.

match. The latest release of VTAM and NCP will dynamically create and add PUs to lines and LUs to PUs at NCP activation if the NCP source and NCP load modules do not match. Figure 11.10 contains the table of NCP definition statements and their associated operands that affect dynamic reconfiguration.

11.3.2 Communication Management Configuration (CMC)

In a multi-domain environment, control and management of the remote network can be further simplified by having a single VTAM host own all of the remote network resources. This type of configuration is called Communication Management Configuration (CMC) and is diagrammed in Figure 11.11. The advantage to this

Network Management and Problem Analysis 225

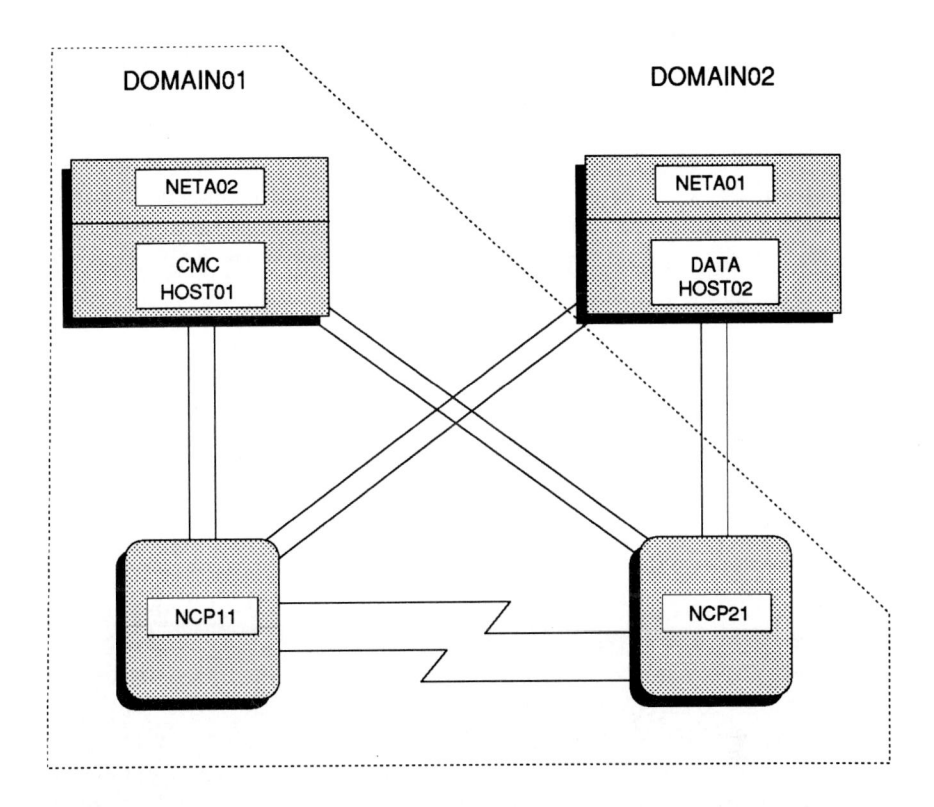

Figure 11.11 CMC network configuration with a CMC host and a data host.

is that all network resources are defined under one VTAM, which centralizes problem analysis and determination. Only the CNM applications and timesharing applications for the systems programming staff are usually found on a CMC host. The other hosts in this configuration are dedicated to end-user application processing and can be referred to as "data hosts". The data host is, however, responsible for control and management of all network resources that are channel-attached to the data host processor.

The CMC host contains the code for each NCP in the network. It activates and loads each NCP just as in any normal configuration. What really makes this configuration unique is the ability of the data hosts to contact the NCPs without activating them. Consequently, the data hosts do not require copies of the NCP generations. The data host uses the channel-attached major node definition

226   Network Management and Problem Analysis

for contacting the NCP. This capability is found in VTAM V2R2 or later for MVS and VSE environments, or VTAM V3R1.1 for VM.

To define the channel-attached major node for the NCP we must code VBUILD, GROUP, LINE and PU definition statements. Figure 11.12 details a sample major node definition for a channel-attached NCP. The one operand that identifies this major node as a definition for a channel-attached NCP is the LNCTL=NCP operand. By defining this major node, the network operator can contact the NCP(s) by issuing the VTAM operator command:

VARY NET,ACT,ID=CANCP

The activation of this major node allows the data host VTAM to communicate with the NCP and its resources without ownership. Therefore, all LU-LU sessions from the remote network are considered to be cross-domain sessions as viewed from the data host.

11.3.3 Extended Recovery Facility (XRF)

A further means of backup and recovery for LU-LU sessions is provided by the Extended Recovery Facility (XRF) of MVS/XA. This software product allows two IMS applications in different VTAM hosts to check-point the LU-LU sessions between IMS and the terminal LU. One of the IMS applications is the primary or active application. The second IMS application is the alternate or secondary application. If the primary application should experience a host related failure (e.g., MVS/XA, IMS, VTAM), then the alternate application will take over the active sessions with reduced impact.

XRF supports all SNA terminals attached to a BNN NCP V4 or higher and with VTAM V3 or higher on the host. The support XRF provides is for the primary LU (PLU) IMS application, the second-

```
      NETA01 Major Node:  CANCP
                          VBUILD    TYPE=CA
            CAGRP         GROUP     LNCTL=NCP,ISTATUS=ACTIVE,
                                    CHANCON=COND
            CALINEA       LINE      MAXBFRU=20,ADDRESS=A01
            CAPUA         PU        PUTYPE=4
            CALINEB       LINE      MAXBFRU=20,ADDRESS=B01
            CAPUB         PU        PUTYPE=4
```

Figure 11.12 Sample NCP channel-attached Major Node for CMC data host.

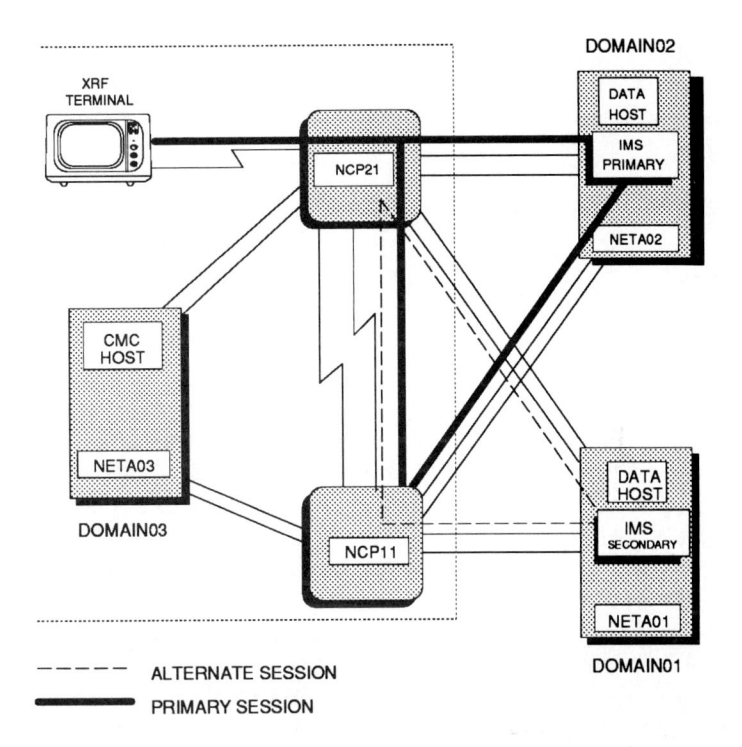

Figure 11.13 Using both CMC and XRF to provide backup and recovery for lost sessions.

ary LU remote terminal and switched SNA resources including X.25 terminals. XRF does not provide recovery support for the channel-attached SNA terminals or the NCP and the telecommunications lines.

In order for an IMS application to support XRF, the VTAM APPL definition statement that defines the IMS application must specify the operand HAVAIL=YES. This specifies to both VTAM and the IMS application that they are participating in an XRF complex. To include the support for the terminals that obtain a session with IMS, the NCP BUILD definition statement must have the BACKUP=n operand specified. The BACKUP operand defines the number of LUs in this NCP that may participate in the XRF complex. The value for "n" may range from 0 to 65535.

The recommended configuration for XRF is using CMC. As we discussed in the previous section, CMC provides the capability of one host controlling and owning all remote network resources. The remaining hosts in the network serve as data hosts. This configuration is a perfect arrangement for XRF. Figure 11.13 demonstrates the use of both CMC and XRF in a network. Note that the data hosts can provide backup using XRF for the IMS applications, while the CMC host concentrates on managing the network.

11.3.4 Dynamic Path Update

This enhancement of VTAM V3R2 and NCP V4R3/V5R2 allows the dynamic addition or deletion of SNA paths without the need for an NCP generation and subsequent loading of the NCP load module into the front-end. There are two types of dynamic path updates. You can delete previously defined explicit routes that are inoperative from their transmission group and add new explicit routes to transmission groups. The combination of the two allows you to move an explicit route from one transmission group to another. In addition, since the VTAM path table can be updated dynamically, you can now modify the virtual route pacing window size dynamically for inoperative routes. The only prerequisite to this capability is that the links used must be defined. If the links have to be previously defined, then why use dynamic path update since an NCP generation is required to add links? Well, the answer to that question is shown in Figure 11.14.

Suppose our network was originally configured as in Diagram A in Figure 11.14. The network has grown and a new communications control unit is coming in the door tomorrow. You just got back from your two week vacation in Hawaii, memories of wind surfing on a board rented from WindSurfer Jay's on Waikiki Beach. What will you do? You use dynamic path update, of course.

Diagram A shows us the links that currently exist between NCP11 and NCP 21 With dynamic update we can utilize these existing links. To do this we must first physically attach TG121 and TG122 to the new communications controller. Then we define the dynamic path statements in VTAMLST.

The path table member in VTAMLST is identified as a dynamic path table by the first non-comment line. If the first non-comment statement contains the VPATH or NCPPATH definition statement, VTAM will process this member using dynamic path update. As you can see in Figure 11.14 we have coded the dynamic path update members for the new configuration. The name of the VPATH definition statement must be the same as the value specified on the SSCPNAME start list option found in this VTAM's ATCSTR00 member of VTAMLST. If the name does not match,

Network Management and Problem Analysis 229

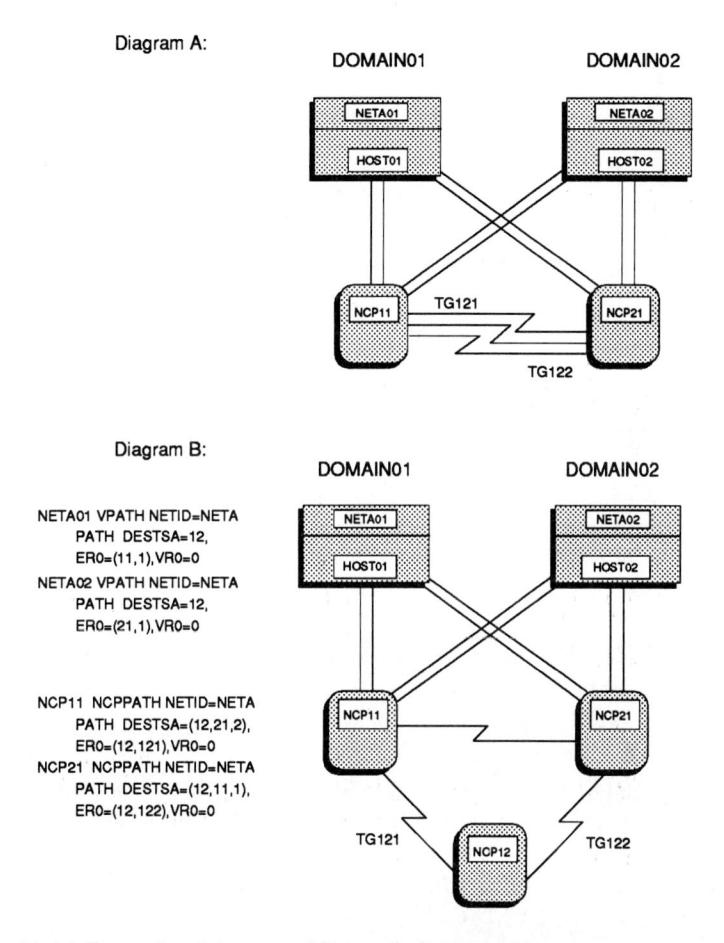

Diagram A:

```
           DOMAIN01              DOMAIN02
           ┌─NETA01─┐            ┌─NETA02─┐
           │ HOST01 │            │ HOST02 │
           └────────┘            └────────┘
                    ╲    ╱
                     ╲  ╱
                     ╱  ╲
           ┌──────┐ ╱ TG121 ╲ ┌──────┐
           │ NCP11│───────────│ NCP21│
           └──────┘           └──────┘
                      TG122
```

Diagram B:

```
NETA01 VPATH NETID=NETA
       PATH DESTSA=12,
       ER0=(11,1),VR0=0
NETA02 VPATH NETID=NETA
       PATH DESTSA=12,
       ER0=(21,1),VR0=0


NCP11 NCPPATH NETID=NETA
      PATH DESTSA=(12,21,2),
      ER0=(12,121),VR0=0
NCP21 NCPPATH NETID=NETA
      PATH DESTSA=(12,11,1),
      ER0=(12,122),VR0=0
```

Figure 11.14 Example of the use of Dynamic Path Table updates.

VTAM will ignore the following PATH and DELETER statements until a VPATH name has a matching SSCPNAME. Similarly, the name of the NCPPATH definition statement must be the same as that specified on the NEWNAME operand of a BUILD definition statement in an NCP that this VTAM has an active session with. If the name does not match, VTAM will ignore any following PATH and DELETER statements until a matching NEWNAME value of an active NCP is found.

There are four ways to invoke the dynamic path update. The first is by issuing the following operator command:

```
VARY NET,ACT,ID=dpumembr
```

230 Advanced SNA Networking

where *dpumembr* is the name of the dynamic path update member in the VTAMLST data set. The second approach is also an operator command:

VARY NET,ACT,ID=ncpname,NEWPATH=dpumembr

where the NEWPATH parameter allows you to enter from one to three dynamic path update member names when activating an NCP. The third way to invoke dynamic path updates is through the NEWPATH operand of the PCCU definition statement. This operand applies only to VTAM V3R2 or higher. The operand permits the specification of up to three dynamic path update members. The updates are sent to the NCP before any of the peripheral links are activated. The member names found on the PCCU NEWPATH parameter are overridden by the operator if the NEWPATH operand is specified on the VARY ACTivate command for this NCP. The fourth and final way is through the inclusion of the dynamic path update member names of VTAMLST in the ATCCON00 member of VTAMLST. In this case, you can specify as many dynamic path update members as are necessary. But, these are only used during VTAM initialization.

In order for the NCP to handle dynamic path updates, three operands were added to NCP V4R3/V5R2. These are the PATHEXT, TGBXTRA and the VRPOOL. The PATHEXT operand specifies the number of rows available in the NCP's Transit Routing Table (TRT) and the explicit route to virtual user route mapping, for this network after the path definition statements have been processed. The values range from 0 - 254. The default is 254. The TGBXTRA operand indicates the number of additional transmission group control blocks (TGBs). These TGBs are indexed by the subarea vector tables (SVT) that are generated after the path statements have been processed. The range is from 0 - 255. The default is the number of subarea links and subarea channels defined in the NCP. A second value has been added to the VRPOOL operand. This value specifies the number of flow control threshold (FCT) rows needed by the NCP. The minimum value coded may be 0; the maximum value is the value of the first parameter of the VRPOOL operand. The default is the first parameter. It is safe to say that your best bet is to allow all these operands to default.

11.3.5 Dynamic Table Replacement

Prior to VTAM V3R2, the following four tables associated with an LU were static. That is, the LU's major node would have to be

Network Management and Problem Analysis

inactivated, then reactivated, for the new table definitions to be incorporated into VTAM. These tables are the USS table (USSTAB), logon mode table (MODETAB), interpret table (INTTAB) and the class of service table (COS).

There are two types of dynamic table replacement (DTR). These are table loads and table associations. Both are accomplished through the MODIFY TABLE command. By specifying the following command, all resources currently using the logon mode table MODETAB1 will now use MODETAB2:

```
MODIFY VTAMPROC,TABLE,OPTION=LOAD,
NEWTAB=MODETAB2,OLDTAB=MODETAB1
```

The OPTION=LOAD operand tells VTAM to load the link-edited module named MODETAB2 into VTAM's address space from VTAMLIB. This OPTION=LOAD is only available for USSTAB, INTTAB and MODETAB. VTAM determines the type of table being requested. The OLDTAB operand is optional for this command. If OLDTAB is omitted, VTAM assumes it is the same as the NEWTAB value. You can also use the same name for NEWTAB and OLDTAB. This will cause VTAM to load a new copy of the table into memory.

A second DTR method is through dynamic association. Suppose we entered the previous command and decided that other LUs should also use this new mode table. Since it is already in VTAM's memory, there is no reason to reload it again. Instead, we can issue the following command:

```
MODIFY VTAMPROC,TABLE,TYPE=MODETAB,
OPTION=ASSOCIATE,NEWTAB=MODETAB2,ID=PUB01,OLDTAB=*
```

The result of this command is the association of all mode tables for LUs under PU PUB01 to the new mode table, MODETAB2. The TYPE operand indicates the type of table to replace. The other possible options for this operand are USSTAB and INTTAB. The OLDTAB=* operand indicates to VTAM that all logon mode tables for resources under PU, PUB01 will be replaced with the value in NEWTAB, MODETAB2. If an NCP name is specified in the ID operand, then every LU's logon mode table will be replaced with MODETAB2. If we were replacing a session-level USSTAB then the new USS message would appear on the terminal after any current LU-LU sessions end.

We can also associate a new class of service table with VTAM and a gateway NCP through this facility. Look at the following command:

232 Advanced SNA Networking

```
MODIFY VTAMPROC,TABLE,OPTION=ASSOCIATE,
TYPE=COSTAB,NEWTAB=COSTAB01,NETID=NETB,ORIGIN=NCP11
```

The new COS table is associated with the gateway NCP, NCP11 NETID NETB. NETB is the non-native network to this NCP gateway. The COS table for the native network does not change. Another attractive feature of this command is that it allows you to update ISTSDCOS dynamically by specifying the following command:

```
MODIFY VTAMPROC,TABLE,OPTION=ASSOCIATE,
TYPE=COSTAB,ORIGIN=hostpuname
```

This will tell VTAM to load the default COS table, ISTSDCOS, into memory by specifying the *hostpuname* as ISTPUS or the value assigned to the HOSTPU start option. Previously, VTAM would have to be taken down to reload this class of service table.

11.4 USING VTAM COMMANDS TO MANAGE THE SNA NETWORK

Management of an SNA network through VTAM is accomplished by using three operational commands. These are the DISPLAY, MODIFY and VARY VTAM operator commands. The DISPLAY command is used to obtain the current status of the network resources and to request route test information for display on the network operator's console. The MODIFY command can be used to alter VTAM start list options while VTAM is executing. The VARY command is used to alter the state of a network resource.

11.4.1 The DISPLAY Command

The DISPLAY ID command is by far the most commonly used VTAM command when operating an SNA network. The results of the command provide the operator with the current status of the resource selected, the desired status as a result of a VARY command, the name of the major node that this resource is associated with if it is a minor node, and LU-LU session data if the resource is so capable. Figure 11.15 outlines the format of the DISPLAY ID command.

The DISPLAY ID command is commonly used to view the current status of resources. For instance, if the command entered is:

Network Management and Problem Analysis   233

```
VM prefix   {DISPLAY|D}  NET,ID=name
                        [,NETID=netid]   <-- MVS|VM only
                        [,SCOPE=ACT|ALL|INACT|ONLY]
                        [,ACT|[EVERY|E],INACT|NONE]
```

Figure 11.15 Format of the DISPLAY ID VTAM command.

D NET,ID=NCP11

only information specific to the node named NCP11 will be displayed. In this example, only the status of NCP11 itself is displayed. If more information about the NCP were needed we could have entered:

D NET,ID=NCP11,E

to obtain the status of the links attached to the NCP as well as receiving the status of the NCP itself. We could have entered the

D NET,LINES

command to obtain the status of all links in the domain.

Use the SCOPE operand or the equivalent standing operand to limit the resource display to a specific status. An example is using the INACT operand to quickly determine which subordinate resources of the requested resource are currently inactive.

So, as you can see, by using the DISPLAY ID command we can determine the current state of any network resource. The resource can be a major or minor node, an application name or an NCP, PU, LU or LINE name.

Let's look at some DISPLAY commands that have built-in functions for specific types of resources. Figure 11.16 contains a list of VTAM DISPLAY commands frequently used to gather status infor-

```
VM prefix   {DISPLAY|D}    NET,MAJNODES
                       D   NET,APPLS
                       D   NET,PENDING
                       D   NET,PATHTAB
```

Figure 11.16 Some of the compounded VTAM commands.

mation of related resources. The formats listed can be used as written.

The D NET,MAJNODES command will display the current status of all major nodes known to this VTAM. That is, major nodes that were activated at start up or activated by the operator. The display shows only those major nodes that are currently active and those that were active but are now in another state. This command does not display major nodes that were never active.

The D NET,APPLS command displays the state of all application minor node names of active application major nodes, including application minor node names that were never activated when the application major node was activated. This display supplies session information for the application minor node only. If the status is CONCT, the application is in a connectable state waiting for the application program to issue an OPEN for the application ACB-name. In most cases this means that the application program has not been started by the operator.

There are some 69 pending states for resources in an SNA network, far too many to include in this book. The display from the VTAM command D NET,PENDING is useful in obtaining the status of all resources that are pending some type of action. Two of the more common pending states are pending activate PU (2) PAPU2 and pending contacted (2) PCTD2. You may see these states during activation of a peripheral PU. PAPU2 specifies that the ACTPU has been sent to the device but the device has not yet responded. The PCTD2 indicates that VTAM has started the activation of the PU but VTAM has not received the CONTACTED reply from the device. The PU address may be inconsistent with that defined in VTAM or the device may not be initialized. The (2) on these states refers to the state of the secondary link station.

Throughout this book we have referred to the PATH table used by VTAM to route data through the network. The D NET, PATHTAB command requests VTAM to display the current path table on the operator's console. The display will identify the destination subarea (DESTSUB), the adjacent subarea (ADJSUB) to reach the DESTSUB, the explicit route (ER) used to reach the ADJSUB, the status of the ER, and the virtual routes (VRs) that have the ER mapped. Take note that this display does not list the transmission group number (TGN). A common status for the ER STATUS column is INOP. This indicates that the ER is defined to VTAM, but there is no physical connection between VTAM and the adjacent subarea.

Network Management and Problem Analysis

There is one more DISPLAY command that we need to discuss, especially when debugging a route problem. The command is the DISPLAY ROUTE command. Figure 11.17 outlines the format.

Using this command, we can determine the routes defined to specific subareas from specific subareas. For example, we can request the display of routes from NCP to NCP, or from SSCP to SSCP, or SSCP to NCP, or NCP to SSCP. This is accomplished by using the DESTSUB and ORIGIN operands of the DISPLAY ROUTE command. Refer back to Figure 11.13. To verify that routes from the CMC host named NETA01 has routes available to the data host named NETA02, we enter the command:

D NET,ROUTE,DESTSUB=2,ORIGIN=NET02PU

This will display the routes defined for the SSCP at NETA01 to communicate to the SSCP at NETA02. The display will identify the origin and destination PU names. It also displays the VRs, the transmission priority (TP), and their status along with the ER status. This display will assist you in mapping the exact paths that are active and available for use. By adding the TEST=YES operand, VTAM performs explicit route tests for each explicit route defined in the route tables. This is because we defaulted to ER=ALL. The results of this test are displayed and provide the operator with the status of the ER, the number of subareas traversed to perform the test for the ER and the TG used for the test. The results also indicate if the test succeeded or failed. An all too common result is the explicit route tested was non-reversible. That is, a reverse route through the same subareas was not defined properly. Remember, data can traverse different forward and reverse explicit routes, but the ERs must pass through the same subareas.

Now that you have a feel for how you can display the status of network resources, let's look at how we can alter the state of these resources.

```
VM prefix    {DISPLAY|D}  NET,ROUTE
                          ,DESTSUB=subarea number
                          [,COSNAME=name|ER=n|ER=ALL|VR=n]
                          [,NETID=netid]  <-- MVS|VM only
                          [,ORIGIN=subarea pu name]
                          [,TEST=YES|NO]
```

Figure 11.17 Format for the DISPLAY ROUTE command.

```
VM prefix   {VARY|V}    NET,REL,ID=name
                        [,CDLINK=ACT|INACT]
                        [,I]
```

Figure 11.18 Format for the VARY REL command.

11.4.2 The VARY Command

Use the VTAM VARY command to change the state of resources. We have used this command throughout the book in our examples. Here we will concentrate on some of the VARY commands not previously discussed that can be used by the operator to manage network resources. These are the VARY REL, and the VARY NOLOGON commands.

In early sections of this chapter we discussed some backup and recovery scenarios for network outages. In those scenarios we explained the use of the VARY ACQ command. The VARY REL command (Figure 11.18) is issued to relinquish ownership of the acquired resources. The default for the command allows sessions to continue during the release process. You can release the NCP, PUs and LUs by placing their names in the ID operand. The VARY REL command allows you to release lower-level nodes by releasing the higher-level nodes. For example,

```
VARY NET,REL,ID=NCP11
```

will release all of the resources subordinate to NCP11 as well as NCP11 itself.

Previously we discussed the ability to assign an application to an LU by using the VARY LOGON command with the LOGAPPL operand or by the application acquiring the LU. The VARY NOLOGON command (Figure 11.19) allows the operator to remove the auto-logon function. For instance, if LU name B01T00 has a controlling PLU named CICS01, we can remove the controlling PLU from owning the LU by issuing the command:

```
V NET,NOLOGON=CICS01,ID=B01T00
```

```
VM prefix   {VARY|V}    NET,NOLOGON={pluname|*},ID=name
```

Figure 11.19 Format for the VARY NOLOGON command.

```
VM prefix    {MODIFY|F}   procname
                          ,CSALIMIT={value|(value[,F]}
                          [,OPTION=TOTAL|BELOW]
```

Figure 11.20 Format for the MODIFY CSALIMIT command.

If several LUs of a PU are controlled by different applications, we can enter the following command to remove the controlling PLU of each LU on the PU:

`V NET,NOLOGON=*,ID=PUB01`

11.4.3 The MODIFY Command

Of all the MODIFY commands available, the MODIFY CSALIMIT command (Figure 11.20) could make your day. In *Introduction to SNA Networking*, we discussed the CSALIMIT and CSA24 parameters of the start options list in VTAMLST and their use by VTAM. If the values selected during initialization prove to be insufficient during production, VTAM will let you know. In fact, no new requests will be handled by VTAM until the resource shortage has been recovered. The MODIFY CSALIMIT command allows you to alter the address space available for VTAM's region in the host computer. You can increase or decrease the storage available to VTAM. Depending on the operating system, the value can go as high as 2 gigabytes. The value is specified on the CSALIMIT id in kilobytes. The OPTION operand is specific to MVS/XA and determines if the value specified is for the CSA24 start option (OPTION=BELOW) or if it is for the CSALIMIT start option (OPTION=TOTAL).

The MODIFY TNSTAT command (Figure 11.21) can be used to turn off tuning statistics that were started at initialization time. The TNSTAT start option must have been specified in the start options list in order for this MODIFY command to take effect. By specifying NO, the tuning statistics are written to the MVS SMF

```
VM prefix    {MODIFY|F}   procname,TNSTAT
                          [,CNSL=YES|NO][,TIME=n]
```

Figure 11.21 Format for the MODIFY TNSTAT command.

data set, the VSE Trace file and the VM "FILE TUNSTATS A" CMS file, or an alternate file with the DDname TUNSTATS defined with the GCS FILEDEF command. Specifying YES will cause the tuning statistics to also write to the system console. The TIME operand specifies the number of minutes between tuning statistics recording events.

11.5 VTAM TRACE FACILITIES

During the course of managing an SNA network, there comes a time when you must determine a problem by analyzing the actual data that flows between network resources. VTAM provides a means to obtain this data by allowing you to request specific types of VTAM traces. The TRACE start list option can be used to start some of these traces at initialization time. In most instances, you will not know that a trace is required to debug an SNA-related problem until the more common means of problem determination have been exhausted. VTAM provides a command to start or modify traces after VTAM has been initialized. Of course, the command is the MODIFY TRACE command.

The MODIFY TRACE command is used on all three operating systems. The command has several operands and parameters that can request a specific type of trace between two network resources. We will discuss the three most commonly used traces for debugging SNA-related problems that you may encounter at your installation. These are the IO, BUFFER and GPT traces. Figure 11.22 details the complete format of the MODIFY TRACE VTAM command.

During the tracing of a resource, VTAM will write the trace records to a file for later analysis. The file can be read by a print program that is specific to each operating system. More than one trace of a node can be active at a time, but a MODIFY TRACE command must be issued for each type of trace requested.

The specification of TYPE=IO causes VTAM to trace I/O activity associated with the name supplied on the ID= operand. This trace provides the contents of the TH, RH and the first seven bytes of the RU. You should use this trace only when you suspect the problem is caused by a network control (NC), data flow control (DFC) or perhaps a function management data (FMD) request or response unit, since these controls will be found in the beginning of the RU traced. An example of the command is:

Network Management and Problem Analysis   239

```
VM prefix   {MODIFY|F}          procname,TRACE
            ,TYPE={BUF|GPT|IO|LINE|NETCLR|SIT|SMS|TG|TSO|VTAM}
            [,COUNT=n|ALL]
            [,FRAMES=DATA|ALL]
            [,ID=name]
            [,LINE=name]
            [,MODE=INT|EXT]
            [,OPTION=option|(option|,..)|ALL]
            [,PU=physical unit name]
            [,SIZE=size]
            [,SCOPE=ALL|ONLY]
```

Figure 11.22 Format of the MODIFY TRACE command.


```
F NET,TRACE,TYPE=IO,ID=PU11C1
```

This command will start an I/O trace between VTAM and PU11C1. If we also specified the SCOPE=ALL operand, then the LUs associated with PU11C1 would be traced. You should be careful when using the SCOPE=ALL operand during tracing, because if the node being traced has several subordinate nodes, VTAM performance will be seriously impacted.

The TYPE=BUF specification on the MODIFY TRACE command is most useful when the problem appears to be related to the application data flowing on the PLU-SLU session flow. That is, when it appears that the application program or the information received from the SLU by the application program is in error. The buffers traced in VTAM are from the Application Program Interface (API) and the Transmission Subsystem Component (TSC) of VTAM. The buffer trace provides you with up to 256 bytes of RU data.

The final TYPE=GPT trace is called the NCP generalized PIU trace. This trace provides PIU information for NCP resources including switched and nonswitched lines, switched and nonswitched PUs and LUs, and the NCP itself. This trace can provide you with the full PIU, both inbound and outbound to the host from the specified name in the ID=operand. The trace data does not include link-level protocols.

11.5.1 VTAM Trace Procedure for MVS

Before the MODIFY TRACE command is issued in an MVS operating system environment, the Generalized Trace Facility (GTF) must be started. This trace facility is used by VTAM to record the trace records in a specific format in a file for later reference. The file name on an MVS system is usually SYS1.TRACE, but check with your installation's MVS systems programmer for the proper file name.

To start the generalized tracing facility of MVS you must first determine the name of the JCL procedure. Usually this is GTF, and it is found in the MVS library SYS1.PROCLIB. You can start this trace procedure by entering the command:

```
START GTF,MEMBER=GTFVTAM
```

Be sure to check with your installation for the actual procedure names and appropriate parameters. The GTF procedure runs as an MVS subtask. To stop GTF, first display the GTF task and observe the output. The number on the display refers to the device address that GTF is using to record the trace records. For example, use the MVS STOP command to end GTF by entering: P 242. The address 242 is the device on which the SYS1.TRACE data set resides.

There are three GTF options that can be specified for recording VTAM traces. The GTF parameter TRACE= must have at least one of these options specified. The RNIO option must be specified for the VTAM I/O trace (MODIFY TRACE TYPE=IO) to record NCP or peripheral PU trace records. The IO or IOP option is used for the I/O trace of channel-attached devices. The USR option must be specified for GTF to record a VTAM internal trace, buffer trace, line trace and SMS trace.

There are two print programs available on MVS to create a report from the trace formatted trace records: the print dump service aid, PRDMP, and the Trace Analysis Program, often referred to as ACF/TAP. The preferred method is ACF/TAP. ACF/TAP reports contain the trace records in a clean orderly format, with the information of record broken down to its parts for easier analysis. TAP will break down all the fields of the TH, RH and RU if the RU is a Management Services RU. The reports include Line trace summary and detail, SNA analysis summary and detail, network data traffic, network error, and GPT summary reports.

11.5.2 VTAM Trace Procedure for VSE

In the VSE environment, the VTAM trace data is recorded and printed by a print utility that can be run as a subtask of VTAM or as a VSE job step. The utility is named TPRINT. Under normal circumstances, the trace utility is started as a subtask under VTAM by using the VTAM command:

MODIFY NET,SUBTASK,ID=TPRINT,FUNCTION=ATTACH

The TPRINT utility must have the SYSLST DDname assigned to a printer, tape, or disk with the device name of IJSYSLS. It is wise to assign the SYSLST statement to a device such as a tape drive, which will prohibit the possibility of wraparound. Wraparound occurs mainly on disk drive files where a limited amount of space has been assigned to that file. This wraparound can occur for GTF as well. GTF can also be used under VSE for the recording of TRACE TYPE=VTAM,MODE=EXT and TYPE=GPT. ACF/TAP can be used on the TPRINT format to print out the trace records or you can use the TPRINT print format. However, like the PRDMP utility of MVS, the TPRINT print format does not break down the bits and bytes of the trace records.

11.5.3 VTAM Trace Procedure Under VM

Under VM, the VTAM trace records are handled by the Group Control System (GCS) and Control Program (CP). When using GCS, the records are placed in an internal wraparound table. It is preferable to use CP, which records the data on a special CP file.

To start the process, the following commands must be issued on the machine:

1. Start CPTRAP only if it is not started by issuing the command CPTRAP START.
2. CPTRAP ALLOWID userid must then be issued to specify which group or userid will handle the trace requests.
3. CPTRAP 3D specifies the event code request for the trace.

Now that CPTRAP has been started and properly initialized, GCS must be made aware of the trace events. To do this, the GCS ETRACE command is used to identify which trace event must be passed to CPTRAP. Note the following:

4. ETRACE GTRACE GROUP must be entered to specify that all GTRACE requests from any virtual machine in the group are to be passed to CPTRAP.
5. ETRACE GTRACE userid is now entered to specify that all GTRACE requests from this userid are to be passed to CPTRAP.

Once all of this is accomplished, you may then issue the MODIFY TRACE commands. To stop VM VTAM from tracing, the CPTRAP STOP command can be issued, causing a reader file to be created, which is then closed and all tracing ceases.

The printing of VM VTAM trace data can be performed by using a VM VTAM provided exit that formats the CPTRAP reader file by using the TRAPRED command. This exit formats the trace records into a format similar to that of MVS, which can then be processed by TAP.

After halting all of the trace facilities available to the operating systems, the MODIFY NOTRACE command must be issued to inform VTAM that tracing is no longer requested. The command is similar in format to the MODIFY TRACE command.

We have only discussed a few of the possible trace and print operations available to VTAM. You should take the time to learn the procedures, learn how to read the traces and become familiar with the formats before you encounter a dire need to use the facilities. A good exercise is to trace normal flows (e.g., SSCP-PU, SSCP-LU, LU-LU, Link activation, NCP activation, SSCP-SSCP). In this way, when a problem does occur, you can go back to a formatted printout of a valid trace to compare with the problem trace.

11.6 SUMMARY

In this chapter we reviewed various functions available within VTAM to manage your network. We discussed how using the ISTATUS, OWNER, BACKUP and LOGAPPL VTAM parameters can be used to manipulate resource management and control. Advanced dynamic reconfiguration for network resources has improved the flexibility of SNA network management. This is accomplished using Dynamic Reconfiguration, Dynamic Table Replacement and Dynamic Path Update. We also reviewed managing an SNA network with VTAM commands.

As you have seen, VTAM commands can provide you with the basic status and health of the network. But as networks grow, managing them becomes more complex and requires an application that is dedicated to network management. The next chapter will review the most widely used communication network management application, IBM's NetView.

Chapter

12

NetView and NetView/PC

The importance of managing an SNA network became evident after IBM introduced the concept of multi-domain networks in the late 1970's with the Multi-System Networking Facility (MSNF). MSNF provided VTAM hosts with the ability to communicate and share resources between them. SNA networks have since migrated from single-domain to multiple domain, and in 1984 to multiple network configurations with SNA Network Interconnection (SNI). The complexity of managing these networks has increased even further by including the management of the network facility equipment. A comprehensive network management system is needed as the focal point to manage and control all of the variables that comprise today's complex networks.

NetView is IBM's strategic tool for managing these highly complex SNA networks. NetView resides under SNA's Open Network Management (ONM) architecture as the cornerstone for a full, comprehensive network management system that incorporates five major network management functions:

1. Configuration Management.
2. Problem Management.
3. Performance Management.
4. Accounting and Availability Management.
5. Distribution Management.

To support a multi-vendor environment, non-IBM equipment and non-SNA resources must be included for true end-to-end cen-

245

tralized network management. NetView/PC provides this functionality under ONM. It allows a user or vendor to create an application that executes on a PC that can collect and generate architected network management alerts for non-IBM and non-SNA resources. These alerts can then be processed by NetView or a similar host-based CNM application.

Before we describe the functions and facilities of NetView and NetView/PC, we must introduce you to the architecture and message flows utilized by them.

12.1 OPEN NETWORK MANAGEMENT ARCHITECTURE

Open Network Management (ONM) through published network management architectures allows users and vendors to incorporate non- IBM and non-SNA resource management under SNA. An Application Program Interface (API) is provided under ONM that allows users and vendors to access network management data and commands. This facilitates the notion of centralized network management which includes both voice and data. Finally, network management products that can interpret the architecture and utilize the API are supported. These network management products have three distinctive roles which are the focal point, entry point and service point.

12.1.1 Focal Point

A focal point provides central network management for the domain. It resides in the host and can be a product or a set of products that supply comprehensive support for managing the network. The network operator, along with the focal point, determines the actions necessary for managing the network. In Figure 12.1 we see that a focal point is residing on a host computer that is running VTAM. The figure indicates that NetView is the focal point for this network. However, any CNM application that has the AUTH=CNM operand specified on the APPL definition statement possesses the ability to be a focal point. More than one focal point application can reside on a host. An example of other focal points are System Center's Net/Master, IBM's Netview Performance Monitor (NPM) and IBM Information Management

(Info/Man). Each of these focal point applications can coincide with NetView or operate without NetView.

12.1.2 Entry Point

An entry point transports network management data and session data to a host over the same link. An SNA PU is an entry point. The PU performs the functions of network management as well as those functions concerned with transporting session data for its peripheral resources. The entry point is in the same domain as the focal point. This is because the focal point works in conjunction with VTAM and VTAM owns any entry point that it activates. The entry point supports the SNA architected management formats

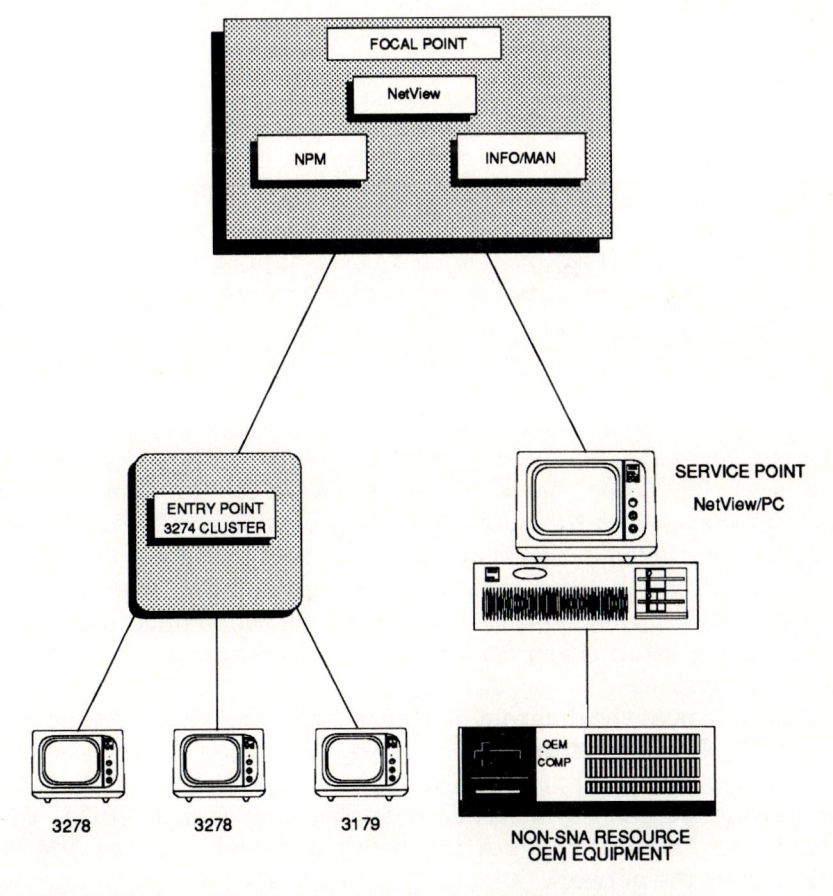

Figure 12.1 Diagram featuring the three roles of ONM architecture.

and protocols to the focal point. Examples of an entry point are IBM 3274 and 3174 cluster controllers.

12.1.3 Service Point

The service point rounds out the ONM architecture roles by providing SNA network management for non-SNA products. Non-SNA products do not have SNA addressability and do not implement the SNA network management services formats and protocols. The service point converts native vendor protocols to SNA formats and then transmits them to the focal point. As with the entry point, the service point must be in the same domain as the focal point. The service point communicates with the focal point on an SSCP-PU session. NetView/PC and applications that can execute with NetView/PC are examples of a service point.

12.2 SNA NETWORK SERVICES FLOW

Prior to Open Network Management, information pertaining to non-SNA resources (e.g., modems, multiplexers, matrix switches) were not consolidated by the SNA CNM application. A different management system outside of the main processor of the computer center handled the management of non-SNA resources. ONM now eliminates the need for two separate management systems to ascertain and diagnose network problems. The consolidation of network fault messages and control under one single application can greatly decrease the time needed to resolve network problems. However, ONM does not eliminate the need for the management system that passes the network fault to NetView/PC. But it does impose a requirement on the non-SNA resource vendor: to write a NetView/PC application that can translate non-SNA alerts to the ONM NMVT format and to allow NetView commands to initiate and request information from the non-SNA resource vendor management system.

Take a look at the diagram in Figure 12.2. This figure provides a typical ONM flow using SNA network management services. In this diagram, a focal point CNM application resides in a MVS/XA operating system. The NetView application named NPDA, the Hardware Facility, receives all unsolicited and solicited NMVT alerts from the network.

NetView and NetView/PC   249

Notice that we have two forms of network management service (NS) request units (RU) that can flow to the focal point. Prior to NMVTs, an NS RU named Record Formatted Maintenance Statistics (RECFMS) was used for unsolicited alerts. In fact, this format is still used by many devices for both unsolicited and solicited RUs. RECFMS is sent to the focal point as a solicited reply in response to the Request Maintenance Statistic (REQMS) NS RU.

Once the NetView/PC application has received and translated the proprietary protocol of the vendor's alarms into an NMVT, both the Service Point and the Entry Point flows are the same. Each transmits the alarm to the focal point via the SSCP-PU session. The SSCP receives the NS RU and must determine the recipient CNM application for this NS RU. It does this by scanning the

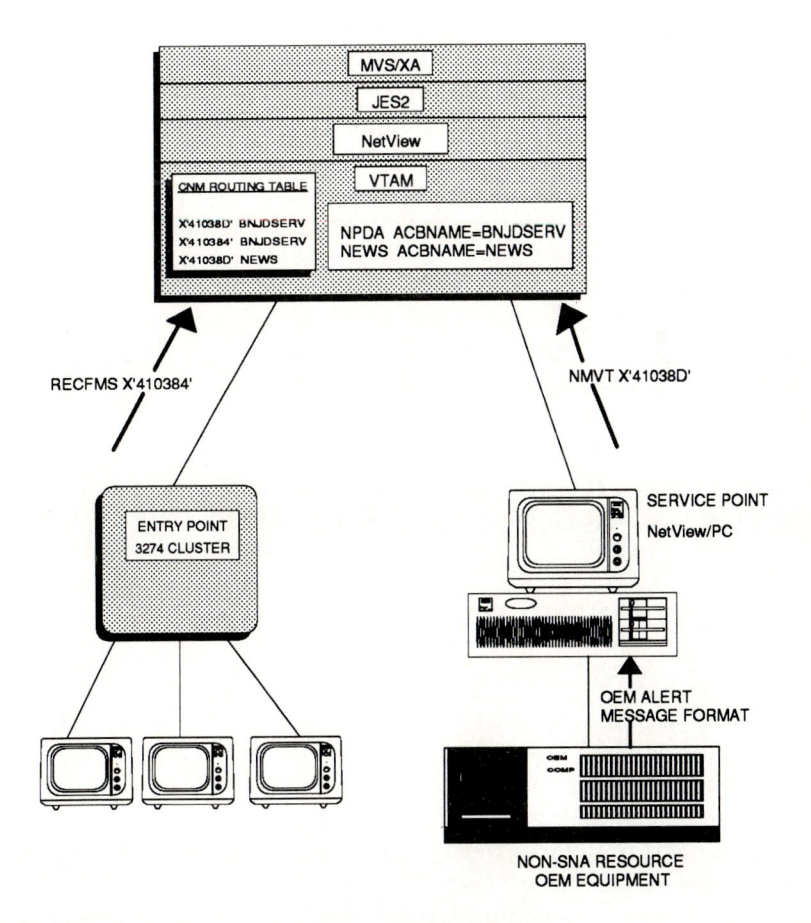

Figure 12.2 SNA Network Management Services flow.

CNM Routing Table. Comparing the NS RU header received from the network with values defined in the CNM Routing Table, the SSCP can then deliver the NS RU to the associated CNM application.

In our example, the CNM application is NPDA, which has an ACB named BNJDSERV. The BNJDSERV ACB is defined to receive both RECFMSs and NMVTs. After determining the receiving application, the SSCP delivers the NS RU to the named ACB which will then process the alarms. Notice that we have also defined an ACB named NEWS for receiving NMVTs. A stipulation for SSCP routing of NS RUs, is that only one CNM application can receive an NS RU. In this case, the ACB for NPDA (BNJDSERV) was opened and participating in an SSCP-LU session with VTAM before the NEWS ACB was opened. To allow NEWS to receive the NMVT alerts from the network, the ACB BNJDSERV must be closed and the NEWS ACB must be opened. This can be accomplished by using the NetView Command Facility operator command STOP TASK=BNJDSERV command to close the BNJDSERV ACB and the VARY ACTivate command to open the NEWS ACB. The NEWS CNM application is not a task of NetView, but rather an independent CNM application. Therefore, the NetView command START TASK=NEWS will not accomplish activation of the NEWS ACB. Once the NEWS ACB is successfully opened by VTAM, it will process all NMVT NS RUs that are received by the SSCP. However, the RECFMS NS RUs are lost because the ACB for BNJDSERV was closed to allow NEWS to receive NMVTs. We can overcome this by issuing the NetView command START TASK=BNJDSERV to open the BNJDSERV ACB once again. In this case, the BNJDSERV will not receive the NMVTs since NEWS is already receiving them, but it will receive the RECFMS NS RUs.

12.3 NETVIEW RELEASE 1 OVERVIEW

In May, 1986, IBM launched their long-range plan for centralized network management. At the core of the plan is NetView. In this initial release, NetView is a conglomeration of previously independent communications network management (CNM) program products. This repackaging of CNM program products allowed IBM to deliver a comprehensive network management package at a reasonable price. There are five main functions provided with NetView R1: Network Command Control Facility (NCCF) was released in 1979 as a program product along with the Network Problem

Determination Application (NPDA); Network Logical Data Manager (NLDM) was released in 1984; and the VTAM Node Control Application (VNCA) and Network Management Productivity Facility (NMPF) which were both originally offered as field-developed programs (FDP). All five applications were released as supported CNM program products in 1986.

12.3.1 Network Command Control Facility (NCCF)

At the heart of the NetView CNM programs is the Network Command Control Facility, now known as the NetView Command Facility (Figure 12.3). This program encompasses the role of the VTAM Primary Program Operator (PPO). The PPO is allowed to issue VTAM operator commands and receive solicited and unsolicited VTAM operator messages. These messages are not the same as solicited and unsolicited NS RUs. The operator messages are of the VTAM IST type found in the VTAM Messages and Codes manual. The Command Facility provides points of entry into the CNM interface for end-users to capture and modify network management data. These customizable points of entry are known as exits. The exit routines must be coded in IBM ASSEMBLER Language. The facility also provides an interpretive language called Command List (CLIST). The CLIST provides a rudimentary means of

```
* NVA01     MAJNODES
C NVA01     DISPLAY NET,MAJNODES
NVA01       IST097I DISPLAY ACCEPTED
' NVA01
IST350I     VTAM DISPLAY - DOMAIN TYPE = MAJOR NODES
IST089I
IST089I
IST089I
IST089I
IST089I
IST089I     NVA01      TYPE = APPL SEGMENT      , ACTIV
IST089I     NCP11      TYPE = PU T4/5 MAJ NODE  , ACTIV
IST089I     SWRJE      TYPE = SW SNA MAJ NODE   , ACTIV
IST089I     CDRM01     TYPE = CDRM SEGMENT      , ACTIV
IST089I     CDRSC01    TYPE = PU T4/5 MAJ NODE  , ACTIV
??? ***
MAJNODES
```

Figure 12.3 Sample display of NetView's Command Facility.

252 Advanced SNA Networking

simplifying and automating the network operator's responsibilities.

12.3.2 NETVIEW HARDWARE MONITOR

The NetView Hardware Monitor (previously known as Network Problem Determination Application, NPDA) receives SNA network management services data that concerns hardware faults for resources in an SNA network. In addition to SNA resources, link level diagnostic data can be received by the Hardware Monitor from modems that support IBM's Link Problem Determination Aid (LPDA) facility. This capability marks IBM's entrance into managing network facilities as well as SNA resources. The Hardware Monitor application notifies a network operator of resource outages and their probable cause, and recommends actions to rectify the problem (Figures 12.4 and 12.5). The Hardware Monitor receives unsolicited and solicited network management services data from SNA resources (e.g., PUs, LUs). This data comprises a formatted request unit (RU) that contains code points and is known as the Network Management Vector Transport (NMVT) or Record Formatted Maintenance Statistics (RECFMS). The code points are used to display pre-defined alert display messages and accompanying recommended actions that reside in files on the host

```
N E T V I E W                                          OPER1     03/28/89 15:22:29
NPDA-BNIFFE25 * RECOMMENDED ACTION FOR SELECTED EVENT *          PAGE 1 OF 1
NVA01             NCP11        L2411
                  +--------+
DOMAIN            ! COMC   !----LINE----
                  +--------+
USER    CAUSED - LOCAL MODEM POWER OFF
                 ACTIONS - D001 - CORRECT THEN RETRY
INSTALL CAUSED - CABLE
                 ACTIONS - D022 - CHECK PHYSICAL INSTALLATION
FAILURE CAUSED - LOCAL MODEM
                 LOCAL MODEM INTERFACE CABLE
ACTIONS-         D022 - CHECK PHYSICAL INSTALLATION
                 D002 - RUN MODEM TESTS
                 D005 - CONTACT APPROPRIATE SERVICE REPRESENTATIVE

ENTER D TO VIEW DETAIL DISPLAY

???
CMD== >
```

Figure 12. 4 Recommended Action display from NetView's Hardware Monitor.

```
N E T V I E W                                            OPER1   03/28/89 15:26:16
NPDA-43B     * EVENT DETAIL FOR SDLC STATION *                     PAGE 1 OF 1
NVA01           NCP11        L2411
                +--------+
DOMAIN          ! COMC   !----LINE----
                +--------+
DATE/TIME: 03/28 15:20
OPERATION - RUN - INITIATES NORMAL SEND/RECEIVE OPERATIONS ON THE SDLC LINK;
ERROR WHILE SENDING TEXT I-FORMAT

PROBABLE CAUSE - MODEM INTERFACE FAILURE
ERROR DESCRIPTION - TRANSMIT CLOCK OR CTS FAILURE


0381000E 83250400 00000001 C0203000 00000AF2 00000000 000B0071 00232200
00016666 40A10000 00800000 00C3000B 008F000B 00000000 1E00FC00 00000000
00000000 00000000 00000000 00000000 00000000 00000000 00000000 00007100
ENTER A TO VIEW ACTION DISPLAY

???
CMD== >
```

Figure 12.5 Sample Event Detail display from NetView's Hardware Monitor.

processor's peripheral storage devices. These files can be customized by end-users to suit their network management needs. The resulting alert errors are logged to the Hardware Monitor alert data base and to an external logging file, such as IBM's System Management Facility (SMF) for further processing and analysis at a later time.

12.3.3 NetView Session Monitor

To assist in trouble shooting SNA session errors, NetView has incorporated the Network Logical Data Manager (NLDM) program product under the guise of the NetView Session Monitor (Figure 12.6). Depending on the NLDM initialization parameters, all SNA sessions may be traced to gather session information, including SSCP-SSCP, SSCP-PU, SSCP-LU and LU-LU sessions. This session information includes session partners, explicit and virtual routes, and specific error and reason codes for session failures. This facility also provides the capability of tracing SNA Path Information Units (PIUs) that travel between the session partners. This data is logged and recalled by the operator for further in-depth analysis of the session error. The Session Monitor is also

254 NetView and NetView/PC

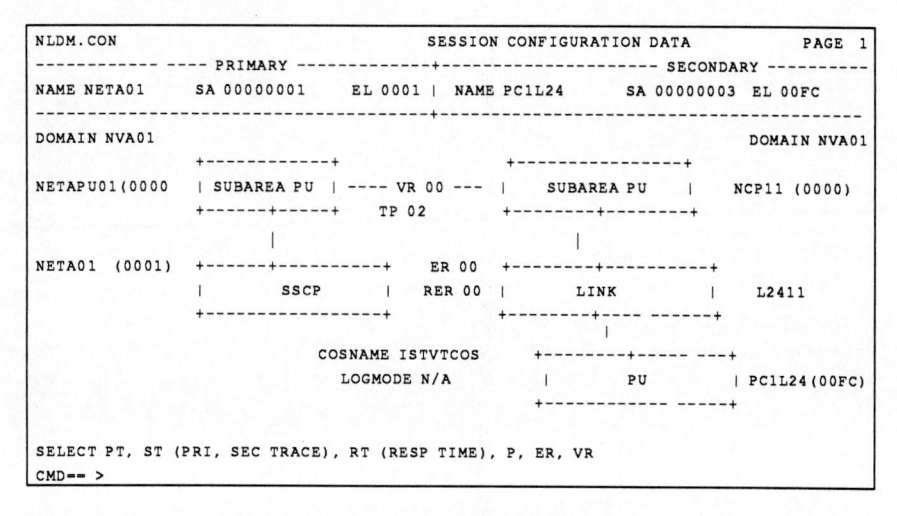

```
NLDM.CON                        SESSION CONFIGURATION DATA              PAGE 1
------------ ---- PRIMARY -------------+--------------------- SECONDARY ----------
NAME NETA01      SA 00000001      EL 0001 |  NAME PC1L24      SA 00000003  EL 00FC
-----------------------------------------+-------------------------------------------
DOMAIN NVA01                                                            DOMAIN NVA01
                 +------------+                    +----------------+
NETAPU01(0000    | SUBAREA PU | ---- VR 00 ---     |   SUBAREA PU   |   NCP11 (0000)
                 +------+-----+      TP 02         +--------+-------+
                        |                                   |
NETA01  (0001)   +------+----------+    ER 00     +--------+----------+
                 |      SSCP       |    RER 00    |       LINK        |   L2411
                 +-----------------+              +--------+----- ------+
                                                           |
                        COSNAME ISTVTCOS          +--------+----- ---+
                        LOGMODE N/A               |       PU         |  PC1L24(00FC)
                                                  +------------- -----+

SELECT PT, ST (PRI, SEC TRACE), RT (RESP TIME), P, ER, VR
CMD== >
```

Figure 12.6 Sample Session Monitor display from NetView.

used in conjunction with the Response Time Monitor (RTM). RTM provides solicited and unsolicited response time reporting to the Session Monitor. Again, this data is logged and can be used by the operator for further analysis.

12.3.4 NetView Status Monitor

The NetView Status Monitor (STATMON) provides the network operator with a "quick glance at the network" for the status of network resources (Figure 12.7). STATMON is comprised of functions from the VTAM Node Control Application (VNCA). This application uses a hierarchical display of the SNA resources in the operator's network. If the status of a resource has changed, STATMON will update its display appropriately. NCCF command lists can be incorporated into STATMON's monitoring capability to automate the recovery procedure for resources that have become inactive. To enhance a network operator's control of the network, STATMON can be used with a light-pen for issuing VTAM commands on SNA resources, simplifying the operator's interface with VTAM. No longer does the network operator have to memorize the format of every VTAM command. Data obtained from STATMON can be logged to an external logging file system (e.g., IBM's SMF) for further report processing on resource availability.

12.3.5 Network Management Productivity Facility (NMPF)

NMPF added several features to the base NetView product as separate features. These features include the NetView Browse Facility, the Help Desk Facility (Figure 12.8) and a library of CLists. The Browse Facility aids the network operator in retracing VTAM solicited and unsolicited operator messages by allowing the operator to view the NetView NCCF log. It can also be used to view certain data files that may aid in problem determination. The Help Desk Facility assists the network operator in gathering problem information for an end-user. This facility can be customized to fit network management requirements. The CLists

```
STATMON.DSS                             DOMAIN STATUS SUMMARY
10:56
HOST: NETA01               *0*      *1*      *2*     *3*     *4*
                         ACTIVE  PENDING    INACT   MONIT  NEVACT    OTHER

...4   NCP/CA MAJOR      ....4    .....    .....   .....   .....    .....
.152         LINES       ...78    .....    ....1   .....   ...71    ....2
.172    PUS/CLUSTERS     ...40    ...41    ....1   .....   ...88    ....2
2116    LUS/TERMS        ..295    ..166    ....7   .....   .1636    ...12
...2   SWITCHED MAJ      ....2    .....    .....   .....   .....    .....
..23       SWITCHED PUS  .....    .....    .....   .....   .....    ...23
.245       SWITCHED LUS  .....    .....    .....   .....   .....    ..245
...4   LOCAL MAJ NDS     ....4    .....    .....   .....   .....    .....
...1            PUS      .....    ....1    .....   .....   .....    .....
..25         LUS/TERMS   ...15    .....    .....   .....   ....2    ....8
...3   APPL MAJ NDS      ....3    .....    .....   .....   .....    .....
.105        APPLICATIONS ...17    .....    .....   .....   .....    ...88
...1   CDRM MAJ NDS      ....1    .....    .....   .....   .....    .....
...4          CDRMS      ....4    .....    .....   .....   .....    .....
...2   CDRSC MAJ NDS     ....2    .....    .....   .....   .....    .....
..15         CDRSCS      ...15    .....    .....   .....   .....    .....
-----  -----------------  -------  -------  ------  -----  -------  ------
2874   TOTAL NODES       ..480    ..208    ....9   .....   .1797    ..380

CMD==>
1=HELP 2=END 3=RETURN 4=BROWSE LOG 6=ROLL                          9=REFRESH
```

Figure 12.7 Sample Status Monitor display from NetView.

```
CNMHDESK                    HELP DESK

SELECT             To Get Information about

      1            A terminal not working

      2            A transaction or an application not working

      3            Slow response time

      4            Problems identified through network monitoring

      5            System message cross-reference

Type a number (1 through 5), then press ENTER.

          PF1 -->- Recommendations for the Set UP and Use of the Help Desk
                          HELP NETVIEW --- NetView Help Menu
ACTION===>
                   PF1= Help   PF2= End    PF3= Return   PF4= Top    PF5= Bottom
                   PF6= Roll   PF7= Backward  PF8= Forward   PF11= Entry Point
```

Figure 12.8 Sample display of the Help Desk facility in NetView.

provided enable the network operator to expand his/her proficiency with VTAM operator commands and control of the network.

12.4 NETVIEW/PC VERSION 1

The integration of third-party vendor network management alerts in NetView for centralizing network management was made possible by a PC-based system from IBM called NetView/PC. This product offering is IBM's second step in advancing the notion of centralized network management. The introduction of NetView/PC further demonstrated IBM's Open Network Management architecture not only to users, but to third-party DCE vendors as well. The Application Program Interface (API) architecture of NetView/PC permits third-party vendors to transmit their proprietary alarms to NetView/PC for conversion to IBM's NMVT format, which is then sent to VTAM over the PU-SSCP session for interpretation by NetView's Hardware Monitor. The code-point information supplied in the third-party vendor's NMVT is used to access customized alarm messages and recommended action displays specific to the vendor's resource(s). For the first time, non-

SNA equipment could be integrated into SNA management. This capability has now become a standard requirement of many corporations when issuing a request for proposal (RFP). As of now, over 25 DCE suppliers have announced NetView/PC support. Among these are MCI, ROLM, Timeplex, Bytex, Racal-Milgo, GDC, DCA, to name a few.

12.5 NETVIEW RELEASE 2

The scope of NetView was expanded under Release 2 to include management of systems and network operations. The focus of NetView Release 2 is on automating both systems and network operations, distributed control with central management, support for monitoring SNA Node T2.1, functional control of non-SNA resources, and further support of IBM's Open Network Management architecture by providing an extensive set of generic alarms to eliminate vendor-specific descriptions and recommended action displays on the host.

12.5.1 Automation and Central Management

The inclusion of operating system, subsystem, and network automation under MVS is accomplished by the use of the MVS Subsystem Interface (SSI). Executing as a subsystem of MVS, all system messages can be examined for automation. Any NetView console can act as an MVS operator console by issuing MVS system and subsystem commands directly or by executing a NetView CList that contains the system commands. Likewise, any NetView command or CList can be entered on any MVS system console, excluding full screen function commands for Session Monitor, Status Monitor and Hardware Monitor. These commands still require a NetView operator's console. Under VM operating systems, functionality similar to that of the MVS SSI is provided by the VM Programmable Operator facility (PROP). For the VSE operating system, NetView utilizes the facilities of the program product VSE/Operator Communication Control Facility (OCCF). However, NetView command entry on the VM or VSE system console is not supported. NetView's new position not only includes enhanced network management, but also the management of all computer operations.

12.5.2 Automation Enhancements

NetView R2 automation facilities can be enabled at both the distributed system (e.g., IBM 9370) and at the focal point. A major enhancement to the Hardware Monitor is the ability to automate responses to solicited and unsolicited alert notification messages. A NetView CList can be executed automatically based upon additional information in the alert notification message format. This ability combined with the central management enhancements discussed in the next paragraph is a formidable base for future automated control using an expert system.

12.5.3 Central Management Enhancements

The introduction of the IBM 9370 distributed processor had a direct influence on CNM enhancements for NetView R2. The 9370 processor is being touted as an inexpensive powerful mainframe processor that can be operated by technically untrained personnel. However, central management and control of these distributed processors and other large mainframe processors in the SNA network can be accomplished through several new CNM enhancements. These are the Message and Alert Notification Routing facility, the Message Driven Alert facility, support for LANs and the Communications Network Management (CNM) Router Function. Each of these functions, either independently or in combination, greatly improves both central network management and automation of a composite network.

12.5.4 Message and Alert Notification Routing Facility

Message and alert information pertinent to a distributed processor can be routed to the NetView focal point operator console by the Message and Alert Notification Routing facility. This facility consists of a supplied CList that can be modified to route specific messages and alerts from the distributed processor to the NetView focal point. This means, of course, that NetView R2 must also be active on the distributed processor. Based on the information of the message or alert received from the distributed processor, the focal point can execute a CList to automate the operator's action for that particular message or alert.

12.5.6 Message-Driven Alert Facility

Any system, subsystem, or network operator console message that is viewed by the NetView command facility can now generate an alert to the NetView Hardware Monitor. The Hardware Monitor then treats the alert like any other alert it receives. The alert is displayed on the Alerts Dynamic screen for viewing by the operator. This incorporates not only network hardware and facility fault alerts, but also the operating system and subsystem faults. By using the Hardware Monitor Alert Automation facility, system and subsystem faults can be corrected automatically. Refer back to Section 12.5.1 on the Hardware Monitor Alert Automation capabilities.

12.5.7 LAN Support

Faults detected on a LAN can now be forwarded to the NetView focal point using the methods mentioned above. In addition, the fault data has been enhanced to include fault domain alerts, LAN errors occurring on the adapter addresses and a filtering scheme based on the adapter addresses. The extended support for LANs is increasingly important for LANs positioned off of a distributed processor.

12.5.8 Communications Network Management Router Function

In VTAM, the CNM Routing table is used to direct the unsolicited network services alerts (NMVTs, RECFMs, RECMSs) to the unsolicited command processor responsible for handling unsolicited alerts. VTAM requires that only one unsolicited command processor can be active at one time for each network service request unit. With this facility, the CNM Router Task (DSICRTR) receives all network service alerts. This allows NetView to interpret the alert in finer detail. Using this facility, the various NetView functions can each receive the same network service RU. For instance, the NMVT has several different types of major vectors within it. CNM Router Task can scan the NMVT received from the network and then re-route the alert to the appropriate NetView task. For example, an Alert Major Vector (x'0000') within an NMVT is routed to the Hardware Monitor, and the Response Time Monitor (RTM) Major Vector (x'0080') is routed to the Session Monitor.

12.5.9 Session Monitor SNA Node Type 2.1 Support

SNA Node Type 2.1 supports IBM's Low Entry Networking (LEN) architecture for peer-to-peer communication. This new SNA node type is supported by the NetView R2 Session Monitor in conjunction with VTAM V3R2 only. This allows the monitoring of primary logical units (PLUs) that are not under VTAM control over an SNA backbone network. Support of SNA Node Type 2.1 is furnished by new session awareness data (SAW) records under VTAM V3R2. The new SAW data contains a unique procedure correlated identifier (PCID) value. The PCID is used to identify each session the PLU has with a session partner. In this way, independent LUs (with multiple concurrent sessions) of SNA Node Type 2.1 can be monitored and tracked for each session by VTAM and NetView's Session Monitor.

12.5.10 Generic Alerts

Under NetView R2, the Hardware Monitor display panels and messages have been enhanced by the new Generic Alert format of the Network Management Vector Transport (NMVT). The implementation of this new format eliminates the customization of NetView Hardware Monitor display panels and messages for product-specific alerts. Instead, the alerts dynamic message, event detail and recommended action screens are built upon the text identified by the generic alert code-points. The code-points are used as indices into tables that reside at the host on disk. This provides individualized alert text for each type of alert received, as opposed to NetView R1 pre-defined alert messages and displays that were indexed by a component identifier and an alert descriptor code.

In keeping with IBM's Open Network Management architecture, NetView R2 provides a facility for vendors to add their own generic alert code-points. A code-point text table can be created to provide product-specific code-point text that can be used with IBM's code-point text to create the Hardware Monitor alert messages and screen displays. Prior to NetView R2, only IBM's text or the product specific text could be displayed. Using generic alerts, product-specific and IBM code-point text can be combined on the same message and/or screen display.

NetView R2 will, however, continue to support non-generic alert formats that were supported under NetView R1 and the individual CNM program products.

12.6 SERVICE POINT COMMAND SERVICE

Management of non-IBM equipment from NetView is now possible from the newly added function of the NetView Command Facility. This new function is called Service Point Command Service (SPCS). Using the command facility, a NetView operator can enter four supported commands that are to be executed by an application program of a service point. IBM's NetView/PC is an example of a service point. The supported commands are:

RUNCMD
LINKDATA
LINKTEST
LINKPD

12.6.1 SPCS RUNCMD Command

The RUNCMD is a generic command that is recognized by the NetView Command Facility and transported to the service point for processing. For example, RUNCMD can be used by the network operator to obtain the status of the vendor's equipment. Command syntax checking is not performed by NetView and must be in agreement with the vendor's application executing on NetView/PC. The vendor's application must be coded to handle command errors, as well as to execute the requested command. The response from the service point is displayed under the command facility function of NetView.

12.6.2 SPCS LINKDATA Command

This command is used to request control, error and statistical data maintained by the service point application. The service point application responds to this command with an architected record. The information supplied in this record is displayed by NetView in full-screen mode.

12.6.3 SPCS LINKTEST Command

Using this command from NetView R2, an application executing on the service point will request DCE tests. The results of the tests will then be sent to NetView in an architected record for presentation by NetView in full-screen mode.

12.6.4 SPCS LINKPD Command

Problem determination analysis can be performed by the service point application for a given element. Using the LINKPD command, the network operator can request the service point application to perform alert correlation for a specific problem. The response to this command is a generic alert. The generic alert is then processed by NetView R2 in the same manner as solicited and unsolicited NMVTs. In this case, the NMVT is solicited.

12.7 NETVIEW/PC VERSION 1.1

Support for the enhanced alert and command extensions of NetView R2 is provided by the IBM service point product named NetView/PC Version 1.1. This new release of NetView/PC enables NetView to extend network management and control to non-IBM equipment. The intent of this release is to further solidify IBM's Open Network Management architecture by having NetView/PC support both generic alerts and SPCS.

12.7.1 NetView/PC Generic Alert Support

NetView's new generic alert architecture places more responsibility on the vendor service point application than the previous non-generic alert format. The current number of code-points supported by NetView R2 without vendor-specific code-point values is quite extensive. Each piece of text displayed on the Hardware Monitor screens can be selected by code-point values. This increases the detail of code needed in the vendor application to support all the possibilities. The current base plus further expansion of the code-point values to increase the detail of the alert message may become overwhelming. The non-generic alert format is upwardly compatible with NetView/PC V1.1.

12.8 SERVICE POINT COMMAND SERVICE SUPPORT NETVIEW/PC V1.1

The previous release of NetView/PC was used by most vendors to consolidate their DCE alarms on NetView. With this release, a NetView operator can, in fact, control the DCE equipment from the NetView console using SPCS. The vendor's application must be developed with the new API/CS interface to support the encoded commands received from NetView. Partial or perhaps total operational and managerial control of their equipment by NetView is possible. Of course, this support is dependent on the vendor's willingness to provide this service to the customer. By providing the capability of NetView to actually operate and test non-IBM DCE by using NetView/PC, IBM is supplying the means for total network management.

12.9 TOKEN-RING NETWORK MANAGER FOR NETVIEW/PC

The IBM Token-Ring Network Manager V1.1 for NetView/PC V1.1 executes as an application under NetView/PC. Alerts generated on the Token-Ring Network can be forwarded automatically to the SNA focal point application (e.g., NetView). Alerts are of the generic alert format. Alert forwarding from a Token-Ring manager executing under NetView/PC, coupled with SPCS functionality, can therefore provide workgroup management from a NetView console.

12.10 NETVIEW R3 ENHANCEMENTS

NetView R3 has added several features to enhance its functionality. Namely, the addition of IBM PL/I and IBM C programming languages and the Restructured Extended Executor (REXX) language. The addition of these languages eases the burden on the communications systems programmer from having to code all NetView user exits and command processors in assembler language.

Both PL/I and C can be used to write the various NetView exits. Using PL/I however, allows communication to IBM's Knowledge-Tool, an expert system for handling complex operating system and networking problems. The REXX language is a 4GL originally developed for the VM operating system. This language is an interpretive language that far exceeds the current capabilities of NetView's Command List (CList) language. REXX provides you with the ability to write complex procedures to assist in automating network operations. CLists are basically IF...THEN...ELSE statements. REXX provides a full function set of commands that allow file processing, arithmetic and terminal screen handling. To increase the performance of this interpretive language, NetView now keeps a copy of the executable module in memory rather than re-interpreting the source code with each execution of the procedure. REXX, however, cannot be used to support NetView exit routines.

In compliance with its Systems Application Architecture (SAA), IBM has added new functionality to the NetView Panel Manager. The NetView Panel Manager now supports all IBM 3279 screen display attributes. With REXX (also SAA) and the added Panel Manager functionality, ISPF-like panels can be presented to the NetView operator with little coding effort by the communications systems programmer. ISPF and its panel presentation also supports SAA. With this new feature, a NetView operator can execute a REXX procedure which can then display a full screen menu or panel with several input fields available to the operator. The interface can be fully conversational between the operator and the REXX procedure. The procedure may also issue a VTAM or NetView command in response to the operators input. The message returning from the command can then be parsed and formatted for presentation to the operator. To use REXX, the MVS operating system must have TSO/E V2 installed while the VM operating system must be at VM/SP R6. There is no indication of REXX support under the VSE operating system.

12.11 NETVIEW/PC V1.2

This latest release of IBM's supreme service point greatly increases its ability to consolidate non-SNA and non-IBM equipment alarms into NetView. With this release, NetView/PC can execute under the OS/2 Extended Edition 1.1 operating system on an IBM PS/2 workstation. This removes a pressing constraint of the previous versions, that of executing a vendor program in under 100K bytes of memory. Under the OS/2 operating system, Netview/PC can execute several vendor programs at the same time. In earlier releases the NetView/PC was dedicated to one vendor. Additionally, with the use of the Communication Manager of OS/2 EE 1.1,

NetView/PC can communicate with several different non-IBM network management systems concurrently.

To ease the management of non-IBM network resources, the NetView/PC Service Point Command Facility (SPCF), in concert with NetView R3's Service Point Command Services (SPCS), allows for more than a 512 byte SPCS command response NetView. This is accomplished by providing a chaining mechanism for the NMVT response to the SPCS RUNCMD, LINKPD, LINKSTAT and LINKTEST commands. Coordinate this new capability with the REXX facility and the responses can be presented to the operator in a clear, concise and informative manner.

12.12 SUMMARY

In this chapter we reviewed IBM's NetView and NetView/PC. We discussed the capability of each and their roles in Open Network Management architecture. NetView serves as a focal point and NetView/PC plays the role of a service point. Together they can assist you in managing a multi-vendor network. The functions provided by both are primarily for problem management. In the next chapter we will discuss the importance of performance management.

Chapter

13

Network Performance and Tuning

When determining network performance in SNA, it must be understood that the network is contiguous, from the application residing on an SNA host out to the logical unit perceived by the end-user as his terminal or printer. Along this path are several network components that must be analyzed through monitoring and reporting mechanisms. Performance tools can assist you in determining if the desired service agreed to in a Service Level Agreement is being met. These performance tools provide you with performance data from cycle and storage to queuing and capacity to the ultimate determinant factors of performance throughput and response time. To effectively analyze the performance data, a methodology must be implemented.

13.1 PERFORMANCE AND TUNING METHODOLOGY

The design and implementation of a methodology for performance and tuning of your SNA network is dependent on many interrelated factors. The topology of your network, the characteristics of end-user interface and the application mix are just some of the factors that must be considered. The following sections discuss three major topics of any performance and tuning methodology:

268 Advanced SNA Networking

1. Performance monitoring.
2. Analysis.
3. Performance objectives.

Products available to assist you in obtaining performance data are discussed in a later section of this chapter.

13.1.1 Performance Monitoring

Before you can implement a Service Level Agreement, the current service level of the network must be determined. It is imperative that you collect as much performance data as possible to allow an accurate analysis. Figure 13.1 outlines some of the performance concerns for performance monitoring. Data from VTAM will pro-

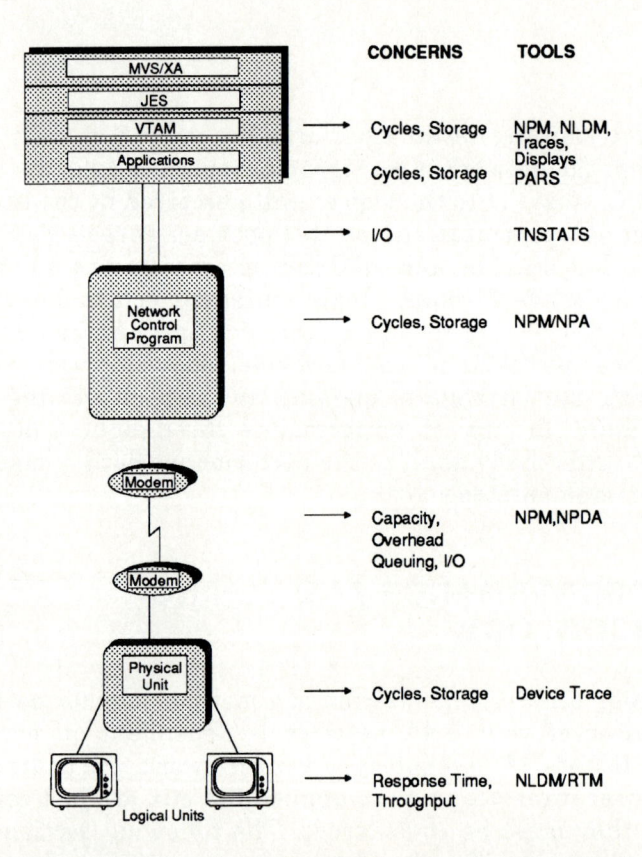

Component	Concerns	Tools
MVS/XA, JES, VTAM	Cycles, Storage	NPM, NLDM, Traces, Displays
Applications	Cycles, Storage	PARS
	I/O	TNSTATS
Network Control Program	Cycles, Storage	NPM/NPA
Modem (line)	Capacity, Overhead, Queuing, I/O	NPM, NPDA
Physical Unit	Cycles, Storage	Device Trace
Logical Units	Response Time, Throughput	NLDM/RTM

Figure 13.1 Typical concerns for network performance and some tools to assist in monitoring performance.

Network Performance and Tuning   269

vide the needed information of buffer usage, I/O to a channel-attached NCP, or VTAM over a CTC adapter. In the NCP, boundary data between the NCP and its peripheral units will supply data on queuing and throughput. LU-LU session data flows will allow us to get a feel for the actual traffic flows between session partners. Network flow control data will provide the information necessary to analyze the routes used in the network. Each of these will be discussed in greater detail with concentration on the key factors that contribute to performance and tuning in an SNA network.

13.1.2 Analyze and Report Performance

During the process of reporting and analysis it is imperative that you correlate time frames. This will allow you to track changes in throughput and response time over the course of the selected time period. It is suggested that the initial time periods of monitoring and reporting be quite extensive so as to provide a good basis for detailed analysis of your current service levels. The data provided should be used to create both table summaries and graphs for yourself and management to allow ease of tracking trends. Once you have the summaries and graphs, you can analyze them for important factors of network performance. These factors are:

- Response time
- Throughput
- Utilization
- Outages
- Trends
- Peaks

Analysis of the reports can provide some clear answers to network bottlenecks, sudden consumption of resources, and over committed resources. However, some underlying causes may not be so apparent and this is where network modeling tools come into play. Using the data collected during performance monitoring, the modeling tools can assist you in optimizing the network by providing the mechanism for "What if ..?" types of scenarios for tuning parameters. This saves time and possible problems that may be caused by implementing parameter changes on a live network. Appendix E contains a list of the VTAM/NCP parameters that most affect performance in an SNA network.

13.1.3 Performance Objectives

After analysis, we should have the current throughput, response time and utilizations for all network components. Based on these figures, we can then set obtainable measurable objectives for Service Level Agreements. These objectives should include throughput, availability and response time. Once the agreements are implemented the process must start all over. Monitoring, analysis and tuning are, from here on in, an ongoing process that may be expected to be daily, weekly, monthly and yearly. As the collected performance data is accumulated, you will be able to predict trends that occur in the network. Using this data you can then tune the network for the maximum loads for not only daily peaks but for weekly, monthly and yearly usage peaks. Let's look at how data for the network can be collected and analyzed to assist you in your network tuning efforts.

13.2 VTAM PERFORMANCE AND TUNING CONSIDERATIONS

As with most subsystems operating on a mainframe, storage allocation is crucial for performance. Under-allocation of mainframe storage as well as over-allocation of storage for VTAM may be detrimental. For VTAM, it is more efficient to keep storage to a minimum rather than over-allocating VTAM buffers and control blocks. The highest pay back that you will receive from tuning VTAM only are those parameters that affect the transfer of data between VTAM and NCP, and VTAM and VTAM. This is done by implementing channel queuing and coat-tailing. By tweaking and massaging the parameters that we are about to discuss, you may save some cycles in milliseconds and some storage, but not in megabytes.

13.2.1 VTAM Buffer Pool Usage

The buffer pools of VTAM are used for passing end-user data to LU partners and for the control blocks that are needed to track VTAM and LU processes. Figure 13.2 diagrams the usage of the I/O buffer pool of VTAM. As data comes into VTAM from a secondary LU (SLU), VTAM places the data in an IO buffer. This IO buffer is fixed, meaning that it is always in the computer's memory. For the

Network Performance and Tuning 271

MVS, MVS/XA and VM operating systems, the VTAM IO buffer pool is called IOBUF, and in a VSE operating system it is called LFBUF. If the application issues a VTAM RECEIVE command, the data is passed directly to the application's designated receive area. If, on the other hand, a RECEIVE command has not been issued by the application, VTAM under MVS, MVS/XA and VM operating systems will move the data to a subpool of memory. For applications in these operating systems, the memory is called SUBPOOL 229. In a VSE environment, the data is moved to the VPBUF buffer pool of VTAM. The VPBUF buffer pool is a pageable area, meaning that the buffer pool does not exist in computer memory, but on the operating system auxillary storage devices, usually a magnetic disk drive. The application can subsequently issue a VTAM RECEIVE command and VTAM will then fetch the buffer and pass it to the application's named receive area. When

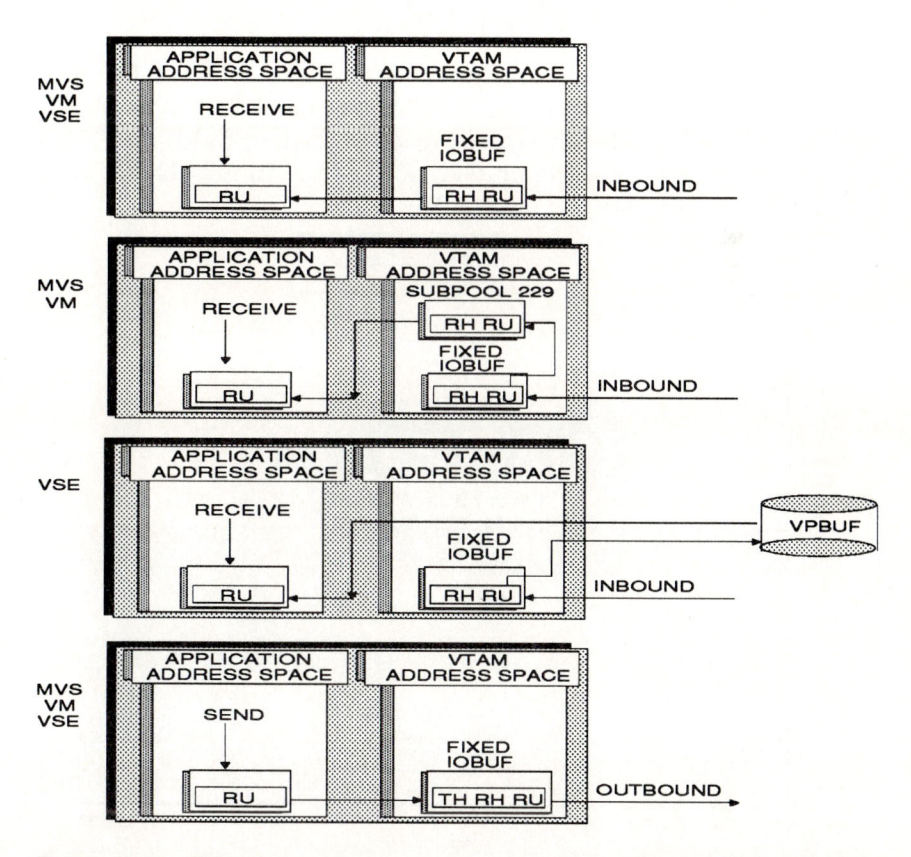

Figure 13.2 VTAM I/O buffer pool usages for MVS, VM and VSE operating systems.

272 Advanced SNA Networking

the application issues the VTAM SEND command, VTAM places the data in the fixed buffer pool before sending the data to the LU partner.

13.2.2 Buffer Pool Specification

All VTAM buffer pool allocations are defined in VTAM's start list ATCSTR00. The format of the buffer pool specification is as follows:

`buffer pool name = (baseno,bufsize,slowpt,,xpanno,xpanpt)`

The format defines two types of buffer allocation. The *baseno*, *bufsize* and *slowpt* operands define the BASIC allocation. The *xpanno* and *xpanpt* operands define the DYNAMIC allocation. Figure 13.3 diagrams the effect of buffer pool expansion on VTAM buffer pools.

When determining the amount of storage to allocate for each buffer pool, you must be aware of VTAM's implementation of allocation. For each buffer in a pool there is a header field. In VTAM V2R2 and earlier, there is an 8 byte header. In VTAM V3, a 16

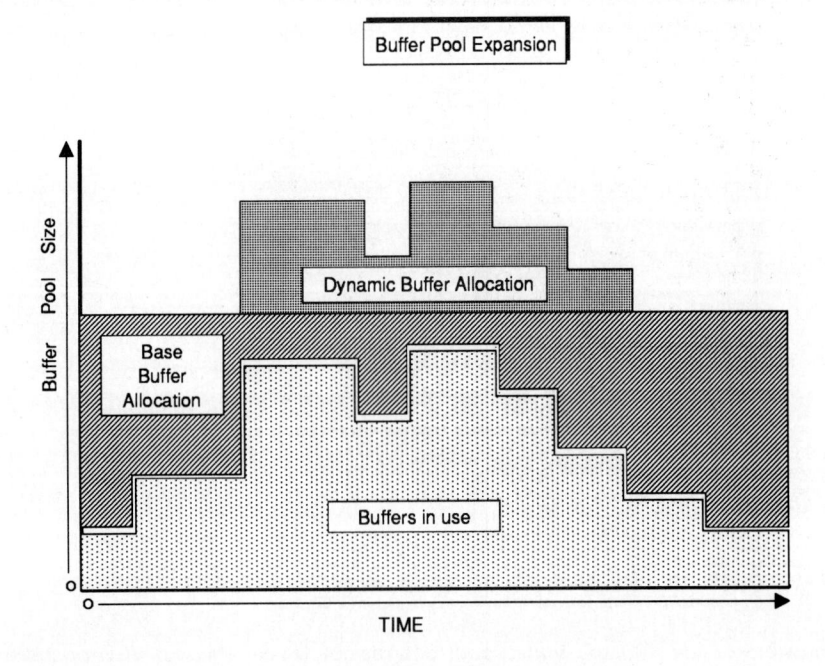

Figure 13.3 Buffer pool expansion effect on VTAM buffer pools.

byte header is appended and each buffer is addressed to a doubleword address boundary. That is, the address of the storage location in memory is divisible by 8. For IO buffers, this header field is also accompanied by another field called a DATA FIELD HEADER.

During initialization, VTAM will get as much storage as required to allocate all buffers according to the basic allocation values specified in ATCSTR00. This storage in memory is allocated in pages. A page of memory is defined as 4096 contiguous bytes. As VTAM begins to fill the memory pages, it is not bound to dedicating a page of storage to a specific type of buffer pool. As long as the buffers are similar in their characteristics (e.g., pageable or fixed), VTAM will utilize the space it has allocated for buffer pools.

The dynamic allocation of buffers is dependent on the *xpanno* and *xpanpt* values specified for each buffer pool. When VTAM requests buffers, it checks the *xpanpt* value. This value defines to VTAM the number of buffers that must be left available at all times. If *xpanpt* buffers or less will remain after the buffer request, VTAM will obtain at least the number of buffers specified by the *xpanno* operand. We say at least because VTAM obtains a minimum of a full page of storage for each expanded pool. For example, if 8 buffers can be allocated in a page of memory, then any *xpanno* value between 1 and 8 will get 8 buffers. Any *xpanno* value between 9 and 16 will get 16 buffers (2 pages of memory). This buffer pool expansion will be noticeable during peak hours of the day. The pools do, however, contract based on the following equation:

```
((2 * xpanno) + xpanpt) = unused buffers in pool
```

The contraction does not take place on individual buffers but on pages. In other words, if the equation is true and there are no used buffers in the expanded page(s) then the page will be released. VTAM facilitates the release of buffers from the dynamic allocation by attempting to use buffers in the basic allocation, thus freeing buffers in the expansion pages.

To monitor buffer usage, the VTAM command DISPLAY NET,BFRUSE is used. This command returns a display like the ones in Figures 13.4a (V3.1.1) and 13.4b (V3.2). This display provides you with the current values of buffer allocation and availability, the maximum allocated and the maximum used, the number of times expansion took place and the expansion/contraction thresholds reached. The one problem with this type of monitoring is that it is not recorded in any type of data base. However, you may go outside of VTAM and use VTAM monitoring packages provided by third party program houses that can collect, store and report on buffer use for analysis.

Some recommendations for VTAM buffer performance and tuning are as follows. Take the default buffer size for all buffers except the IO buffer. For this buffer, some analysis of PIU size should be performed to find the average PIU size, then set the IO buffer *bufsize* operand accordingly. For *baseno*, determine the steady buffer state allocation for peaks and then set the *baseno* equal to that number plus the value chosen for *xpanpt*. Also, define more than one page of initial buffers on the *baseno* value. For the *slowpt* operand on the IO buffer pool specification, make sure that the (*xpanpt - slowpt*=MAXBFRU). This allows expansion without reaching the specified *slowpt* value. The largest PIU (MAXBFRU) candidates in your network are the MAXBFRU values for VTAM and NCP, the NetView Session Monitor (NLDM) trace buffer size and the JES/NJE TPBFSIZ operand. Allowing for this will avoid excessive expansions, which create fragmentation. Fragmentation, in turn, increases buffer search time and control block usage.

13.2.3 Coat-Tailing

Optimizing the exchange of data between two VTAMs or VTAM and an NCP attached by a channel connection provides the great-

```
a.)
IST350I   VTAM     DISPLAY - DOMAIN TYPE = BUFFER POOL DATA
IST632I   BUFF     BUFF     CURR     CURR     MAX      MAX      TIMES    EXP/CNT          EXP
IST633I   ID       SIZE     TOTAL    AVAIL    TOTAL    USED     EXP      THRESHOLD        INCR
IST356I   IO00     00203    00100    00060    00100    00057    00000    00020/-----      00018
IST356I   LP00     01344    00064    00060    00064    00007    00000    00001/-----      00003
IST356I   WP00     00184    00078    00052    00078    00030    00000    00001/-----      00020
IST356I   LF00     00068    00104    00091    00104    00013    00000    00001/-----      00046
IST356I   CRPL     00116    00208    00187    00208    00024    00000    00016/-----      00030
IST356I   SF00     00064    00163    00154    00163    00009    00000    00001/-----      00051
IST356I   SP00     00112    00002    00002    00002    00000    00000    00001/-----      00032
IST449I   CSALIMIT = NOLIMIT, CURRENT = 0000414K, MAXIMUM = 0000417K
IST790I   MAXIMUM CSA USED = 0000417K
IST449I   CSA24 LIMIT = NOLIMIT, CURRENT =0000045K, MAXIMUM = 0000049K
IST790I   MAXIMUM CSA24 USED = 0000049K
IST595I   IRNLIMIT = NOLIMIT, CURRENT = 0000000K, MAXIMUM = 0000000K
IST314I   END
```

Figure 13.4*a* D NET,BFRUSE display from VTAM V3.1.1

```
b.)
IST920I   IO00    BUFF SIZE     00203           EXP INCREMENT     00036
IST921I           TIMES EXP     0000000000      EXP/CONT THRESH   00002/*N/A*
IST922I           CURR TOTAL    0000000160      CURR AVAILABLE    0000000092
IST923I           MAX TOTAL     0000000160      MAX USED          0000000159
IST924I           ----------------------------------------------------------
IST920I   LP00    BUFF SIZE     01344           EXP INCREMENT     00003
IST921I           TIMES EXP     0000000000      EXP/CONT THRESH   00001/*N/A*
IST922I           CURR TOTAL    0000000064      CURR AVAILABLE    0000000058
IST923I           MAX TOTAL     0000000064      MAX USED          0000000014
IST924I           ----------------------------------------------------------
IST920I   WP00    BUFF SIZE     00208           EXP INCREMENT     00018
IST921I           TIMES EXP     0000000006      EXP/CONT THRESH   00001/00037*
IST922I           CURR TOTAL    0000000114      CURR AVAILABLE    0000000023
IST923I           MAX TOTAL     0000000150      MAX USED          0000000137
IST924I           ----------------------------------------------------------
IST920I   LF00    BUFF SIZE     00084           EXP INCREMENT     00039
IST921I           TIMES EXP     0000000000      EXP/CONT THRESH   00001/*N/A*
IST922I           CURR TOTAL    0000000104      CURR AVAILABLE    0000000076
IST923I           MAX TOTAL     0000000104      MAX USED          0000000046
IST924I           ----------------------------------------------------------
IST920I   CRPL    BUFF SIZE     00116           EXP INCREMENT     00030
IST921I           TIMES EXP     0000000000      EXP/CONT THRESH   00016/*N/A*
IST922I           CURR TOTAL    0000000208      CURR AVAILABLE    0000000153
IST923I           MAX TOTAL     0000000208      MAX USED          0000000122
IST924I           ----------------------------------------------------------
IST920I   SF00    BUFF SIZE     00076           EXP INCREMENT     00042
IST921I           TIMES EXP     0000000000      EXP/CONT THRESH   00001/*N/A*
IST922I           CURR TOTAL    0000000163      CURR AVAILABLE    0000000152
IST923I           MAX TOTAL     0000000163      MAX USED          0000000011
IST924I           ----------------------------------------------------------
IST920I   SP00    BUFF SIZE     00112           EXP INCREMENT     00032
IST921I           TIMES EXP     0000000001      EXP/CONT THRESH   00001/00065
IST922I           CURR TOTAL    0000000034      CURR AVAILABLE    0000000034
IST923I           MAX TOTAL     0000000034      MAX USED          0000000008
IST924I           ----------------------------------------------------------
IST920I   AP00    BUFF SIZE     00064           EXP INCREMENT     00051
IST921I           TIMES EXP     0000000000      EXP/CONT THRESH   00003/*N/A*
IST922I           CURR TOTAL    0000000016      CURR AVAILABLE    0000000016
IST923I           MAX TOTAL     0000000016      MAX USED          0000000000
IST924I           ----------------------------------------------------------
IST449I   CSALIMIT = NOLIMIT, CURRENT = 0000689K, MAXIMUM =0000740K
IST790I   MAXIMUM CSA USED = 0000740K
IST449I   CSA24 LIMIT = NOLIMIT, CURRENT =0000016K, MAXIMUM =0000028K
IST790I   MAXIMUM CSA24 USED = 0000028K
IST595I   IRNLIMIT = NOLIMIT, CURRENT = 0000000K, MAXIMUM = 000000K
IST314I   END
```

Figure 13.4b D NET,BFRUSE display from VTAM V3.2.

est payback on VTAM performance. Coat-tailing is a mechanism used by VTAM and an NCP that allows them to send more than one PIU at a time. Both VTAM and the NCP use channel programs to send data. VTAM can write to the NCP at any time. When building the channel program, VTAM always builds a combination WRITE/READ channel program if there are available buffers. Upon a write, VTAM can send multiple PIUs depending upon the current queue limit. The queue limit for VTAM is determined by the formula: Queue Limit = (3 * n)/4 where "n" is the number of PIUs in the last DELAY. The NCP allocates its buffers after receiving the write command. The NCP can request VTAM to write by issuing a READ request. The VTAM/NCP parameters that have a commanding impact are MAXBFRU and DELAY.

VTAM will always allocate MAXBFRU buffers for a read from the NCP. Hence, VTAM may receive up to MAXBFRU PIUs. To fully utilize the positive effects of coat-tailing, set the DELAY parameter to a value greater than zero. This will allow for PIU queuing making it possible to send more than one PIU per read. The MAXBFRU value must be large enough to accommodate multiple PIUs in MAXBFRU x UNITSZ, which results in the PCCU parameter value MAXDATA. As of VTAM V1R3 and NCP V1R3, the MAXBFRU value in the NCP source file may be changed and placed into effect without executing a new NCP load module. This is only if the MAXBFRU value is increased. The value coded on the MAXBFRU parameter is passed in the XID when VTAM and the NCP first contact each other.

A starting point for the DELAY operand is a value of .2 seconds and for MAXBFRU is 16. After defining these values, a way of recording the effects must be instituted. You can do this by using the following VTAM command:

```
MODIFY NET,TNSTAT,TIME=10,CNSL=YES
```

This command provides the necessary tuning statistics (TNSTAT) between VTAM and any other channel-attached SNA device. The command must be specified in VTAM's start list ATCSTR00. The CNSL operand of the command allows the statistics to be displayed on the operator console. In addition, the statistics are written to the System Management Facility (SMF) in a formatted record. This record is called an SMF Type 50 (x'32'). This record can then be analyzed by such programs as MICS, SAS and SLR to produce reports on the channel activity. Figure 13.5 provides a sample display of the TNSTAT operator console message.

There are two basic displays for TNSTAT. Statistics are produced for VTAM-NCP and VTAM-Local SNA, and VTAM-VTAM over a CTC configuration. Each display is slightly different from the other. A noticeable difference is the inclusion of the TIMERS

```
IST440I      TIME=14075721    DATE =89042     ID   =3A0-L
IST441I      DLRMAX=1         CHWR =256       CHRD =243
IST442I      ATTN=243         RDATN=0         IPIU =243
IST443I      OPIU=256         RDBUF=243       SLODN=0
IST314I      END
```

Figure 13.5 Tuning statistics display for a channel-attached NCP communications controller.

value on the CTC display. TIMERS is used to identify the number of times the DELAY value expired. For a CTC, the DELAY value can have serious performance implications because of the MAXBFRU value. The MAXBFRU value, as of VTAM V3.1.1, tells VTAM to allocate the maximum number of buffers for every WRITE/READ. A low DELAY value, in this instance, is not taking advantage of sending multiple PIUs in one channel program. Similarly, for an NCP, a low DELAY value will cause excessive ATTN commands. This attention will cause VTAM to read NCP buffers. The NCP will issue the attention if the DELAY value and/or the MAXBFRU value has been reached. Therefore, if you find that TNSTAT indicates that the ATTN value is high, the DELAY value and/or the MAXBFRU value is too low. One other indicator of poor channel performance is the OPIU and CHWR values. If the outbound PIU (OPIU) value equals the channel write (CHWR) value, then there is no coat-tailing in effect. Hence, for every write and read, only one PIU is transmitted. This drastically reduces the performance of the channel transmission media, which can handle 4.5 megabytes per data transfer.

13.3 NCP PERFORMANCE AND TUNING CONSIDERATIONS

The link configurations and the characteristics of the data load through the network are of major concern to the performance of the NCP. The parameters defined for an NCP have a major impact on link and application performance. These parameters can be tuned to control the data flow through the NCP. The data flow inbound and outbound from VTAM are greatly affected by these NCP parameters. Internal to the NCP are tuning parameters

278 Advanced SNA Networking

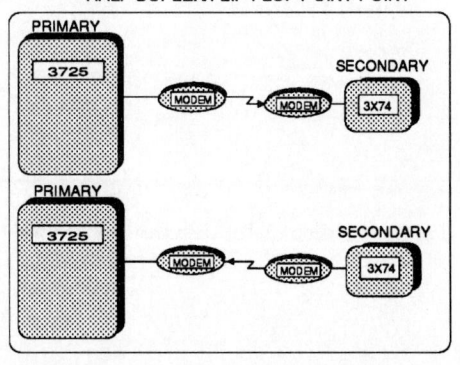

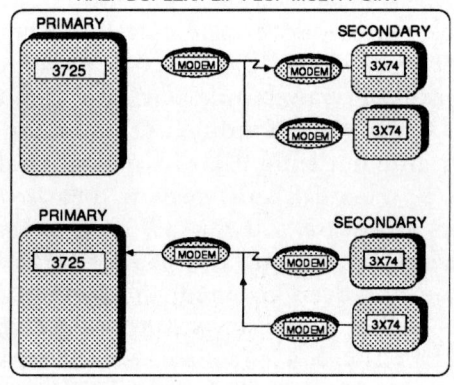

Figure 13.6 The effect of specifying DUPLEX=HALF on NCP LINE definition statements for point-to-point and multi-point lines.

which affect the number of buffers used, service of the link scheduler and the queuing of PIUs on a transmission group, to the response time seen by the end user.

13.3.1 Facility and Link Configurations

The actual physical connection between the peripheral PU and the NCP is defined by the DUPLEX parameter of the NCP LINE definition statement. The values for this parameter identify to the NCP whether this facility is a 2-wire or 4-wire circuit. As depicted in Figure 13.6, the specification of DUPLEX=HALF on the LINE definition statement impacts the link configurations. For point-to-point and multi-point configurations, the primary link station can only transmit and then receive information from one secondary link station at a time. Even in a multi-point configuration, the transmission of data is always in one direction. This is often referred to as half-duplex/flip-flop. However, most facilities in use today are 4-wire. In this case, to increase the efficiency of transmission over the facility, DUPLEX=FULL is specified. This indicates to the NCP that the possibility of simultaneously sending and receiving data exists. The specification of DUPLEX=FULL also tells the NCP to keep the READY-TO-SEND (RTS) signal high on the NCP modem. This reduces modem turnaround time even when the secondary link station is not capable of full duplex transmission.

Most peripheral PUs are not capable of full duplex data transmission. That is, they cannot send and receive data concurrently. This characteristic is defined on the PU definition statement by the DATMODE parameter. The default value, HALF, indicates to the NCP that the defined PU is a flip-flop data transmission device. Typical DATMODE=HALF devices are the IBM 3274 and 3174 control units. These devices can only send or receive, but may exist on a duplex facility. The duplex facility is utilized in a multi-point configuration of these type of devices.

As seen in Figure 13.7, although the secondary link station is DATMODE=HALF, the primary link station (NCP) can send data to secondary link stations while receiving data from another. The NCP is in two-way simultaneous mode, while each secondary link station is in two-way alternate mode. Devices that can support DATMODE=FULL, or simultaneous send/receive transmissions, require another NCP parameter to take full advantage of a complete full duplex transmission. This is the ADDRESS parameter of the LINE definition statement.

The ADDRESS=(n,HALF|FULL) parameter defines the actual transmission capabilities used on this link. The specification of HALF tells the NCP that this is a half-duplex transmission link and to expect all traffic to flow over the specified address. By defining FULL on this parameter, the NCP assigns an even/odd pair of internal addresses for transmission. The even address is used for sending data (outbound) and the odd address for receiving data (inbound). IBM devices that can support a full duplex transmission are the IBM 3705, 3720, 3725, 3745 Communications Control Units and the IBM 3710 Network Controller. Figure 13.8 provides examples of the various configurations for DUPLEX and DATMODE operands.

280 Advanced SNA Networking

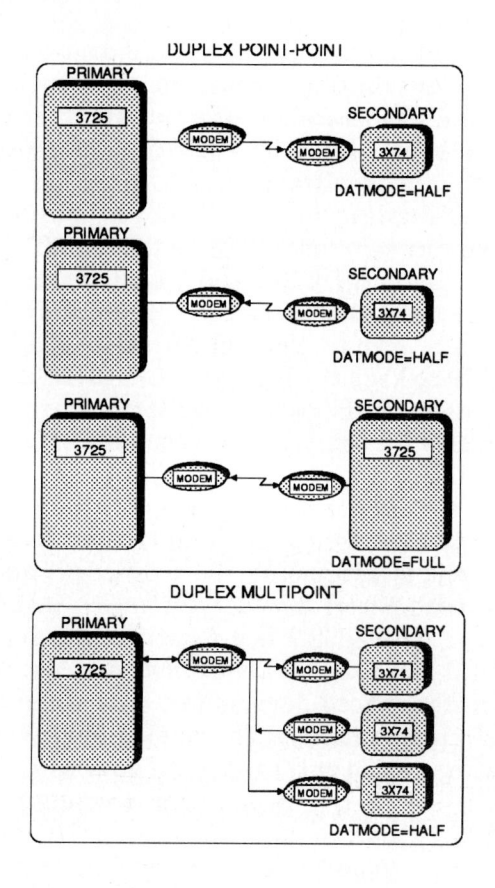

Figure 13.7 The effect of specifying DUPLEX=FULL on the LINE definition statement and DATMODE=HALF|FULL on the PU definition statement.

13.3.2 NCP Inbound Data Flow

Several parameters coded in the NCP affect the number of buffers used. The BFRS and AVGPB parameters of the BUILD definition statement are two such parameters. The BFRS parameter defines the size of the NCP buffers that will be used for data. The optimal size for an NCP buffer to enhance link-level performance is 128 bytes. However, if data on the network indicates that the average PIU is much less than 128 or the NCP is short of storage, use a smaller size. The size must be a multiple of 4 and, for optimization, divide into 256 as evenly as possible. The default value of 88 bytes does not divide into 256 for optimization. Three buffers will

Network Performance and Tuning 281

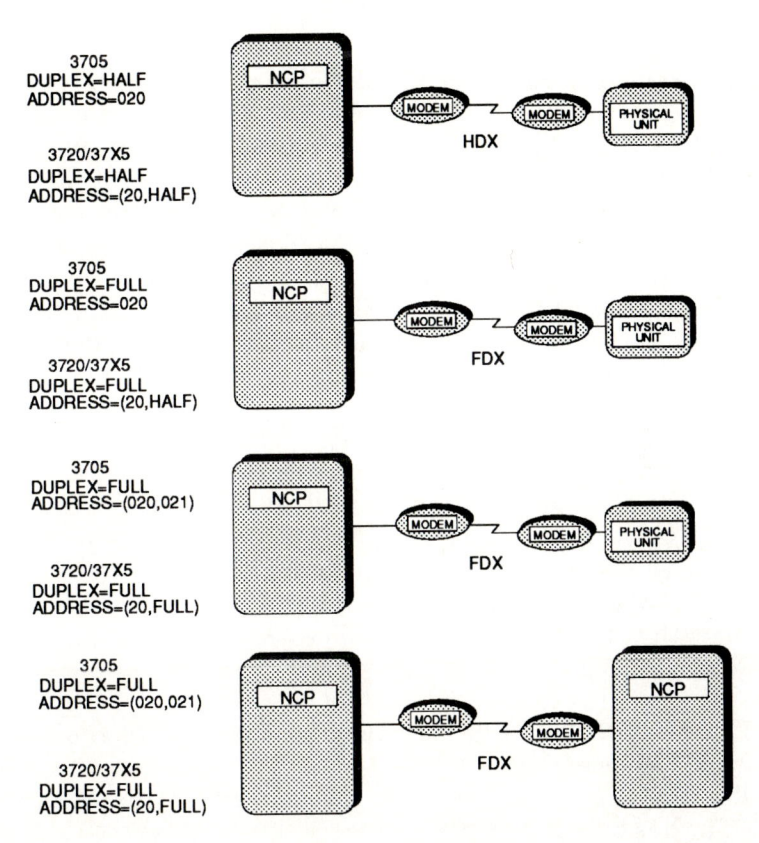

```
3705
DUPLEX=HALF
ADDRESS=020

3720/37X5
DUPLEX=HALF
ADDRESS=(20,HALF)
```
[NCP — MODEM — MODEM — PHYSICAL UNIT, HDX]

```
3705
DUPLEX=FULL
ADDRESS=020

3720/37X5
DUPLEX=FULL
ADDRESS=(20,HALF)
```
[NCP — MODEM — MODEM — PHYSICAL UNIT, FDX]

```
3705
DUPLEX=FULL
ADDRESS=(020,021)

3720/37X5
DUPLEX=FULL
ADDRESS=(20,FULL)
```
[NCP — MODEM — MODEM — PHYSICAL UNIT, FDX]

```
3705
DUPLEX=FULL
ADDRESS=(020,021)

3720/37X5
DUPLEX=FULL
ADDRESS=(20,FULL)
```
[NCP — MODEM — MODEM — NCP, FDX]

Figure 13.8 Possible configurations using DUPLEX and DATMODE operands.

be used to handle 256 bytes of data; the third buffer leaving 8 bytes of storage unused. Multiply that by the number of PIUs that travel through the NCP and you can see that large amounts of NCP buffer space will go unused. The AVGPB parameter of the BUILD definition statement specifies to the NCP the number of buffers required to satisfy the average amount of data received on a poll from a device. Before polling, the NCP checks this number against the number of available buffers above the slowdown value specified on the SLOWDOWN parameter of the BUILD definition statement. If the AVGPB value is not available, the NCP will forgo the poll at that time, waiting until the AVGPB value is available. The default for AVGPB is one NCP buffer size. However, again for optimization, it is better to analyze the average PIU size and then specify a value that is coherent with BFRS. Again, a good check is the divisibility into 256 evenly.

The parameters on the HOST definition statement in the NCP also affect the number of buffers used by the NCP. Out of these parameters there are three that directly influence buffer usage. The UNITSZ parameter defines to the NCP the size of the VTAM I/O buffer. This value must match the IOBUF operand in the VTAM start list named ATCSTR00. The MAXBFRU parameter specifies the number of buffers VTAM will use to receive a read request. By multiplying the MAXBFRU * UNITSZ, the NCP can determine the largest PIU that can flow between VTAM and the NCP. This value must also be less than or equal to the MAXDATA value of the PCCU definition statement. The MAXDATA value of the PCCU definition statement defines to VTAM the maximum sized PIU that can traverse this subarea path. The final parameter that can affect buffer usage directly is the DELAY value. The value specified here determines the amount of time, in seconds, the NCP will wait before sending an ATTENTION to VTAM requesting a READ operation. This value is important because it is tied in with the MAXBFRU value. The NCP will issue an ATTENTION only when:

- The MAXBFRU value has been reached before the DELAY value has been reached.
- The DELAY value has been reached before the MAXBFRU value has been reached.
- Both MAXBFRU and DELAY values have been reached simultaneously.

It is important to note this because if the MAXBFRU and DELAY values are large, the NCP buffers will be used to store data awaiting an unsolicited VTAM WRITE/READ combination. Optimal values are network specific, but a starting point value for MAXBFRU is MAXBFRU * UNITSZ = 1 VTAM I/O buffer page, and for DELAY, a value of .2 seconds.

A final HOST definition statement parameter used by the NCP is the INBFRS parameter. This parameter defines to the NCP the number of NCP buffers to allocate when receiving data from a VTAM WRITE operation. This value, multiplied by the BFRS value, will result in the number of buffer storage bytes needed for allocation for a VTAM WRITE operation. It is highly recommended that the number specified here be conservative. This value is coupled with the communications wall (CWALL) parameter of the BUILD definition statement. The CWALL value is the minimum number of NCP buffers needed to operate. If the product of INBFRS * BFRS results in a buffer pool reduction below that of the CWALL value, the NCP will not honor the VTAM WRITE request. The VTAM WRITE request will be honored when this product indicates a value of CWALL or greater of buffers remaining in the buffer pool.

13.3.3 NCP Outbound Data Flow

Data flowing to peripheral PUs from the NCP are affected by many NCP parameters. The MAXDATA parameter of the PU definition statement defines the largest PIU that the PU link buffer can handle. For PU Type 1 devices the value is 261, for IBM 3274 PU Type 2 devices, it is 265. For the special case of the IBM 3770 PU Type 2, the MAXDATA value is 521 bytes. For the IBM 3174, MAXDATA can be either 265 or 521 bytes. The value specified for the PU Types 1 and 2 is the result of the PU link buffer size plus the bytes that make up the Transmission Header (TH) and the Request/Response Header (RH) of the FID Type 1 and 2 formats respectively.

Applications, however, usually send data sizes much larger than the MAXDATA value. This results in what is know as segmentation. Segmentation occurs between the NCP and peripheral PUs. Data from the application is sent to the NCP in one large PIU up to the PCCU MAXDATA value. The NCP must then break the large PIU down into PIUs the size of MAXDATA on the PU definition statement. This process of reducing the larger PIU into smaller PIUs is called segmentation. Both PU Type 1 and Type 2 support segmentation. However, the IBM 3770 PU Type 2 does not support it. Figure 13.9 outlines the mechanism of segmentation.

One drawback of SDLC is the unsightly affect it has on the display screen of a 3270 LU type. The data display results in a painting or shading effect on the end-users terminal. This gives the end user the false impression of poor response time when just the opposite is true. To circumvent this painting effect, two PU parameters can be used for tuning. The MAXOUT parameter defines to the NCP the number of SDLC frames that the NCP will send to the PU before polling again. In general, this value is dependent upon the transmission modulus in effect. For normal NCP-PU connections over standard facilities, the modulus used is MODULO8. This means that up to 7 frames can be transmitted before polling the device. The other alternative is utilized for

284   Advanced SNA Networking

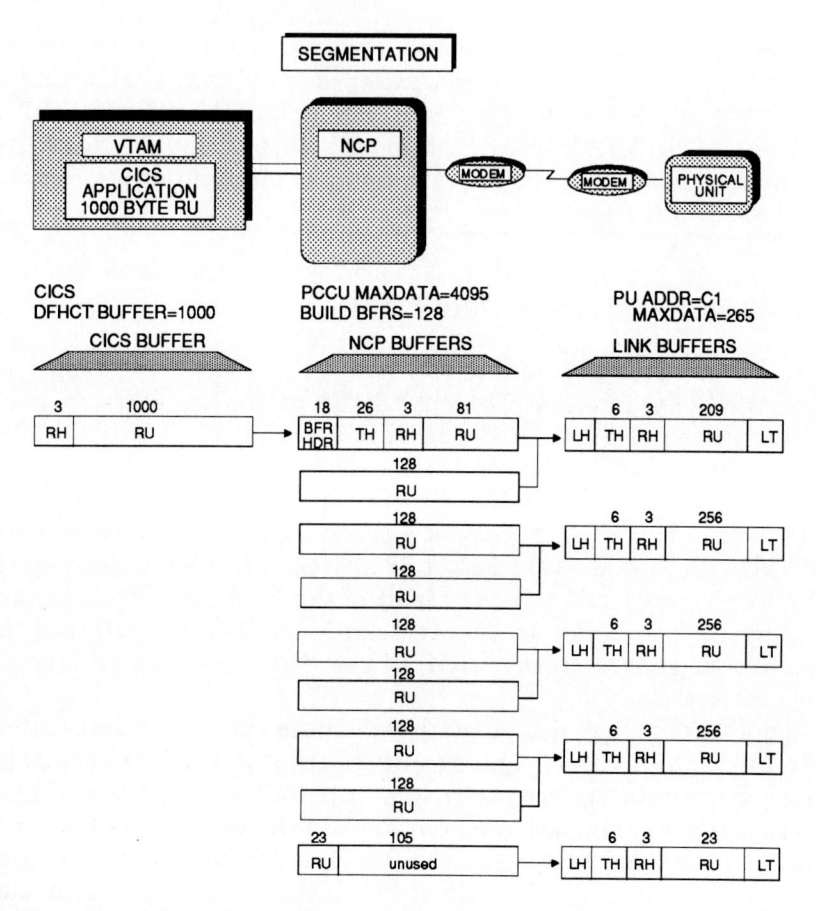

Figure 13.9 Diagram depicting the mechanism of segmentation.

NCP-NCP connections and those configurations that use satellite links. In these cases, MODULO 128 can be used and it indicates that up to 127 frames may be transmitted before the polling bit in the Receive-Ready (RR) SDLC frame is turned on. The rule of thumb for MAXOUT is to code the highest value possible.

The second parameter is PASSLIM. The value specified here dictates the maximum number of frames to send to a PU before servicing the next PU in the Service Order Table (SOT) of a multi-drop line. This parameter can be used in two ways. The first is to reduce the amount of service obtained by a high volume PU on a multi-point line. The second assists in reducing the painting effect of 3270 type displays. Defining a PASSLIM large enough to accommodate a full 3270 screen display will reduce the painting

Network Performance and Tuning   285

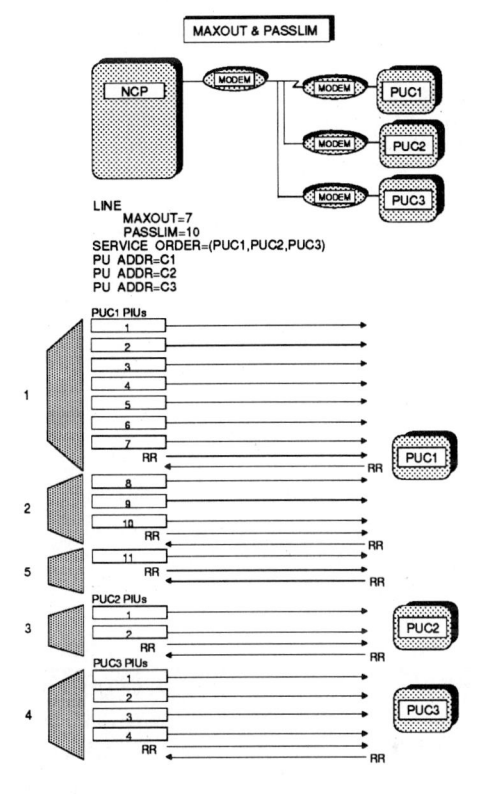

Figure 13.10 The effect of MAXOUT and PASSLIM values on delivering PIUs to peripheral nodes.

effect, but at a small performance cost to the other PUs and LUs of a multidrop line. Generally, for a point-to-point configuration, code the maximum value of 254. This will allow the NCP to transmit as many SDLC frames as possible while servicing the link defined to this PU. For a multi-point configuration, a good starting value is PASSLIM=MAXOUT. This will ensure the transmission of as many frames as possible before a link-level response (RR or RNR) is solicited by the NCP from the PU. Figure 13.10 diagrams the effect of PASSLIM and MAXOUT.

13.3.4 Link Scheduler Service

The function in the NCP that schedules service to resources attached to defined links is performed by the Link Scheduler. Checks are made on the number of frames sent and are compared to the MAXOUT and PASSLIM values specified for this PU. The PU itself is serviced based on its position in the Service Order Table (SOT) defined by the SERVICE definition statement. The SOT is used primarily for multi-point lines. The SOT defines the order in which each PU on the link is serviced by the link scheduler. If a specific PU needs more service than some of the others, it can be coded more than once in the SOT. The service provided to a PU is classified into two categories by the link scheduler:

1. Special service.
2. Normal service.

During SSCP-PU session establishment, the PU may not immediately respond to the activation request. This is reflected by VTAM posting the PU in a pending contacted state (e.g., PCTD2). To the link scheduler this is a special service. A special service processes all SDLC commands except Receive-Ready (RR) and Receive-Not-Ready (RNR). The amount of special service is determined by the SERVLIM parameter of the LINE definition statement. The value coded here tells the link scheduler to provide normal service to active PUs through the SOT SERVLIM times before processing special service requests such as Set-Normal-Response-Mode (SNRM). The higher the SERVLIM value, the less impact special service requests have on active users of a multipoint line. For a point-to-point line it does not have much purpose. The default for PU Type 1 and 2 is 4 and for PU Type 4 it is 254.

Normal service provided by the link scheduler differs between half-duplex and full-duplex transmission. For a half-duplex (HDX) link, whether point-to-point or multi-point, output to the PU has priority. The transmit and receive pointers of the link scheduler are the same for an HDX line. As the pointer is moved through the Service Order Table, the link scheduler checks the outbound queue of the PU. If it is not empty, the NCP will keep transmitting frames until the outbound queue is empty, the PASSLIM value has been reached, or the MAXDATA value has been reached. If MAXDATA has been reached, the NCP will poll the device. At that time, the PU may then send data to the NCP. Once the data is processed by the NCP, the link scheduler resumes sending the remaining frames left in the PASSLIM count, assuming the PASSLIM count has not been reached. The procedure continues for the remaining active PUs for SERVLIM times before special link scheduler service is processed. Figure 13.11 details the different services and pointers used by the Link Scheduler.

Network Performance and Tuning 287

LINK SCHEDULER

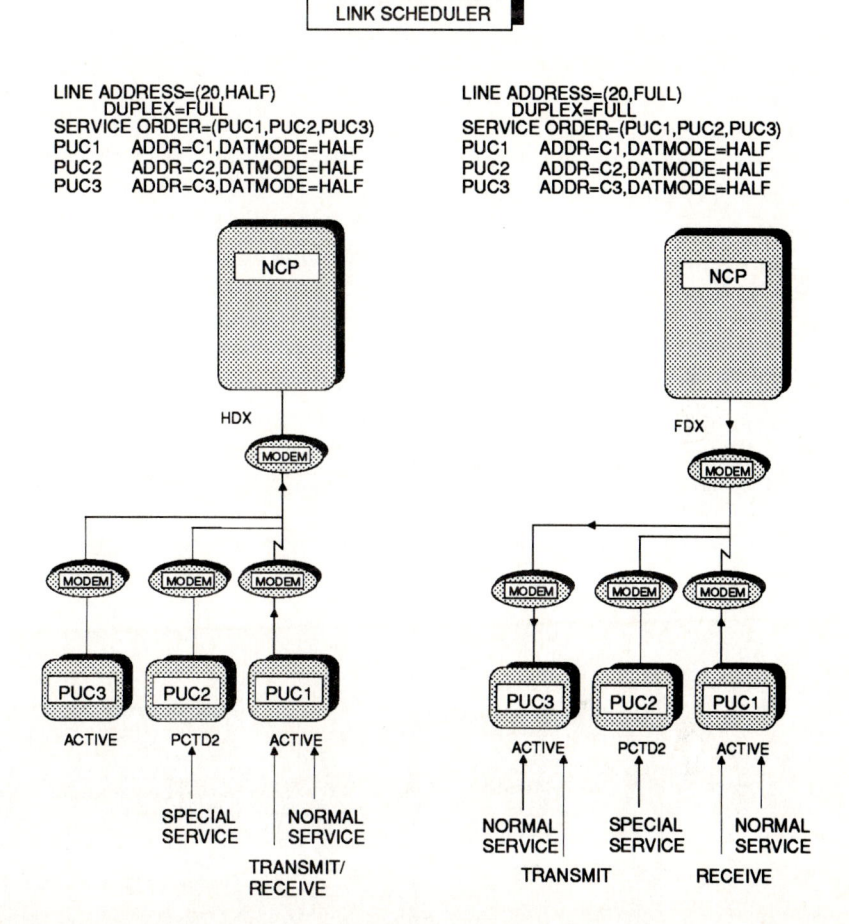

```
LINE ADDRESS=(20,HALF)              LINE ADDRESS=(20,FULL)
      DUPLEX=FULL                         DUPLEX=FULL
SERVICE ORDER=(PUC1,PUC2,PUC3)      SERVICE ORDER=(PUC1,PUC2,PUC3)
PUC1    ADDR=C1,DATMODE=HALF        PUC1    ADDR=C1,DATMODE=HALF
PUC2    ADDR=C2,DATMODE=HALF        PUC2    ADDR=C2,DATMODE=HALF
PUC3    ADDR=C3,DATMODE=HALF        PUC3    ADDR=C3,DATMODE=HALF
```

```
        NCP                                  NCP
         |                                    |
        HDX                                  FDX
       MODEM                               MODEM
     /   |   \                           /   |   \
  MODEM MODEM MODEM                   MODEM MODEM MODEM
    |    |    |                         |    |    |
  PUC3 PUC2 PUC1                       PUC3 PUC2 PUC1
 ACTIVE PCTD2 ACTIVE                  ACTIVE PCTD2 ACTIVE

 SPECIAL  NORMAL                    NORMAL  SPECIAL  NORMAL
 SERVICE  SERVICE                   SERVICE SERVICE  SERVICE
          TRANSMIT/
          RECEIVE                   TRANSMIT         RECEIVE
```

Figure 13.11 Diagram depicting the Link Scheduler normal/special services and transmit/receive pointer usage.

In a full duplex configuration supporting concurrent transmit and receive, the link scheduler has a transmit pointer and a receive pointer. The transmit pointer remains on the current PU being serviced until the outbound queue is empty or PASSLIM has been reached. A poll is sent whenever the receive pointer points to the PU entry in the SOT. As the pointers move independently through the SOT, they may catch up with each other. The transmit pointer will pass over the PU entry being polled. If, however, the PU device can support concurrent transmit and receive (e.g., IBM 3725), then both pointers can be servicing the same PU entry.

13.3.5 Transmission Group Queuing/Resequencing

Multiple explicit and virtual routes are served by the transmission group (TG). For each TG defined in an NCP there is one queue. As the PIUs arrive in the NCP, they are placed in the TG queues only if all the links defined to that TG are busy. The PIUs are queued within a TG queue on a first-in-first-out (FIFO) basis within the virtual route priority assigned by the class of service table entry for the session. Figure 13.12 details the queing and resequencing of PIUs. The links that make up the TG are searched in activation order when sending PIUs. Ultimately, this is the order in which the links are defined in the NCP, especially when the ISTATUS parameter value is specified as ISTATUS=ACTIVE. The first available link in this order will be used to transmit the data.

Recall that TGs can have as many as 8 links defined to them. As the PIUs are sent over the TG, their sequence may be disturbed on

TG QUEUEING & RESEQUENCING

DATA INBOUND		NCP		TG	NCP
PIU	VR PRIORITY	TG TRANSMIT QUEUE			Sequence Number Checking
1	0	PIU	VR PRIORITY		
2	0	4	2		Equal 1
3	1	5	2		High 2
4	2	6	2		Low 3
5	2	3	1		
6	2	7	1		
7	1	1	0		
		2	0		

1. Sequence number matches expected receive number. No resequencing required.
2. Sequence number received higher than expected receive number. Resequencing required.
3. Sequence number received lower than expected receive number. Duplicate PIU. Transmission error.

Figure 13.12 Diagram outlining the queuing and resequencing algorithm for TGs.

the receiving NCP. The size of the PIUs (MAXDATA), the speed of the individual links, the characteristics of the links (e.g., HDX or FDX) and error recovery all play a role in determining if resequencing is needed. You can reduce the amount of resequencing in your network by architecting the links with the same line speed and characteristics for the TG. The size of the PIUs that traverse this TG can be restricted to dedicated traffic through prudent VR mapping. Implementing these will improve response time, throughput, reduce NCP cycles and buffer usage and thereby lead to better network performance.

13.4 LOGICAL DATA FLOW PERFORMANCE

The most noticeable performance factor in a network is the response time perceived by the end-users during their LU-LU sessions. That time is measured by the end-user according to the speed in which he receives a response from an interactive application under CICS, for example, or the time in which it takes to receive a printed report at his local printer. Both scenarios, interactive and batch, are typical in any SNA network.

To facilitate this logical data flow, the movement of data between the LUs must be controlled and coordinated. This movement is orchestrated by VTAM and the NCP implmenting SNA Data Flow Control (DFC) mechanisms. These mechanisms are outlined in Figure 13.13. The table is listed in order of importance for tuning considerations of LU-LU sessions.

CONSIDERATION	INTERACTIVE	BATCH LARGE RU SIZE
PACING	2	1
CHAINING vs. SEGMENTATION	2	1
DEFINITE RESPONSE	2	1
FLIP-FLOP vs. CONTENTION	1	2
COMPRESSION	3	1
COMPACTION	3	1
NULL RUs & CICS	1	2

1 - Heavy 2 - Light 3 - Not Applicable

Figure 13.13 LU-LU session considerations implemented by VTAM and NCP.

13.4.1 Chaining and Segmentation

Two functions of SNA that can greatly influence response time and throughput are chaining and segmentation. Figure 13.14 diagrams the basic differences between the two functions. Chaining occurs within the host, either at the application level or at VTAM. Segmentation occurs in the NCP. Previously, we discussed segmentation and how it segments an RU size that is larger than the receiving MAXDATA value of the secondary LU's controlling PU. Segementation offloads data transmission from the host to the NCP. It is not uncommon in an SNA network to utilize both chaining and segmentation concurrently to a LU. In one instance

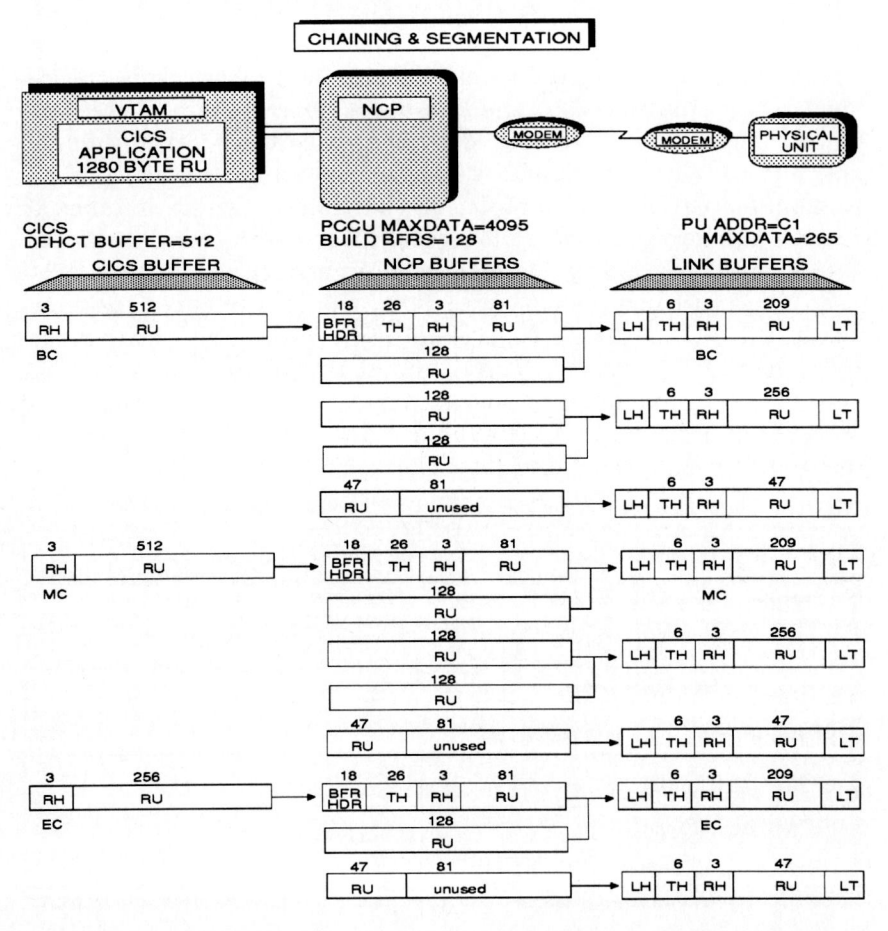

Figure 13.14 Detailed flow of using both chaining and segmentation for an LU-LU session.

Network Performance and Tuning 291

it is up to the application to provide the chaining. An enhancement to VTAM V2.1 in conjunction with CICS V1.6 called the Large Message Performance Enhancement Outbound (LMPEO), allows VTAM to perform the chaining of the outbound RU on behalf of the CICS subsystem application.

Chaining is commonly performed for RJE/RJP and batch type of sessions. This is because these sessions are usually involved with print data or data transfer. For these, and some interactive sessions, a large chain achieves higher throughput than smaller chains. To effectively use chaining, the application must implement multiple chain elements. A chain element is a section of a full chain. For instance, in Figure 13.14, an application sends 1280 bytes of information to an SLU. The first PIU has the Begin Chain (BC) and First-In-Chain (FIC) indicators on in the RH. The following elements are described as Middle-In-Chain (MIC) chain elements by the RH. The final chain element is indicated in the RH by the End-of-Chain (EC) and Last-In-Chain indicators turned on. Chaining of data in this fashion allows a grouping of RUs into one entity for error-recovery purposes. The receiving LU returns to the sender one response for the entrie chain rather than a response for each individual RU. This can save considerable overhead where immediate-mode response or definite-response (DR) session protocols are in use.

The size of the chain is determined by the application's outbound/inbound buffer size. Chaining is implemented by analyzing the average RU size sent to the SLU by the application. Once this data is compiled, tuning can begin. For CICS this is the BUFFER/RU SIZE value in the TCT; in IMS it's the OUTBUF/RECANY value; in JES2 the BUFSIZE value of the RMTnnnn definition; and in TSO the RUSIZE value in the session parameter BIND definition. If the transaction creates an outbound buffer larger than the values specified above then chaining will occur. Optimal throughput with chaining can be achieved by using a chain that results in approximately 10 chain elements. Chains larger than this may not help, especially during error recovery since the entire chain must be retransmitted. However, large chains can virtually eliminate the possible performance improvement.

For JES2, the chain size is acutally determined by the check-point pages (CKPTPGS) and check-point lines (CKPTLNS) parameters of the printer definition (Rnn.PRnn) of the RJE station. The values specified here determine the size of the chain. The values of the two parameters are multiplied together. The product is then multiplied by the number of characters per line to determine the

292 Advanced SNA Networking

number of bytes that are transmitted. This number is then divided by the BUFSIZE value of the RMTnnn RJE definition statement, which results in the number of elements in a chain. The BUFSIZE parameter should equal the maximum RU size that the RJE station can accept. All RJE sessions operate in definite-response mode. Thus, at the end of the last chain element, the RJE station will respond with a positive or negative reponse indicating successful or unsuccessful transmission. Figure 13.15 diagrams the RJE scenario.

13.4.2 Session-Level Pacing

SNA has a coordinated mechanism for protecting SNA resources on session-level communications. This protection mechanism is called pacing. Pacing is used to prevent one partner of an LU-LU

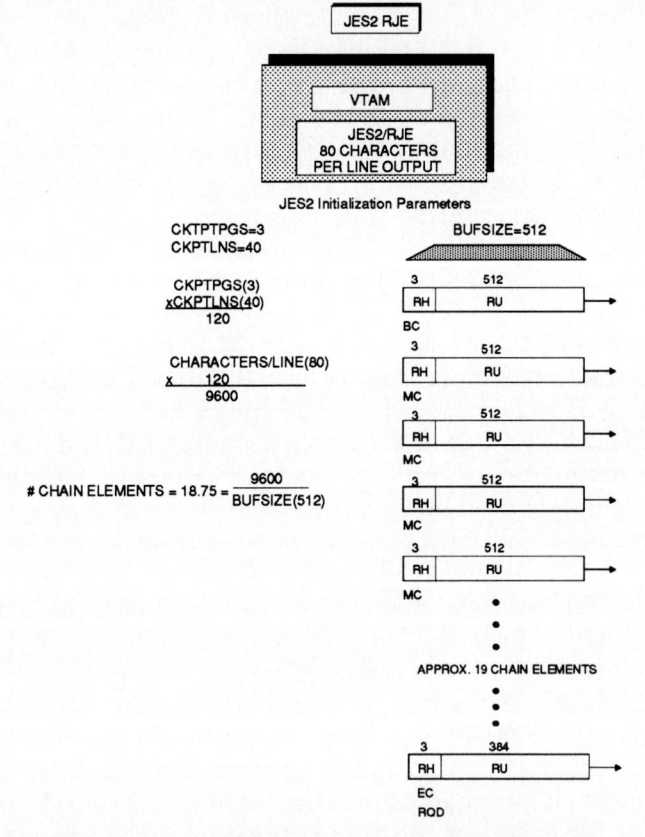

Figure 13.15 Algorithm for determining the number of elements in a chain.

Network Performance and Tuning 293

session from overwhelming the other partner with data. This is necessary to protect the PU's device buffer from LU "hogging".

The pacing is performed in one or two stages. One-stage pacing involves locally attached devices to the host computer. Two-stage pacing is categorized as pacing between the host and a boundary function subarea node and from the boundary function subarea node to the receiving LU. Figure 13.16 depicts one-stage and two-stage pacing. Pacing in both configurations is handled for inbound and outbound transmission.

Pacing is specified by the session parameters passed in the BIND request and by VTAM/NCP parameters. In the session parameters, there are two that define VTAM outbound pacing. These parameters are the Primary-Send (PSNDPAC) and the Secondary-

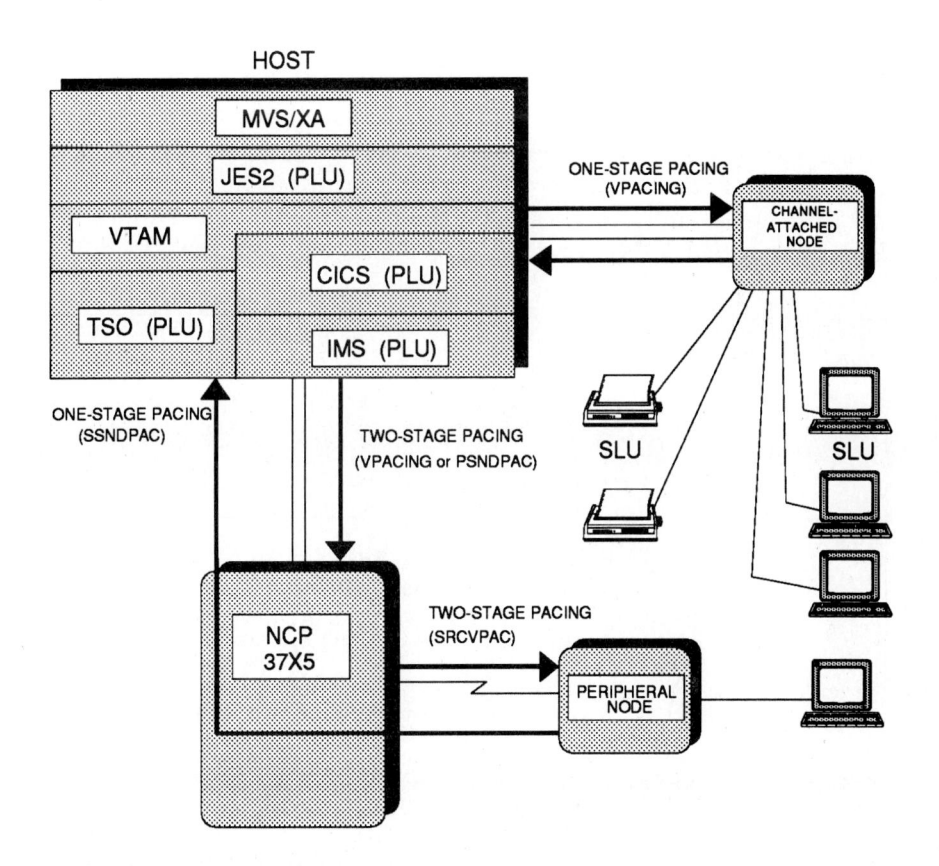

Figure 13.16 Diagram of one-stage and two-stage session pacing.

Receive (SRCVPAC) parameters. The PSNDPAC parameter specifies the number of PIUs that VTAM can send to the NCP before expecting a pacing response. This value can also be defined by the VPACING VTAM parameter. The SRCVPAC parameter defines the number of PIUs that can flow from the boundary function subarea node (VTAM or NCP) to the receiving LU before waiting for a pacing response. The VTAM/NCP parameter that can also be used for this is called PACING. The Secondary-Send (SSNDPAC) parameter of the session parameter of the BIND request serves as the inbound value of data flowing from the LU to VTAM on behalf of this LU-LU session and as the outbound value from the boundary function LU to the VTAM. In certain situations, the VPACING value specified on the application (APPL) definition statement is used as the inbound pacing value. The algorithm for selecting these pacing values is involved.

The rules for pacing value selection can get quite confusing. The selection path used by VTAM for each of the three types of session pacing, 1) VTAM to NCP (VPACING and PSNDPAC), 2) NCP to LU (PACING and SRCVPAC), 3) LU to VTAM (VPACING and SSND) is detailed in Figures 13.17, 13.18, 13.19, 13.20. For each value there are three sources to determine the pacing count. A logon mode entry in the mode table of the LU will supply the PSNDPAC, SRCVPAC and SSNDPAC values through the BIND

SRCVPAC Value in LOGMODE Entry	NCP Source PACING Value	NCP Load PACING Value	SRCVPAC Value in BIND Image
0	1	1	0
7	1	1	0
0	5	5	2
7	5	5	5
0	0	0	0

Rules:
- If SRVCPAC=0 is defined in LOGMODE entry, then the NCP Load PACING value is used in the BIND image.
- If SRVCPAC value in LOGMODE entry is greater than 0, then the SRCVPAC value specified in the LOGMODE entry is used in the BIND image.
- If SRVCPAC=0 and the NCP source PACING value is greater than the NCP Load PACING value, then the NCP source PACING value is used in the BIND image.

Figure 13.17 VTAM outbound SRVCPAC value selection rules for insertion into the BIND image at session establishment.

Network Performance and Tuning

SRCVPAC Value in LOGMODE Entry	PLU VPACING Value	SSNDPAC Value in BIND Image
0	2	0
0	1	0
2	2	2
7	5	5
0	0	0

Rules:

- If SSNDPAC=0 in LOGMODE entry, then 0 will be used in the BIND image.

- If SSNDPAC=0, then the VPACING value specified on the Primary Logical Unit (PLU) definition is used in the BIND image at session establishment.

- RU size specified for PLU should be large enough to accept the VPACING inbound value from the SLU.

Figure 13.18 VTAM inbound SSNDPAC value selection rules for insertion into the BIND image at session establishment.

request. For both the PSNDPAC and SRCVPAC paramters a non-zero value will override the VTAM/NCP source value of the VPACING and PACING parameter values and the NCP load module values. If the PSNDPAC and SRCVPAC values are zero, then then the values specified on the VTAM/NCP source definitions are inserted into the BIND request. However, if the VTAM/NCP source value for PACING is zero, then the NCP load module value will be used. The SSNDPAC value takes on a different meaning. If the

SRCVPAC Value in LOGMODE Entry	PLU VPACING Value	SSNDPAC Value in BIND Image
0	2	0
0	1	0
2	2	2
7	5	5
0	0	0

Rules:

- If PSNDPAC=0 in LOGMODE entry, then the VAPCING value specified on the SLU source definition will be used in the BIND

- If PSNDPAC > 0, then the PSNDPAC value specified in the LOGMODE entry is used in the BINDimage at session establishment.

Figure 13.19 VTAM outbound PSNDPAC value selection rules for insertion into the BIND image.

296 Advanced SNA Networking

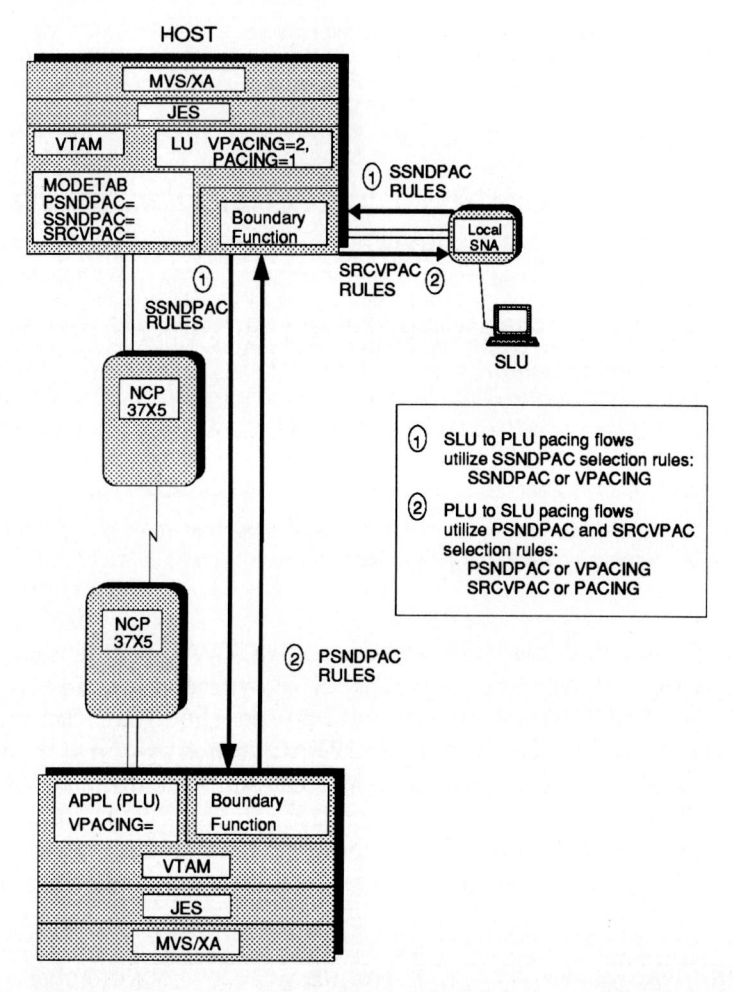

Figure 13.20 Cross-domain LU-LU session between a channel-attached SLU and a remote application PLU. This is the only instance where all session pacing flows are used.

SSNDPAC value in the BIND request is a non-zero value, then the VPACING value specified on the PLU APPL definition statement is used. However, this is only true if you have coded AUTH=VPACE for this application. If AUTH=NVPACE is coded, then SSNDPAC will be set to zero. The NVPACE parameter indicates that no VTAM pacing is to take place.

13.4.3 Compression and Compaction

For VTAM and NCP there are no specific parameters that are defined to include compression and compaction, but they do have a role in the performance of the network, especially for Remote Job Entry (RJE/RJP). Compression can be an effective means of reducing the transmission load of an LU-LU session with little impact on VTAM and NCP cycles. Compression is a mechanism that allows you to compress repetitive characters in a data stream into two bytes of data. The character must be repeated 3 or more times in succession for compression to take place. This is especially useful for print data that has an excessive number of imbedded spaces. The space character (X'40') is the default Prime Compression Character. However, you may assign other characters for compression. Compaction on the other hand can create more overhead than it is worth. A compaction table is created by you, the systems programmer, based on careful analysis of the data streams. The compaction table is used in three distinct places in the network. Before compaction all of the characters are checked for validity, then they are compacted. The compaction algorithm will search for "master characters" defined in the compaction table and compact an 8-bit character into 4-bits. Only up to 16 "master characters" can be compacted. Once transmission begins, a copy of the compact table is sent to the PU of the receiving LU for decompaction. As you can see, the compaction/decompaction of a large amount of data can be exhaustive at the application and PU levels. Consider compaction only if you must reduce transmission volumes, if the data lends itself to compaction, and if the LUs support the mechanism. If the LUs support compression then use it, but avoid compaction until it appears to be unavoidable.

13.5 VIRTUAL ROUTE PACING

The flow of data through an SNA network is controlled by a route pacing mechanism. This mechanism is inclusive to the Virtual Routes (VRs) that map the logical routes of the network. The pacing of virtual routes is implemented in each subarea node along the virtual route. The pacing itself is automated and is not an option when defining the network. Route pacing assists in avoiding network node overload affecting all sessions on a VR while controlling network data flows. Figure 13.21 provides an overview of the VR pacing mechanism.

Virtual Route Pacing:
- Dynamic pacing

- Uses a pacing window size

- Uses VRPWS00=(min,max) to VRPWS72=(min,max) on PATH defintion statements.

- Min and max values determined at VR activation time if not defined on the PATH definition statement.

- VR pacing request (VRPQS) bit in the Transmission Header (TH) of the first PIU indicates VR pacing.

- VR pacing response (VRPRS) bit in the TH flows in an Isolated Pacing Response (IPR) PIU, indicating the complete VR window size has been transmitted.

Figure 13.21 Overview of virtual route pacing.

13.5.1 VR Window Size

The pacing window size of the VR defines the number of PIUs sent over a VR before an isolated pacing response is requested. Requests and responses for VR pacing are indicated in the FID-4 Transmission Header (TH) of the PIU. As of VTAM V2R2 and NCP V3, the minimum and maximum VR pacing values can be specified on the PATH definition statement. The defaults for the minimum and maximum window size are calculated according to the supporting ER and the number of subarea nodes (i.e., hops) the ER passes through to its final destination. For ERs that have several hops, the minimum VR window size equals the number of hops. The maximum default value is equal to 3 times the number of hops taken by the ER. For ERs that have a single channel hop, the minimum value is set to 1. The maximum is the greater of 15 or 256 - (16 * n), where n is the number of ERs that pass through the adjacent subarea but do not terminate there. Once these values are reached, VTAM will wait for the VR Pacing Response bit (VRPRS) indicator in any TH that flows over this VR.

In VTAM, there is a specialized module that handles the VR window size. It is called ISTPUCWC. This module oversees all of the VRs and sets the window sizes accordingly. Initially all window sizes are set to the minimum value. To minimize delay and

Network Performance and Tuning   299

maximize throughput, VTAM would like to see the VRPRS indicator before one window of PIUs has been sent. This reduces the VR idle time and the window size remains unchanged. If VTAM has sent one window of PIUs and is waiting on the VRPRS it will increase the window size by 1 if the maximum value has not been reached. Figure 13.22 details this VR pacing flow example.

13.5.2 VR States

The status of a VR is constantly monitored by both ends of the VR. There are two states that either end can indicate to the other. The HELD VR state occurs when the origin subarea has sent a window of PIUs and is waiting for the VRPRS. While waiting, the originating subarea will accept PIUs up to a full window. The second state is the BLOCKED VR state. This status is more serious than the HELD state. In the BLOCKED state the origin is waiting on a VRPRS after sending a full window of PIUs and has queued up a second window of PIUs for transmission. The blockage may be

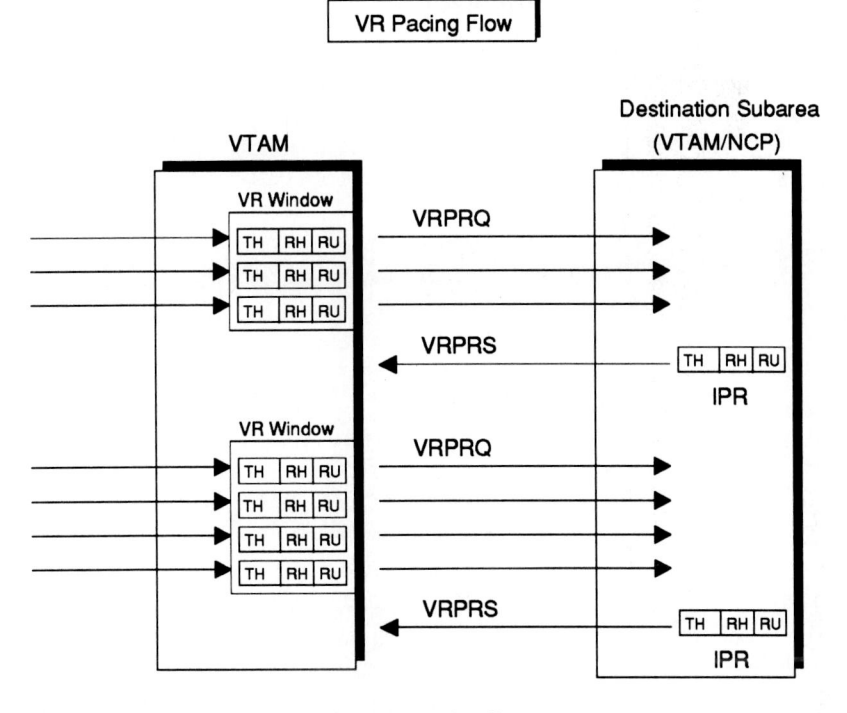

Figure 13.22 Example of virtual route pacing flow.

300 Advanced SNA Networking

caused by several network components. There may be too many intervening hops and transmission groups along the virtual route causing excessive delays in receiving the VRPRS. The specified window sizes may have been miscalculated resulting in a window size that's too small. One problem found in many shops is that all sessions are on the same virtual route. This results in too many sessions and too much traffic over the VR. The transmission groups may also be a cause for the BLOCKED VR. If the TGs are too slow for the amount of data passing through them, it may be reflected in BLOCKED VRs between subarea nodes on the INN links. Figure 13.23 diagrams the two VR states.

Both VTAM and the NCP react quickly to try to circumvent the problem. Both stop LU input from their respective resources.

VR States

VTAM

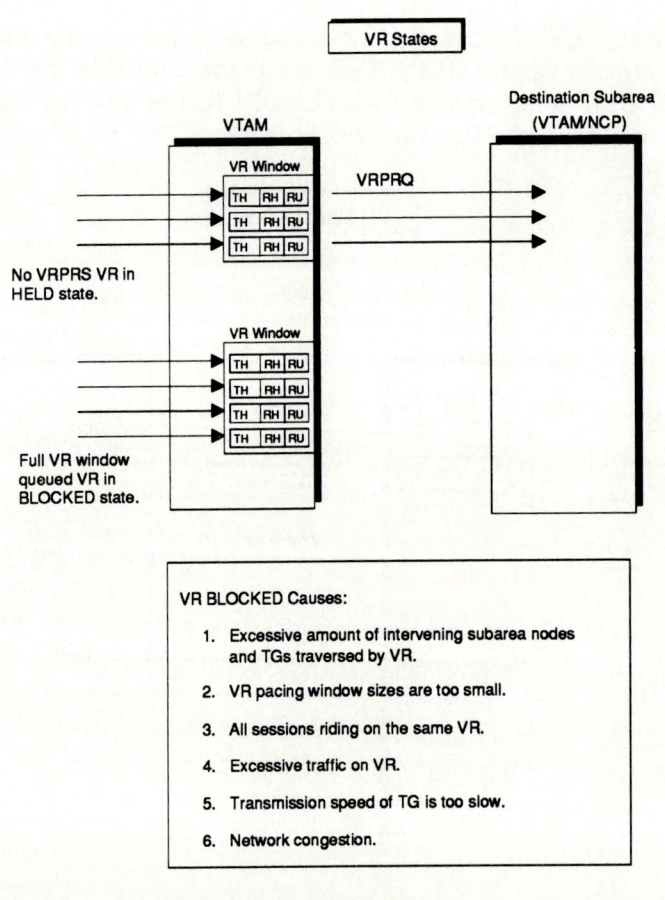

Destination Subarea (VTAM/NCP)

VR Window
TH RH RU
TH RH RU
TH RH RU

VRPRQ

No VRPRS VR in HELD state.

VR Window
TH RH RU
TH RH RU
TH RH RU
TH RH RU

Full VR window queued VR in BLOCKED state.

VR BLOCKED Causes:
1. Excessive amount of intervening subarea nodes and TGs traversed by VR.
2. VR pacing window sizes are too small.
3. All sessions riding on the same VR.
4. Excessive traffic on VR.
5. Transmission speed of TG is too slow.
6. Network congestion.

Figure 13.23 Virtual route states and their causes.

They do, however, service all output requests. A situation can arise where VTAM is waiting for a VRPRS from the NCP and the NCP is waiting for a VRPRS from VTAM for the same VR. In this situation, we have a deadly embrace and the VR must be made inactive to release the deadlock. Stopping LU input from channel-attached devices is accomplished by VTAM not presenting a channel READ command. The NCP, in turn, ceases to POLL non-SNA devices for input and sends a Receive-Not-Ready (RNR) to all PUs. In this way, a TH of one of the PIUs will have the VRPRS indicator on and LU input will then start. These procedures are performed to allow the NCP to deliver queued PIUs to VTAM and vice-versa.

13.5.3 Network Congestion

Excessive buffering in some subarea nodes along the VR may also be a cause for BLOCKED VRs. This congestion comes in two flavors. Moderate congestion is indicated by the Change-Window-Reply-Indicator (CWRI) value in the TH of the VRPRS. Sent by a VR end node, this indicator is specific to INN links only. The CWRI causes the window size to decrement by 1 unless the minimum value has been reached. Severe congestion is indicated by the Reset-Window-Indicator (RWI) in the TH of any PIU from any subarea node along the VR. This indicates that the window size must be set to the minimum immdiately.

Severe congestion is the only type that VTAM will detect. A likely cause of severe congestion in VTAM is VTAM's inability to allocate I/O buffers. Hence, it enters SLOWDOWN. This is because the I/O buffer pool cannot expand fast enough or the CSALIMIT value has been reached. VTAM sends RWI on all PIUs outbound on all VRs.

In the NCP, INN congestion is focused on the threshold counters defined for each TG on the PATH defintion statement ER operand (Figure 13.24). A counter is supplied for each VR transmission priority and a total counter. As data is queued for transmission, the bytes of each PIU are counted and entered in the corresponding threshold counter. Moderate congestion is reached when any of the counters have reached the threshold value. The NCP will then set the Change-Window-Indicator (CWI) on the next PIU sent over the TG. This will cause the destination subarea node to send CWRI, decreasing the window size by one. This continues until the counter falls below the threshold. Severe congestion in the NCP occurs when the total counter has reached its threshold. The

302 Advanced SNA Networking

NCP immediately sets RWI on all PIUs transmitting over this TG until the counter falls below the threshold value. To circumvent NCP INN link congestion problems, consider raising the TG thresholds.

For effective network flow control tuning, take advantage of the VTAM mechanisms described. Utilize VTAM's class of service (COS) table to prioritize session flows and to separate applications. If you do not feel that users or applications on the same VR need to be separated, then define the COS to provide the highest transmission priority for every user. Sessions that flow primarily over channel links should have the minimum and maximum window sizes set high. For VRs that flow over a communications network, monitor for held/blocked VRs. Use the VTAM command:

NCP INN Congestion

Moderate Congestion

PATH DESTSA=n,ERn=(adjsa,TG,5000,5000,5000,15000)

TG VR priority counters:	Priority 0	Priority 1	Priority 2	TOTAL
	5000	2000	3500	10500

Origin Subarea → INN NCP → Destination Subarea
CWI
CWRI

Severe Congestion

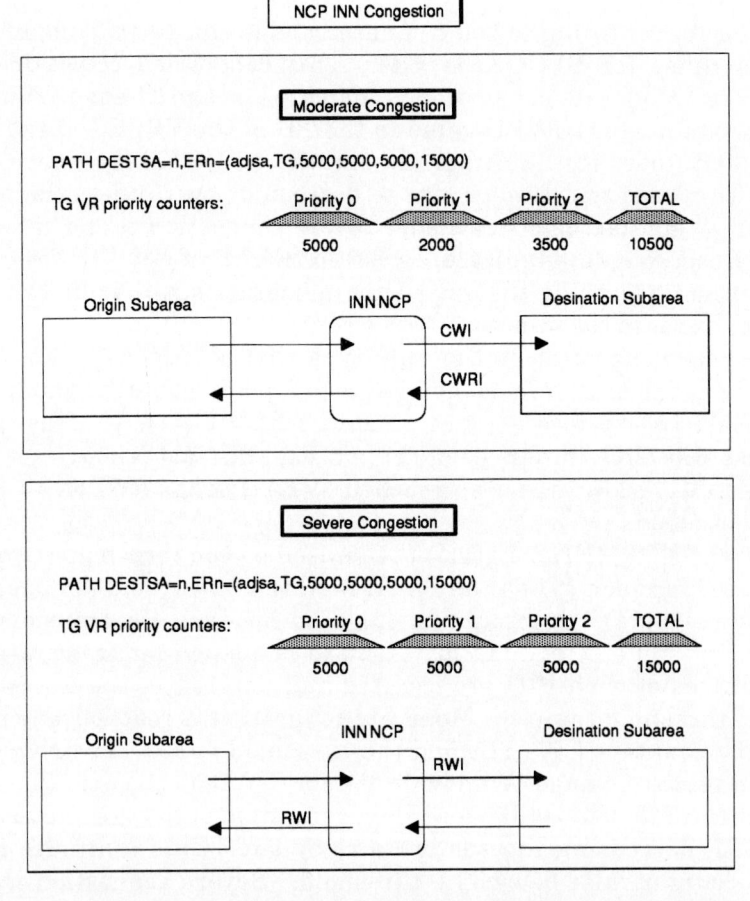

PATH DESTSA=n,ERn=(adjsa,TG,5000,5000,5000,15000)

TG VR priority counters:	Priority 0	Priority 1	Priority 2	TOTAL
	5000	5000	5000	15000

Origin Subarea → INN NCP → Destination Subarea
RWI
RWI

Figure 13.24 INN congestion between NCP and boundary function subarea nodes.

    D NET,ROUTE,DESTSUB=n,VR=n

to identify these states as VTAM sees them. For an NCP this is more difficult. We must first have the address of the Virtual Route Control Block (VRB) in the NCP. This can be obtained from the link-edited output of the NCP generation. Once it is known, you can enter the VTAM command:

    D NET,NCPSTOR,ID=ncpname,ADDR=nnnnn

If you want to go to extremes, you can automate these displays with NetView command lists or REXX procedures. In this way, the command list or REXX procedure can diagnose the displays and take any corrective action necessary to circumvent the problem.

Monitor NCPs for Receive-Not-Ready (RNR) polling, which indicates that the minimum window size may be too small. To do this, execute a trace on the NCP PU. The RNR polling indicates that inbound pacing should be used wherever possible and set at a high value. Another possible corrective action is to raise the minimum window size.

Determine if your subareas are overusing CWI, CWRI, RWI and using VRPRS. These conditions indicate network congestion. To obtain this data, execute VTAM TYPE=IO traces on the NCPs and VTAM's PU name. The NCP trace will show CWI, RWI CWRI and VRPRQ indicators, while the VTAM PU name trace will show the VRPRS indicator.

13.6 SUMMARY

In this chapter, we introduced you to a methodology for SNA network performance and tuning. We discussed the three major topics of this methodology — performance monitoring, analysis and deciding on performance objectives. We reviewed VTAM's buffer pools and how they are used by VTAM, and what you can do to improve VTAM's performance by tuning these buffer pools. We also reviewed the role of the NCP in network performance and how the NCP's Link Scheduler utilizes PACING, chaining and segmentation to transmit data to remote resources. This chapter concludes our section on network performance and management. The following section details two of the most recent networking enhancements available to SNA. These are Low Entry Networking and Token-Ring Networking.

Part 4

New Connectivity Issues

Chapter

14

Low Entry Networking

Prior to distributed office processing, corporations maintained a central depository for all corporate data. As departments in the corporation grew, so did their demand for quick access time and data control. To meet this requirement, departmental processors provided by such computer giants as IBM, DEC and WANG were installed. These systems were much smaller and easier to maintain than the large mainframe computing environments, hence they lent themselves quite well to departmental computing. The need for quick access time and local control of the deparment's data was answered by migrating the information from the central mainframe computer to the smaller departmental computer.

Problems arose for applications executing on the mainframe computer in need of this departmental data. These mainframe applications had to be provided with the departmental data. The immediate solution was to duplicate the data. A data base at the local department computer and a data base at the central computer. Further developments in the PC arena made it possible for departments to have distributed processing within the department groups. These tiers of shared data and processing, coupled with differences in the equipment used at each tier, led IBM to develop Low Entry Networking (LEN). Figure 14.1 illustrates the three tiers of distributed processing.

308 Advanced SNA Networking

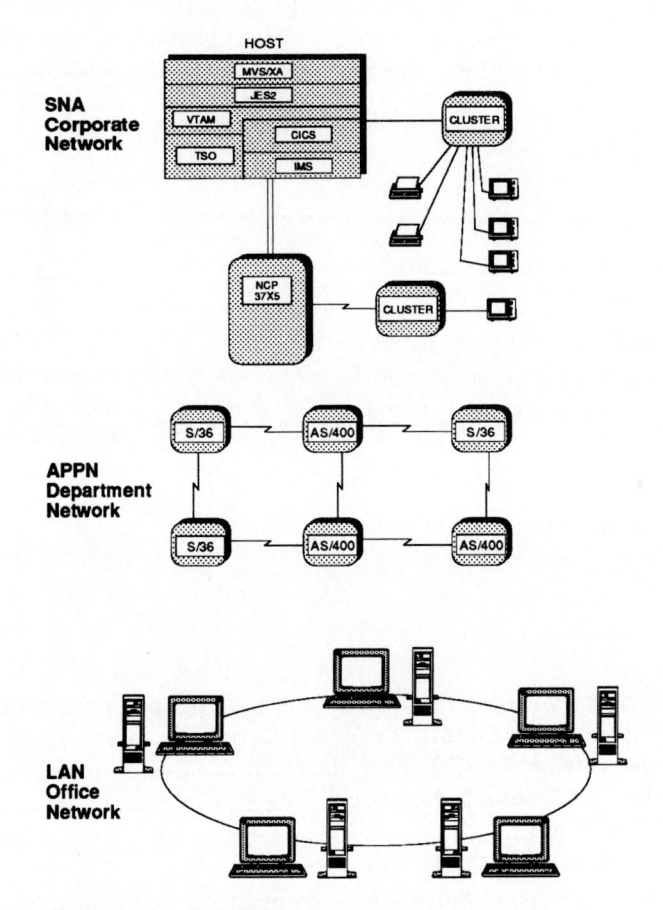

Figure 14.1 The three tiers of distributed processing.

14.1 LEN ARCHITECTURE

The theory behind LEN is to allow any device of any network to communicate and access any application and or data in all connected networks. In short, any-to-any communications regardless of operating system software and hardware and regardless of the physical connectivity. In essence, peer-to-peer relationships. This is the stated telecommunications network direction for all future products developed by IBM.

This directive is accomplished by implementing two types of architectures — Open Communications Architecture (OCA) and Systems Application Architecture (SAA). OCA is implemented across all 7 layers of SNA. Distributed services are defined for

SNA Layer 7 by various IBM products such as SNADS, DIA, and DDM. Layers 4, 5 and 6 of SNA are concerned with transmission and presentation services. Under OCA, these layers are used by SNA Logical Unit Type 6.2. This LU type provides for peer-to-peer session capabilities between applications. This ability of peer-to-peer sessions is also known as Advanced Program-to-Program Communication (APPC). The lower 3 layers of SNA are directly supported by LEN. The support for these path control layers comes from SNA Node Type 2.1. Common Communications Support of SAA is used to provide the connectivity architecture for any-to-any communications. This support implements the architected protocols of OCA for consistent connectivity across designated session protocols. The various functions and facilities of these architectures indicates the evolutionary direction of SNA, from that of a hierarchical arrangement to that of peer-to-peer (Figure 14.2).

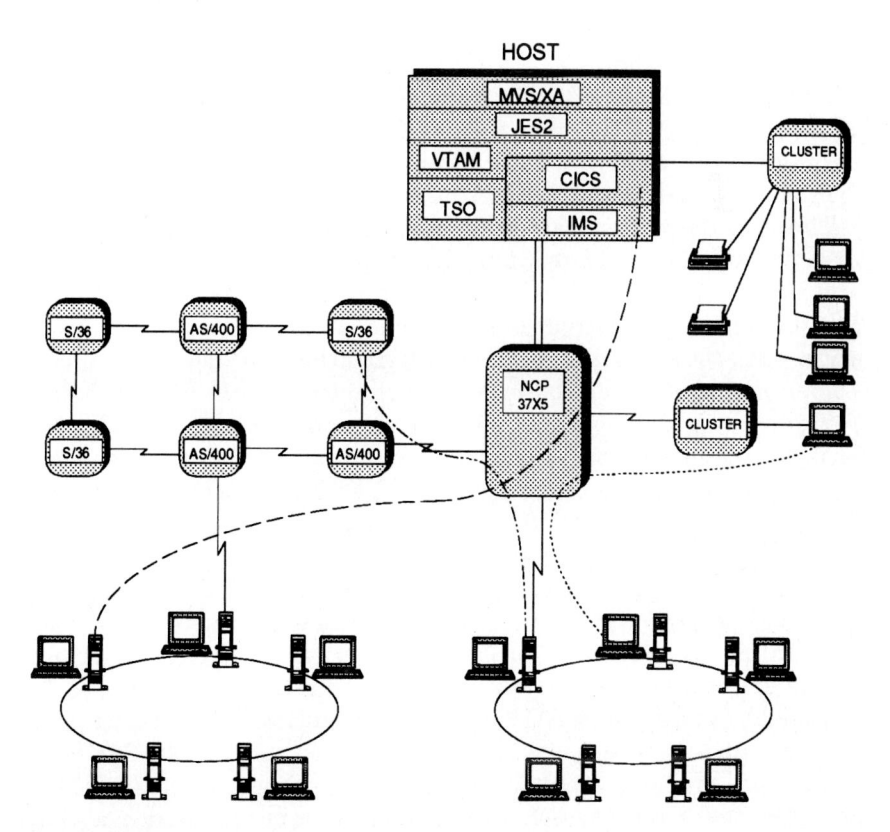

Figure 14.2 Any-to-any communications using LEN.

14.1.2 SNA Node Type 2.1

The T2.1 node has been architected to support peer-to-peer communications between adjacent T2.1 nodes. This capability is implemented on the IBM AS/400, S/36, S/38, APPC/PC and other third-party devices. Low Entry Networking is significant because it incorporates the basic T2.1 architectural components into the cornerstones of SNA. VTAM and NCP support of T2.1 nodes allows multiple concurrent peer-to-peer LU6.2 sessions over the SNA subarea backbone network. These sessions can occur between peripheral T2.1 nodes and/or T2.1 nodes and APPC/VTAM applications.

Support for T2.1 nodes and LU6.2 was incorporated into VTAM V3R2 and NCP V4R3, and NCP V5R2. The different NCP versions reflect the communications controller in which the NCP executes. NCP V4R3 is used for the IBM 3725, NCP V5R2 in the IBM 3720 and IBM 3745 Communications Controllers. Together VTAM and the NCP act as a T2.1 node referred to as a "composite" T2.1 node. VTAM/NCP incorporates the Control Point (CP) component and subcomponents, Path Control, and the Data Link Control components of the T2.1 node.

Logically, the CP of a T2.1 node has similar attributes to the SSCP found in VTAM. The CP in T2.1 nodes is comprised of three subcomponents: Configuration Services, Session Services and Address Space Manager (Figure 14.3).

The Configuration Services subcomponent maintains a data base of definitions for resources in this T2.1 node including links and their characteristics, local LUs, and LUs residing in adjacent T2.1 nodes. The activation/deactivation and link failure procedures are also a function of the Configuration Services component.

The initiation and subsequent termination of LU-LU sessions is performed by the Session Services subcomponent of T2.1 nodes. This service maps the requested session partner name to the controlling node which contains the LU. The link to which the node is attached is also mapped. Session Services interfaces to the Configuration Services subcomponent to ensure that the link is active prior to session initiation. Another function is to identify and associate the LU with a path that describes the route to the node containing the requested session partner. This capability of providing session establishment services has eliminated the need for the SSCP residing in VTAM to establish an SSCP-PU session with the T2.1 node. In fact, the T2.1 node participates in an SSCP-PU session only for network management data flows. Instead, VTAM provides the directory services to locate resources and associate

Low Entry Networking   311

```
                    ┌─────────────────────────────┐
                    │  SNA Node Type 2.1 Architecture  │
                    └─────────────────────────────┘

                         ┌────┐            ┌────┐
                         │ LU │------------│ LU │
                         └────┘            └────┘

                         ┌──────────────────────┐
                         │    CONTROL  POINT    │
                         └──────────────────────┘
                        /            |            \
              ┌──────────────┐   ┌──────────┐   ┌──────────────┐
              │ CONFIGURATION│   │ SESSION  │   │ ADDRESS SPACE│
              │   SERVICES   │   │ SERVICES │   │   MANAGER    │
              └──────────────┘   └──────────┘   └──────────────┘

              ┌──────────┐                      ┌──────────┐
              │   PATH   │----------------------│   PATH   │
              │ CONTROL  │                      │ CONTROL  │
              └──────────┘                      └──────────┘

              ┌──────────┐                      ┌──────────┐
              │ DATA LINK│----------------------│ DATA LINK│
              │ CONTROL  │                      │ CONTROL  │
              └──────────┘                      └──────────┘
```

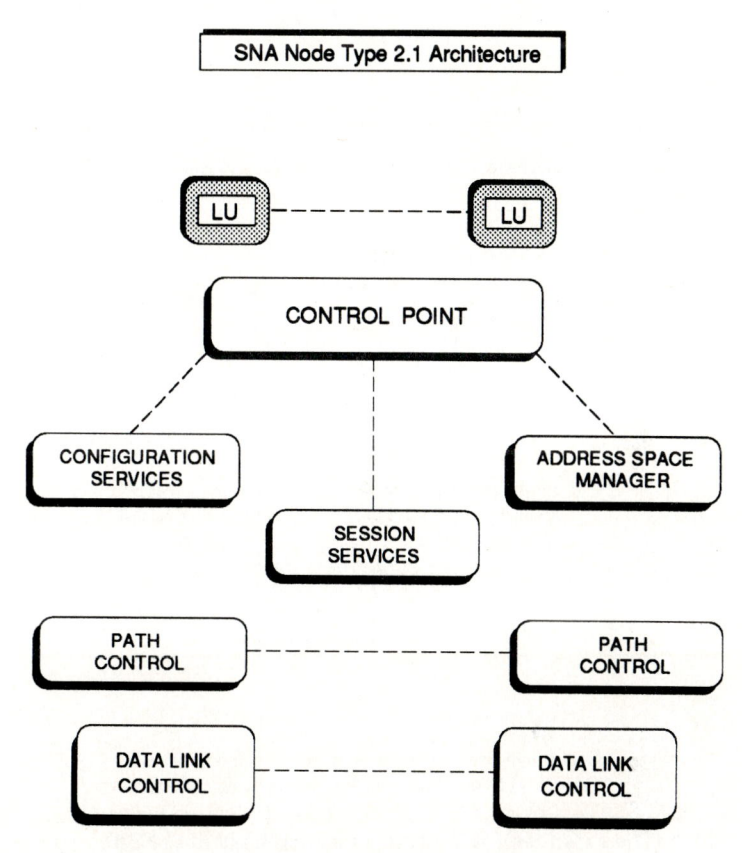

Figure 14.3 Overview of the SNA Node Type 2.1 architecture.

paths for use in the SNA subarea network. The path is selected via the Class of Service (COS) Table entry defined for this LU from the DLOGMOD parameter defined on the LU definition statement.

Finally, the third subcomponent is the Address Space Manager. This subcomponent dynamically assigns the session address during session initiation and subsequently frees the assigned address at session termination. The address is known as the Local Form Session Identifier (LFSID). The LFSID is assigned dynamically to a session that uses the link and corresponding path control component associated with the LFSID. The LFSID is used as an index into the Session Connector Block (SCB) table, which associates a session with a path with an address. It is these associations that are used to route messages between the LU and the path control

312 Advanced SNA Networking

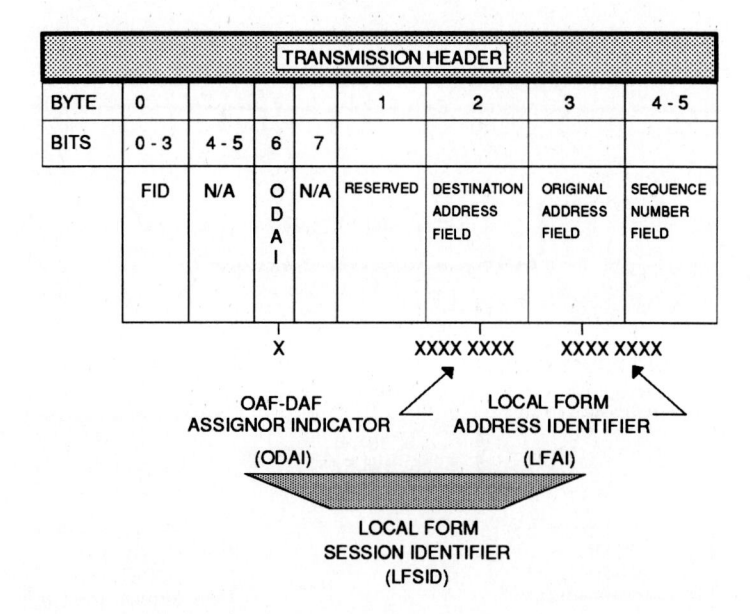

Extended FID2

		TRANSMISSION HEADER			
BYTE	0		1	2	3	4 - 5
BITS	0 - 3	4 - 5	6	7				
	FID	N/A	ODAI	N/A	RESERVED	DESTINATION ADDRESS FIELD	ORIGINAL ADDRESS FIELD	SEQUENCE NUMBER FIELD

```
              X                XXXX XXXX       XXXX XXXX
        OAF-DAF                   LOCAL FORM
    ASSIGNOR INDICATOR        ADDRESS IDENTIFIER
         (ODAI)                      (LFAI)

                        LOCAL FORM
                     SESSION IDENTIFIER
                           (LFSID)
```

ODAI=0 Indicates primary link station assigned address.
ODAI=1 Indicates secondary link station assigned address.

Figure 14.4 The extended FID2 format and location of the LFSID.

component for transmission over the appropriate link for this session.

The LFSID is used in the extended Format Identifier Type 2 (FID2), which provides the communications between T2.1 nodes for transmitting PIUs. The extended FID2 format is similar to that used for T2.0 nodes, but the address field is used differently. For T2.0 nodes, the address field uses an 8 bit PU address and 8 bits for the LU address, restricting the number of LU sessions to 255. Under a T2.1 node, the FID2 address field (Figure 14.4) uses the 17 bit LFSID assigned by the Address Space Manager for each session that utilizes a link. The LFSID is unique for each session over the link. It is comprised of the OAF-DAF Assignor Indicator (ODAI) and the 16 bit Local Form Address Identifier, allowing a maximum of 65,535 (64k) unique sessions over the link to the adjacent T2.1/LU6.2 node. This is far greater than T2.0 nodes that support a maximum of 255 sessions, where LU types in a T2.0 node, including LU6.2, are restricted to the role of secondary logical units each capable of only one session. The session capabilities of the LU6.2 in a T2.1 node allow the LU to initiate sessions and respond to session requests.

Recall that a session in SNA consists of a Primary LU (PLU) and a Secondary (LU). An LU initiating a session by sending an SNA BIND request is always considered to be the PLU for the session. The LU in the T2.1 node receiving the SNA BIND request is always the SLU. Since an LU6.2 in a T2.1 node can have multiple/parallel concurrent sessions with other LU6.2s, the primary and secondary roles can exist for one or all of the sessions. The ODAI bit in the transmission header of the T2.1 FID2 indicates primary-to-secondary or secondary-to-primary flow direction. Couple this with the LFSID addressing scheme, and we now have the capability of 128K sessions between T2.1 nodes.

14.1.2 Logical Unit Type 6.2

The inclusion of T2.1 nodes in an existing SNA subarea network has fostered the concept of an independent LU (ILU). An independent LU does not support nor require an SSCP-LU session, whereas a dependent LU (DLU) requires an SSCP-LU and, inherently, an SSCP-PU session for the controlling PU of the dependent LU. Most independent LUs are LU Type 6.2. Figure 14.5 lists the differences between ILUs and DLUs.

SNA logical units are the interfaces between the end users and the SNA Path Control Layer. The LU functions as the manager of resources and services available to the end-user. LU6.2 is a more robust logical unit in that it supports end-users with a super

Attributes Of Independent LUs and Dependent LUs	
INDEPENDENT LUs (ILUs)	DEPENDENT LUs (DLUs)
Multiple/parallel sessions PLU and SLU capability No SSCP-LU session required Supported by T2.1 nodes only Most ILUs are LU6.2 (TPF uses LU Type 2)	Single LU-LU session SLU capability only SSCP-LLU session required Supported by T2.1 and T2.0 nodes Examples: LU Types 1,2,3, 6.2

Figure 14.5 Attributes of independent LUs and dependent LUs.

highway to other end-users in your SNA network. The LU6.2-LU6.2 sessions between T2.1 nodes serve as the super highway. Transaction Programs (TPs) residing in the T2.1 nodes call upon the LU6.2 services to exchange data. The TP issues LU6.2 Protocol Attributes Of Independent LUs and Dependent LUs

The Transaction Processing Facility (TPF) uses LU Type 2 Boundary verbs to obtain the LU6.2 services. This "conversation" between the TPs utilizes one of the LU6.2 sessions between the T2.1 nodes. The control point of a T2.1 node will initiate a session with another T2.1 node for an LU if a session between the LU partners does not currently exist.

Each LU-LU session is thought of as long-term. TP conversations, on the other hand, are considered to be short-term, a brief exchange of data between TPs on an existing session. The LU-LU session is serially reusable. Only one conversation per session is allowed. As a conversation ends and releases the session, another conversation may begin. Although the conversation may go away, the LU-LU session remains intact waiting for a TP to request a conversation over this session. In this way, the overhead of session initiation and termination is significantly reduced for the exchange of data between two TPs. At most, there can be only two TPs on a single session per conversation. Parallel sessions between LU6.2s will allow the same TP partners to engage in multiple concurrent conversations, each conversation on a different LU-LU session. Figure 14.6 diagrams the various LU session and conversation configurations.

These enhancements to the SNA architecture of LU6.2 in T2.1 nodes now provide the capability for true distributed processing between host nodes and peripheral nodes through the SNA subarea network.

14.2 LEN ENHANCED CONNECTIVITY SUPPORT

Together, VTAM V3R2 (LEN/VTAM) and NCP V4R3/V5R2 (LEN/NCP) support the "composite" T2.1 node. The T2.1 architecture implements peer-to-peer communications between adjacent T2.1 nodes. As such, the entire SNA subarea network is viewed by a T2.1 node attached to an NCP as an adjacent T2.1 node. This includes SNI networks. All T2.1 nodes and their corresponding LUs must enter the SNA subarea network through the LEN/NCP. Direct attachment to the LEN/VTAM is not supported since the T2.1 Boundary Function interface is found in the LEN/NCP.

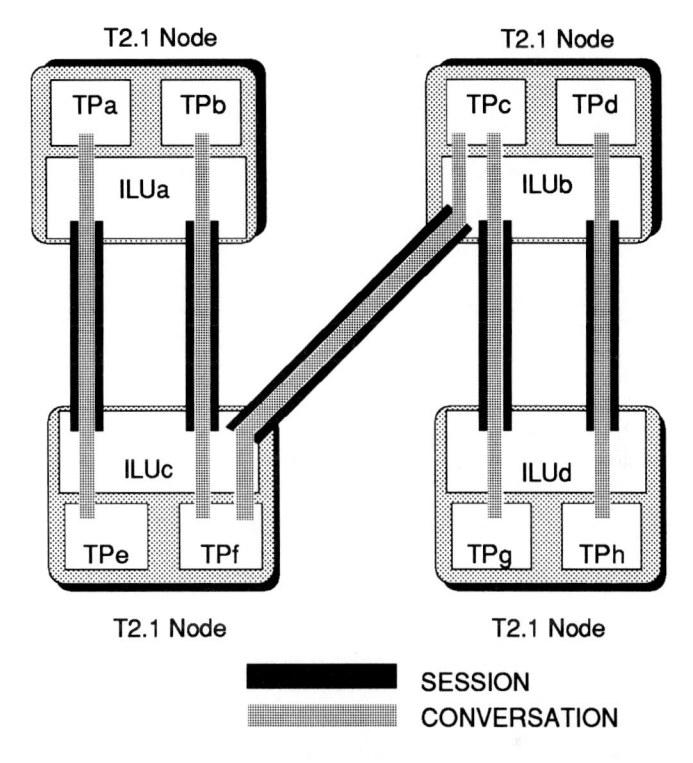

Figure 14.6 Diagram showing multiple/parallel ILU sessions. Note that TPf is participating in multiple concurrent conversations.

14.2.1 LEN/VTAM/NCP Support

The T2.1 architecture supports connectivity of a T2.1 node to multiple adjacent T2.1 nodes through a single link to each adjacent node. Multiple links between two adjacent nodes is not currently implemented. The link facilities can vary. The only requirement is that T2.1 nodes must be attached to a LEN/NCP. In Figure 14.7 we see that every facility connection supported in SNA is or will be supported for LEN. For example, channel connections are used between the LEN/NCP and the IBM 9080 mainframe processor. This processor executes the Transaction Processing Facility (TPF), formerly the Airline Control Program (ACP). The TPF can be defined as a T2.1 node to the LEN/NCP. However, the TPF T2.1 node does not utilize LU6.2. Instead it uses LU T2, which allows only one SLU session. All telecommunications facilities are supported. A T2.1 node may be connected via a switched or leased line. The leased link may be configured as a point-to-point or a

316 Advanced SNA Networking

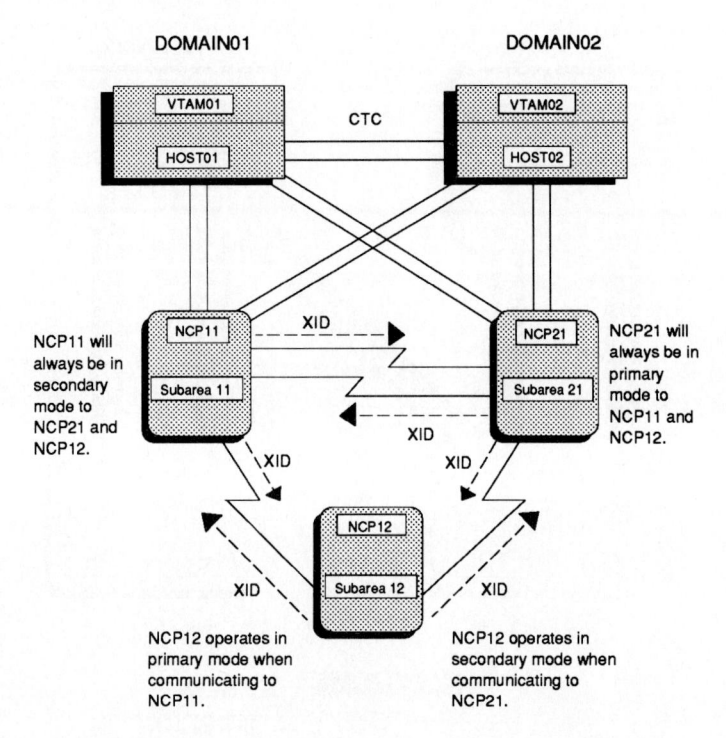

```
                    DOMAIN01                              DOMAIN02
                   ┌─────────┐         CTC          ┌─────────┐
                   │ VTAM01  │═══════════════════════│ VTAM02  │
                   │ HOST01  │                      │ HOST02  │
                   └─────────┘                      └─────────┘

                   ┌─────────┐    XID ─ ─ ─ ─►      ┌─────────┐
  NCP11 will       │  NCP11  │                      │  NCP21  │   NCP21 will
  always be in     │         │                      │         │   always be in
  secondary        │Subarea11│                      │Subarea21│   primary
  mode to          └─────────┘    ◄─ ─ ─ ─ ─         └─────────┘   mode to
  NCP21 and              \           XID              /           NCP11 and
  NCP12.                  \ XID                 XID /              NCP12.
                           ▼                       ▼
                                ┌─────────┐
                                │  NCP12  │
                                │Subarea12│
                                └─────────┘
                      XID                       XID

         NCP12 operates in              NCP12 operates in
         primary mode when              secondary mode when
         communicating to               communicating to
         NCP11.                         NCP21.
```

Figure 14.7 LEN attachment support for T2.1 nodes to the SNA network.

multi-point line. The Token-Ring interface capability of an NCP can also be used for T2.1 connectivity. An added feature of token-rings for T2.1 nodes is the enhanced connectivity within the ring. Each T2.1 node residing on the ring is seen as an adjacent node. Hence, regardless of the number of intermediate nodes on a ring, each is seen as being connected directly.

The peripheral LUs can have multiple and parallel sessions acting as the PLU or SLU or both. All of these sessions can occur through the SNA subarea network. They can occur between peripheral node applications residing on departmental computers or PCs and VTAM applications residing on the LEN/VTAM host computer.

14.2.2 Advanced Peer-to-Peer Networking (APPN)

Recall our scenario of departmental computing in the beginning of this chapter. When processing within departments came into being, they were already calling for a way to network these small

Low Entry Networking   317

systems without using the SNA subarea network. A new networking scheme that possesses the capability of dynamic connectivity, address assignment, topology and session establishment was developed.

APPN was primarily developed for small system networking between IBM S/36 minicomputers. In APPN there are two types of network nodes. The first is the End Node (EN), which is a T2.1 node that does not possess the capability of supporting network function requests for topology updates, route selections, or session establishment. Under APPN, this node is likened to the SNA peripheral node, a node that is dependent upon another node for networking services. APPN networking services is provided by the Network Node (NN). The dynamics of APPN is provided by the Network Node Control Point (NNCP). Figure 14.8 diagrams an APPN network.

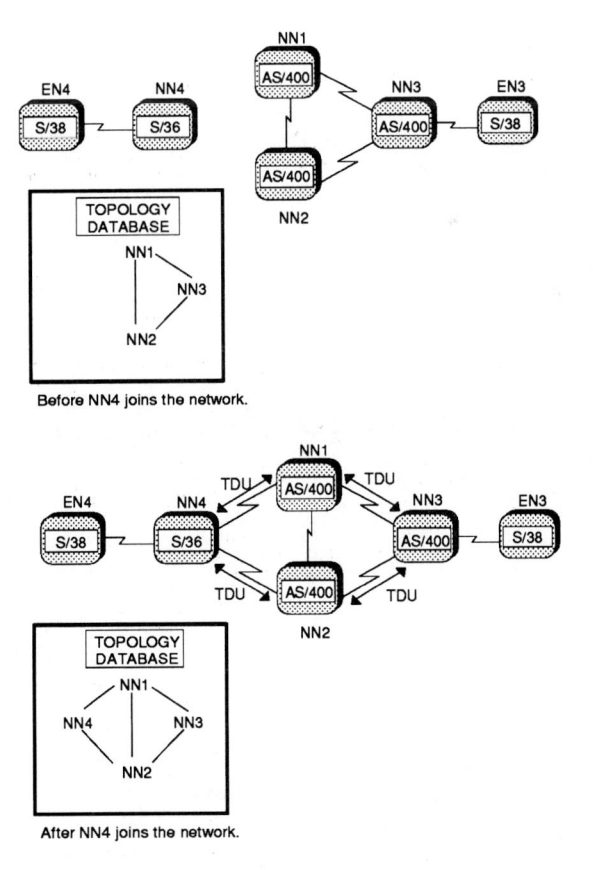

Figure 14.8 APPN network showing network nodes and end node connectivity.

318 Advanced SNA Networking

The NNCP uses LU6.2 to establish sessions with adjacent NNCPs in the network. This CP-CP session is similar to the SSCP-SSCP session found in the SNA subarea network. Using this session, the NNs exchange topology data bases, thereby informing each other about adjacent and nonadjacent nodes in the network. This allows each node to join a network dynamically, building a topology data base as each NN is contacted. Each adjacent NN in APPN exchanges the topology data base using the Topology Data Exchange Unit (TDU) whenever a new NN joins the network. The only static definitions required are those that define the communication links between adjacent NNs.

Due to the enhanced networking capability of APPN and LEN, complex subarea connections can be configured. Figure 14.9 details such a configuration. ANN networks can be connected to a

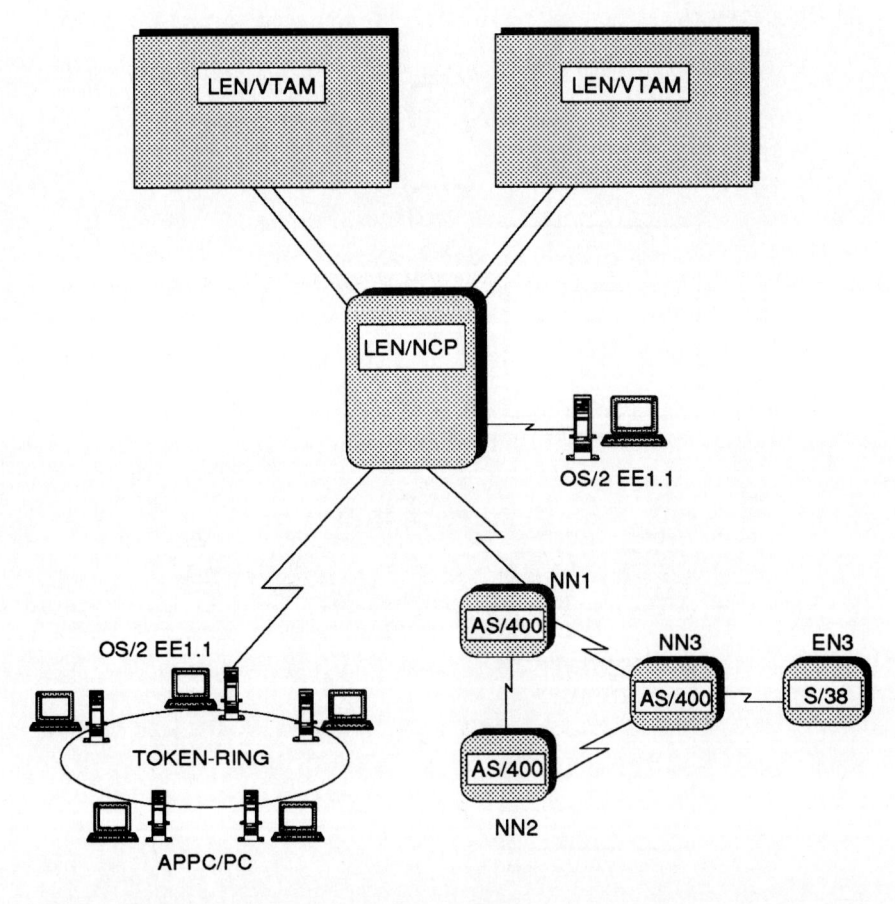

Figure 14.9 Complex peer-to-peer connectivity configuration involving LEN, APPN and APPC/PC.

LEN/Composite Node (LEN/CN) comprised of a LEN/VTAM and a LEN/NCP. Each LEN/CN supports only one APPN connection. This is done to remove the possibility of duplicate names in the network. A S/38 acting as an EN off of an APPN AS/400 NN can participate in peer-to-peer sessions with a PC executing IBM's OS/2 Extended Edition 1.1 (OS/2 EE1.1). This release of OS/2 contains the Communications Manager which includes, among other functions, the APPC/PC facility. APPC/PC supports T2.1 and LU6.2 protocols on an IBM PC, PS/2 or equivalent clone. The PC can be connected to the LEN/NCP directly or indirectly through the Token-Ring interface. As you can see, the configurations have been greatly enhanced to support any-to-any communications.

14.3 DEFINING A T2.1 NODE TO LEN/NCP

There are two changes for LEN/NCP when coding the PU definition statement. The first is the deletion of the MAXLU parameter. The second is a new parameter, XID=YES|NO. The exchange ID (XID) parameter is specified on all PU definitions in the NCP. The default value is XID=YES. When VTAM issues an ACTPU command to the NCP for this node, XID=YES tells the NCP to contact the node, not with an SNA ACTPU command, but rather a "null" XID command.

An XID in response to this indicates to the LEN/NCP that the peripheral node is a T2.1 resource. Consequently, the NCP then sends a real XID populated with the values defined on the PU definition statement. One of these values is the name of the LEN/CN control point. The LEN/NCP will include the name of the T2.1/LU6.2 SSCP owner in the XID3. Due to this, the SSCPNAME option in the LEN/VTAM start list is now required. Pre-LEN/VTAM, this option indicated SNI capabilities only.

During this exchange, LEN/NCP identifies itself as the Primary Link Station (PLS). This means that the NCP will always poll the T2.1 node. This is true for all T2.1 nodes entering the SNA sub-area network using LEN.

If, however, the peripheral node responds negatively to the "null" XID, the NCP will then issue the SNA ACTPU command and interpret this to address all requests and responses to/from this peripheral node with PU T2.0 formats and protocols. In this way the LEN/NCP can dynamically determine the node type, allowing for flexible network reconfigurations.

320 Advanced SNA Networking

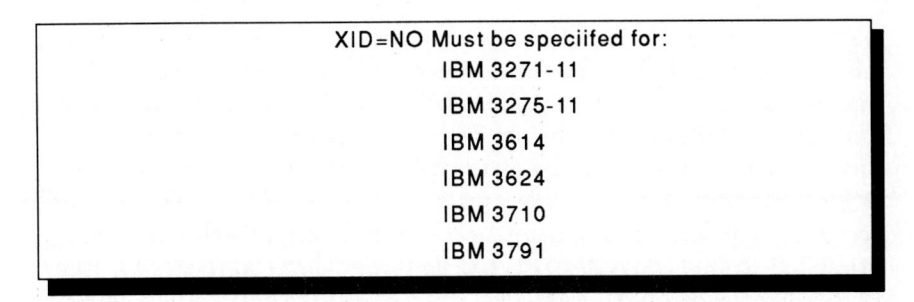

```
              XID=NO Must be speciifed for:
                       IBM 3271-11
                       IBM 3275-11
                       IBM 3614
                       IBM 3624
                       IBM 3710
                       IBM 3791
```

Figure 14.10 List of some IBM products that require XID=NO specification.

The fields of the XID format 3 used for T2.1 nodes provide negotiable values for former static parameters. The MAXDATA, MAXOUT, MODULO and DATMODE values of the PU definition statement are used in the initial contact, but can be negotiated by the T2.1 node. The PASSLIM parameter, however, is non-negotiable. This allows the NCP to maintain control of servicing T2.1 nodes on a multi-point line, preventing a single T2.1 node from dominating the link. Figure 14.10 specifies the peripheral nodes which cannot handle the "null" XID format. For these nodes, XID=NO must be specified.

14.4 DEFINING T2.1/LU6.2 TO LEN/NCP

The LU definition statement under LEN/NCP also has some minor changes. The PACING parameter format has been altered by eliminating the second operand. Previously, PACING=(n,f) was used to identify the number of frames (n) that can be sent before waiting for an Initial Pacing Response (IPR), and of these frames, which frame (f) contained the IPR indicator. The new format removes the need for the second parameter, since the IPR indicator always flows on the first PIU of the pacing sequence. The LOCADDR parameter now allows the address value of 0 to be defined. A value of LOCADDR=0 specifies to LEN/NCP that this LU definition statement defines an independent LU6.2. Remember that LU6.2 can act as either an independent or dependent LU. The RESSCB parameter on the LU definition statement defines the number of Session Control Blocks guaranteed for this ILU to support multiple and parallel sessions. The default is 0 and the range is 0 - 5000. By defining a value here you are guaranteeing that this ILU will have a specified number of SCBs to assign LFSIDs. When using the default or requiring more SCBs than are specified, additional SCBs will be taken from a pool specified by the ADDRESS parameter on the BUILD definition statement.

Another change is that the BATCH=YES|NO parameter has been deleted. This is because the LEN/VTAM and LEN/NCP use the Transmission Priority value assigned to this session through the COS table entry down to the peripheral node over the route extension. This name is found by VTAM using the logmode entry name specified on the DLOGMOD parameter of the LU definition statement. The path defined in the COS entry identifies the VR and TP the LEN/NCP will assign to this session.

During session establishment, the T2.1 LU can send a BIND command to LEN/NCP for a specific LEN/CN LU. The bind image is expanded to accommodate the added features of T2.1/LU6.2. This extended BIND contains the fully-qualified network name of the session partners. This network name is similar to the resource names used in an SNI network. The fully-qualified name has the following format:

NETID.LUNAME

The NETID is derived from the VTAM start list option NETID. For pre-LEN/VTAM, this option indicated SNI capability along with the SSCPNAME option. In LEN/VTAM these two options are now required. The SSCPNAME is used by the LEN/NCP during the XID with a T2.1 node. Recall that the SSCP is similar in function to the T2.1 Control Point (CP). Because the session partner names are included in the extended BIND, LUnames assigned in the LEN/NCP must be coordinated with the LU names assigned in the T2.1 adjacent peripheral node.

In Figure 14.11, NODE A is considered to be an adjacent T2.1 node to the LEN/NCP. All of the LUs known by this APPN network node are defined to the LEN/NCP as if they are directly attached to NODE A. It is the responsibility of the routing services in NODE A to correctly route session information to the actual LU. NODE A, acting as a network node (NN), views LEN/NCP and LEN/VTAM as a "composite" node (CN) and is, therefore, regarded as an end node (EN) in NODE A's APPN1 network. The same holds true for the NN NODE D in APPN2.

The LU resources within an NN or EN of an APPN network are defined as if they are attached to the adjacent node. For example, the EN NODE C defines all the LUs in NODE B, NODE A and the LEN/CN as if they are in NODE B. We must point out here that resources of the LEN/CNs of the SNA subarea network must be

322 Advanced SNA Networking

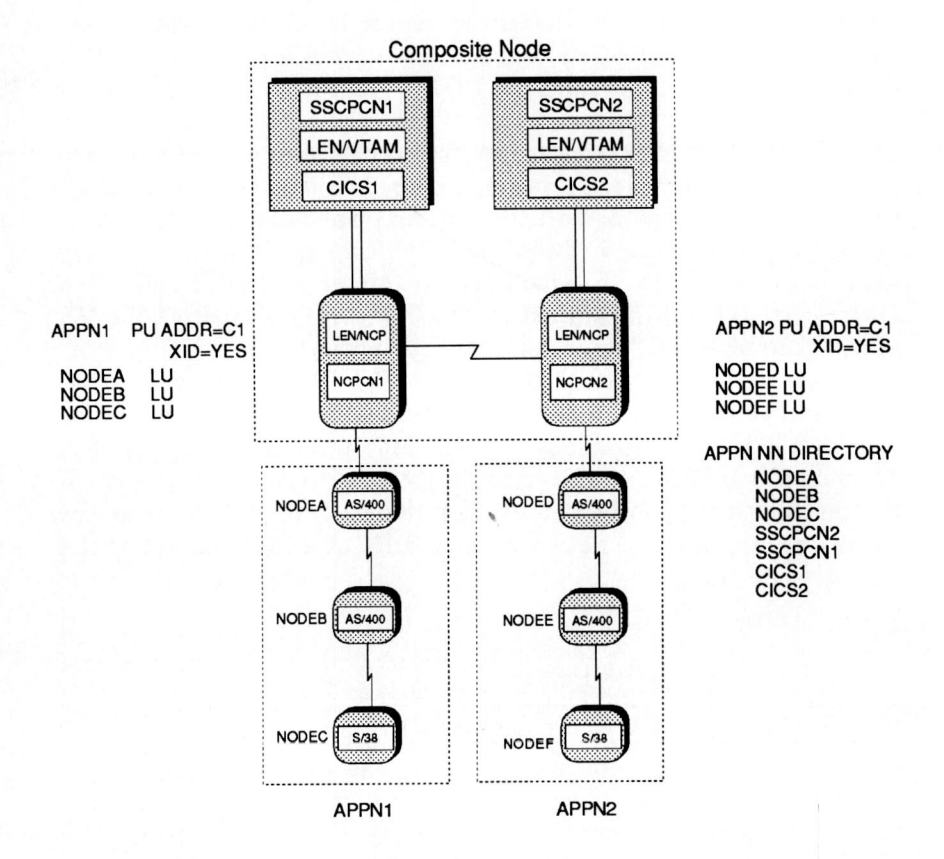

Figure 14.11 Example of a LEN network configuration and definition

explicitly defined to the APPN NNs since the LEN/CN SSCP does not participate in a CP-CP session with the T2.1 adjacent node. In addition, the APPN network name must match the owning SSCP network name (NETID). Also, in the NN configuration, the administrator specifies the SSCP name of each LEN/VTAM host with which this NN can communicate. This includes all resources that are attached to a LEN/CN through the SNA subarea network. For instance, resources of APPN1 that need to communicate to resources of APPN2 must be explicitly defined in the directory list. The name defined is the name assigned to the node in NCPCN1,

```
              LEN / NCP BUILD PARAMETERS
                              ADDRESS=(0-5000)
                              MAXSESS=(1-5000)
                              AUXADDR=(0-5000)
                              NAMETAB=(10-5000)
```

Figure 14.12   BUILD parameters to support LEN.

i.e., NODEA, NODEB, NODEC. And so on, down the APPN network for cross-subarea-network sessions.

14.5 LEN/NCP BUILD DEFINITION PARAMETERS

Several new parameters have been added to the BUILD definition statement to support LEN. Figure 14.12 lists the new BUILD parameters. The ADDRESS parameter defines a pool containing Session Control Blocks (SCB) for LU-LU boundary sessions between independent LUs. These blocks are used in conjunction with the SCBs reserved by the RESSCB parameter of the LU definition statement. The range is 0 - 5000. If RESSCB is coded for an LU, the SCB pool is accessed only when the LU control point must increase the number of LU-LU sessions between the two T2.1 nodes. The CP issues a change-number-of-sessions (CNOS) command. CNOS can be used to increase or decrease the number of sessions between any T2.1 nodes.

The MAXSESS parameter specifies the number of LU-LU sessions any ILU can have through this LEN/NCP. This restricts the number of sessions to below the architected value of 64K PLU and 64K SLU. This is done to ensure the NCP resource availability for other ILUs that may exist in the network.

Each ILU is assigned a network address. However, for the NCP and VTAM to manage the multiple sessions an ILU can have, a dynamic address is created. The number of additional addresses assigned to any ILU is specified by the AUXADDR parameter.

The final parameter is NAMETAB. This parameter reserves entries in a network name table. This table contains the names of all networks, SSCPs and T2.1 nodes that form a session with the NCP. There is one for each network if the NCP is a gateway-NCP, one for each SSCP that can have a session with the NCP, and one for each T2.1 node that joins the SNA subarea network using LEN.

14.6 DR AND SWITCHED LEN SUPPORT

The support for dynamic reconfiguration in VTAM V3.2 and NCP V4.3/V5.2 has greatly enhanced network availability (Figure 14.13). For a LEN, these features are covered by the LUDRPOOL of the NCP and the VTAM switched major node. In the LUDRPOOL, a new parameter, NUMILU, has been added to define to the NCP the number of independent LUs that may use dynamic reconfiguration or switched configurations. Associated with the LUDRPOOL is the PUDRPOOL. The MAXLU parameter of the PUDRPOOL definition statement has been deleted to support the new dynamics of the SNA network.

Switched support for T2.1 nodes is also supported. The switched GROUP definition statement now defines a transmit delay value (XMITDLY). The XMITDLY value indicates to the NCP a delay value before sending an XID to the PU after a successful switched connection. This assists in avoiding XID collisions on the link stations. Accompanying this, the VTAM switched major node contains the CPNAME parameter. The value specified here is the name of the control point of the T2.1 node dialing-in to the NCP. The IDBLK and IDNUM values can still be used, but are not necessary when a T2.1 node uses a switched connection. Enhancing the availability of switched connections, VTAM V3.2 and NCP V4.3/V5.2 support continued service of a switched cross-domain session. This is specified by the ANS=CONTINUE parameter, which is now available to switched links. Previously, only leased connections supported continued service during ANS.

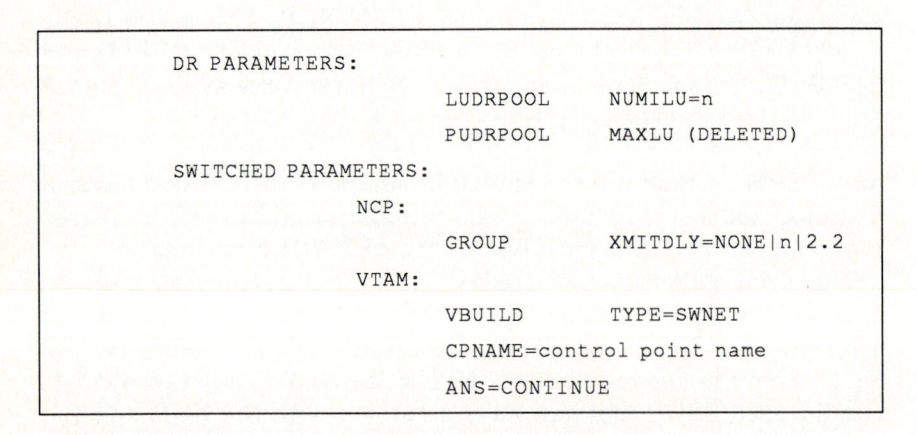

```
DR PARAMETERS:
                        LUDRPOOL    NUMILU=n
                        PUDRPOOL    MAXLU (DELETED)
SWITCHED PARAMETERS:
    NCP:
                        GROUP       XMITDLY=NONE|n|2.2
    VTAM:
                        VBUILD      TYPE=SWNET
                        CPNAME=control point name
                        ANS=CONTINUE
```

Figure 14.13 DR and Switched LEN parameter support.

14.7 SUMMARY

In this chapter we explored the usage of Low Entry Networking. We reviewed the origins of SNA Node Type 2.1 and Logical Unit Type 6.2. The architecture of SNA Node Type 2.1 allows for LU-LU sessions without the use of VTAM's SSCP. It also allows LU Type 6.2 to handle multiple sessions with a conversation on each session simultaneously. We described how this capability is leading the way for distributed and cooperative processing information systems. In the next chapter we will discuss a technology that has also greatly influenced the overall configuration of an SNA network. This technology is Token-Ring Networking.

Chapter

15

Token-Ring LAN Networking

Before we learn the details of the token-ring LAN, let's see what a Local Area Network (LAN) is. As the name suggests, a LAN provides connectivity for various devices for a unit of area called a local area or limited area. In a true sense, a LAN provides a physical and logical connection for data treminal equipment (e.g., a computer, an IBM 3174 controller) within a local area. Normally, we describe a local area as limited to the distances between the floors of a building or a few adjacent buildings. However, we may increase the distances to suit a campus-like environment by using repeaters and may extend such distances to about 5 or 6 miles.

15.1 WHAT IS A TOKEN RING LAN?

A token-ring LAN is a local area network that uses token passing protocols for communicating on the LAN. Such protocols have been precisely defined by the Institute of Electrical and Electronics Engineers (IEEE) standard 802.5 and International Standards Organization (ISO) standard 8802.5. It is beyond the scope of this book to go into the details of these protocols, that is a subject for a book in itself. Since this book is oriented towards implementors, we will look at only the practical aspects of this topic.

A misconception. Traditionally, people consider a LAN to be a communications methodology *only* for personal computers, file servers, print servers, etc. This was true in the past when LANs were only used for networking PCs. It is not true anymore. LANs provide high-speed communications between workstations, PCs, IBM 3174s, IBM 3745s, IBM 3720s, IBM 9370s and AS/400s.

How was it done in the past? Before IBM introduced Token-Ring Networks for connecting non-PC equipment, the traditional way of connecting IBM data processing hardware and data communications hardware was either through channel-attached or link-attached media. Channel-attached equipment from the communications perspective were local cluster controllers like the 3274-41D and 3274-41A, or channel-attached communications controllers like IBM 37x5s or IBM 3720s. Channel connectivity also provided linkage for two or more hosts using channel-to-channel communications. A channel puts severe limitations on the distance between the computer channel and the communications equipment. Normally, this limitation was 200 feet, although it could be extended to some extent by using various IBM supported features. Channel connectivity is still used for connecting computer equipment in a limited distance environment.

When the distances involved were outside the range of what was permitted by a computer channel, connectivity was provided by connecting to the communications ports of communications controllers (i.e., IBM 37X5s). If the equipment was spread over a long distance, the services of a common carrier were used. Otherwise, an EIA cable system over limited distance modems or modem eliminators was used. This kind of connectivity is still used.

Where does the LAN fit in? In a limited distance environment, connectivity between a communications controller and cluster controllers was possible through a link between a 3274 and a port on the communications controller. If you had 20 cluster controllers, you probably ran 20 point-to-point lines from each one of these to the front-end processor ports. In most cases, line speed was limited to 9,600 bps.

A token-ring LAN environment will let you link these cluster controllers (e.g., 3174s) over a high speed link of 4 or 16 million bits per second and connect them to the communications controller. This not only provides a high-speed bandwidth for exchanging data, but also eliminates the need for having multiple point-to-point links. Needless to say, these are not the only advantages of a

LAN and 3174s are not the only devices that can use a token-ring LAN. Other IBM hardware, such as AS/400s, 9370s, 3745s, 3720s, Series/1, PS/2s, and low-end models of the ES/9000 can also use LAN connectivity for intercommunications.

15.2 TOKEN-RING SUPPORT HARDWARE

In order to interconnect and support various devices on a token-ring, support equipment must be in place. This equipment includes physical transmission media, nodes for connecting devices to the ring, and repeaters for carrying signals over relatively large distances. Figure 15.1 shows a sample token-ring local area network which we will use to understand how various network components fit together in a configuration.

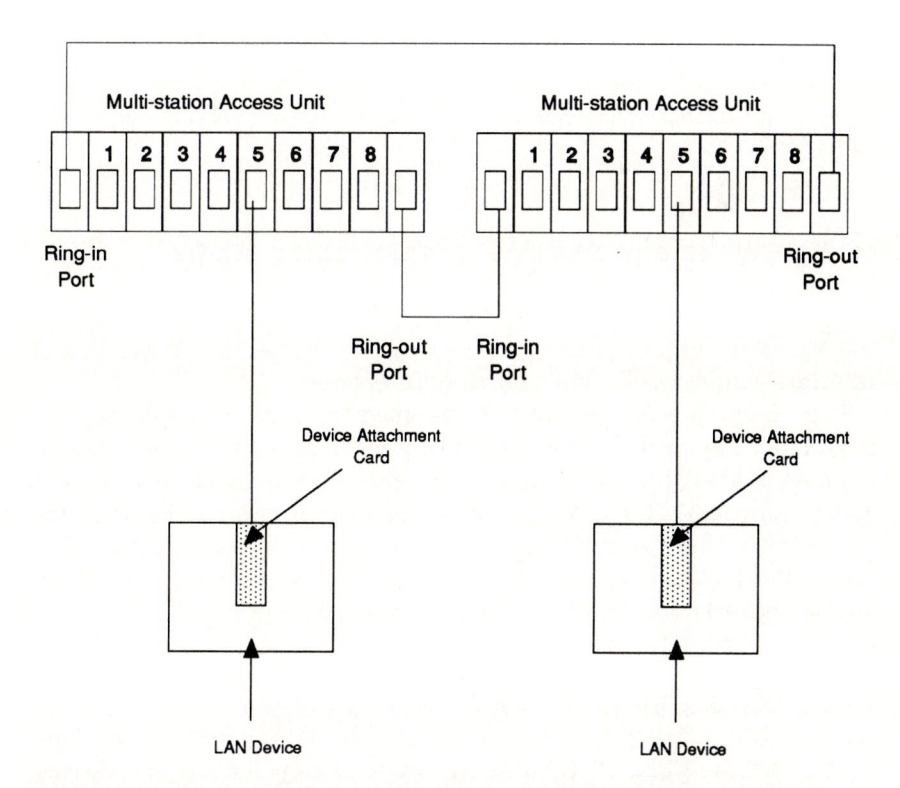

Figure 15.1 A sample Token-Ring Network LAN showing MAU, connecting cables, a hypothetical LAN device (e.g., 3174 Model 1L) and a device attachment card.

330   Advanced SNA Networking

Cable	Type and Shielding	Material	Suitability for Outdoors
Type 1	Braided Two American Wire Guage 22 Twisted	Copper	Yes
Type 2	Braided Two American Wire Guage 22 Twisted	Copper	No
	Unshielded Four Telephone Twisted Pair		
Type 3	Unshielded Four Telephone Twisted Pair	Copper	No
Type 5	Unshielded Two Fiber 110/140	Fiber Optics	Yes
Type 5J	Unshielded Two Fiber 50/125	Fiber Optics	Yes
Type 6	Braided Two American Wire Guage 26 Twisted	Stranded Copper	No
Type 8	Braided Two American Wire Guage 26	Copper	No
Type 9	Braided Two American Wire Guage 26	Copper	No

Figure 15.2 Suitable cable types and their characteristics for Token-Ring Network LANs.

15.2.1 Cables and Physical Transmission Media

There are a multitude of cable types that can be used to connect the various components of a Token-Ring Network. Figure 15.2 tabulates those cable types for easy reference.

Type 1 or Type 2 cable should be used for connecting devices to the MAU. Type 5 (in addition to Types 1 and 2) can be used to connect MAUs themselves. Type 3 cable can be used to connect a device to a MAU for 4Mbps LANs, however it can not be used for LANs with 16Mbps speed. Bear in mind that Type 3 (unshielded telephone twisted pair) should already be wired in most existing buildings and additional expenses may not be incurred.

15.2.2 Multi-station Access Unit - IBM 8228

MAUs are the hubs of token-ring LANs. They consist of a device with 10 connecting ports. Two of those 10 ports are the ring-in port and ring-out port and are used to connect to other MAUs. The remaining eight ports provide connectivity to the devices on the

LAN. Thus, a total of eight devices may be attached to a MAU. A number of MAUs can be connected together to put more devices on a single ring. In Figure 15.1, we have two MAUs joined together and could put a total of 16 devices, although we have shown only two devices on it.

15.2.3 Token-Ring Cards

A token-ring card (or a device attachment card) provides the connectivity between the MAU port and the device itself. Such a card fits in one of the empty slots of the device, the device being a PS/2, a 3174, a 37X5, a AS/400 or any other LAN eligible hardware. The card and its associated microcode together implement the IEEE 802.2 link level protocols and IEEE 802.5 token-ring LAN protocols.

15.2.4 Repeaters and Converters

The transmission media consisting of twisted wires or cables (Figure 15.2) limit the distance between the devices depending upon the attenuation properties of the medium itself. Even though a device may not have data of its own to send, its adapters regenerate the signals. If there is no device over a long distance of cable, the signal cannot be regenerated and may get weak. Under these circumstances, hardware, called a repeater, is needed to regenerate the signal. If a copper wire-based cable is being used between a device and the MAU, you may not use a repeater in between. However, for providing connectivity between two MAUs over a long distance, you may need repeaters to amplify the signal.

When placing repeaters between two consecutive MAUs, you must anticipate the fact that the repeaters in the connecting cable might fail. In such cases, the signal will be transmitted over an alternate path which may be longer and might need repeaters in anticipation of failures in the primary path.

Repeaters used for copper wire connection are the IBM 8218 and for optical fiber, the IBM 8219. IBM 8220 optical fiber converters may be used if you need the converters to not only amplify the signal, but also to provide for automatic recovery and alternate path fall-back in case of errors. Thus, a converter is a sophisticated repeater with additional functions.

332 Advanced SNA Networking

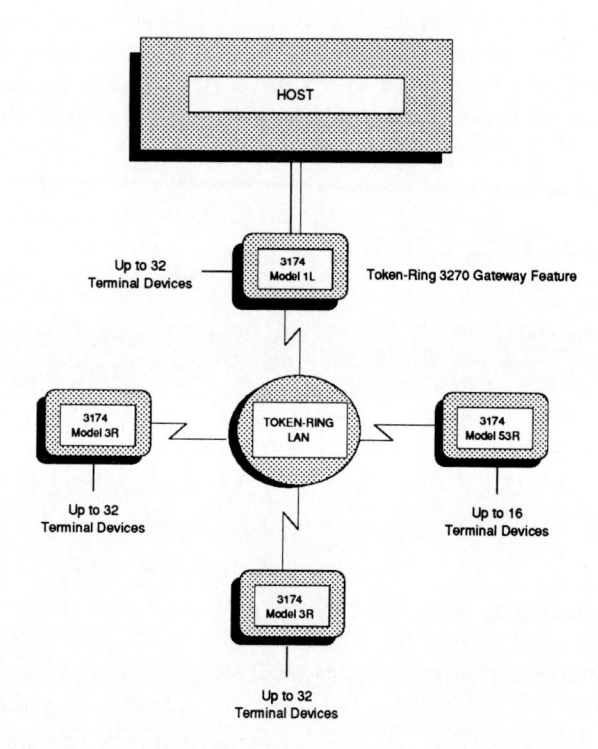

Figure 15.3 A sample Token-Ring Network in which a single 3174 Model 1L acts as a gateway for itself and three other 3174s on the LAN.

15.3 TOKEN-RING LAN DEVICES

In the past, token-ring LANs were used to provide connectivity between personal computers (i.e., PCs, PS/2s) and the servers. Those servers could be file servers, print servers, application servers, etc. Now, in addition, token-ring LANs are used to provide connectivity for other IBM and non-IBM devices such as 9370s, 3745s, 3720s, AS/400s, 3174s, etc. They provide data transmission between those devices at a speed of 4Mbps or 16Mbps, depending on the adapter they use. Keep in mind that LAN connectivity is limited to a local area environment such as a building, a cluster of buildings or a small campus environment. Long distance connectivity still falls within the realm of communications lines and common carriers.

15.3.1 IBM 3174 EC

Traditionally, cluster controllers are linked to a host either via a host channel or via a communications link to a port of the communications controller. In the latter case, unless a multipoint configuration was used, each cluster controller had to have a separate port on the communications controller for connectivity. Now, in a limited distance environment, we can put various 3174s on the Token-Ring Network and provide a single gateway to the host channel or the communications controller.

Figure 15.3 shows a sample Token-Ring Network in which a single channel-attached 3174 Model 1L provides connectivity to three other 3174s on the same LAN. In this case, terminal devices (e.g., 3278s) attached to the gateway 3174 and other 3174s will have connectivity to the host. There are certain models of the 3174 that are eligible to have a Type 3 or Type 3A adapters which can provide them with connectivity to the LAN's MAU. Type 3 adapters operate at 4Mbps, while Type 3A adapters operate at 4 as well as 16Mbps speed. A 3174 which is eligible for LAN connectivity does not necessarily become a gateway controller. There are only certain models that can function as a Token-Ring Network Gateway. However, any 3174 that can function as a gateway always has connectivity to the token-ring LAN. Figure 15.4 shows 3174s that are eligible to have gateways, 4Mbps connectors, and 16Mbps connectors.

15.3.2 IBM Communications Controllers

IBM Communications Controllers also provide the gateway function to various devices on the Token-Ring Network. In Figure 15.5, the communications controller is channel-attached to the host. It is also connected to the token-ring LAN via a Token-Ring Adapter (TRA)/Token-Ring Interface Coupler (TIC). Other devices on the ring are a 3174 Model 3R, a 3174 Model 53R and a PS/2 workstation. The communications controller provides connectivity to the 3174s and their terminal devices through its host gateway support. Notice that the 3174s do not require a communications port on the controller for connectivity; they interact through the LAN. *NOTE: Also notice that there is no gateway 3174 as we had shown in Figure 15.3. The gateway function is being taken care of by the controller itself.*

Although we have shown a channel-attached communications controller, we could also have shown the same functionality

3174 Model	4 Mbps Type 3 Adaptor Support	4/16 Mbps Type 3 A Adaptor Support	Token-Ring Gateway Support
1 L	O	O	O
11 L	N	O	O
1 R	O	O	O
11 R	N	O	O
2 R	O	O	O
12 R	N	O	O
3 R	O	O	N
13 R	N	S	N
51 R	O	O	O
61 R	N	O	O
52 R	O	O	O
62 R	N	O	O
53 R	S	O	N
63 R	N	S	N
81 R	N	N	N
91 R	N	N	N
82 R	N	N	N
92 R	N	N	N

Note: S = Standard Feature
O = Optional Feature
N = Not Supported

Figure 15.4 A table showing Type 3 connector, Type 3A connector and Gateway feature eligibility for different 3174s.

through a link-attached controller. In such a case, although various devices on the LAN will be communicating with the controller at 4/16 Mbps, data will be transferred from the controller to the host (obviously through another controller) at the transmission line speed, which could be anywhere from 9.6 Kbps to T1 line speeds (1.544 Mbps).

Now, let's look into the token-ring capabilities of various communications controllers.

IBM 3745. The token-ring subsystem of a high-end 3745 consists of up to four Token-Ring Adapters (TRAs). Since each TRA has two Token-Ring Interface Couplers (TICs), there can be up to eight TICs. Two types of TICs are supported for a 3745, TIC Type 1 and TIC Type 2. While Type 1 supports 4Mbps LAN

Token-Ring LAN Networking 335

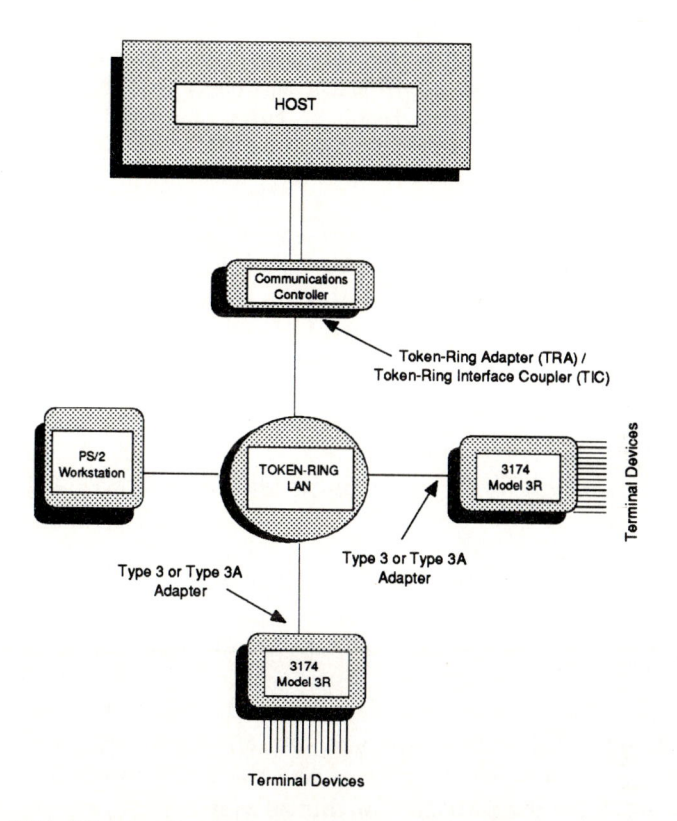

Figure15.5 A Token-Ring Network in which a communications controller (e.g., 3745) acts as a gateway for various 3174s on the LAN.

speed, Type 2 supports switchable 4/16 Mbps. TIC Type 1 and Type 2 adapters can be used in the same controller.

IBM 3720. The Token-Ring Subsystem (TRSS) is supported on Models 11 and 12 only. It provides one TRA (i.e., two TICs) at 4 Mbps speed.

IBM 3725. TRSS is not a standard in any model of 3725 but can be acquired through an RPQ (Request for Price Quotation). TICs operate at 4Mbps speed only.

NTRI. A communications controller must support IEEE 802.2 connection-oriented services to become eligible for token-ring connectivity. Those services are part of the NCP and are created by the NCP generation option, NCP Token-Ring Interconnection (NTRI). Each physical connection appears to VTAM as a full duplex, nonswitched, point-to-point line. Each PU looks like a half-duplex, switched, point-to-point line.

Frame Sizes. The MAXTSL parameters of the BUILD macro (transmission frame size) for TIC Type 2 has a different set of default values than TIC Type 1. Its minimum value is 265 bytes and the default is 2012 bytes. At a speed of 4 Mbps (switchable in TIC Type 2), the maximum value for MAXTSL is 4060 bytes and for 16 Mbps it is 16,732 bytes.

Token-Ring Network communication is also permitted between communications controllers themselves. In such a case, both NCPs look like a PU Type 4 on a single leased link to VTAM.

15.3.3 IBM 9370 Token-Ring Subsystem

IBM 9370s are System/370-based minicomputers that are more suitable for departmental computing in a distributed environment. In September 1990, IBM announced a new series of computers called ES/9000, whose low-end models were replacements for the 9370. Since their capabilities are the same, we will still use the term 9370 for the purposes of this section.

Since 9370s are low-end models, all the benefits of their low cost would be lost if one had to spend a lot of money to provide them with communications capabilities. As a matter of fact, the top of the line 9370 is cheaper than the high-end 3745 communications controller. Provision for inexpensive communications capabilities for 9370s is extensive. They support SDLC, X.25, TCP/IP, token-ring and a host of other protocols. As a matter of fact, the Token-Ring Subsystem (TRSS) is one of the four communications subsystems for a 9370.

There are two types of Token-Ring Adapter cards supported in a 9370 - a 4Mbps card or a 16/4 Mbps card. The TRSS consists of an adapter card and a 9370 Communications Processor Card. It complies with IEEE 802.5 and 802.2 standards. Host software looks at the Token-Ring Adapter card as three different channel address groups. Each group in this case represents four contiguous channel addresses.

Token-Ring LAN Networking 337

Figure 15.6 shows two 9370s, a 3720 and a 3174 on a Token-Ring Network. In general, the connectivity options provided by a 9370 in an SNA network are as follows:

- PU Type 5 to PU Type 5 — this is what 9370s support to communicate with each other.
- PU Type 5 to PU Type 4 — this is the connectivity between the 9370s and 3720s in the example.
- PU Type 5 to PU Type 2.0 — this is the connectivity option between the 9370 and the 3174.

VTAM. For a particular 9370 on a Token-Ring Network, other 9370s (PU Type 5) and NCPs (PU Type 4) provide Intermediate Network Node (INN) functionality. In Figure 15.6, the 3174 Establishment Controller looks like a Downstream PU (DSPU) to the 9370. This interface is a Boundary Network Node (BNN).

INN = Intermediate Network Node
BNN = Boundary Network Node
DSPU = Downstream PU

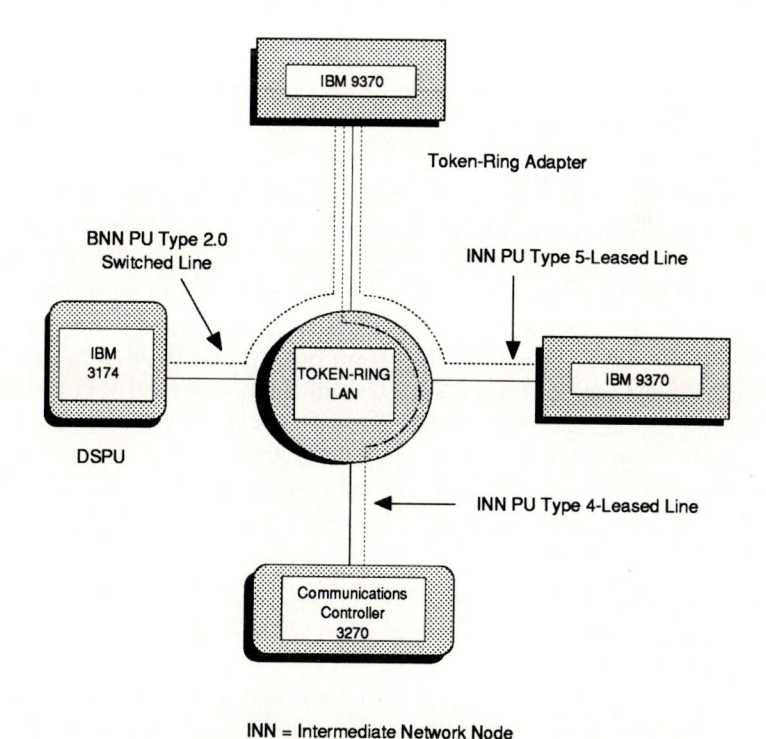

Figure 15.6 A Token-Ring Network with two 9370s, a 3720 and a 3174.

The PU Type 2.0, instead of being a 3174, could have been an AS/400, a LAN workstation or a System/36. A TRSS can support up to 64 PUs. Data transmission related to BNN and INN can exist on the same TRSS as is shown in Figure 15.6. Notice that an INN interface between the 9370/9370 and a 9370/3720 looks to VTAM like a "leased line", while a 9370/3174 looks like a "switched line". The INN is defined in a LAN Major Node while a BNN is defined in a LAN Major Node plus in switched major nodes.

TCP/IP. The Transmission Control Protocol/Interconnect Protocol (TCP/IP) offering for VM supports communications between 9370s and workstations as well as 9370s themselves over a token-ring LAN.

TSAF. The Transparent Access Control Facility (TSAF) for VM supports communications between 9370 members over the Token-Ring Network.

15.3.4 IBM AS/400

AS/400s are a series of minicomputers that run under the OS/400 operating system and are the successors to the old System/36 and System/38 minicomputers. They share a common SAA platform with MVS/ESA, VM and OS/2 Extended Edition operating systems. Their success has prompted many large companies to downsize their data processing from large mainframes to AS/400s. They provide connectivity over Token-Ring Networks not only for themselves, but also for a host of other devices. Figure 15.7 shows a sample Token-Ring Network with AS/400s. The capabilities of an AS/400 in this environment can best be understood by looking at a few connectivity examples.

1. Shows a peer-to-peer high-speed link between two AS/400s.
2. Shows a high-speed link between AS/400 and a 3174 as a host gateway.
3. Shows a high-speed link between AS/400 and a 3720 as a host gateway.
4. Shows a high-speed link between AS/400 and a 3745 as a host gateway.

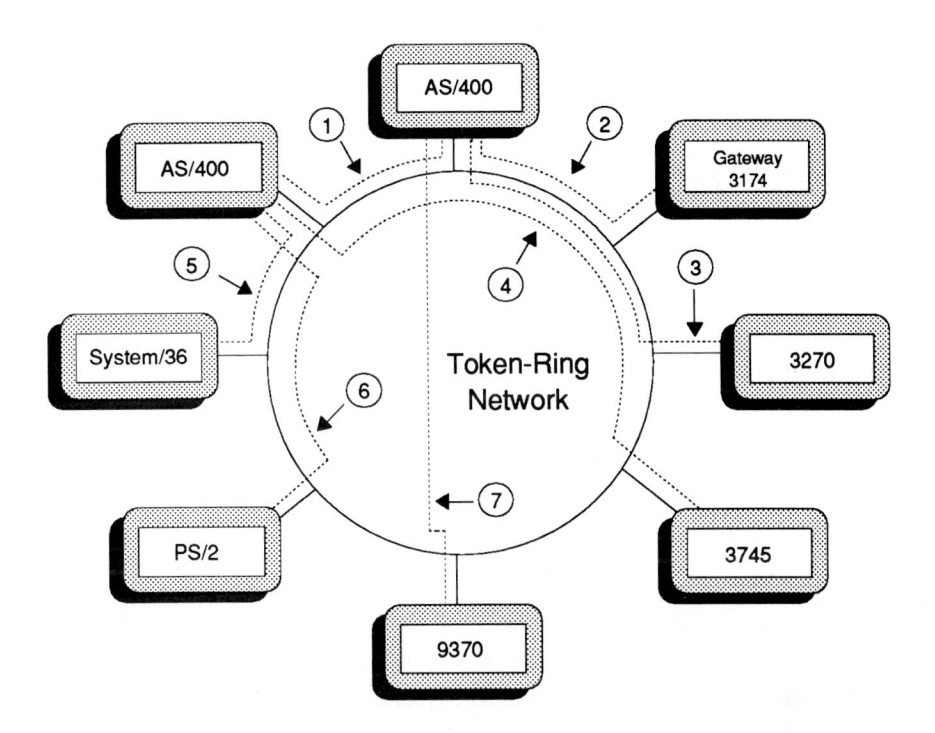

Figure 15.7 A Token-Ring Network involving AS/400s, System/36, 3174s, 9370s, 3720s and workstations.

5. Shows a high-speed peer-to-peer link between an AS/400 and a System/36.
6. Shows connections between AS/400 and a PS/2 (could be a PC, as well) running AS/400 PC Support programs.
7. Shows a high-speed link between an AS/400 and a 9370 as a host gateway.

High-speed peer-to-peer links between two AS/400s or between an AS/400 and System/36 provide various services as follows:

- Advanced Program-to-Program Communications (APPC) based on LU6.2 and PU Type 2.1
- Advanced Peer-to-Peer Networking (APPN) to network AS/400, S/36, S/38, PCs and Node Type 2.1 systems

340 Advanced SNA Networking

- Distributed Data Management (DDM) to access files at a remote AS/400, S/3X or CICS as if they were local files
- SNA Distribution Services (SNADS) to exchange messages, files and documents with other AS/400s, S/3Xs, workstations, S/370 systems

High-speed links between an AS/400 and an S/370 host gateway provide various services as follows:

- OS/400 SNA 3270 Device Emulation to make an AS/400 look like an IBM 3274 or 3174 controller with attached terminals and printers.
- Distributed Host Command Facility (DHCF) to make an AS/400 look like a host system for terminals attached to an S/370.
- Distributed Systems Node Executive (DSNX) to allow AS/400 to receive programs, procedures, files and screen formats from Netview/DM running on a S/370.
- SNA Upline Facility (SNUF) to allow AS/400 users to communicate with CICS/VS or IMS/DC.

15.4 DEFINING A TOKEN-RING TO VTAM/NCP

Token-Ring Networks provide a unique platform for connecting and communicating to an SNA host. The top speed for a TRN is currently 16Mbps using the Token-Ring Adapter Type 2. This significantly improves performance over normal, dedicated SDLC lines running at speeds of 56Kbps or even 256Kbps. As we will see, the TRN is extremely flexible. It allows for virtually uninterruptible changes to network resources because VTAM and NCP view TRN communications as switched connections.

15.4.1 The OPTIONS and BUILD Definition Statements for NTRI

During an NCP generation, the OPTIONS statement specifies to the Network Definition Facility (NDF) certain options that the systems programmer would like added to the generation. The NEWDEFN parameter indicates whether or not we would like NDF to include resource definitions and parameters that the systems programmer does not want to define manually. By coding the NEWDEFN parameter as follows:

```
OPTIONS NEWDEFN=YES
```

the NDF will include all NCP Token-Ring Interconnection (NTRI) definitions and parameters, whether they are explictly or implicitly defined.

The BUILD defintion statement in the NCP has two parameters that specify the number of real (physical) and virtual (logical) NTRI connections to an NCP. These parameters are the MXRLINE and the MXVLINE keywords. The MXRLINE keyword specifies the number of physical lines attached to the TICs and the MXVLINE keyword specifies the number of logical lines that are mapped to the physical lines defined. For example:

```
BUILD  MXRLINE=2,MXVLINE=255
```

This definition defines two physcial lines with 255 logical lines that will be mapped to the physical lines. Prior to NCP V5R3, the systems programmer would have to count all of the physical and logical lines and then code the MXRLINE and MXVLINE values. Under NCP V5R3 and the System Support Program (SSP) V3R5, the NCP generation process will implicitly code the MXRLINE and MXVLINE values. This automatic count overrides any manually coded values.

15.4.2 Defining the Physical GROUP Definition Statement for NTRI

In Figure 15.8 we have diagrammed a typical TRN configuration. The IBM 3174 is defined as a downstream physical unit (DSPU) to the TRN gateway, NCP11. NCP12, in Figure 15.8, is also attached to the same ring as the IBM 3174 DSPU. For this scenario to work, the TIC labeled TICB must be a Token-Ring Adpater Type 2 (TRA-2) on an IBM 3745 Communications Controller. There are three keywords of the NTRI GROUP definition statement that need defining. These are: ECLTYPE, ADAPTER and TRSPEED as shown in Figure 15.9.

The ECLTYPE keyword defines to the NCP the type of connection that will be used. In our example from Figure 15.8, the GROUP is defining the physical connection and the fact that both subarea and peripheral node communications will be used on TICB.

342 Advanced SNA Networking

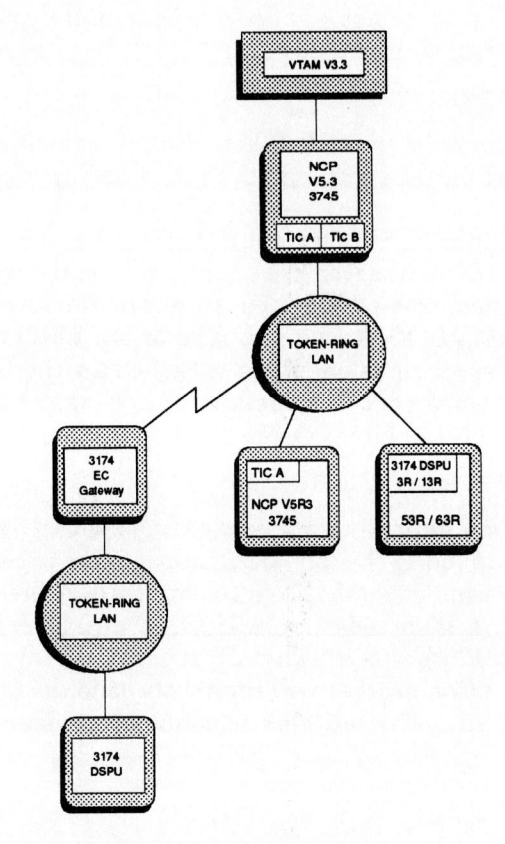

Figure 15.8 Sample configuration for a Token-Ring Network.

The ADAPTER keyword can specify either a Token-Ring Adpater (TRA) Type 1 or Type 2. Remember that the TRA-1 supports only 4Mbps and that TRA-2 supports both 4 and 16Mbps under NCP V5R3. Since in our example we are using an IBM 3745 and mixing subarea and peripheral node traffic on the token-ring, we have chosen a TRA-2 to support the higher speed TRN. TIC1 is the

```
name        GROUP ECLTYPE=(PHYSICAL|LOGICAL,
                    ANY|PERIPHERAL|SUBAREA)          *
                   ,ADAPTER=TIC1|TIC2                *
                   ,TRSPEED=4|16
```

Figure 15.9 NTRI GROUP definition keywords.

```
TRGR1        GROUP ECLTYPE=(PHYSICAL,ANY)            *
                   ADAPTER=TIC2,                     *
                   TRSPEED=16
```

Figure 15.10 Sample NTRI GROUP definition statements for the physical group definition.

default unless you coded ANY on the ECLTYPE keyword. In this instance the default is TIC2. *NOTE: Both the IBM 3720 and 3725 Communication Controllers support only 4Mbps TRNs and therefore can only have a TRA-1.* The IBM 3745 supports both TRA-1 and TRA-2.

The TRSPEED keyword (new in NCP V5R3) defines to the NCP the speed at which the TRSS is to clock the TIC. Since we would like to use the higher speed TRN, we will code a value of 16 for the TRSPEED. A value of 4, the default, can also be specified but the TRN will operate at the slower 4Mbps speed. All stations on the token-ring must run at the same speed or unexpected errors will occur. Figure 15.10 details the NTRI GROUP definition for the physical NTRI connection. Next we must define the physical line attributes.

15.4.3 Defining the Physical LINE Definition Statement for NTRI

As with SDLC lines, the LINE definition defines the physical attributes of the NTRI (Figure 15.11) to the NCP. Just as with other SDLC lines, an ADDRESS keyword is needed. Recall that the ADDRESS keyword specifies the relative line number (physical port) address on the communications controller and whether the line being defined can support full duplex or half-duplex transmission. For NTRI in an IBM 3720, this address must be 16 or 17. In an IBM 3725, the value specified is related to the LABC position and the TRA installed in that position. In an IBM 3745, the value coded can be from 1088 to 1095. The FULL parameter must be coded for the NTRI.

An associative mechanism is used to relate the physical NTRI line definition to the logical NTRI definition. This is the function of the PORTADD keyword. The value specified here is a logical entity and can range from 0 to 99. In our example we will use 1.

344 Advanced SNA Networking

```
name        LINE ADDRESS=(n,FULL),                    *
                 ,PORTADD=n(where n is 0-99)          *
                 ,LOCADD=4000abbbbbbb                 *
                 [,MAXTSL=692|n]                      *
                 [,RCVBUFC=n]
```

Figure 15.11 Format of the physical NTRI LINE definition. See Appendix A for details on the MAXTSL and RCVBUFC values.

The LOCADD keyword is required on the physical NTRI GROUP definition statement. The value coded here is used as the TIC address. The format of this value is 4000*abbbbbbb*. The *a* value can be in the range of 0 to 7. The *bbbbbbb* value can be a combination of numbers with values of 0 to 9. Using this format of the LOCADD keyword allows systems programming personnel to establish a TRN addressing scheme. A useful scheme is worth the effort, since a TRN can proliferate resources at an incredible rate. Management of these resource definitions will become extremely important for configuration and problem management. Using the LOCADD value is one means of accomplishing this.

The LOCADD value of the physical NTRI LINE definition of the NTRI GROUP must also be specified in all TRN resources if they want to gain access to this specific TIC. For example, the DSPU in Figure 15.8 must specify the value of the LOCADD for TICB during the customization procedure. Specifically, question 107 of the customization feature requests a twelve-character hexadecimal address that represents the TRN gateway. In our example, the value coded here identifies NCP11 TICB as the TRN gateway.

The MAXTSL keyword of the physical NTRI LINE definitions specifies the maximum frame size that can be transmitted over the TIC. For a TRA-2 at a speed of 4Mbps the range of the MAXTSL is 265 to 4096 bytes. At 16Mbps, the range is 265 to 16,732 bytes. The default for TRA-2 is 2012. For TRA-1, the range is 265 to 2044 and the default is 692.

The RCVBUFC value is the maximum buffer size for a TRA during a single data transfer. For TRA-1, the range is found by multiplying the NCP BFRS keyword value by 6. The maximum allowed for a TRA-1 is 4096. The default for TRA-1 is 1440. For a TRA-2, the maximum value is 32,000 bytes. The minimum value here is also calculated by multiplying the NCP BFRS value by 6. If

```
    TRBNNGRP       GROUP ECLTYPE=(LOGICAL,PERIPHERAL),        *
                         PHYPORT=1,                            *
                         CALL=INOUT,                           *
                         AUTOGEN=140
```

Figure 15.12 Example of a logical NTRI GROUP definition for peripheral nodes.

the SUBAREA or ANY parameters of the ECLTYPE physical GROUP statement are specified then the default is 4072. Otherwise, it is 1400 bytes (see Appendix A).

The ADAPTER and TRSPEED keywords can be specifed on the physical NTRI LINE definition statement. If you code them, they will override the values set in the physical NTRI GROUP definition statement. Figure 15.11 details the format of the physical NTRI LINE definition statement.

15.4.4 Defining the Physical NTRI PU

It is a requirement that lines have physical units attached to them. NTRI lines are no exception. For these lines, a Physical Unit Type 1 is defined.

15.4.5 Defining a DSPU to NTRI

In Figure 15.8, the DSPU is attached to the token-ring and interfaces with an IBM 3745 executing NCP V5R3 on a TRA-2. On this same token-ring, another NCP V5R3 IBM 3745 communications controller is communicating with NCP11. The NCP in NCP11 must delineate communications between the DSPU and the NCP. The DSPU in our example is an IBM 3174 Subsystem Controller. Recall from our previous discussion that the customization of the DSPU specifies a twelve-digit hexadecimal address that represents the TRN gateway controller that matches the LOCADD value of the physical NTRI LINE definition statement.

Figure 15.12 details sample definitions for this configuration. The ECLTYPE keyword indicates that this group identifies logical resources and that these resources are peripheral Boundary Network Node (BNN) type resources (e.g., cluster controllers, PU Type 2). The PHYPORT keyword value is the link back to the physical NTRI LINE definition. The association is made by specifying the

PORTADD value coded on the physical NTRI LINE definition statement as the value on the PHYPORT keyword. The CALL keyword indicates to the NCP that resources using this logical NTRI line will be using switched protocols. VTAM defines these resources in a switched major node discussed in Section 15.5.7. The AUTOGEN keyword value specifies the number of logical LINE and PU pairs that NDF will create during NCP generation. The maximum value for the AUTOGEN keyword is 3000. We have defined 140 logical LINE and PU pairs. These resources are defined using an algorithm that concatenates the NCP subarea number specified of the SUBAREA keyword on the NCP BUILD definition statement using a base 32 representation and a hexadecimal NTRI resource counter. The resource network names created by NDF for these resources begin with either the letters J or K.

15.4.6 Defining Subarea Connections Over Token-Ring

Intermediate Network Nodes (INN) can communicate over a token-ring just as BNN resources can. The main difference here is that the INN definitions are not defined in VTAM switched major nodes. Instead each NCP defines the LOCADD value of the other NCP's physical NTRI LINE definition in its own logical NTRI PU definition using the ADDR keyword. Figure 15.13 outlines sample code for the INN NTRI definitions. Here again, we see how the ECLTYPE keyword indicates the type of connection to the NCP. In this instance for both NCP11 and NCP12, the ECLTYPE value identifies this group for subarea communications. The PHYPORT keyword is also used to relate this logical definition to the physical NTRI LINE definition. The SDLCST keyword should also be specified, since this line defines an SDLC subarea link. See Chapter 6 for more information on the SDLCST keyword and its usage. The LINE definition statement following the logical NTRI subarea group need only define the transmission group number (TGN) used for this SDLC subarea link. Token-ring subarea links must be single link transmission groups. The PU definition statement of the NTRI subarea link defines this physical unit as a PU Type 4. This is required if the NTRI LINE definition specifies a TGN value. The ADDR keyword of the PU definition is the key to associating this NCP NTRI definition with the remote NCP NTRI definition. The ADDR has the format *ss*4000*abbbbbb*. The *ss* value is the service access point (SAP) of the token-ring defined by this

```
In NCP11:
S11TRGR         GROUP ECLTYPE=(PHYSICAL,ANY),            *
                      ADAPTER=TIC2,                      *
                      TRSPEED=16
S11TRLNE        LINE ADDRESS=(1088,FULL)                 *
                      LOCADDR=40041000111,               *
                      PORTADD=1,                         *
                      MAXSTL=4096,                       *
                      RCVBUFX=4096
S11TRPU1        PU    PUTYPE=1
S11TRLOG        GROUP ECLTYPE=(LOGICAL,SUBAREA),         *
                      PHYPORT=1, RELATES TO PORTADD=1    *
                      SDLCST=(PRIGRP,SECGRP)
S11S12LN        LINE  TGN=11           TRANSMISSION GROUP
S11S12PU        PU    PUTYPE=4,                          *
                      ADDR=044000410000121
S11BNN          GROUP ECLTYPE=(LOGICAL,PERIPHERAL)       *
                      PHYPORT=1,                         *
                      CALL=INOUT,                        *
                      AUTOGEN=140                        *
In NCP12:
S12TRGR         GROUP ECLTYPE=(PHYSICAL,ANY),            *
                      ADAPTER=TIC2,                      *
                      TRSPEED=16
S12TRLNE        LINE ADDRESS=(10088,FULL)                *
                      LOCADD=40041000121,                *
                      PORTADD=1,                         *
                      MAXSTL=4096,                       *
                      RCVBUFX=4096
S12TRPU1        PU    PUTYPE=1
S12TRLOG        GROUP ECLTYPE=(LOGICAL,SUBAREA),         *
                      PHYPORT=1,                         *
                      SDLCST=(PRIGRP,SECGRP)
S12S11LN        LINE  TGN=11           TRANSMISSION GROUP
S12S11PU        PU    PUTYPE=4,                          *
                      ADDR=044000410000111
```

Figure 15.13 Sample code for token-ring subarea and peripheral node connectivity definitions.

PU statement. The *ss* value is always X'04' when the INN link is attached to another NCP. If the INN link is attached to an IBM 9370 host, the ss value must be a multiple of X'04'. The 4000*abbbbbbb* value must match the LOCADD keyword value of the physical NTRI LINE definition found in the attached subarea.

15.4.7 Defining the DSPU to VTAM

Downstream physical units attached to an NCP over a token-ring are defined to VTAM in a switched major node. The switched major node identifies the physical units and their associated LUs that can "dial" in to the SNA network. Figure 15.14 details the code for a switched DSPU major node. The IDBLK keyword value identifies the actual resource type. In this case, an IDBLK of 017 indicates that the resource attached is an IBM 3x74 type of device. The IDNUM value indicates the unique identifier that the DSPU sends in an XID to VTAM so that it can identify itself as a defined resource. In our example, the IDNUM value is E1101. This value must also be specified during the customization of the DSPU. The specific customization question is 215 and the value here must match an IDNUM value defined to VTAM in a switched major node. MAXDATA is set at 2042, since the connection is made through a TRA-2. The PATH definition keyword DIALNO identifies the address of the DSPU to VTAM. The format of this value is $xxyy4000abbbbbbb$. The xx value specifies the actual TIC position in the NCP. In our example, TICB is in position 1 so we code 01. The yy value is the service address point (SAP). In this case, the SAP is an NCP so we code 04. The $4000abbbbbbb$ matches the value specified for question 106 during the customization of the DSPU. In our example, the value coded is 400031741101. *NOTE: The LUDRPOOL definition statement must have a value large enough to support not only token-ring resources, but normal switched SDLC resources as well.*

15.4.8 Defining a Remote 3174 Establishment Controller Gateway

In Figure 15.8, an IBM 3174 Establishment Controller is link-attached to NCP11. The 3174 EC acts as a gateway for a DSPU 3174 attached to the 3174 EC over the Token-Ring Network. Figure 15.15 defines the 3174 EC gateway. In the figure, you can see that the 3174 EC is defined to a physical port on the NCP, unlike the previous DSPU example. The LINE definition is the same as other SDLC LINE definitions that we have discussed throughout the book. Looking at the definition, you will note that the line is defined as a multi-point connection. The first PU definition identifies the actual 3174 EC gateway controller. The 3174 EC customization process specifies several values that are needed for connectivity to take place. During the customization of the EC gateway, there

```
TRSWNET         TYPE=SWNET
                DSPU1101  PU    IDBLK=017,
                IDNUM=E1101,
                MAXDATA=2042
PATH            DIALNO=0104400031741101
                DSPULU01  LU    LOCADDR=02
                DSPULU02  LU    LOCADDR=03
```

Figure 15.14 VTAM switched major node for DSPU token-ring resource.

are several questions asked that are specific to the gateway feature. The EC gateway identifies the lowest and highest SDLC station addresses that can use this EC gateway. Question 900 on the EC gateway is the token-ring address used by the downstream PUs to access the EC gateway through the token-ring. The downstream PU specifies this value in question 107. Question 940 on the EC gateway specifies the token-ring address of the downstream PU. This value must match the value for question 106 on the downstream PU. On the EC gateway, question 912 specifies the general polling address that the EC gateway will respond to when polled by the NCP. This value must match the GP3174 value specified on the EC gateway PU definition statement. The general polling address should be less than or greater than the values

```
    In NCP11:
    ECGWLNE         LINE  ADDRESS=(000,HALF),              *
                          DIAL=NO,                         *
                          LNCTL=SDLC
    ECGWPU          PU    ADDR=C1,  EC GW HAS LOW ADDRESS  *
                          GP3174=CF,    GENERAL POLLING ADDRESS  *
                          SECNET=NO
    ECGWLU01        LU    LOCADDR=02
    ECGWLU02        LU    LOCADDR=03
    DSPU01          PU    ADDR=C2,  EC GW HIGH ADDRESS     *
                          SECNET=YES                       *
    DSPULU01        LU    LOCADDR=02
    DSPULU02        LU    LOCADDR=03
```

Figure 15.15 Sample definition of a 3174 Establishment Controller gateway with one downstream PU defined to NCP11.

specified for EC gateway low and high SDLC station address values. In our example, the general polling address is defined as X"CF".

15.5 SUMMARY

In this chapter we learned about the Token-Ring Networking facilities in an SNA environment. Token-ring LANs are implemented using appropriate token-ring cards for various devices, and repeaters/converters. Devices eligible for token-ring connectivity are IBM 3174s, 3725s, 3720s, 3745s, 9370s, AS/400s, System/36s, and PS/2s. Wherever possible, Token-Ring Networks are replacing the traditional link-attached networks or channel-attached devices in a limited distance environment. They provide communication between the attached devices at a speed of 4Mbps and 16Mbps.

Appendix A

The following table defines the maximum and minimum values for MAXSTL and RCVBUFC for NCP V5R3 for each type of Token-Ring adapter. These keywords are used on the LINE definition statement to define the maximum send and receive frame size that may be sent over the NCP Token-Ring Interconnection (NTRI). The MAXSTL keyword is used to indicate the maximum frame size that can be transmitted. The RCVBUFC is the maximum buffer size used by the TRA during a single data transfer.

Maximum and Minimum Values for MAXSTL and RCVBUFC in NCP V5R3

	ADAPTER	MINIMUM	MAXIMUM	DEFAULT
MAXSTL	TRA1	265	2044	692
	TRA2 @ 4 Mbps Peripheral	265	4060	2012
	TRA2 @ 4 Mbps Subarea/Any	265	16732	2012
	TRA2 @ 16 Mbps Peripheral	265	16732	2012
	TRA2 @ 16 Mbps Subarea/Any	265	4095	2012
RCVBUFC	TRA1	6*NCP BFRS=value	4095	1440
	TRA2	6*NCP BFRS=value	32000	1400 (Peripheral) 4072 (Subarea) 4072 (Any)

Appendix B

IBM Default USS Table

The following table is an IBM-supplied default USS table for VTAM V3R2. If you plan to customize your own USS table, be sure to link-edit your table with a name other than ISTINCDT.

```
ISTINCDT   USSTAB     TABLE=STDTRANS
LOGON      USSCMD     CMD=LOGON,FORMAT=PL1
           USSPARM    PARM=APPLID
           USSPARM    PARM=LOGMODE
           USSPARM    PARM=DATA
LOGOFF     USSCMD     CMD=LOGOFF,FORMAT=PL1
           USSPARM    PARM=APPLID
           USSPARM    PARM=TYPE,DEFAULT=UNCOND
           USSPARM    PARM=HOLD,DEFAULT=YES
IBMTEST    USSCMD     CMD=IBMTEST,FORMAT=BAL
           USSPARM    PARM=P1,DEFAULT=10
           USSPARM    PARM=P2,DEFAULT=ABCDEFGHIJKLMNOPQRSTUVWXYZ0123456789
MESSAGES   USSMSG     MSG=1,TEXT=' INVALID COMMAND SYNTAX'
           USSMSG     MSG=2,TEXT=' % COMMAND UNRECOGNIZED'
           USSMSG     MSG=3,TEXT=' % PARAMETER EXTRANEOUS'
           USSMSG     MSG=4,'% PARAMETER VALUE INVALID'
           USSMSG     MSG=5,TEXT=' UNSUPPORTED FUNCTION'
           USSMSG     MSG=6,TEXT=' SEQUENCE ERROR'
           USSMSG     MSG=7,TEXT='%(1) UNABLE TO ESTABLISH SESSION-%(2) FAILED
                          WITH SENSE %(3)
           USSMSG     MSG=8,TEXT=' INSUFFICIENT STORAGE'
           USSMSG     MSG=9,TEXT=' MAGNETIC CARD DATA ERROR'
           USSMSG     MSG=11,TEXT=' % SESSIONS ENDED'
           USSMSG     MSG=12,TEXT=' REQUIRED PARAMETER OMITTED'
           USSMSG     MSG=13,TEXT=' IBMECHO %'
           EJECT
```

```
STDTRANS    DC      X'000102030440060708090A0B0C0D0E0F'
            DC      X'101112131415161718191A1B1C1D1E1F'
            DC      X'202122232425262728292A2B2C2D2E2F'
            DC      X'303132333435363738393A3B3C3D3E3F'
            DC      X'404142434445464748494A4B4C4D4E4F'
            DC      X'505152535455565758595A5B5C5D5E5F'
            DC      X'606162636465666768696A6B6C6D6E6F'
            DC      X'707172737475767778797A7B7C7D7E7F'
            DC      X'80C1C2C3C4C5C6C7C8C98A8B8C8D8E8F'
            DC      X'90D1D2D3D4D5D6D7D8D99A9B9C9D9E9F'
            DC      X'A0A1E2E3E4E5E6E7E8E9AAABACADAEAF'
            DC      X'B0B1B2B3B4B5B6B7B8B9BABBBCBDBEBF'
            DC      X'C0C1C2C3C4C5C6C7C8C9CACBCCCDCECF'
            DC      X'D0D1D2D3D4D5D6D7D8D9DADBDCDDDEDF'
            DC      X'E0E1E2E3E4E5E6E7E8E9EAEBECEDEEEF'
            DC      X'F0F1F2F3F4F5F6F7F8F9FAFBFCFDFEFF'
            END
```

Appendix

C

Product Support of SNA Network Addressable Unit Types

The two tables provided in this appendix correlate IBM product types to SNA network addressable unit types. This is not a complete list, but rather a list of the most widely used products that support the various SNA network addressable units.

NODE TYPES

PU 1	PU 2	PU 2.1	PU 4	PU 5
3271	3174	S/36	NCP	VTAM
6670	3274	S/38	37X5	4300
3767	3276	3174	3720	308X
	PC	PC		3090
	3770	TPF		
	AS/400	AS/400		

355

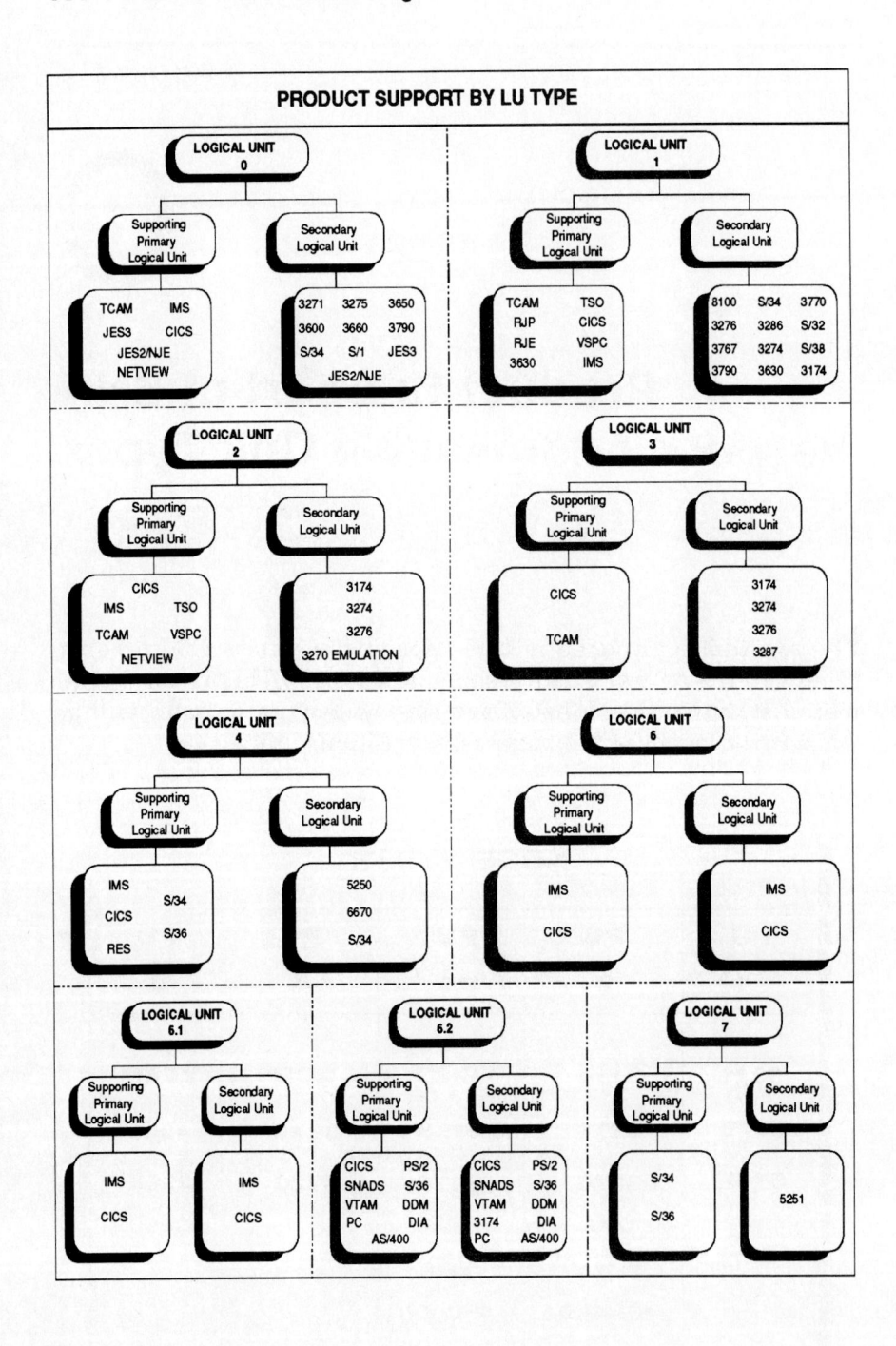

PRODUCT SUPPORT BY LU TYPE

LOGICAL UNIT 0

Supporting Primary Logical Unit
- TCAM
- IMS
- JES3
- CICS
- JES2/NJE
- NETVIEW

Secondary Logical Unit
- 3271, 3275, 3650
- 3600, 3660, 3790
- S/34, S/1, JES3
- JES2/NJE

LOGICAL UNIT 1

Supporting Primary Logical Unit
- TCAM
- TSO
- RJP
- CICS
- RJE
- VSPC
- 3630
- IMS

Secondary Logical Unit
- 8100, S/34, 3770
- 3276, 3286, S/32
- 3767, 3274, S/38
- 3790, 3630, 3174

LOGICAL UNIT 2

Supporting Primary Logical Unit
- CICS
- IMS
- TSO
- TCAM
- VSPC
- NETVIEW

Secondary Logical Unit
- 3174
- 3274
- 3276
- 3270 EMULATION

LOGICAL UNIT 3

Supporting Primary Logical Unit
- CICS
- TCAM

Secondary Logical Unit
- 3174
- 3274
- 3276
- 3287

LOGICAL UNIT 4

Supporting Primary Logical Unit
- IMS
- S/34
- CICS
- S/36
- RES

Secondary Logical Unit
- 5250
- 6670
- S/34

LOGICAL UNIT 6

Supporting Primary Logical Unit
- IMS
- CICS

Secondary Logical Unit
- IMS
- CICS

LOGICAL UNIT 6.1

Supporting Primary Logical Unit
- IMS
- CICS

Secondary Logical Unit
- IMS
- CICS

LOGICAL UNIT 6.2

Supporting Primary Logical Unit
- CICS, PS/2
- SNADS, S/36
- VTAM, DDM
- PC, DIA
- AS/400

Secondary Logical Unit
- CICS, PS/2
- SNADS, S/36
- VTAM, DDM
- 3174, DIA
- PC, AS/400

LOGICAL UNIT 7

Supporting Primary Logical Unit
- S/34
- S/36

Secondary Logical Unit
- 5251

Appendix

D

IBM 3720 and 3745 Line and Channel Adapter Considerations

These tables provide you with the line and channel adapter definition values that require special attention for the IBM 3720 and 3745 communications controllers. This is partly because of the differences between the IBM 37X5 communications controllers and the enhanced features of the IBM 3720 and 3745 communications controllers.

HISPEED=YES for 3720 LINE Definition

Line Adapter Base	*Inbr* value for one scanner	*Inbr* value for two scanners
1	0	*
2	32	32 or 48

* Only one scanner is permitted on this line adapter base.
For hispeed lines on the IBM 3720, the Inbr value must be the lowest position on that scanner.

Inbr value for IBM 3745

Adapter Type	*Inbr* values	USGTIER Notes
LSS	0 - 511	
HSS	1024 - 1039	USGTIER1 & 2 do not support High Speed Scanners.
TRA	1088 - 1095	Only 1088 & 1089 are valid for USGTIER1 & 2. Only first TRA is supported.

channl adapt addr value for IBM 3745

One CCU — CCU A or B			Two CCUs — CCU A and B			USGTIER Notes				
Physical Adapter Position	*channl adapt addr* value		CCU	Physical Adapter Position	*channl adapt addr* value	1	2	3	4	5
1	8		A	1	8	*	*	*	*	*
2	9		A	2	9			*	*	*
3	10		A	3	10			*	*	*
4	11		A	4	11			*	*	*
5	0		B	5	0	*	*	*	*	*
6	1		B	6	1			*	*	*
7	2		B	7	2			*	*	*
8	3		B	8	3			*	*	*
9	12		A	9	12				*	*
10	13		A	10	13				*	*
11	14		A	11	14				*	*
12	15		A	12	15				*	*
13	4		B	13	4				*	*
14	5		B	14	5				*	*
15	6		B	15	6				*	*
16	7		B	16	7				*	*

Appendix

E

VTAM and NCP Performance Tuning Tables

The following tables have been supplied for your reference. They contain information on performance factors for VTAM, NCP, LU-LU flows, Network Data Flows and communication links.

TUNING TABLE

NETWORK COMPONENT	PERFORMANCE FACTOR	SPECIFIED IN
VTAM	Buffer Expansion	VTAM Start List
	Buffer Sizes	VTAM Start List
	ITLIM (Transient)	VTAM Start List
	EAS	VTAM Start List
	VTAMEAS	VTAM Start List
	VTAM Internal Trace (VIT)	VTAM Start List
	SONLIM (Transient)	VTAM Start List
	CSALIMIT/CSA24	VTAM Start List
	MAXPVT	Application Minor Node
	UNITSZ, MAXBFRU	NCP HOST Definition Statement
	DELAY, MAXBFRU	VTAM CTC Definition Statement
NCP	PAUSE	NCP Source LINE Definition
	NEGPOLP	NCP Source LINE Definition
	RETRIES	NCP Source LINE Definition
	ADDRESS=(n,FULL)	NCP Source LINE Definition
	NCP BUFFER size	NCP Source BUILD Definition
	MAXOUT (Modulus 8|128)	NCP Source PU Definition
	MAXDATA (Segmentation)	NCP Source PU Definition
	PASSLIM	NCP Source PU Definition
	SERVLIM	NCP Source GROUP Definiton
	REPLYTO	NCP Source LINE Definition
	Service Order Table (SOT)	NCP Source SERVICE Definition
	DELAY	NCP Source BUILD Definition
	TG Activation Sequence	NCP Source TG Definitions

TUNING TABLE

NETWORK COMPONENT	PERFORMANCE FACTOR	SPECIFIED IN
LU-LU Flows	Chaining	Application Definitions
	PACING, VPACING	LOGMODE Table, NCP Source, Appl. Definition
	Type of Response (Definite or Exception)	LOGMODE Table, Appl. Definition
	Compaction and Compression	Application Definitions
	Flip-Flop vs. Contention	Appl. Definitions, LOGMODE Table
Network Data Flows	INN Congestion Thresholds	NCP Source PATH Definition
	VR Window Sizes	VTAM/NCP Source PATH Definition
	VR Priority	LOGMODE Table COS Table
	Message Size	Application Definitions
	Alternate Routing	COS Table, PATH Tables
Links	Line Speed	Modem clocking, NCP clocking
	BSC vs. SDLC	NCP Source LINE Definition
	DUPLEX=FULL	NCP Source LINE Definition
	Point-point vs. Multi-point	NCP Source LINE and PU Definitions

Appendix

F

Subsystem and Device Performance Considerations

This appendix contains several tables relating to network performance for subsystems and devices. The information in the tables does not represent definitive values. These tables are provided as a reference. For accurate values, consult the respective subsystem and device manuals.

SUBSYSTEM CONSIDERATIONS

CONSIDERATION	CICS	IMS	JES2	JES2/NJE
LU TYPE	DFHTCT TYPE = TERMINAL TRMTYPE= SESTYPE=	TYPE UNITYPE= SLUTYPEP SLUTYPE1 SLUTYPE2 SLUTYPE4 LUTYPE6	RMTnn LUTYPE1	INHERENTLY LU TYPE 0 i.e., NOT DEFINED USES FDX
TYPE OF RSP (PLU-TO-SLU)	DFHPCT TYPE=OPTGRP MSGOPT= (MSGINTEG)	NONREC NONREC - RQE RECOV - RQD	RQD	RQE
TYPE OF RSP (SLU-TO-PLU)	SESSION PARM. CODED RQD/RQE	(SEE IMS TABLE)	RQD	RQE
MAXRU (PLU-TO-SLU)	DFHTCT TYPE=TERMINAL BUFFER=	TERMINAL OUTBUF=	RMTnn BUFSIZE =	INIT. STATE & TPBUFSZ=nn i.e., NO LIMIT
MAXRU (SLU-TP-PLU)	DFHTCT TYPE=TERMINAL RUSIZE=	COMM RECANY=	RMTnn BUFSIZE=	see above
BID	ALWAYS	TERMINAL OPTION (SLUP)		NO BRACKETS
COMPRESSION	N/A	N/A	COMP / NOCOMP	STANDARD
COMPACTION	N/A	N/A	CMPCT / NOCMPCT	APPL COMPACT=
CHAIN SIZE	DEPENDS ON MSG SIZE & BUFFER	DEPENDS ON MSG SIZE & OUTBUF	Rnn.PRnn CKPTPGS= CKPTLNS=	USES SINGLE ELEMENT CHAINS

CICS LU TYPE DEFINITION EXAMPLES

DEVICE	LOGICAL UNIT	TRMTYPE=	SESTYPE=
3270	3270 - DS	3275 3270	
	3270 - PRT	3270P	
	LU 2	LUTYPE2	
	LU 3	LUTYPE3	
	SCS PR	SCSPRT	
3770	INTER-FLIP FLOP	3770I	
	INTER-CONTENTION	3770C	
	BATCH-FLIP FLOP	3770 3770B BCHLU	
	FULL FUNCTION	3770 3770B	USERPROG
	BATCH DATA INTER	3770	BATCHDI

IMS RESPONSE TYPES

	DATA TYPE	UNITYPE= SLUTYPE, 3600 ACK	UNITYPE= SLUTYPE, 3600 OPTACK	3790	3767, 3770 SLUTYPE1	SLUTYPE2
INPUT	UPDATE TRANS	DRX	DRX/EXCP DRX	N/A	DR1/EXCP DR1	EXCP DR1
INPUT	RECOV INQ TRANS	DRX	DRX/EXCP DRX	N/A	DR1/EXCP DR1	EXCP DR1
INPUT	NONRECOV INQ TRANS	DRX/EXCP DRX	DRX/EXCP DRX	EXCP DRX	DR1/EXCP DR1	EXCP DR1
INPUT	IMS MSG SWITCH	DRX	DRX/EXCP DRX	EXCP DRX	DR1/EXCP DR1	EXCP DR1
INPUT	IMS COMMAND	DRX/EXCP DRX	DRX/EXCP DRX	EXCP DRX	DR1/EXCP DR1	EXCP DR1
INPUT	SNA COMMAND	DR1	DR1	DR1	DR1	DR1
INPUT	MFS CTL REQUEST	DRX/EXCP DRX	DRX/EXCP DRX	N/A	N/A	EXCP DR1
OUTPUT	BROADCAST OUTPUT / MSG SWITCH / REPLIES (RECOV) / /FOR,/DIS,/RDIS / LAST MFS PGED OUTPUT	DR2	DR2	DR2	DR2	DR2
OUTPUT	ALL OTHER IMS CMDS / REPLIES (NONRECOV) / MFS PAGED OUTPUT	EXCP DR2	EXCP DR2	EXCP DR2	EXCP DR2	EXCP DR2
OUTPUT	SNA COMMANDS	DR1	DR1	DR1	DR1	DR1

SUBSYSTEM CONSIDERATIONS

CONSIDERATION	POWER	TSO	RES	BDT(MVS)
LU TYPE	PRMT TYPE = LUT1	BIND	TDESCR=	LU TYPE 0
TYPE OF RSP (PLU-TO-SLU)	RQD	RQD	RQD	RQE
TYPE OF RSP (SLU-TO-PLU)	RQD	BIND	RQD	RQE
MAXRU (PLU-TO-SLU)	FIXED 256	BIND	TERMINAL BUFSIZE=	4K MAX INIT. DECK
MAXRU (SLU-TP-PLU)	FIXED 256	BIND	TERMINAL BUFSIZE=	4K MAX
BID	N/A			
COMPRESSION	OUT - BIND IN - NO	N/A	RTAM SNACOMP=	YES
COMPACTION	PRMT CMPACT= name	N/A	RTAM CAPCT=	NO
CHAIN SIZE	PRINT DATA SET	APPLICATION & MAXRU DEPENDENT	TERMINAL VBUF=	NO CHAINING

DEVICE CONSIDERATIONS

CONSIDERATION	3174	3274/3276	MLU 3770	3770
PU TYPE	2/2.1	2	2	2
NUMBER OF PUs	1	1	1	1
FDX or HDX PU	HDX	HDX	FDX	HDX
TYPE OF LOGON	UNFORMATTED	UNFORMATTED	UNFORMATTED	UNFORMATTED
LU TYPES	1 - SCS PRTR. 2 - 3270 D.S. 3 - 3270 PRTR. 6.2 - DLU/ILU	1 - SCS PRTR. 2 - 3270 D.S. 3 - 3270 PRTR.	1	1
RJE (SINGLE OR MULTIPLE LUs)	N/A	N/A	MULTIPLE (1 - 6)	SINGLE
COMPRESSION	NO	NO	YES	YES
COMPACTION	NO	NO	YES	YES
CONTENTION or FLIP-FLOP	FLIP-FLOP	FLIP-FLOP	BOTH	BOTH
ENCRYPTION	YES	YES	YES	NO
NUMBER OF LUs	MULTIPLE	MULTIPLE	DEPENDS ON MAXRU & PACING	1
TS PROFILE	3	3	3	3
MAX. RUSIZE OUTBOUND FROM HOST	REMOTE - ANY LOCAL - 1536	REMOTE - ANY LOCAL - 1536	512	512
MAX. RUSIZE INBOUND TO HOST	1K or 2K	3274 - 1K 3276 - 2K	512	512

DEVICE CONSIDERATIONS

CONSIDERATION	3174	3274/3276	MLU 3770	3770
MAXDATA	265 or 521	265	265 or 521	265 or 521
SEGMENTATION	YES	YES	NO	NO
MAX. # SEGMENTS	NO LIMIT	NO LIMIT	N/A	N/A
MAXOUT	7	7	7	1
PACING TO DEVICE	LU 1 - ANY LU 2 - ANY LU 3 - RQD LU 6.2 - ANY	LU 1 - ANY LU 2 - ANY LU 3 - RQD	VARIABLE	1
PACING FROM DEVICE	ANY	ANY	VARIABLE	VARIABLE
LINE SPEED	T1 or 56kps	T1 or 56kps	19.2bps	4.8bps 3770 19.2bps 3776, 3777
LU LOCADDR	2 - n	2 - n	1 - 6	1
ACTPU/ACTLU ERP	YES	YES	YES	YES
MULTIPLE ELEMENT CHAINS	YES	YES	YES	YES
SLU-PLU RSP DEFINITION	BIND	BIND	BIND	BIND
SLU-PLU RSP DEFAULT	RQE	RQE	RQD	RQD

Appendix

G

Bibliography of Suggested IBM Manuals

VTAM

SC23-0111	VTAM Installation and Resource Definition
LY30-5614	VTAM Customization
GC31-6403	VTAM Directory of Programming Interfaces for Customers
SC23-0113	VTAM Operation
SC23-0114	VTAM Messages and Codes
SC23-0115	VTAM Programming
SC30-3400	VTAM Programming for LU 6.2
LY30-5601	VTAM Diagnosis
LY30-5592	VTAM Data Areas for MVS
LY30-5593	VTAM Data Areas for VM
LY30-5594	VTAM Data Areas for VSE
LY30-5600	VTAM Reference Summary

NetView

SK2T-0292	Learning About Netview
SC30-3476	NetView Installation and Administration Guide
SC30-3361	NetView Administration Reference
SC30-3462	Netview Customization
GC31-6005	NetView Directory of Programming Interface sfor Customers
SC30-3423	NetView Command Lists
SC30-3363	NetView Operation Primer
SC30-3364	NetView Operation

SC30-3365	NetView Messages
SX27-3620	NetView Command Summary
LY30-5587	NetView Diagnosis
SC30-3366	NetView Hardware Problem Determination Reference
LD21-0023	NetView Problem Determination Supplement For Management Services Major Vectors 0001 and 0025
SD21-0016	NetView 5822 Supplement

NetView/PC

SC30-3408	NetView/PC Planning and Operation Guide
SC30-3482	NetView/PC Installation Guide
SC30-3313	NetView/PC Application Program Interface/Communication Services Reference

NCP

SC30-3348	NCP, SSP, and EP Generation and Loading Guide
SC30-3440	NCP Migration Guide
SC30-3447	NCP, SSP, and EP Resource Definition Guide
SC30-3448	NCP, SSP, and EP Resource Definition Reference
LY30-5603	NCP and EP Reference Summary and Data Areas
LY30-5606	NCP Customization Guide
LY30-5607	NCP Customization Reference
LY43-0021	SSP Customization
GC31-6202	NCP and Related Products Directory of Programming Interfaces
SC30-3169	NCP, SSP, and EP Messages and Codes
LY30-5591	NCP, SSP, and EP Diagnosis Guide
LY30-5605	NCP and EP Reference

Miscellaneous

Ranade, Jay and Sackett, George. *Introduction to SNA Networking: A Guide for Using VTAM/NCP*

Appendix H

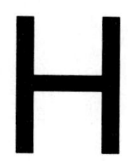

List of Abbreviations

ACB	Access method control block or application control blocks.
ACF	Advanced Communications Function.
ACTLU	Activate logical unit.
ACTPU	Activate physical unit.
ACU	Auto calling unit.
API	Application program interface.
APPL	Application program.
APPC	Advanced Peer-to-Peer Communications.
APPN	Advanced Peer-to-Peer Network.
BER	Box event records.
BIU	Basic information unit.
BNN	Boundary network node.
BSC	Binary synchronous communications.
BTU	Basic transmission unit.
CA	Channel adapter.
CCITT	Consultative Committee on International Telegraph and Telephone.
CCU	Central control unit.
CDF	Configuration data flow.
CDRM	Cross-domain resource manager.
CDRSC	Cross-domain resource.
CLSDST	Close destination.
CMC	Communications management configuration.
CN	Composite node.
CNM	Communications network management.
COS	Class of service.
CP	Control Program.
CSP	Communications scanner processor.
CSU	Channel service unit.

CTCA	Channel-to-channel attachment.
CUA	Channel unit address.
CUT	Control unit terminal.
CVT	Communications vector table.
DAF	Destination address field.
DCE	Data communications equipment.
DDS	Digital data service.
DFC	Data flow control.
DLU	Destination logical unit.
DMA	Direct memory access.
DMUX	Double multiplexer.
DSTINIT	Data services task initialization.
DSU	Data service unit.
EBCDIC	Extended binary-coded decimal interchange code.
ECC	Enhanced error checking and correction.
EN	End node.
EP	Emulation program.
ER	Explicit route.
EREP	Environmental recording editing and printing.
FID	Format identification.
GTF	Generalized trace facility.
ILU	Independent logical unit.
IML	Initial microcode load.
INN	Intermediate networking node.
IOC	Input/ouput control.
IPL	Initial program load.
IRN	Intermediate routing node.
LAB	Line attachment base.
LAN	Local area network.
LIB	Line interface base.
LIC	Line interface coupler.
LSS	Low-speed scanner.
LU	Logical unit.
MAU	Multistation access unit.
MOSS	Maintenance and operator subsystem.
MSNF	Multi-system Networking Facility.
MVS	Multiple Virtual Storage.
MVS/XA	MVS for Extended Architecture.
MVS/370	MVS for System/370.
NAU	Network addressable unit.
NCB	Node control block.
NCCF	Network Communications Control Facility.
NCP	Network control program.
NCTE	Network channel-terminating equipment.
NIB	Node Identification Block.
NLDM	Network logical data manager.
NN	Network node.
NPDA	Network Problem Determination Application.

OAF	Origin address field.
OPNDST	Open destination.
OS	Operating system.
PCCU	Physical communications control unit.
PEP	Partition emulation program.
PIU	Path information unit.
PLU	Primary logical unit.
PTF	Program temporary fix.
PU	Physical unit.
PUT	Program update tape.
RDT	Resource definition table.
RFP	Request for proposal.
RFQ	Request for price quotation.
RH	Request/response header.
RPL	Request parameter list.
RSF	Remote support facility.
RTS	Ready to send.
RU	Request/response unit.
SBA	Set buffer address.
SDLC	Synchronous data link control.
SIO	Start I/O.
SLU	Secondary logical unit.
SMF	System management facility.
SMP	System Modification Program.
SNA	Systems Network Architecture.
SNI	SNA network interconnection.
SSCP	Systems services control point.
SVA	Shared virtual area.
TAP	Trace Analysis Program.
TCB	Task control block.
TG	Transmission group.
TH	Transmission header.
TIC	Token-Ring Interface Coupler.
TPS	Two processor switch.
TRA	Token-Ring adapter.
TRSS	Token-Ring Subsystem.
TSC	Transmission subsystem controller.
TSO	Time-sharing option.
TSS	Transmission subsystem.
USS	Unformatted systems services.
VM	Virtual machine.
VM/SNA	Virtual machine with SNA function
VM/SP	Virtual Machine System Product.
VR	Virtual route.
VRPWS	Virtual route pacing window size.
VSCS	VM SNA console support.
VTAM	Virtual Telecommunications Access Method.
XID	Exchange identification.

Glossary

ACB. In context of VTAM, it refers to application control block. In context of NCP, it refers to adapter control block.

ACB name. Name specified in the ACBNAME parameter of VTAM's APPL statement.

access method. Software responsible for moving data between the main storage and I/O devices (e.g., disk drives, tapes, etc).

acquire. Process by which a VTAM application program (e.g., CICS) initiates and establishes a session with another LU.

adapter control block. A control block of the NCP having control information and the current state of operation for SDLC, BSC and start/stop lines.

Advanced Communications Function. A group of SNA-compliant IBM program products such as ACF/VTAM, ACF/TCAM, ACF/NCP and ACF/SSP.

alert. Occurrence of a very high priority event that requires immediate attention and response.

alias name. A name defined in the name translation program when alias name does not match the real name. It is primarily used for an LU name, Logon mode table name and class of service name in a different SNA network.

API. See application program interface.

application control block. A control block linking a VTAM application (e.g., CICS) to VTAM.

application program. A program (e.g., CICS) using the services of VTAM to communicate with different LUs and providing a platform for users to perform business-oriented activities.

application program identification. A name specified in the APPLID parameter of the ACB macro. VTAM identifies an application program by this name.

application program interface. Interface through which an application program interacts with VTAM.

application program major node. A group or collection of application program minor nodes. It is a partitioned data set (PDS) member of MVS containing one or more APPL statements.

ASCII. American Standard Code for Information Interchange.

automatic logon. A process by which VTAM automatically starts a session request between PLU and SLU.

begin bracket. An indicator in the request header (RH) indicating the first request in the first chain of a bracket. (Also see end bracket).

binary synchronous communication. A non-SNA link-level protocol for synchronous communications.

bind. Request to activate session between a PLU and SLU.

BIU. A request header (RH) followed by all or part of a request/response unit (RU).

boundary function. Capability of a subarea node to provide support for adjacent peripheral nodes.

bracket. One or more RUs exchanged between two LU-LU half-sessions which must be completed before another bracket can be started.

BSC. See Binary Synchronous Communication.

buffer. A portion of main storage for holding I/O data temporarily.

CCP. Configuration Control Program.

CDRSC. Cross-Domain Resource.

chain. See RU chain.

channel-attached. Attachment of a device directly to the computer's byte or block multiplexer channel.

CICS. Customer Information Control System.

class of service. Designation of transmission priority, bandwidth and path security to a particular session.

cluster controller. A channel-attached or link-attached communications device (e.g., 3174) which acts as an interface between a cluster of terminal devices and the CPU or communications controller.

CNM. Communication Network Management.

communication adapter. An optional hardware available on IBM 9370 and IBM 4331 that allows communication lines to be directly attached to it thus alleviating need for a communications controller.

communications controller. Communications hardware that operates under the control of an NCP and manages communication lines, cluster controllers, workstations and routing of data through a network.

Configuration Control Program (CCP). An interactive application program used to define and modify the configuration of an IBM 3710.

COS. See class of service.

cross-domain. Pertaining to more than one domain.

Cross-Domain Resource (CDRSC). A resource owned and controlled by a cross-domain resource manager (CDRM) of another domain.

cross-network. Resources involving more than one SNA network.

Customer Information Control System (CICS). A database/data communication teleprocessing and transaction management system which runs as a VTAM application.

Data Link Control (DLC) layer. A layer of SNA implemented in the SDLC protocol which schedules data transfer over a pair of links and performs error checking.

deactivate. To render a network resouce inoperable by taking it out of service.

definite response. Value in the RH directing the receiver to respond unconditionally.

DFC. Data Flow Control.

disabled. An indication to SSCP that a particular LU is unable to establish an LU-LU session.

disconnected. Loss of physical connection.

domain. An SSCP and the PUs, LUs, links and other resources that are controlled by that SSCP.

duplex. Capability to transmit in both directions simultaneously.

EBCDIC. Extended Binary Coded Decimal Interchange Code.

element. A resource in a subarea.

enabled. An indication to SSCP that a particular LU is ready to establish an LU-LU session.

end bracket. A value in the RH indicating an end of the bracket.

ER. See Explicit Route.

Explicite Route (ER). A set of one or more TGs that connect two subarea nodes.

FID. See Format Identification.

FMH. Function Management Header.

Format Identification Field (FID). A field in the TH indicating its format.

formatted system services. A segment of VTAM providing certain service that pertain to receiving field-formatted commands.

gateway NCP. An NCP connecting two or more SNA networks.

half-duplex. Ability to transmit data in one direction at a time only.

IMS/VS. Information Management System/Virtual Storage.

Intermediate Routing Node (IRN). A subarea node with an intermediate routing function. A subarea node may also be a boundary node.

local address. Address used by the peripheral node (e.g., cluster controller, terminals). Boundary function of a subarea node translates network address to local address and vice versa.

local-attached. A channel-attached device.

logical unit. A port through which an end-user accesses the SNA network and communicates with another logical unit.

logon mode table. A VTAM table containing one or many logon modes name.

LU. Logical Unit.

major node. A set of resouces (minor nodes) that are given a unique name which can be activated or deactivated by a single command.

minor node. A resource within a major node.

multiple-domain network. A network with more than one SSCP.

Multiple Virtual Storage (MVS). An IBM mainframe operating system.

NAU. Network Addressable Unit.

NCCF. Network Communications Control Facility.

negotiable BIND. Capability of two LU-LU half-sessions to be able to negotiate parameters of a session.

NetView. An IBM network management product consisting of old NCCF, NPDA and NLDM and a few new enhancements.

network address. An address consisting of subarea and element fields.

Network Addressable Unit (NAU). An SSCP or an LU or a PU.

Network Management Vector Transport (NMVT). A record of information sent to a host by an SNA resource. It contains information about errors, alerts and statistics.

Network Terminal Option (NTO). A program product that runs in the communications controller and allows certain non-SNA devices to have a session with VTAM application programs.

NMVT. Network Management Vector Transport.

node name. A symbolic name for a major or minor node.

NTO. Network Terminal Option.

pacing. Pertaing to control of data transmission by the receiving station so that the sending station does not cause buffer overrun.

parallel sessions. Capability of having two or more concurrently active sessions between the same set of two LUs.

Path Information Unit (PIU). A message consisting of TH and BIU.

Physical Unit (PU). A network addressable unit (NAU) that manages attached resources and acts as a routing node for communications between LUs. Examples of PUs are SSCP, Communications Controllers and Cluster Controllers.

PIU. Path Information Unit.

PLU. Primary Logical Unit.

Primary Logical Unit (PLU). In an LU-LU session, a PLU is the LU which is responsible for bind, recovery and control.

PU. Physical Unit.

Request Header (RH). Control information prefixed to the request unit (RU).

Request Parameter List (RPL). A control block containing parameters pertaining to a data transfer request or session initiation/termination request.

Request Unit (RU). A message unit containing user data or function management headers (FMH) or both.

return code. A code pertaining to the status of the execution of a particular set of instructions.

RH. Request/Response Header.

RPL. Request Parameter List.

RU. Request/response Unit.

SDLC. Synchronous Data Link Control.

session. A logical connection between two network addressable units (NAUs).

single-domain network. A network with one SSCP.

SLU. Secondary Logical Unit.

SMF. System Management Facility.

SSCP. System Services Control Point.

System Support Program (SSP). An IBM program product to support an NCP.

TAP. Trace Analysis Program.

TCAS. Terminal Control Address Space.

Terminal Control Address Space (TCAS). The address space of TSO/VTAM that provides logon services for TSO user address spaces.

TG. Transmission Group.

TH. Transmission Header.

TIC. Token-Ring Interface Coupler.

Token-ring Interface Coupler (TIC). An adapter to connect a communications controller to an IBM Token-Ring Network.

Trace Analysis Program (TAP). A program service aid to help in analyzing trace data produced by VTAM and NCP.

Transmission Group (TG). A group of one or more links between two adjacent subarea nodes that appears as a single logical link.

Transmission Header (TH). Information created and used by path control and used as a prefix to a basic information unit (BIU).

transmission priority. Priority by which the transmission group control component of path control selects a PIU for transmission to the next subarea.

unbind. Request to terminate a session between two LUs.

Unformatted System Services (USS). An SSCP facility that translates character coded request (e.g., logon or logoff) into a field formatted request for processing by formatted system services (FSS).

user exit. A user written program which can be given control at a determined point in an IBM program.

USS. Unformatted system services.

Virtual Route (VR). Logical connection between two subareas to provide for transmission priority and underlying explicit routes.

Virtual Route (VR) pacing. A technique used by VR control component of path control to regulate PIUs flow over a virtual route.

VM SNA Console Support (VSCS). A VTAM component for VM providing SNA support and providing for SNA terminals to be VM consoles.

VM/SP. Virtual Machine/System Product.

VR. Virtual Route.

VSCS. VM SNA Console Support.

VSE. Virtual Storage Extented operating system.

VTAM. Virtual Telecommunications Access Method.

VTAM application program. A program that can issue VTAM macro instructions and is known to VTAM through an ACB.

VTAM operator. A human being or a program authorized to issue VTAM operator commands.

XRF. Extended recovery facility.

X.21. CCITT's recommandations for an interface between the DTE and DCE for synchronous communications (e.g., HDLC) over a data network.

X.25. CCITT's recommandations for an interface between the DTE and packet switching networks.

X.25 NCP Packet Switching Interface (NPSI). A program product which runs in the communications controller that allows VTAM applications to communicate over an X.25-compliant network to SNA or non-SNA equipment or end users.

Index

Abandon Connection (ABCONN), 198
ACF/TAP, 240
ACTCDRM command, 187
ACTCONNIN procedure, 184
Activate physical unit, 178
Activating Routes, 178
Activation of Explicit and Virtual
    Routes, 181
ACTLINK command, 175
ACTLINK command, 180
ACTLU command, 184
ACTLU(ERP), 218
ACTPU, 203
ACTPU command, 178, 183
ACTPU(ERP), 218
ADDLINK command, 174, 175
ADDLINKSTA command, 175
Address Space Manager, 311
Adjacent SSCP Table, 157
Adjacent SSCP Table (ADJSSCP),
    76, 77, 83
    cdrmname operand, 86
    non-gateway VTAM, 136
    start list options, 85
ADJCDRM Definition Statement, 86
ADJSSCP Major Node
    gateway-capable VTAM, 158
Advance Program-to-Program
    Communication APPC, 309, 321, 339
Advanced Peer-to-Peer Networking
    (APPN), 316, 339
Airline Control Program (ACP), 315
Alert Major Vector, 259
Alias Name Translation
    ALIASMEM statement, 143
    APPL definition statement, 141
    NetView, 141
    ORIGNET statement, 144
    use in SNI, 142
APA - All Points Addressability
    See IBM 3174 Establishment
        Controller
API/CS interface, 263

Application Program Interface (API),
    246, 256
APPN, 321
Asynchronous Emulation Adapter, 20
    as a feature on an IBM 3174, 13
    IBM 3174 Establishment
        Controller, 8
ATCCON00, 172
ATCSTR00, 272
    CSA24 start options, 237
    HOSTPU start option, 232
    IOBUF operand, 282
    NETID start list option, 321
    SSCPNAME start list option,
        228, 319, 321
    TRACE start list option, 238
ATCSTR00 start list, 80
ATCSTR00 start option
    CONFIG operand, 172
    SSCPID operand, 171
ATCVT table, 172
Auto Calling Unit (ACU), 118
AUTODMP operand, 101
AUTOIPL operand, 101
AUTOSYN operand, 101

Back-to-Back Gateway
    ADJNET operand, 164
    ADJNETEL operand, 164
    ADJNETSA operand, 164
    COSTAB operand, 166
    cross-network path table, 168
    for NCP, 166
    Gateway NCP definition, 166
    Gateway VTAM, 165
    Gateway-capable VTAM, 163
    GWNAU definition statement, 167
    NETID, 166
    NETWORK definition statement,
        167
    non-gateway VTAM, 163
    null network, 162, 166
    PATH definitions, 162

388 Index

SNI, 162
SUBAREA operand, 166
BACKUP operand
  PCCU, 217
Begin Chain (BC), 291
Bi-synchronous Control (BSC),15, 35
Boundary Network Node (BNN), 99, 337, 345
Boundary_Function_Control_Initiate (BFCINIT), 205
Boundary_Function_Initiate (BFINIT), 204
Boundary_Function_Session_Start (BFSESSST), 205
BROWSE facility, 255
BTAM, 209
BUILD definition statement, 102
  ADDRESS parameter, 321, 323
  AUXADDR parameter, 204, 323
  AVGPB parameter, 280
  BFRS, 280
  communications wall parameter (CWALL), 282
  COSTAB operand, 150
  example of, 102
  HSBPOOL operand, 150
  MAXSESS parameter, 323
  MAXSSCP operand, 103
  MAXSTL parameter, 336
  MAXSUBA value, 102
  multi-domain network operands, 102
  NAMETAB, 323
  NCPCA operand, 102
  NETLIM operand, 151
  NEWNAME operand, 229
  NUMHSAS operand, 103
  operands of, 102
  RESSCB parameter, 323
  SESSLIM operand, 151
  SLOWDOWN parameter, 281
  TRANSFR operand, 102
  VRACT operand, 151
  VRPOOL operand, 103

CCITT V.24 Interface, 41, 65
CCITT V.25 Interface, 65
CCITT V.35 Interface, 34
CCITT X.21 Interface, 34
CDINIT command, 79, 84
CDINIT request, 192
cdrmname operand, 78
cdrscname operand, 81
CDSESSEND request unit, 194
CDTERM request unti, 193
Chaining, 290
  implementation, 291
Change-number-of-session (CNOS) command, 323
Change-Window-Indicator (CWI), 301
Change-Window-Reply-Indicator (CWRI), 301
Channel Adapter Board (CAB), 54
Channel-to-Channel Attachment (CTCA), 87
  ADDRESS operand, 89
  DELAY operand, 89
  GROUP definition statement, 88
  I/O GEN statement, 89
  LINE definition statement, 88
  MAXBUFR operand, 89
  PU Definition statement, 89
  PUTYPE operand, 90
Check point lines (CKPTLNS), 291
Check point pages (CKPTPGS), 291
CINIT request, 190
CL-MENU, 216
Class of Service table (COS), 93, 130, 165, 231, 302
CNM Router Task (DSICRTR), 259
CNM Routing Table, 250
Coat-tailing, 274
Command Facility, 250, 251
Command List (CList), 251, 258,264
Common Communications Support, 309
Communication Management Configuration (CMC) , 218, 224, 225
Communication Subsystem, 33
  High Performance Transmission Subsystem (HPTSS), 33
  Token-Ring Subsystem (TRSS), 33
  Transmission Subsystem (TSS),33
Communications adapters
  use with an IBM 3174, 14
Communications Control Unit, 56
Communications Network Management (CNM), 209
  Router Function, 258
Communications Scanner Processor (CSP), 62
Compaction, 297
Composite node (CN), 321
Composite T2.1 node, 314
Compression, 297
CONFIG operand
  ATCSTR00 start options, 172

CONFT table, 172
Connect Out Request (CONNOUT)
  CONNOUT procedure, 184
CONTACT command, 176, 186, 203
CONTACTED command, 181
Control Initiate (CINIT), 192
Control Initiate request unit (CINIT), 189
Control Point (CP), 321
Control Program (CP), 241
Control Subsystem
  cache buffers, 29
  Central Control Unit (CCU), 28
  Channel adapters, 30
  direct memory access (DMA), 30
  enhanced error checking and correction (ECC), 30
  input/output control, 30
  main storage, 29
  storage control, 30
  two-processor switch (TPS), 31
Control Terminate (CTERM), 193, 194, 196
Converter, 331
CP-CP session, 318
CPTRAP, 241
Cross-Domain Initiate Request (CDINIT), 189,192
Cross-Domain Control Initiate (CDCINIT), 192
Cross-Domain Control Initiate Request (CDCINIT), 190
Cross-Domain Resource Manager (CDRM), 76, 77, 173
  ADJNET operand, 140
  ADJNETEL operand, 140
  ADJNETSA operand, 140
  CDRDYN operand, 79
  CDRSC operand, 79
  definition statement, 78
  GWN operand, 140
  GWPATH statement, 140
  NETWORK statement, 139
  RECOVERY parameter, 80
  statement format, 78
  SUBAREA operand, 80
  use in defining gateway VTAM, 130
  VBUILD statement, 77
Cross-Domain Resources (CDRSC), 76,81
  CDRM operand, 82
  definition statement, 81
  definition statement format, 82
  use in SNI, 130

VBUILD statement, 81
Cross-Domain Session Ended (CDSESSEND), 193
Cross-Domain Session Started (CDSESSST), 191, 192
Cross-Domain Takedown (CDTAKED), 195
Cross-Domain Takedown Complete (CDTAKEDC), 196
Cross-Domain Terminate (CDTERM), 193
Cross-Network (CDRM), 140
Cross-network communications, 126
CSA24 operand, 172
CSALIMIT operand, 172
Control Unit Terminal (CUT), 14

DACTLINK, 200, 202
DACTLU, 198
Data Circuit-Terminating Equipment (DCE), 5,34,52
Data Flow Control (DFC), 289
Data Service Unit/Channel Service Unit (DSU/CSU), 34
Data Terminal Equipment (DTE), 34
DCE suppliers, 257
Deactivate CDRM (DACTCDRM), 196
Deactivate LU (DACTLU), 197
Deactivate PU (DACTPU), 198, 201
Deactivate Virtual Route (DACTVR), 201
Deactivation of explicit and virtual routes, 199
DEC/VAX, 14
Delete Network Resource (DELETNR), 202
Dependent LUs (DLU), 203, 313
Determining Link Station Roles, 111
  MONLINK operand, 112
  NCP V4R3 / V5R2, 111, 112
  predefined configuration, 111, 112, 114
Digital Data Service (DDS), 34
DISCONTACT, 198, 199
DISPLAY ID command, 232
  INACT operand, 233
  SCOPE operand, 233
Distributed Data Management (DDM), 340
Distributed Host Command Facility (DHCF), 340
Distributed Systems Node Executive (DSNX), 340
Domain, 75

390 Index

Double Multiplexer (DMUX), 63, 64, 66,
Downstream physical unit (DSPU),
    337, 341, 348
DSU/CSU, 67
Dynamic Path Update, 218, 228
    DELETER statement, 229
    NCPPATH definition statement, 228
    NEWPATH parameter, 230
    PATH statement, 229
    PATHEXT operand, 230
    required NCP operands, 230
    TGBXTRA operand, 230
    VPATH, 228
    VRPOOL operand, 230
Dynamic Reconfiguration (DR), 218, 324
    dynamic reconfiguration data set
        (DRDS), 220
    enhancements, 221
    MAXLST operand, 222
    MAXPU operand, 222
    operands that affect DR, 224
Dynamic Table Replacement (DTR),
    218, 230
    class of service table (COS), 231
    dynamic association, 231
    interpret table (INTTAB), 231
    logon mode table (MODETAB), 231
    USS table (USSTAB), 231

EIA-547 Interface, 34
End Node (EN), 317, 321
End-of-Chain (EC), 291
Entry Point, 246, 247
Establishment Controller
    see IBM 3174 Establishment
    Controller
    IBM 3174, 4
Exchange ID (XID), 176, 319
Explicit Route (ER), 91, 121, 179, 234
Extended BIND, 203
Extended Format Identifier Type 2
    Local Form Address Identifier, 312
    LocalForm Session Identifier
        (LFSID), 311
    OAF-DAF Assignor Indicator, 312
    Session Connector Block (SCB), 311
Extended Network Addressing (ENA),
    102, 129
Extended Recovery Facility (XRF), 218,
    226
    recommended configuration, 227
    support for, 227
Fallback, 58
First-In-Chain (FIC), 291

Focal Point, 246, 258
Fragmentation, 274
Frame Reject Command (FR-REJ), 181
Free Network Address (FNA), 197
Full-duplex configuration, 287

Gateway NCP
    assigning subareas, 129
    element address, 129
Gateway VTAM, 130, 137, 143
    ADJNET operand, 140
    ADJNETEL operand, 140
    ADJNETSA operand, 140
    Back-to-Back Gateway, 165
    CDRM major node, 138
    CDRM statement, 130
    CDRSC name, 130
    changes to the CDRM Major Node,
        159
    class of service table, 130
    definition updates, 159
    GWN operand, 140
    HOSTPU option, 138
    HOSTSA option, 138
    logon mode table, 130
    NETID, 130
    NETWORK definition statement,
        130
    NETWORK statement, 139
    SSCPID parameter, 130
    SSCPNAME option, 138
    SSCPNAME parameter, 130
Gateway-Capable Host, 155, 158
Gateway-Capable VTAM, 156
    ADJSSCP major noe, 158
    change to the CDRM Major Node,
        157
    PATH table, 158
Generalized Trace Facility (GTF), 240
Generic Alert format, 260, 262
Group Control System (GCS), 241
GROUP definition statement, 341
    ADAPTER keyword, 342
    AUTOGEN keyword, 346
    ECLTYPE keyword, 341
    PHYPORT keyword, 345
    SDLCST keyword, 346
    TRSPEED keyword, 343
GWNAU definition statement, 151
    back-to-back gateway, 167
    ELEMENT operand, 153
    NAME operand, 153
    NETID operand, 153
    NUMSESS operand, 153

Index   391

Half-duplex link (HDX), 286
Half-duplex/flip-flop, 279
HALT command, 193
Hardware Facility, 248
Hardware Monitor, 252, 256, 259
Help Desk Facility, 255
High Performance Transmission
  Subsystem (HPTSS), 30, 33, 34
    direct attachment, 34
    limitations, 34
    physical interfaces, 34
    T1 and CEPT, 34
High-Speed Scanners (HSS), 30, 54, 62
Host Definition Statement, 103
    for multi-domain NCP, 103
    INBFRS parameter, 282
    UNITSZ parameter, 282

IBM ES/9000, 336
    Establishment Controller, 4
IBM 3174 Establishment Controller,
  3, 4, 333, 337, 348
    advantages over 3274s, 9
    All Points Addressability (APA), 9
    ASCII host connectivity, 12
    Asynchronous Emulation Adapter,
      6, 17
    base memory size, 6, 17
    concurrent communications
      adapter (CCA), 6
    channel-attachment, 9
    cluster controllers, 11
    Communications Adapter, 8, 17, 18
    control unit terminal attachment
      to Model 1L, 14
    Disk drives, 5
    diskette drive, 6
    Encrypt/Decrypt Adapter, 7
    Features, 5
    Functions, 4
    host connectivity, 9
    how 3174s fit in a local area
      network, 11
    Intelligent Printer Data Stream
      (IPDS), 9
    large 3174 models, 14
    link-attachment, 10
    medium-size models, 16
    Model 92R, 20
    Models 1L and 11L, 14
    Models 1R and 11R, 15
    Models 2R and 12R, 15
    Models 3R and 13R, 15
    Models 51R and 61R, 17

Models 52R and 62R, 18
Models 53R and 63R, 18
Models 81R and 91R, 18
Models 82R and 92R, 19
Multi-station Access Unit, 12
Multiple Logical Terminals, 9
Terminal Multiplexer Adapter, 9
Single Link Multi-Host Support, 6
small models, 18
Token-Ring attachment, 11
Token-Ring Network gateway,
  7, 17
Token-Ring SNA Gateway, 4
IBM 3174 Cluster controller, 248
IBM 3174 control unit, 279
IBM 3174 Subsystem Controller, 3
IBM 3274
    Cluster Controllers, 5, 248
    control unit, 279
    host connectivity, 9
IBM 3279, 264
IBM 3710 Network Controller, 279
IBM 3720
    use in LAN, 335
IBM 3725, 335
IBM 3745 Communications
  Controller, 21, 23, 25, 27, 29, 31, 33,
  35, 37, 39, 41, 43, 45, 47, 49, 51, 53,
  55, 57, 59
    3745 Model 410, 56
    3746 Model A11, 54
    3746 Model A12, 55
    3746 Model L13, 55
    3746 Model L14, 56
    architecture, 25
    channel interface (CI), 31
    characteristics, 46
    Communications Subsystem, 26, 33
    components, 61, 63, 65, 67, 69, 71
    Concentrator, 25
    configuration, 61
    configuration rules for line weights,
      70
    Control Subsystem, 26, 28
    expansion units, 53
    features of expansion units, 55
    features of the Model 130, 49
    features of the Model 150, 50
    features of the Model 170, 50, 51
    features of the Model 210, 52
    features of the Model 410, 54
    Front End Processor (FEP), 24
    functional categories, 23
    hierarchy of components, 63

392 Index

High Performance Transmission Subsystem (HPTSS), 34
IBM 3705, 22
IBM 3720, 22
IBM 3725, 22
Intelligent Switch, 25
LIC Type 1, 65
Maintenance and Operator Subsystem (MOSS), 27
major functions, 22
Model 130, 47
Model 130 upgrades, 48
Model 150, 49, 67
Model 170, 50
Model 210, 47, 51
Model L15, 56
scanner overload, 71
support of full duplex transmissions, 279
Token-Ring Subsystem, 36
Transmission Subsystem (TSS), 35
types of attachment, 25
use in Token-Ring LAN, 334
IBM 3745 Model 410, 56
modes of operation, 56
twin-backup mode, 59
Twin-Dual Mode, 56
twin-standby mode, 57
IBM 8218, 331
IBM 8220, 331
IBM 8228, 330
IBM 9370, 22, 258
Token-Ring subsystem, 336
IBM AS/400, 332, 338
use in LEN, 310
IBM Communications Controllers
use in Token-Ring LAN, 333
IBM Information Management (Info/Man), 246
IBM NetView Performance Monitor (NPM), 246
IBM System 36
use in LEN, 310
IBM System 38
use in LEN, 310
IBM's Knowledge Tool, 263
IEEE protocols, 331
INBFRS operand, 103
independent LUs, 313
INITEST operand, 101
Initial Microcode Load (IML), 27
Initial Program Load (IPL), 27
Initial Program Load Initialization (IPLINIT), 181

Initiate self request unit (INIT-SELF), 189
Integrated Clock Controller (ICC), 62
Integrated Communications Adapter, 115, 120
Intensive mode recording, 178
Intermediate Network Node (INN), 99, 337, 346
Intermediate Routing Node, 114
IO buffer, 270
IOBUF operand, 271, 282
IPDS - Intelligent Printer Data Stream
See IBM 3174 Establishment Controller
IPLFINAL request unit, 181
IPLINIT command, 181
IPLTEXT request unit, 181
ISPF, 264
ISTATUS operand, 216
ISTINCNO, 211
ISTPUCWC, 298

JES2
chaining, 291

Large Message Performance Enhancement Outbound (LMPEO), 291
Last-In-Chain, 291
LFBUF, 271
LIC Interface Unit (LIU), 27
LIC weight value, 67
Line Attachment Base (LAB), 27, 51, 62, 63
Line Configuration
determination of line weights, 68
LINE definition statement
ADAPTER keyword, 345
ADDRESS keyword, 343
DUPLEX parameter, 278
LOCADD keyword, 344
MAXSTL keyword, 344
PORTADD keyword, 343
RCVBUFC value, 344
SERVLIM parameter, 286
transmission group number (TGN), 346
TRSPEED keyword, 345
Line Interface Base (LIB), 27, 67, 69
LIB Type 1, 67
LIB Type 2, 67
LIB Type 3, 67
Line Interface Coupler (LIC), 35, 62, 63, 64, 65

Index 393

LIC Type 2, 66
LIC Type 3, 66
LIC Type 4A, 66
LIC Type 5, 66
LIC Type 6, 66
Line Interface Coupler Units (LIU), 52, 66
Line Weights
    configuration rules, 70
    considerations, 67
    determining for a LIB in an IBM 3745, 69
    Rule # 1, 70
    Rule #2, 70
    total line weight, 70
Link Problem Determination Aid (LPDA), 252
LINKDATA Command, 261
LINKPD Command, 262
LINKTEST Command, 262
LOCADDR operand, 186
Local Area Network (LAN), 11, 327
    support under NetView, 259
LOGAPPL operand, 214, 236
Logical Unit Type 6.2, 309
    LOCADDR parameter, 320
    RESSCB parameter, 320
Logon Mode Table, 130
Low Entry Networking (LEN), 202, 260, 307
    architecture, 308
Low-Speed Scanner (LSS), 30, 51, 54, 62, 66
LU Type 6.2, 313
LU-LU session, 189
LUDRPOOL definition statement, 348
    NUMILU parameter, 324

Maintenance and Operator Subsystem (MOSS), 37
    alternate console, 41
    console sharing, 41
    control panel, 39
    diskette drive, 39
    hard disk drive, 39
    initial program load, 37
    intitial microcode load, 37
    local console, 41
    MOSS console, 40
    MOSS components, 38
    MOSS functions, 43
    MOSS microprocessor, 38
    network control program, 37
    remote console, 41
    Remote Support Facility (RSF), 42

Master Characters, 297
MAXBFRU operand, 103
Maximum line speed, 70
Message and Alert Notification Routing facility, 258
Message Driven Alert facility, 258, 259
Middle-In-Chain (MIC), 291
Multiple Logical Terminals (MLT)
    See IBM 3174 Establishment Controller
MODIFY command, 237
MODULO128, 110, 284
MODULO8, 110, 283
Multi-Domain NCP
    ACTIVTO operand, 110
    determining link station roles, 111
    GROUP definition statement, 105
    GROUP definition stement, 108
    HOST definition statement, 103
    MODE operand, 109
    MODULO128, 110,284
    MODULO8, 110,283
    path statement updates, 121
    REPLYTO operand, 109
    SDLCST definition statement, 104
    SUBAREA operand, 103
    TEXTTO operand, 109
Multi-Domain Network
    channel-to-channel attachment (CTCA), 87
Multi-point Subarea Link
    DUPLEX operand, 116
Multi-Point Subarea Links, 113, 114
    ADDR operand, 115
    DATMODE operand, 115
    IPL operand, 117
    MODE operand, 116
    MODULO operand, 115
    SDLCST operand, 116
    SERVICE statement, 114
    TGN operand, 116
    TADDR operands, 116
Multi-station access unit (MAU), 36,330
    use with an IBM 3174 Establishment Controller, 5, 12
Multi-System Networking Facility (MSNF), 75, 245
Multiple Domain, 75, 99, 101, 103, 105, 107, 109, 111, 113, 115, 117, 119, 121,123

394 Index

definitions for NCP, 99, 101, 103, 105, 107, 109, 111, 113, 115, 117, 119, 121, 123
Path table considerations, 90
Multiple Gateway, 155
Multiple Gateway for NCP, 160
Multiple Gateway NCP
   GWNAU definition statement, 161
Multiple Gateway VTAM
   effect on CDRM definitions, 156
MVS
   VTAM Trace Procedure, 240

Name operand, 88
NC-ACTVR command, 179
Network Command Control Facility (NCCF), 133, 141, 250, 251
   ALIASMEM statement, 142
   DSIDMN member, 141
   DSTINIT parameters, 142
   MEM operand, 142
   TASK statement, 141
NCCF command lists, 254
NCP Token-Ring Interconnection (NTRI), 336
NCP V4R3 / V5R2
   dynamic reconfiguration under, 221
NCPPATH definition statement
   Dynamic PATH Update, 228
Net/Master, 246
Net/Master EASINET, 216
NetView, 141, 211, 245
   BROWSE facility, 255
   Command Facility, 261
   R1, 260
   R2 automation enhancements, 258
   R2 generic alerts, 260
   release 2, 257
   release 3 enhancements, 263
   Status Monitor (STATMON), 254
NetView Panel Manager, 264
NetView/PC, 246, 248, 261
   version 1, 256
   version 1.1, 262
   Version 1.2, 264
Network Addressable Units (NAU), 75
Network Channel-Terminating Equipment (NCTE), 34
Network Control Explicit Route Activation Request(NC-ER-ACT), 178
Network Control Program (NCP), 100, 174, 178, 216
   activating routes to remote NCP, 181

inbound data flow, 280
link scheduler service, 285
levels required for SNI gateway, 128
performance and tuning considerations, 277
Network Control Request Unit, NC-ER-OP, 176
Network Control Request Virtual Route Deactivation (NC-DACTVR), 199
Network Control-Explicit Route Activation Reply Request Unit NC-ER-ACT-REPLY, 178
Network Definition Facility (NDF), 340
NETWORK Definition Statement, 130, 152, 192
   ACTPU operand, 152
   back-to-back gateway, 167
   COSTAB operand, 152
   NETID operand, 152
   NETLIM operand, 152
   NUMHSAS operand, 152
   SESSLIM operand, 152
   SUBAREA operand, 152, 167
Network Logical Data Manager (NLDM), 251, 253
Network Management Productivity Facility (NMPF), 251, 255
Network Management Vector Transport (NMVT), 248, 252, 256, 259, 260
Network Node (NN), 317, 321
Network Node Control Point (NNCP), 317
Network Performance and Tuning Methodology, 267, 269, 271, 273, 275, 277, 279, 281, 283, 285, 287, 289, 291, 293, 295, 297, 299, 301, 303
   performance objectives, 270
Network Problem Determination Application (NPDA), 248, 250, 252
Network Services (NS), 174
Node T2.1
   switched major node, 324
Non-gateway NCP, 130
   NUMHSAS operand, 131
   SNI, 160
   VRPOOL operand, 131
Non-Gateway VTAM
   ATCSTR00 updates, 135, 139
   PATH statement, 137
Null Network, 168

Index 395

Back-to-Back Gateway, 162
NULL XID, 203

One-stage pacing, 293
Open Communications Architecture (OCA), 308
Open Network Management (ONM), 245, 260
    architecture, 246
OPTIONS definition statement, 340
    NEWDEFN parameter, 340
OWNER operand, 216

PACING parameter, 292, 295
Pacing window size, 298
Parallel Transmission Groups, 94, 95
    channel-attached major node, 95
    CUADDR keyword, 96
    defining, 95, 97
    multiple single-link transmission groups, 94
    PCCU definition statement, 96
    SUBAREA keyword, 96
    TGN keyword, 96
PATH definition statement, 298
PATH information unit (PIU), 275, 288
    outbound PIU (OPIU), 277
PATH Table
    definition of the multi-domain, 91
Physical Communcations Control Unit (PCCU), 77
    BACKUP operand, 217
    CUADDR operand, 176
    definition statement for add'l hosts, 100
    MAXDATA operand, 276, 283
    NEWPATH parameter, 230
    OWNER operand, 216
    RNAME operand, 180
PCCU definition statement, 282
    GWCTL operand, 149
    NETID operand, 149
    SUBAREA operand, 149
Peer-to-peer communication, 260, 309
Pre-VTAM V3R2, 222
Primary Link Station (PLS), 203, 319
Primary LU (PLU), 203, 313
Primary Program Operator (PPO), 251
Primary-send (PSNDPAC), 293
Prime Compression Character, 297
Procedure correlated identifier (PCID), 260
Programmable Operator Facility (PROP), 257

PSNDPAC parameter, 294
PU definition statement
    ADDR keyword, 346
    DATMODE parameter, 279
    GP3174 parameter, 349
    MAXDATA parameter, 283
    MAXOUT parameter, 283
    PASSLIM parameter, 284, 320
PUDRPOOL definition statement
    MAXLU parameter, 324
PUTYPE
    valid values for multi-point, 115

Ready-To-Send (RTS)
    use with DUPLEX operand, 116
Receive-Not-Ready (RNR), 286, 301
Receive-Ready (RR), 286
Record Formatted Maintenance Statistic (RECFMS), 249, 252
Remote Support Facility (RSF), 37, 41, 42
Repeater, 331
REPLYTO operand, 88
Request Contact (REQCONT), 185
Request Maintenance Statistic (REQMS), 249
Request_Network_Address_Assigment (RNAA), 186, 192, 204
Reset-Window-Indicator (RWI), 301
Resource Definition Table, 172, 220
    resource definition table segment (RDTS), 172
Resource Defn. Table Segment (RDTS)
    possible formats, 173
Resource Vector Table (RVT), 220
Response Time Monitor (RTM), 254
Response Time Monitor (RTM) Major Vector, 259
Restructured Extended Executor (REXX), 263
RUNCMD Command, 261

SAMON, 216
SDLC, 15, 22, 35, 104, 108, 198, 219, 284
    DIAL operand, 109
    LNCTL operand, 109
    nonswitched SDLC nodes, 182
    switched SDLC nodes, 184
    TYPE operand, 109
SDLC Subarea Link
    ANS operand, 113
    configurations and definition example, 112

396 Index

Line definition statement, 110
    MAXOUT operand, 112
    MODULO operand, 112
    SDLCST operand, 110
    TGN operand, 113
SDLCST definition statement, 105
    GROUP operand, 105
    MAXOUT operand, 105
    MODE operand, 105
    MODULO8, 105
    MODULO128, 105
    PASSLIM operand, 105
    primary mode, 105
    REPLYTO operand, 106
    RETRIES operand, 106
    secondary mode, 105
    SERVLIM operand, 107
    TADDR operand, 107
Secondary (LU), 313
Secondary Link Station (SLS), 203
Secondary LU (SLU), 203
Secondary-Receive (SRCVPAC) parameter, 293
Secondary-Send (SSNDPAC) parameter, 294
Segmentation, 290
Selective Scanning, 68
Service Level Agreement, 267
Service Order Table (SOT), 286, 287
Service Point, 246, 248
Service Point Command Facility (SPCF), 265
Service Point Command Service (SPCS), 261, 263
Session awareness data (SAW), 260
Session Control Block (SCB), 320, 323
Session End (SESSEND), 193, 194
Session Monitor, 253, 274
Session-pacing
    types of, 294
Session Start command (SESSST), 189, 190, 192
    types of, 294
Set Control Vector Command (SETCV), 178, 185, 192
Set Initialization Mode command SET-INIT-MODE, 181
Set-Normal-Response-Mode command (SNRM), 181, 186, 286
Single-Gateway, 134
    ACTPU operand, 152
    COSTAB operand, 150, 152
    cross-network PATH definition, 154
    gateway NCP, 146
    gateway NCP definition, 148
    GWCTL operand, 148, 149
    GWNAU definition statement, 153
    HSBPOOL operand, 150
    NCP, 145, 147, 149, 151, 153
    NETID operand, 148, 149, 152
    NETLIM operand, 151
    NETWORK definition statement, 152
    non-gateway NCP definition, 145
    non-gateway VTAM definition, 135
    NUMADDR operand, 150
    NUMHSAS operands, 145
    PATH statement, 148
    PCCU definition statement, 148
    SESSLIM operand, 151
    SUBAREA operand, 149
    TGN operand, 147
    VRACT operand, 151
    VRPOOL operands, 145
SNA Distribution Services (SNADS), 340
SNA Network Interconnection (SNI), 245
SNA Node Type 2.1, 257, 260, 309
    Address Space Manager, 311
    Configuration Services, 310
    Control Point (CP), 310
    overview of architecture, 311
    Session Services, 310
SNA PATH Control Layer, 313
SNA PATH Information Units (PIU), 253
SNA terminals, 226
SNA Upline Facility (SNUF), 340
SNI, 125, 127, 129, 131, 133, 135, 137, 139, 141, 143
    alias name translation table, 141
    assigning subarea under gateway NCP, 129
    Back-to-Back Gateway, 162
    BUILD definition statement, 131
    CDRM major node, 136
    considerations, 126
    cross-network sessions, 126
    defining gateway to NCP, 130
    defining gateway to VTAM, 130
    determining gateway location, 127
    example of a single-gateway configuration, 129
    gateway NCP, 126, 128, 160
    gateway SSCP, 126
    gateway VTAM, 126
    gateway VTAM definition, 137

Index 397

GWNAU definition statement, 151, 153
  level of software required, 126
  multiple Gateway, 160
  native network, 126
  network autonomy, 132
  network definition statement, 152
  non-gateway NCP, 128, 160, 161
  non-native network, 126
  principal idea of, 126
  single gateway NCP, 145, 147, 149, 151, 153
  SNI link, 131
SSCP-PU session, 217, 310
SSCP-SSCP session, 83, 187
SSCPDYN option, 85
SSCPID option, 136
SSCPORD option, 85
Start Data Traffic Command (SDT), 178, 188, 189
STATMON - NetView Status Monitor, 254
Storage Mangement Services (SMS), 171
SUBPOOL 229, 271
Subsystem Control Units, 3
Subsystem Interface (SSI), 257
Switched Major Node, 346
  CPNAME parameter, 324
  IDBLK keyword, 348
  IDNUM value, 348
  node T2.1, 324
  PATH definition statement, 348
Switched Subarea Links, 117
  "dummy" PU, 118
  ACTIVTO parameter, 118
  ADDRESS operand, 120
  ANSWER operand, 118
  AUTO operand, 118, 120
  BRKCON operand, 118
  CALL operand, 118
  DIAL parameter, 118
  PUTYPE parameter, 118
  SUBADIAL operand, 120
  SUBAREA operand, 120
  switched major node, 119
  TGN operand, 119
Symbol Resolution Table (SRT), 174
System Center Net/Master, 246
System Management Facility (SMF), 253, 276
System Services Control Point (SSCP), 77
System Support Program (SSP), 341
Systems Application Architecture (SAA), 264, 308

T1 Line, 62, 64
T2.1 Node
  defining to NCP, 319
TERM-SELF request unit, 194
Terminal Control Table (TCT), 134
Terminate Self (TERM-SELF), 193
Token-Ring gateway, 3, 4, 328
  defining to NCP, 340
  hardware support, 329
Token-Ring adapter, 30, 48, 51, 333, 336, 340
Token-Ring card, 331
Token-Ring connectivity
  use with an IBM 3174
    Establishment Controller, 12
Token-Ring gateway
  3270 gateway connectivity with an IBM 3174, 12
Token-Ring Interface, 316
Token-Ring Interface Couplers (TIC), 48, 333
Token-Ring LAN
  MAU as hub, 330
Token-Ring Network, 22, 348
  Establishment Controller, 4
  sample, 332
Token-Ring Network Gateway, 333
Token-Ring Network Manager, 263
Token-Ring Subsystem (TRSS), 33, 36, 335, 336
  adapters, 37
  Token-Ring Interface Couplers (TIC), 37
Topology Data Exchange Unit (TDU), 318
TPBFSIZ operand, 274
TPRINT, 241
Trace Analysis Program, 240
Transaction Processing Facility (TPF), 315
Transmission Control Protocol/ Interconnect Protocol, 338
Transmission group (TG), 288
Transmission Group (TR), 92
Transmission Subsystem (TSS), 33, 35, 61
  components, 36
Transmission Subsystem Controller (TSC), 120
Transparent Access Control Facility (TSAF), 338
Two-Processor Switch (TPS), 31, 32
Two-stage pacing, 293

398 Index

Unformatted System Services (USS), 210
UNITSZ operand, 103
Unnumbered Acknowledgement command (UNACK), 181, 186, 203
USSMSG statement
    Description Code operand (DESC), 212
    MCSFLAG operand, 212
    MSG operand, 211
    OPT operand, 212
    ROUTCDE operand, 212
    SUPP operand, 212
    TEXT operand, 212, 213
    USSTAB, 211
USSTAB
    USSMSG statement, 211

VARY ACT command, 89
VARY command, 236
VBUILD statement, 77, 81, 87
Virtual Route (VR), 91, 234, 297
Virtual Route Control Block (VRB), 303
Virtual route pacing, 297
VM
    VTAM Trace Procedure for, 241
VPACING, 295
VPATH
    Dynamic PATH Update, 228
VPBUF, 271
VR pacing response, 298
VR States
    BLOCKED VR state, 299
    HELD VR state, 299
VSE
    VTAM Trace Procedure for, 241
VSE/Operator Communication Control Facility (OCCF), 257
VTAM, 24, 75, 77, 78
    advanced configuration facilities, 218
    buffer pool specification, 272
    buffer pool usage, 270
    defining gateway under SNI, 130
    initialization, 171
    network management and problem analysis, 209
    path table considerations, 90
    performance and tuning considerations, 270

Token-Ring LAN, 337
trace facilities, 238
VTAM initialization
    activating a channel-attached NCP, 177
    activating an NCP subarea, 177
    activating an SSCP-LU session, 186
    activating switched SSCP-PU sessions, 186
    establishing a cross-domain LU-LU session, 189
VTAM message identifier, 212
VTAM Node Control Application (VNCA), 251, 254
VTAM Operator Commands
    DISPLAY, 211, 232
    DISPLAY BFRUSE, 273
    DISPLAY NCPSTOR, 211
    DISPLAY PATHTAB, 211
    DISPLAY ROUTE, 211
    DISPLAY ROUTE command, 235
    DISPLAY STATIONS, 211
    MODIFY, 211
    MODIFY CSALIMIT, 237
    MODIFY DR, 222
    MODIFY NOTRACE , 242
    MODIFY TABLE, 231
    MODIFY TNSTAT, 237
    MODIFY TRACE , 238
    redefining, 213
    VARY ACQ, 218, 236
    VARY ACT , 230
    VARY DRDS, 220
    VARY LOGON, 236
    VARY NOLOGON, 236
    VARY REL, 236
    VARY TERM, 211
VTAM Trace Procedure
    for MVS, 240
    for VM, 241
    for VSE, 241
VTAMLST, 78, 135, 172, 222, 230

X.21 Interface, 66
X.25, 15
XID, 181, 184
XID Type 3 (XID3), 202
XID3, 319

ABOUT THE AUTHORS

Jay Ranade is an Assistant Vice President at Merrill Lynch, New York, and is a Series Editor-in-Chief for McGraw-Hill.

George C. Sackett is President and Chief Consultant at ASAP Technologies, Inc., a Rutherford, New Jersey consulting and educational firm specializing in strategic network design and network management.